RESUME WINNERS FROM THE PROS

Books and audios by Wendy S. Enelow:

100 Winning Resumes For $100,000+ Jobs

201 Winning Cover Letters For $100,000+ Jobs

1500 KeyWords For $100,000+ Jobs

Resume Explosion (audio)

Resume Winners From the Pros

RESUME WINNERS FROM THE PROS

177 of the Best From the Professional Association of Resume Writers

Wendy S. Enelow

IMPACT PUBLICATIONS
Manassas Park, VA

Library of Congress Cataloging-in-Publication Data

Enelow, Wendy S.
    Resume winners from the pros: 177 of the best from the
Professional Association of Resume Writers / Wendy S. Enelow
      p.   cm.
    ISBN 1-57023-097-8 (alk. paper)
    1. Resumes (Employment) I. Professional Association of
Resume Writers. II. Title.
HF5383.E479   1998
808'.06665—dc21   98-17709
                                                 CIP

For information on quantity discounts, Tel. 703/361-7300, Fax 703/335-9486, or write to : Sales Department, IMPACT PUBLICATIONS, 9104-N Manassas Drive, Manassas Park, VA 20111-5211. Distributed to the trade by National Book Network, 15200 NBN Way, Blue Ridge Summit, PA 17214, Tel. 800/462-6420.

CONTENTS

Dedication And Acknowledgements

This book is dedicated to **Rebecca Stokes**, my most valued associate and a successful resume writer in her own right. If it were not for your technical skills, editorial assistance and personal support, this book would never have been published. Your overall contribution to my success and that of my business can never be quantified; it has been enormous. Thank you!

My heartfelt thanks and acknowledgements to:

Jean Schoell Oscarson, the newest member of my staff. You have managed to come into a "unique" intense working environment, and make immediate and valuable contributions. I thank you and my clients thank you. Here's to many years together!

Betsy Suter Gooding. You did an absolutely outstanding job proof-reading all of the resumes. I know that it was a monumental task. Call me when you need your next pair of glasses!

Frank Fox, Executive Director, Professional Association of Resume Writers. Thank you for the opportunities you have provided and for the tremendous impact you have had on the recognition of our industry. PARW will always be a source of pride and respect.

Jay Block, CPRW. You keep my vision moving forward and my energies focused. What an invaluable contributor to temper my "entrepreneurial" bent. Thank you always.

David Grunert, my husband. I don't know how you tolerate my pace, but thanks. I love you so much!

Pierre Viens, my son. At age 14, I already "see" your writing skills, creativity and imagination. I am delighted! You are definitely "my kid" and I love you.

Contributors

A special thank you to each of the following contributors. The superior quality of your resumes, cover letters and other job search communications speaks highly of our industry. I am proud to be associated with a group as professional, talented and devoted as each of you. My personal thanks and appreciation.

To all job search candidates: Each contributor to this book is a member of the Professional Association of Resume Writers (PARW), the industry's national trade association. Many have earned their credential as a Certified Professional Resume Writer (CPRW) through a specialized testing and examination process. Be assured, as you review the resumes in this book, that each contributor is well-known for his/her expertise in resume strategy, writing and presentation.

Many contributors also offer comprehensive job search services including Internet resume postings, targeted direct mail campaigns, job lead reports, career counseling, interview skills training, career coaching and much more. If you would like professional assistance in developing a top-flight resume, accelerating your search campaign and getting more job offers, please contact one of the contributors.

Again, to each contributor, thank you! On behalf of myself and the Professional Association of Resume Writers, we wish you continued success and recognition.

Contributor	*Pages Resumes Appear On*
Georgia Adamson, CPRW ADEPT BUSINESS SERVICES 180 W. Rincon Avenue Campbell, CA 95008-2824 Phone: (408) 866-6859 Fax: (408) 866-8915 Email: peach2000@aol.com	164, 259, 232-233
Elizabeth J. Axnix, CPRW QUALITY WORD PROCESSING 329 East Court Street Iowa City, IA 52240-4914 Phone: (319) 354-7822 / (800) 359-7822 Fax: (319) 354-2220 Email: axnix@earthlink.net	289, 302-303
Mark Berkowitz, NCCC, CPRW CAREER DEVELOPMENT RESOURCES 1312 Walter Road Yorktown Heights, NY 10598 Phone: (914) 962-1548 / (888) 277-9778 Fax: (914) 962-0325 Email: Cardevres@aol.com	156, 218-220, 249, 282-284, 342-343
Beverly Baskin, MA, NCC, CPRW BASKIN BUSINESS & CAREER SERVICES 6 Alberta Drive Marlboro, NJ 07746 Phone: (800) 300-4079 Fax: (732) 972-8846 Email: bbcs@skyweb.net (Other Offices in Iselin, NJ and Princeton, NJ)	214, 215, 159-160, 298-299
Jerry Bills, MBA, CPRW THE RESUME & TAX CENTER 115 North Union Boulevard Colorado Springs, CO 80909 Phone: (719) 632-9050 Fax: (719) 473-3225 Email: Jbillspho@aol.com	146, 199

Contributor	*Pages Resumes Appear On*
Ted Bills THE RESUME & TAX CENTER 115 North Union Boulevard Colorado Springs, CO 80909 Phone: (719) 632-9050 Fax: (719) 473-3225 Email: Jbillspho@aol.com	83, 319, 340
Patricia S. Cash, CPRW RESUMES FOR RESULTS P.O. Box 2806 Prescott, AZ 86302 Phone: (520) 778-1578 Fax: (520) 771-1229 Email: geow@goodnet.com	143-144, 155, 162, 210, 274-276, 343-347, 367
Laura A. DeCarlo, CPRW, ICCC COMPETITIVE EDGE CAREER SERVICE 1600 W. Eau Gallie Blvd., Suite 201 Melbourne, FL 32935 Phone: (407) 752-0880 / (800) 715-3442 Fax: (407) 752-7513 Email: lauraads@aol.com	157-158
Darby Diehl, CPRW D'SCRIBE RESUMES 107 Cimarron Trail #2073 Irving, TX 75063 Phone: (972) 556-1945 Fax: (972) 556-1076 Email: DscribeRes@aol.com	88-89, 198
Karen Wilson-Dooley, CPRW JUST YOUR TYPE Professional Development & Business Center 1633 Dairy View Road Chatham, VA 24531 Phone: (804) 432-3719 Fax: (804) 432-2459 Email: rezuma@gamewood.net	97-98, 141-142, 169, 300-301

Contributor	*Pages Resumes Appear On*

Marta L. Driesslein, CPRW
CAMBRIDGE CAREER SERVICES
300 Montvue Road, Suite B
Knoxville, TN 37919
Phone: (423) 539-9538
Fax: (423) 453-3109
Email: careerhope@webtv.net

117, 149-150,
243-244, 251-252,
370-371

Michelle M. Dumas, CPRW
DISTINCTIVE DOCUMENTS
146 Blackwater Road
Somersworth, NH 03878
Phone: (603) 742-3983 / (888) 894-9694
Fax: (603) 743-6720
Email: resumes@distinctiveweb.com

95-96, 115-116,
145, 185-186, 226

Wendy S. Enelow, CPRW
THE ADVANTAGE, INC.
119 Old Stable Road
Lynchburg, VA 24503
Phone: (804) 384-4600 / (800) 922-5353
Fax: (804) 384-4700
Email: wenelow@aol.com
          wenelow@inmind.com

104-105, 129-133,
192-193, 206-207,
211-214, 216-217,
221-224, 229-232,
235-236, 255,
206-261, 268-269,
285-286, 317-318,
322-323, 330-331,
353-358, 364-365,
368-369

Mark Freedman
THE RESOURCE PLANNING GROUP
31 Purchase Street
Rye, NY 10580
Phone: (914) 921-2110
Fax: (914) 967-6726
Email: Mark_Freedman@msn.com
          rpginc@compuserve.com

137-138, 167-169,
196-197, 324-325,
349-350

Contributor	Pages Resumes Appear On
Louise Garver, CPRW, CMP CAREER DIRECTIONS 115 Elm Street, Suite 104 Enfield, CT 06082 Phone: (860) 253-0432 Fax: (860) 623-9473 Email: CAREERDIRS@aol.com	112-113, 253-254, 308
Meg Guiseppi, CPRW RESUMES PLUS 132 Newton-Sparta Rd. Newton, NJ 07860 Phone: (973) 383-9621 Fax: (973) 383-1974 Email: resumesplus@nac.net	161, 227, 223, 305
E. René Hart, CPRW FIRST IMPRESSIONS RESUME & CAREER DEVELOPMENT SERVICES 7100 Pebble Pass Loop Lakeland, FL 33810 Phone: (941) 859-2439 / (888) 9-RESUME Fax: (941) 859-9718 Email: FLResumes@aol.com	176-178, 279-280, 315-316, 320-321
Beverly Harvey, CPRW BEVERLEY HARVEY RESUME & CAREER SERVICES 815 S. Volusia Avenue, Suite 12 Orange City, FL 32763 Phone: (904) 775-0916 Fax: (904) 775-6886 Email: bhss@n-jcenter.com	91-92, 125-126, 170-171, 200-201, 237-240, 256-257, 326-327
Susan Higgins, CPRW Q RESUME SERVICE 3368 Independence Street Grove City, OH 43123 Phone: (614) 873-3123 Fax: (614) 873-3123 Email: SusanQ@aol.com	81, 93-94, 313-314

Contributor	*Pages Resumes Appear On*
Kim Isaacs, CPRW, NCRW ADVANCED CAREER SYSTEMS 34-41 85th Street, Suite 6G Jackson Heights, NY 11372 Phone: (718) 565-8016 Fax: (718) 565-8016 Email: CareerSys@aol.com	79, 136, 148, 182, 296
Melissa Kasler, CPRW RESUME IMPRESSIONS One North Lancaster Athens, OH 45701 Phone: (740) 592-3993 Fax: (740) 592-1352 Email: mkasler2@eurekanet.com	147, 248, 262, 281, 338
Ann Klint, CPRW ANN'S PROFESSIONAL RESUME SERVICE 1608 Cimmarron Trail Tyler, TX 75703 Phone: (903) 509-8333 Fax: (903) 509-8333 Email: Resumes-Ann@tyler.net	86-87, 127-128, 287-288, 309-310, 311
Myriam-Rose Kohn, CPRW JEDA ENTERPRISES 27201 Tourney Road, Suite 201 Valencia, CA 91355 Phone: (805) 253-0801 Fax: (805) 253-0744 Email: jeda@pacificnet.net	194-195, 362-363
Louise Kursmark BEST IMPRESSION 9847 Catalpa Woods Court Cincinnati, OH 45242 Phone: (513) 792-0030 Fax: (513) 792-0961 Email: Louisekbi@aol.com	52, 54, 208-209, 295, 351

Contributor	*Pages Resumes Appear On*
Carol Lawrence, CPRW A BETTER RESUME P.O. Box 9826 Savannah, GA 31412 Phone: (912) 832-4438 Fax: (912) 832-4385 Email: APlusOSI@aol.com	99-100, 153-154, 297, 341, 328-329
Sally McIntosh ADVANTAGE RESUMES 35 Westfair Drive Jacksonville, IL 62650 Phone: (217) 245-0752 Fax: (217) 243-4451 Email: SallySJM@aol.com	82, 224
Marie Keenen Mansheim SUMMIT CAREER SERVICES 7410 Blueberry Court Wausau, WI 54401 Phone: (715) 359-8089 / (800) 693-8072 Fax: (715) 359-2586 Email: Mansheim@dwave.net	103, 109, 204-205, 265-266
Veronica A.C. Martish CONNECTICUT WORKS 1320 Main Street Willimantic, CT 06226 Phone: (860) 465-2123 Fax: (860) 450-7527	90, 312
Diane McGoldrick BUSINESS SERVICES OF TAMPA BAY 2803 W. Busch Blvd. #103 Tampa, FL 33618 Phone: (813) 935-2700 Fax: (813) 935-4777 Email: mcgoldrk@ix.netcom.com	80, 183-184, 293-294

Contributor	*Pages Resumes Appear On*

Debra O'Reilly, CPRW
A FIRST IMPRESSION RESUME SERVICE
16 Terryville Avenue
Bristol, CT 06010
Phone: (860) 583-7500 / (800) 340-5570
Fax: (860) 585-9611
Email: debra@resumewriter.com

106, 245, 267

Donald P. Orlando, CPRW
THE MCLEAN GROUP
640 South McDonough
Montgomery, AL 36104-5850
Phone: (334) 264-2020
Fax: (334) 264-9227
Email: ORLANDORES@aol.com

250

Walt Schuette, CPRW
THE VILLAGE WORDSMITH
931 South Mission Road, Suite B
Fallbrook, CA 92028
Phone: (760) 728-1884 / (800) 200-1884
Fax: (760) 728-1025
Email: wrschuette@aol.com

101-102, 114,
118-119, 174-175,
225, 258

Deborah L. Schuster, CPRW
THE LETTERSMITH WRITING & DESIGN
P.O. Box 202
Newport, MI 48166
Phone: (734) 586-3335 / (800) 586-3335
Fax: (734) 586-2766
Email: lettersmith@foxberry.net

122-123, 134,
139-140, 165-166,
270-271

Makini Siwatu, CPRW
ACCENT ON WORDS
1601 El Camino Real, Suite 301
Belmont, CA 94002-3943
Phone: (650) 595-2514
Fax: (650) 595-0706
Email: AccentWrds@aol.com

180-181, 272-273,
366

Contributor	*Pages Resumes Appear On*
Rebecca Stokes, CPRW THE ADVANTAGE, INC. 119 Old Stable Road Lynchburg, VA 24503 Phone: (804) 384-4600 / (800) 922-5353 Fax: (804) 384-4700 Email: wenelow@aol.com wenelow@inmind.com	77-78, 84-85, 110, 111, 121-122, 135, 241-242, 290-292, 307
John A. Suarez, CPRW THE RESUME CENTER 807 West Highway 50, Suite 6 O'Fallon, IL 62269 Phone (618) 624-0707 Fax (618) 632-5670 Email: JASuarez@aol.com	52, 56, 107-108, 172-173, 179, 190-191, 277-278, 304, 334-335
Gina Taylor ABOUT THE OFFICE 1111 West 77th Terrace Kansas City, MO 64114 Phone: (816) 523-9100 Fax: (816) 523-6566 Email: GinaResume@aol.com	187-189, 202-203, 246-247, 336-337, 359
Susan Britton Whitcomb, CPRW, NCRW ALPHA OMEGA RESUME SERVICES 1255 West Shaw Avenue, Suite 100-A Fresno, CA 93711 Phone: (209) 222-7474 / (888) 449-7474 Fax: (209) 222-9538 Email: TopResum@aol.com	151-152, 163, 306, 339
Terri Zbick THE WRITE CONNECTION 2541 Monroe Avenue, Suite B3 Rochester, NY 14618 Phone: (716) 244-0390 Fax: (716) 232-1414 Email: ResumeLady@aol.com	53, 55, 228

For more information on the Professional Association of Resume Writers (PARW), contact:

Frank Fox, Executive Director
PARW HEADQUARTERS
3637 Fourth Street North, Suite 330
St. Petersburg, FL 33704
Phone: (800) 822-7279
Fax: (813) 894-1277
Email: PARWHQ@aol.com

RESUME WINNERS FROM THE PROS

Chapter 1

You Can Win!

RESUME WRITING = CAREER MARKETING

*R*esume writing is career marketing! It is understanding that you have a product to sell (YOURSELF) and determining how you can best "merchandise" that product to attract the right audience. Your challenge is to create a top-flight marketing communication – a powerful resume that will open doors, get interviews and help you land that next great job. It is that simple ... yet that complex.

> *Those who win in the "resume writing game" are those who successfully integrate core marketing strategies into their resumes and job search campaigns.*

Your task is to identify the skills, qualifications, experiences and achievements you possess that are most relevant to, and most supportive of, your current job search objectives. In theory, you take every item of your career, "lay it out on the table," and then select what to include, how to include it and where to include it based on your current goals. There must be a strategy behind your resume based on *"who you are and how you want to be perceived."* Then, use that strategy to:

> *Paint the picture you want your reader to see!*

If your objective is a position as a Chief Financial Officer, focus your resume on core financial expertise and related financial achievements. You will, of course, integrate non-financial achievements that may include technology installations, business turn-arounds, start-up ventures, human resource affairs and corporate administration.

If, however, you are that same CFO and your objective is a position as Chief Operating Officer, President or Chief Executive Officer, focus your resume on general management qualifications. These may include multi-site operations, P&L management, organizational leadership, strategic planning and visioning, market development, sales and service management, and much more. Of course, there will be a strong focus on finance (it is your core competency), but your challenge is to "create a picture" of a well-qualified Senior Management Executive.

Look at the difference between each of these summaries for the same job seeker:

Sample 1.

CHIEF FINANCIAL OFFICER
Start-Up, High-Growth, Turnaround & Multinational Companies

Dynamic management career building and leading best-in-class finance and accounting organizations for partnerships, joint ventures and Fortune 100 companies worldwide. Combines expert strategic planning and finance qualifications with strong business development, negotiation and leadership skills.

- Financial Planning & Analysis
- General Accounting & Reporting
- Budgeting (Capital & Operating)
- Tax Planning & Cash Control
- Investment Management
- Equity & Debt Financing
- Corporate Lending
- Asset Yield & Optimization

Sample 2.

SENIOR EXECUTIVE PROFILE

<u>Cross-Functional Leadership Success in:</u>
P&L Management / Multi-Site Operations / Finance
Human Resources / Performance Improvement
IS Technology / Contracts / Legal

Fifteen-year management career building profitable business and marketing organizations throughout emerging nations worldwide. Decisive, proactive leadership style. Harvard MBA.

You can see the dramatic difference in the perceived identity of the same individual based on the two different summaries. We have "printed" two different pictures.

Even if you are a talented sales and marketing executive, it is often difficult to "sell the product" when **you** are the product. Take the time that is necessary to develop a strong resume, ask your colleagues for assistance, carefully review other resumes, or hire a professional resume writer. The time, effort and energy you devote to developing your resume will pay for itself over and over. Remember, your resume is the single most critical tool in your job search campaign!

RESUME WRITING = ACTION

Your drive, energy and enthusiasm is the single most important catalyst in accelerating your search campaign. That same level of energy and confidence must be communicated in your resume, cover letters and other job search materials. Companies want to hire winners. And winners are confident in their performance. Successfully communicate that message within your resume and you will *win at your job search!*

To succeed in the resume writing process, you must identify the features and benefits that "sell" you to a prospective employer. Then, carefully with great thought, present that information in your resume. You must use a format that supports your current career objectives, highlights appropriate qualifications and uses the right KeyWords that will get you noticed, not passed over.

Consider the following scenario: You are CEO of Outdoor Adventures & Expeditions, Inc., a high-growth company ready for further expansion. You have run an advertisement in *The Wall Street Journal* for a Regional Sales Director and within one week you have 829 resumes on your desk and at least 200 phone messages from prospective candidates. It would be easier to just do the job yourself (if you had the time), than to try to work your way through this task.

You spend the next week sifting through resumes that all say the same thing. Each prospective candidate highlights his/her strong presentation, negotiation, sales closing, customer management and product management experience. **YOU ALREADY KNOW ALL THESE THINGS!** They are the job specifications. Nothing is new. Nothing is distinctive. Nothing is unique.

Then you spot resume #628 and something is different. This resume is interesting! It highlights special projects, challenges, achievements, product performance, revenue growth and much more. You are impressed not only with the quality of this individual's qualifications, but with the time and effort that went into preparing the resume. You want to interview this candidate!

Is that candidate you? It certainly can be if you devote the energy to learn the tricks and techniques that will allow you to effectively market your skills, create a top-flight resume and win in today's competitive job search market.

Your objectives when preparing your resume are to:
GENERATE INTEREST AND GET AN INTERVIEW!

RESUME STRATEGIES THAT SELL!

The first recorded history of resumes dates back to cavemen who used pictographic presentations to demonstrate their skills. Later, Egyptians used papyrus to write down their qualifications. Over the centuries, as a large part of the world's workforce industrialized, resumes became "standard" job search tools to highlight employment, education, technical skills and qualifications. Now, as the U.S. employment market has virtually reinvented itself, resumes have become strategic and competitive marketing tools, the cornerstone for every successful job search.

Why? The answer is simple: Resumes are *the tools* that allow you to creatively, aggressively and succinctly "sell" your qualifications to a prospective employer. Resumes are your personal introduction, your opportunity to highlight skills, experience and accomplishments, and open the door to potential career opportunities. Resumes are the backbone of today's sophisticated job search and career management process.

> *The purpose of your resume is to get interviews.*
> *Resumes do not get jobs!*

The most intriguing aspect of resume writing is that *there are no rules*, no definitive procedures that dictate what you must include in your resume and how. The choice is yours. The opportunity is there to "sell" your success and competitively position yourself against other candidates by creating a resume that is aesthetically-sharp, achievement-oriented and a "cut above" other candidates.

There is a specific strategy to resume writing. It is not simply a piece of paper on which you list your employment experience and education. You must think carefully about your professional skills and experiences, and how these support your current career objectives. Use this information as your guiding strategy, and write your resume to highlight those "*features and benefits.*"

Consider the following. You are an innovative new product ready for market launch. What do you do? You:

1. ***Develop a marketing strategy*** ... A plan of action that highlights potential market opportunities and specific action plans to get your product (YOU) in the door.

2. ***Design creative marketing materials*** ... In this case, resume, cover letters and other marketing communications to attract prospective buyers (employers).

3. ***Communicate the features and benefits of the product*** ... If you do not clearly highlight your qualifications and achievements, they will never be noticed. Remember, prospective employers tend only to glance at resumes for 5-10 seconds.

4. ***Communicate the value of the product and potential for positive results*** ... Demonstrate, through achievement, that you have delivered strong operating, financial, revenue, profit and leadership results.

Just as outlined above, resume writing is the same process as selling, marketing and merchandising any other product. Your challenge is to communicate what makes the product of value and why the prospective buyer needs the product. This, specifically, is the function of your resume and cover letter.

Resume Messages To Communicate

- Value
- Energy
- Success
- Technical Skills
- Leadership Skills
- Achievements
- Features
- Contributions
- Professional Skills
- Management Skills
- Results
- Benefits
- Performance
- Power
- Honesty

When writing your resume, you must communicate success and achievement by demonstrating:

- Revenue & Profit Increases

- Market Share Gains

- Productivity, Quality & Performance Improvements

- Process Simplification & Consolidation

- Major Client Successes

- Special Projects & Task Forces

- New Systems Design & Implementation

- Pioneering Technology Advances

- Cost Reductions & Avoidance

- Cash Flow & Yield Improvements

- Team Building & Leadership Success

- Start-Up & Emerging Growth Ventures

- Turnaround & Reengineering Initiatives

- International Expansion & Global Positioning

- Mergers, Acquisitions, Strategic Alliances & Partnerships

The above is just a brief listing of the vast number of accomplishments to highlight in your resume. Consider the strategy behind your resume (aka – your current career objectives) to determine which achievements to include, where, when and how.

Be a winner!

Chapter 2
Anatomy Of A Winning Resume

WINNERS' GUIDELINES

Following are the Top 10 guidelines to resume writing and job search success. Read them carefully and live by them.

1. *If anyone ever tells you that there are rules for resume writing, walk away.* The single most important concept in resume writing is that **THERE ARE NO RULES!** Each individual's situation is unique and must be considered in determining resume style, content, format and presentation.

   Because there are no rules, resume writing can be a challenge. Options are unlimited and may appear unclear. Of course, your resume must communicate certain basic information such as employment history, education, professional licenses, technology skills and more. How you present that information can vary widely in format and presentation based on your particular career history, skills, qualifications and objectives. You must determine:

   - What information you want to communicate.
   - How best to communicate that information.
   - What format to select and why.
   - What typestyle to use and why.
   - The appropriate length for your resume.

This book will help you do just that. All of the resumes that follow have been written by the "best of the best" resume writers nationwide. Many have earned the professional distinction of Certified Professional Resume Writer (CPRW), an examination and certification program sponsored by the Professional Association of Resume Writers. These writers are all professionals and clearly understand what it takes to win in today's competitive job search market.

Review their resumes carefully and you will note a diversity of styles and formats. Each was prepared with a specific objective in mind and was structured to highlight the skills of that individual as they related to his/her objectives. Look at how flexible these documents can be, allowing each individual to structure and present qualifications in a style that is most supportive of his/her current career goals.

Although many consider resume writing to be a cumbersome challenge, it can be fun. It is a creative process that encourages you to review your entire career history, identify your skills and achievements, and present that information in a manner that "sells" you to a particular audience. Use the resumes in this book to get ideas for content, style, format and presentation of your resume. Be one of the winners!

2. ***"Don't just tell it to me ... Sell it to me!"*** is a key concept in resume writing, allowing you to transition your job functions into specific achievements and create a resume that communicates action, results and success. For example:

    TELLING: Supervised 200 production employees.
    SELLING: Trained, mentored and led a team of 200 employees that reached record production volumes.

Which sentence excites you? Which individual appears to be more qualified? Whom would you want to interview?

Here are a few more examples of how to transition job function and responsibility into success and achievement:

For Accounting Positions:

TELLING: Supervised accounting and monthly financial reporting.

SELLING: Managed a staff of 12 responsible for daily accounting operations, monthly financial reporting, special projects and year-end reconciliations.

For Administrative Positions:

TELLING: Managed daily office operations.

SELLING: Streamlined daily office operations, consolidated reporting functions, and implemented new PC software to expedite order processing.

For Health Care Positions:

TELLING: Expanded into emerging health care markets.

SELLING: Negotiated joint ventures and strategic partnerships to launch NNC's entry into emerging home health care, respiratory care and managed care markets. Projecting first year revenues at more than $5 million.

For Manufacturing Positions:

TELLING: Directed a 24x7 manufacturing operation.

SELLING: Redesigned core processes for a 245-person, 24x7 manufacturing operation. Reduced material costs 24%, improved production yields 18% and achieved/surpassed all quality objectives.

For Purchasing Positions:

TELLING: Negotiated purchasing and service agreements.

SELLING: Structured and negotiated over $22 million in annual purchasing contracts and service agreements with suppliers nationwide.

For Sales Positions:

TELLING: Managed growth in the company's Western U.S. markets.

SELLING: Closed $200 million in sales (125% of quota), building Western Region to #1 revenue producer in the company.

For Teaching Positions:

TELLING: Improved classroom performance.

SELLING: Redesigned core curriculum, created new instructional materials and improved students' academic performance.

For Technology Positions:

TELLING: Upgraded IS architecture to better support operations.

SELLING: Championed transition from System 36 to LAN-based client/server system, led software and applications development team, and strengthened IS support to business units worldwide.

The *"Sell It ... Don't Tell It"* concept is also a valuable interviewing tool when you apply the same selling concepts to your verbal presentation. Remember, the impact of your words – either verbally or through written communication – creates a perception of who you are and the value you bring to an organization. Be sure to use the right words and presentation to "sell" your qualifications and differentiate yourself from the crowd.

> *Success in translating your job functions into achievements will be a key factor in the quality and "saleability" of your resume. Work to sell your qualifications without overstating the truth.*

3. ***Be honest, but don't be modest.*** Your resume is your "public speaking platform" – the place to highlight your career performance. You should boast ***nicely***, demonstrate your leadership and management talents ***genuinely*** and "sell" your achievements ***truthfully.*** Resume writing is not a time for humility, but is a time for honesty and integrity.

> ***RESUME CREED:***
> *Sell, Sell, Sell ... But*
> *"always remain in the realm of reality!"*

4. ***Your resume must be bold, aggressive and positive***, clearly communicating your strengths, achievements, qualifications and track record of performance. Often the best place to highlight this information is in a summary section at the beginning of your resume. You can use either a bullet format or paragraph format to quickly communicate your most notable qualifications and achievements as they relate to your current objectives. For more information on summary sections, refer to pages 15-17.

5. ***Your resume must be easy to read and conducive to a quick perusal.*** The first time someone reviews your resume will be with a quick glance. Be sure your that resume highlights (through structure, presentation, format and typestyle), the words, phrases and achievements to immediately capture each reader's attention.

6. ***Your resume must include your professional employment history.*** A prospective employer wants a clean and concise employment history that is quick and easy to review, and includes company names, locations (NOT full addresses), job titles and dates.

    •   Professional and executive job search candidates – Use years only for employment dates.

    •   Graduating students and individuals with fewer than five years of experience – Use both months and years to strengthen your presentation.

    If you are a "more seasoned" job search candidate (50+ years of age), how much of your past experience you include and how you present it will vary dramatically based on your career and current objectives. Please refer to pages 36-39 for more detailed information regarding age and its impact on your resume presentation.

7. ***Your resume must highlight your professional achievements and contributions.*** There is no other document more appropriate than your resume to "toot your own horn." Use it to "sell" your career achievements, successes and contributions, including revenue and profit improvements, cost

reductions, technology installations, major reengineering projects, start-up ventures, successful turnarounds and much more. Refer to pages 25-31 for more information on the content and presentation of career achievements.

8. *Your resume must include your educational credentials, colleges, degrees, certifications, licenses and other academic training.* Be brief, but comprehensive. Whether you choose to include college related activities will depend on your age, number of years of work experience, and significance of each activity. Refer to pages 20-21 for detailed information on presenting your educational credentials.

9. *Your resume must communicate that you are computer literate.* If you are in a technology field, you will most likely include a separate section in your resume detailing your technical qualifications (e.g., hardware, software, networks, applications, operating systems, programming languages).

    If your primary career field is not technology, you still want to communicate in your resume that you are computer literate. Consider one of the following options:

    -   Include a brief statement in your summary that mentions you are computer literate. For example, "PC proficient with Microsoft Office and Windows 95."

    -   Highlight technology skills and achievements within your job descriptions. For example, "Team member on $250,000 PC network installation project to link field sales operations to corporate headquarters."

- Include your email address at the top of your resume. By doing so, you immediately communicate that you are computer and Internet proficient.

10. ***Take everyone's advice with a "grain of salt."*** Everyone, from your wife to your old boss and every recruiter you speak with, will offer differing recommendations for your resume. Listen carefully to what each person has to say and then integrate only those which are of value based on your particular situation, resume strategy and career objectives. Remember, one important rule – ***THERE ARE NO RULES TO RESUME WRITING!***

BUILDING BLOCKS FOR SUCCESS

The above discussion regarding "No Rules" in resume writing is most applicable to this section in which we are going to discuss each of the major resume categories. Two of these sections must be included on virtually every job seeker's resume – Professional Experience and Education. Other sections will only be used in your resume as appropriate to your specific career history, skills and qualifications. Review each section carefully, identify the sections related to your experience, and build your resume from that foundation.

Career Summary

The Career Summary is the apex of your resume. It is the starting point from which the entire document flows. It is the most critical because it is a snapshot of your entire career, your most significant qualifications and your most notable achievements. It is your 5-10 second "commercial" to get noticed.

Career Summaries come in many shapes and sizes. They can be titled Executive Profile, Management Profile, Skills Summary, Professional Qualifications, Professional Profile or Career Highlights. They can be written in paragraphs, bullets or a combination of both. They can be 1-2 lines; they can be 10 lines. They can highlight specific industry or business honors, awards and notable achievements. They can include patents, technology skills, publications, press coverage, leadership performance, significant revenue gains , and more.

Only you can determine what to include in your summary to ensure that you are highlighting the most distinctive aspects of your career. This varies with every job search candidate.

As you review the Career Summaries in this book, you will note the diversity of style, format and presentation. You will also note that many of the resumes begin with a *"Title Header"* which clearly defines "who" the job search candidate is. Look at each of these summaries and you instantly know that the individual is a Senior Finance Executive, Field Sales Representative, Human Resources Manager, Logistics Analyst, etc. Each resume communicates an immediate and specific message.

Here are four sample Career Summaries to give you a sampling of the diversity in style, format and presentation.

**Best Format To Demonstrate
Broad-Based Management Expertise**

SENIOR MANAGEMENT PROFILE
**General Management / P&L Management / Strategic Planning
Sales & Marketing / Customer Service / Client Management
MBA Degree**

**Best Format To Highlight Expertise In
One Core Management Function**

FINANCIAL SERVICES EXECUTIVE
Treasury, Trading & Risk Management
US / Europe / Asia / Africa

Worldwide Financial Services Executive combining financial, credit and investment experience with strong general management, operating management and P&L experience. Creative and decisive "dealmaker." Strong negotiation, presentation and relationship management skills.

NASD Series 7, 24 and 63.
Fluent in English, French and Spanish.
Proficient in Japanese.

**Best Format To Focus On
Core Competencies And KeyWords**

SALES & MARKETING PROFESSIONAL

Top-Producing Sales Professional with excellent qualifications in the planning, implementation and management of sales, marketing and business development programs. Specialization in medical and research products/equipment, health care and pharmaceutical sales. MBA in Marketing. Core competencies include:

- New Client Development
- Territory Management
- Key Account Management
- New Product Introduction
- Sales Administration & Reporting

- Sales Presentations
- Price Negotiations
- Customer Retention
- Competitive Bidding
- Sales Forecasting

Best Format To Highlight Dual Career Paths

CAREER PROFILE:

Construction Management
- Project Planning & Scheduling
- Manpower & Resource Management
- Contract Administration
- Regulatory Review & Compliance

Business Systems & Analysis
- Organizational Design
- Operations Improvement
- Strategic/Tactical Planning
- Information Systems

MBA Degree. Proficient with MS Word, Excel & Project.

Professional Experience

Professional Experience is the most important contributor to the quality and strength of your resume. It is in this section that you can best "sell" your experience, achievements and contributions, creating a picture of action, results and success.

For each position, include job title, company name, location (city and state) and dates of employment. You can write your job descriptions in paragraphs, bullets or a combination of both. Often the most effective presentation is a short paragraph introduction which identifies overall scope of responsibility – budgets, staffs, functions and challenges. Follow each introductory paragraph with a bulleted listing of achievements, highlights and special projects.

There are countless other styles and formats to present your experience. Review the resumes in this book carefully to identify those most appropriate to your career history and your current objectives. Remember, your objectives will dictate what information you include in your resume, how you include it and why. You must focus your resume on the qualifications required for the specific type of position you are seeking.

Best Format To Highlight
Long-Term Career With One Corporation:

BUSCH COMPANIES, INC.   1988 to Present

Fast-track promotion through increasingly responsible industrial engineering, project management and operating management positions. Recruited to each successive position based on consistent contributions to productivity, quality and efficiency improvement. Career highlights:

Plant Manager (1994 to Present)
Assistant Plant Manager (1992 to 1994)
Senior Industrial Engineer (1990 to 1992)
Industrial Engineer (1988 to 1990)

Senior Manager with full P&L responsibility for a $35 million production operation. Scope of responsibility is extensive and includes production operations, equipment, technology, human resources, quality, safety, maintenance and purchasing. Concurrent accountability for corporate-wide performance and productivity improvement projects. Manage $20 million annual budget.

- Delivered strong and sustainable performance results:

  - 30% increase in profitability.
  - 15% reduction in operating costs.
  - 20% improvement in production yields.
  - 56% gain in quality rating.
  - 42% reduction in Workers Compensation costs.

- Implemented self-directed work teams into a unionized facility with full support of union officials and workforce.

- Spearheaded development and implementation of a new safety training program that increased employee retention and reduced training time by an average of 50%.

> **Best Format To Highlight**
> **Broad Responsibilities In One Position**

Director – Human Resources   1994 to 1997
NATIONAL MANAGEMENT ASSOCIATION, Denver, CO

Senior HR Executive for this worldwide trade association. Responsible for three distinct HR operations:

- all generalist affairs for Association and its 110 employees.
- strategic planning and leadership of worldwide HR training.
- HR guidance and consultation to 2800 member organizations.

Achievements:

- Revitalized internal HR organization, implemented new compensation structure, enhanced performance review policy, updated employee manual and reduced turnover 90%.

- Developed and instructed a series of 10 management training programs taught to 1000+ personnel throughout North America.

- Created CD-ROM, self-paced management training program.

International Sales Manager   1995 to Present
BXT MANUFACTURING, Minneapolis, MN
(*High-growth horizontal directional drill & equipment manufacturer*)

Challenge: Accelerate international expansion, increase revenue, capture key accounts and outperform competition.

Results:
- Built global sales from $500,000 to $6 million within two years.
- Expanded market presence throughout Australia, New Zealand, Malaysia, Hong Kong, Europe and Latin America.
- Created an international dealer/distributor network.

Education

Your Education section should include your college degrees, attendance at college courses, seminars, workshops, conferences and any other professional development activities along with the name of the college, university, training institute, foundation or sponsoring organization. Be sure to highlight any distinguished academic achievements (e.g., honors, awards, scholarships, first in graduating class, notable GPA).

College activities may or may not be appropriate based on the number of years of work experience you have. If you are a recent graduate, these activities are important. If, however, you have worked professionally for 10+ years, college activities are generally not necessary, unless they are particularly significant or unique.

MBA – Finance & Technology – Harvard University – 1972
BSBA – Accounting & Economics – Tufts University – 1970

200+ Hours of Professional Education – Executive Leadership, Strategic Planning, Management, Communications, Problem Solving

Best Format For Professional Without College Degree

BARNARD COLLEGE, Barnard, Florida, 1972-1976
Electrical Engineering & Business Administration

Highlights of Continuing Professional Education:

- Center for Creative Leadership
- PC Systems & Technology
- Proactive Project Management
- Financial Management for Non-Finance Professionals

Best Format For Graduating Student

B.S., Electrical Engineering, University of Texas, 1998

- Dean's List, President's List, Cum Laude Graduate
- Member, Varsity Football & Soccer Teams
- Member, Phi Beta Kappa
- Treasurer, Student Government Association

Professional Activities

Professional Activities is a broad category for professional presentations, publications, public speaking engagements, teaching, research projects, conference attendance and industry leadership activities. This section can also include special projects, consulting assignments and other "unique" professional activities.

Professional Activities can be encapsulated into one section (if each section is only 2-3 lines) or divided into separate sections (if each section is more detailed). Use the following as a sample for a dynamic and integrated Professional Activities section.

Best Format To Highlight Professional Activities

PROFESSIONAL PROFILE:

Certification:	Registered Professional Engineer, NY, PA, VA, DE
Affiliations:	National Society of Professional Engineers American Society of Highway Engineers American Society of Industrial Engineers
Publications:	Published Author, *Euromoney* (1993) "Ergonomic Highway Design"
Languages:	Fluent in Spanish and Portuguese.
Personal:	Competitive Triathlete & Skier.

Professional Affiliations

Use this section to include memberships in professional associations and societies, including any leadership roles within these organizations. If any specific activities were particularly prominent (e.g., fiscal responsibility, marketing success, team building), also include that relevant information.

Best Format To Highlight Professional Affiliations

PROFESSIONAL AFFILIATIONS:

ASSOCIATION FOR WOMEN IN SCIENCE (AWIS)

- Board of Directors, 1996 to Present
- Treasurer, 1994 to 1996
- Member, 1992 to Present

AMERICAN ASSOCIATION FOR MEDICAL RESEARCH

- Chair, Exhibits Committee, 1996 to Present
- Member, 1995 to Present

Civic Affiliations

Civic Affiliations, such as Boy Scouts, PTA, a local church organization and the like may be included in your resume if they are highly-visible organizations and/or if you have held a significant leadership position. Other than that, civic affiliations generally do not need to be included. Of course, if you are seeking a position in association management or public appointment within the area, they may be of significant value.

Best Format to Highlight Civic Affiliations

COMMUNITY MEMBERSHIPS:

Troop Leader, Boy Scouts of America
Volunteer, Habitat for Humanity
Volunteer Treasurer, Dayton Revitalization Project
Volunteer Treasurer, Dayton Year 2000 Celebration Committee

Languages

Be sure to include all foreign language skills and levels of proficiency. You can include this information in a separate section at the end of your resume or as part of your Career Summary. Remember, the market is now global and your foreign languages may be of significant value to a prospective employer.

Best Format To Highlight Foreign Language Skills

LANGUAGE PROFICIENCY:

Fluent in French and Spanish. Conversational German & Italian.

Technical Qualifications

If you are seeking a position in a Technical or Engineering field, a Technical Qualifications section is of paramount importance. If you are in Information Systems and Technology, include hardware, software, operating systems, programming languages and network protocols. If you are in Engineering, include relevant technical skills, methodologies, equipment and related qualifications.

If you are not employed in a Technical profession, your technical qualifications can be included in your summary section or integrated into your job descriptions. A separate Technical Qualifications section is not necessary.

Best Format to Highlight Technology Skills

TECHNOLOGY QUALIFICATIONS:

Hardware:	Digital VAX, Unisys 1100, Intel-Based PCs & Servers
Software:	MS Office Suite, SQL, RDBMS, 4th GL
Networks:	DECnet, Novell Netware, LAN, WAN, Windows NT
Languages:	FORTRAN, COBOL, C, C++
Applications:	Closed Loop Manufacturing, Order Entry, Billing, Project Management, General Ledger, Purchasing

Personal Information

Generally, do not include Personal Information in your resume. Your resume is a marketing tool designed to sell your professional qualifications. It is not the platform to note marital status, wife's name, number of children, birth date, the fact that you enjoy reading and golfing, and that you have excellent health (what else would you say). Keep your resume to the "professional" point.

There are instances, however, when personal information will be of significant value. These situations may include:

- Permanent U.S. Residency Status or U.S. Citizenship.
- Country of Birth (if seeking an international position).
- Competitive Athletics (shows teamwork and perseverance).
- Personal Data directly relevant to the position.
- Personal Data requested in an advertisement.

Best Format To Highlight Personal Information

PERSONAL PROFILE:

Born June 15, 1962 in Budapest, Hungary.
Permanent U.S. Resident.
Fluent in English, Hungarian, Italian, French & German.
Competitive Triathlete. 1978 Hungarian Downhill Olympic Team.

"SELLING" YOUR CAREER ACHIEVEMENTS

Career achievements are the centerpiece of your resume. Many are quantifiable accomplishments such as revenue gains, profit increases, operating improvements, labor cost reductions, efficiency enhancements and more. However, there are just as many equally significant achievements that cannot be quantified. These include technology installations, process improvements, leadership training and development, change management initiatives, strategic planning, financial planning, and much more.

> *Career achievements do not have to have a number or percentage attached to it to be notable. Many very impressive accomplishments simply are not quantifiable.*

Carefully review the following list of sample achievements, highlighted for the same professions as the resumes that follow in this book. From this list, you will get a good sampling of the various types of career successes, achievements and contributions that can be incorporated into your resume.

Use the following list to develop your own achievements and then incorporate them into one of three sections in your resume:

1. Your Career Summary or Profile (at the top of your resume).
2. A special section titled Achievements or Career Highlights.
3. Integrated within appropriate job descriptions.

LIST OF SAMPLE ACHIEVEMENTS

Accounting

- Identified cost overrides in contractor fees, renegotiated contracts and saved over $2.3 million in annual costs.

Administration

- Introduced new PC technologies to streamline and consolidate customer tracking, sales order processing, recordkeeping and management reporting.

Association Management

- Led the association through a period of explosive growth and expansion, building national membership from less than 200 to more than 1200 within the first year.

Banking

- Negotiated with creditors, restored investor confidence, and delivered sustainable growth in fee income and asset value.

Customer Service

- Reorganized a 400-employee customer service and call center operation, reduced annual operating costs by 23% and delivered customer satisfaction ratings consistently above 98%.

Engineering

- Led cross-functional engineering team in the specification, design, testing and final production of six new industrial products projected to increase annual sales by a minimum of 15%.

Finance

- Restructured and renegotiated over $100 million in corporate debt while lowering debt carrying fees by more than 8%.

Government

- Prepared RFPs, managed review process and awarded over $92 million in A&E contracts.

Graduating Student

- Maintained a 4.0 GPA while working full-time.

Healthcare

- Transitioned from single site to multi-site provider organization, established preferred provider network and built revenues from $15 million to $800+ million in five years.

Hospitality

- Implemented internal controls which reduced labor costs by 15% and food costs by an additional 18%.

Human Resources

- Introduced performance improvement, quality-driven leadership and corporate culture change to support the organization through a period of massive reorganization.

Human Services

- Lobbied before various political and civic groups, increasing program funding by $200,000 for FY98.

Information Technology

- Developed and implemented new Information Management System to replace obsolete technology. Managed $2 million project from concept through acquisition, customization, configuration planning, installation and user training/support. Delivered project three weeks ahead of schedule.

Insurance

- Introduced commercial lines, launched regional marketing and sales programs, and improved year-over-year results by 35%.

International Business

- Led the company's successful expansion into emerging international markets in Africa, Asia and Latin America. Delivered first year revenues of $20 million (215% of quota).

Investment Finance

- Negotiated $250 million in secured/unsecured loans, debt and equity participations, and acquisitions for Fortune 500 clients.

Law/Attorney

- Won precedent-setting case involving corporate liability relative to international trade and cross-border transactions.

Logistics

- Consolidated distribution, warehousing and transportation into one new division, streamlined process flow, and reduced net costs by more than $3 million annually.

Manufacturing

- Introduced improved materials handling, inventory planning and assembly processes that increased production yields 11%.

Marketing

- Led creative, strategic and tactical team in the global market launch of new PCS technology to regain competitive lead in the telecommunications industry. Achieved $54 million in sales.

Media

- Conceived, designed and produced award-winning multimedia corporate sales and marketing presentations.

Meeting Planning & Special Events

- Planned, staffed, budgeted and directed conferences, symposia, meetings and special events for up to 5000 participants annually at Xerox's Executive Training Institute.

Military Conversion

- Acquired strong qualifications in team building, team leadership, crisis management, problem solving and action planning, easily transferable into commercial and industrial markets.

Public Relations

- Won favorable press coverage with major media nationwide despite company's financial and market instability.

Purchasing

- Sourced vendors worldwide to replace U.S. technology suppliers, lowering annual material costs by better than 18% while increasing overall product quality ratings.

Quality

- Led the corporation to successful ISO 9000 certification (first industrial manufacturer in Pennsylvania to achieve ISO 9000).

Real Estate

- Captured $325 million in venture capital funding for two large real estate development and urban revitalization projects.

Research & Science

- Pioneered the use of radioactive isotopes for broad industrial applications to support the company's transition from military to commercial markets.

Retail

- Drove growth of this new retail venture from one site, 12 employees and $350,000 in annual sales to 10 locations, 250 employees and over $28 million in annual sales.

Sales

- Revitalized dormant sales region and delivered a 34% increase in annual revenues. Closed 1997 at 125% of quota.

Senior Executive

- Credited with providing renewed vision, energy and leadership to transition company from loss to double digit profit within 18 months.

Sports & Recreation

- Led UCLA's basketball team to four consecutive years of top ranked performance.

Teaching

- Introduced new instructional programs and laboratory projects to expand Electronics Technology curriculum.

Achievements are the core message you want to communicate in your resume. Devote the time and energy required to carefully review your career history and identify the experiences, special projects and accomplishments you have to offer to a prospective employer. Integrate that information with your current objective to create a resume that positions you for success.

> *Resume Writing is Merchandising ...*
> *Highlight the Features, Benefits,*
> *Value & Achievements of the Product –*
> *YOU!*

Chapter 3

Meet The Challenges And Beat The Odds

ONE PAGE VERSUS TWO PAGES
What Is The Answer For You?

For as long as people have been writing resumes, there has been controversy over the length of the document. Should all resumes be one page or is a two-page resume just as acceptable? What about three or four pages?

Years ago, it was accepted that most resumes were one page. Keep it short and to the point was the "rule." The resume was just a brief outline for use in a reasonably non-competitive job market. Today, all this has changed. With tremendous competition in virtually all job sectors, resumes have transitioned into high-impact marketing tools, some that are one page, some that are two, and in very select circumstances, some that are even longer.

As before, your goal in resume writing is to be succinct and to the point. However, you must balance that with a focus on "selling" your success. Your ability to market your qualifications and incorporate achievements into your resume is what will differentiate you from the crowd, open the door for interviews and get offers. If this means expanding your resume to two pages, so be it.

Consider the following: If sales professionals simply stated what they sold and to whom, all of their resumes would be virtually the same. What gives a resume competitive distinction is how well those sales functions are performed. The best strategy to communicate results is through demonstrated achievements.

If you have effectively marketed your achievements and qualifications in your resume, it does not matter whether it is one or two pages. Each works equally well. The difference in response rate is entirely dependent on the quality of your resume and the message of success you have communicated. Length **does not** impact results.

If your resume is three or more pages, consider the following:

- Can your message be communicated on just two pages?
- Are your achievements or qualifications so significant that three or more pages are required?
- What do others think about the length of your resume?
- Does your resume make you appear old?
- Did you use a typestyle that is too large?
- Why do you think your resume should be longer than two pages?
- Is your resume getting interviews and results?

If your answers to these questions are the "right" answers, and you are getting strong results, continue to use your resume as is. Remember, there are no rules in resume writing. The key is to sell and merchandise what you have to offer and the value you bring to a prospective employer. If a three or four page resume is an appropriate search tool based on your specific situation, and you are getting strong results, drive forward. You are already winning at the job search game.

NOTE: If you are a clinical health care provider, researcher, scientist or academician, it is acceptable that your resume be longer than two pages. In your professions, it is important to include all academic credentials, research studies, licenses, public speaking engagements, publications, work experiences, internships and other specifics that support your professional standing. Obviously, with the addition of this information, a two-page resume generally becomes virtually impossible.

> *The response to your job search campaign will be directly dependent on how well you have marketed your qualifications and achievements; not on number of pages!*

CHRONOLOGICAL VERSUS FUNCTIONAL RESUMES
And Other Equally Confusing Options

In job search, there has long been controversy among resume writers, career counselors, recruiters and employers regarding chronological versus functional resumes. The debate continues today. You have to make the decision as to which of these two formats is best for you, or if a modified version would be most appropriate based on your specific employment experience and current career goals.

A *chronological resume* is a resume that presents your work experience in a chronological format, from most recent to past. These types of resumes are the most common. Use a chronological resume when your career path has been steady and strong, and you want to paint a clear picture of who you are, where you have worked and what you have accomplished.

A *functional resume* focuses on highlighting skills and either (1) does not include employment history at all, or (2) includes a brief listing of employment history at the end of the resume. Functional resumes are generally **NOT** the preferred resume structure as they can often communicate a vague message. Careful consideration must be given when deciding to use a functional resume to be sure that it is the appropriate job search tool and that your message is clear and concise. Use a functional resume when:

- You are attempting to paint a unique picture about your career history that is more dependent on skills and achievements than on your chronological career track.

- Your employment history has not been progressive and you want to downplay your most recent position.

- Your employment history has been erratic with extensive periods of unemployment.

- You are an older job search candidate attempting to highlight skills and experiences you acquired early in your career.

- You are a recent college graduate with strong internship, volunteer, employment and/or leadership experience to emphasize your professional qualifications and compete more effectively.

A *modified chronological resume* provides you with the "best of both". This type of resume begins with a Career Summary focused on presenting skills and achievements that are most noteworthy and related to your current objectives (much the same as a Functional Resume). However, to offset the potential vagueness of a true functional resume, the next section to follow is Professional Experience, chronologically detailing your positions, responsibilities, achievements and success. Many of the resumes presented in this book use a modified chronological format to best communicate each candidate's qualifications.

An *achievement-oriented resume* can also be a strong marketing tool. These resumes focus on presenting career achievements as the primary benefit you bring to an organization. In achievement-oriented resumes, accomplishments are the primary focus, generally integrated into a section titled Career Highlights or Professional Achievements at the top of your resume. However, be wary! Achievement-oriented resumes can also be vague in nature, leaving your reader with a sense of incompleteness and not a firm grasp of what you have done, for whom and how well. It is critical to communicate achievements in a manner that is easy to comprehend and easy to assimilate into the prospective employer's current needs.

HELP! I'M 50+ YEARS OF AGE!

Age can be a critical concern in resume writing and career marketing if you are an "older" job search candidate (age 50+). You have the unique challenge of "selling" your qualifications while not excluding yourself from consideration because of your age.

If you are 50+ years of age, you must carefully consider your experience, dates of employment, dates of education, and current objectives to determine what information you want to include in your resume and how. You **DO NOT** want to include information that could be potentially exclusionary; specifically, dates prior to 1968 (although as with all things in resume writing, this is not a hard and fast "rule"). Here are some guidelines to live by:

If you graduated from college in 1968 and have been working ever since, include your entire career history (even if you have to summarize at the end to meet your spacing requirements). If, however, you graduated prior to 1968, you will want to give serious consideration to:

- whether or not to include your college graduation date. If you do, you will immediately date yourself. If you do not, you will be masking the fact that you are older, but certainly not fooling anyone.

- whether or not to include employment experience prior to 1968. If the experience is notable because of the employer, your position or your achievements, you may want to summarize at the end of your resume with no dates. Just include the highlights. For example:

Sample 1.

Previous professional experience included a series of increasingly responsible accounting and financial management positions with ***Air France***, ***Swiss Air*** and several other prominent European airlines.

Sample 2.

Previous professional experience was highlighted by consistent ranking as the *#1/#2 sales producer in IBM's nationwide sales organization*.

Sample 3.

Previous Professional Experience: Promoted from Purchasing Assistant to Purchasing Agent to Director of Purchasing & Materials for the Foster Manufacturing Corporation.

By using one of the above scenarios, you can benefit from the success of your past experiences without having to divulge your specific age.

But remember, by not including dates, you are still communicating the message that you are an older job search candidate. However, you are "easing the blow" by leaving off dates that may immediately exclude you. People reviewing resumes often look at dates before they have ever reviewed your qualifications. To counterbalance this, you want to create a resume that focuses on your success and achievements, not on the number of years you have been working.

Do not interpret any of this as a message to lie or misrepresent. Rather, remember what your resume's mission is – to market your qualifications and open the door for interviews. Your resume is designed to highlight your skills, experiences, competencies and successes. It is not a comprehensive biography that details each and every thing you have done since the beginning of your career. Your resume **DOES NOT** have to be comprehensive!

Fortunately for older job search candidates, there is good news! With the increasing prevalence of consultants and interim executives throughout our nation's workforce, age is becoming less of a consideration. Companies are looking to hire (often within unique parameters) the most qualified candidates to solve problems, accelerate growth, increase revenues, strengthen profits, manage special projects, launch new ventures and more. No longer is every job a marriage. More positions are now available in unique settings with non-traditional job titles and varied responsibilities. The explosion in consulting and interim assignments has been a great boost in expanding the opportunities available for the older job search candidate and complementing existing, more traditional employment opportunities.

If you are under 50 years old, your age should not be a major concern in your job search, unless a particularly unusual circumstance. As such, you should proceed with resume development as usual and include all dates.

> *Create a resume that focuses on achievement and success ... Not on your age and years of employment experience.*

NEVER ... NEVER ... NEVER ...

... Except for Unique Circumstances

(*See! There really are no rules in resume writing!*)

---

1. *NEVER prepare a resume that does not include dates of employment.* The entire document becomes too vague and often renders itself worthless. Dates, along with employers and position titles, are the infrastructure of your resume and support everything else. Do not prepare a document that is difficult to interpret. You will, more often than not, become

frustrated with your search and unable to find an opportunity because no one "understands" your resume.

2. ***NEVER prepare a resume that does not include the name of your current employer (if you are employed).*** You want a prospective employer to be willing to take the time to interview you, yet you won't even share the name of your employer? It just doesn't "feel" right and past response to this type of resume has been consistently poor.

   Be assured that 99% of the time, prospective employers will respect your confidentiality and not contact your current employer. But be honest. The potential does exist, no matter how slim. If you are committed to your job search, go for it.

3. ***NEVER include any dates on your resume prior to 1968.*** As discussed in the previous section, dates and age are a critical concern in resume writing and career marketing. Your goal is to include information that will sell you and your qualifications, not eliminate you from consideration. Dates can do just that.

4. ***NEVER lie, misrepresent or mislead.*** If you believe that misrepresenting your educational and/or professional experience will make a significant difference in the success of your job search, you are mistaken. It simply is not worth it. Why risk losing a potentially great career opportunity and hinder your further career progression?

5. ***NEVER include any information that you will have to "defend" in an interview.*** "Sell" your achievements, but be honest and be truthful. Resume writing provides you with

the opportunity to embellish and enhance your performance. Temper that with a commitment to 100% accuracy.

6.   ***NEVER send a resume without an accompanying cover letter.*** Cover letters are part of job search etiquette and a critical component in the success of your job search. Each cover letter allows you the opportunity to highlight the skills, qualifications and achievements you offer that are directly related to that company's needs. Use your cover letters to further sell your performance, highlight related experience and get you in the door for an interview.

7.   ***NEVER include salary on your resume.*** If a prospective employer or recruiter requests salary information, use your cover letter to include the specifics. The only exception is when preparing a resume for submission to the U.S. Federal Government. This type of resume must include your full salary history (beginning and ending for each position), along with other specific data, including supervisor's name and contact information, number of hours worked per week and complete mailing address. Refer to pages 127-133 for an example of a Federal Government resume.

8.   ***NEVER print your resume double-sided***. The quality of the visual presentation of your resume is generally quite poor if printed on both sides and can appear as though you were trying to save money on your printing costs. If your resume is two pages (or more), print single-sided pages and staple them together in the upper left hand corner. A clean, neat and conservative presentation is the preferred resume style for virtually all job seekers. Exceptions to this include per-

forming artists, broadcast personalities, graphic designers and other "creative" careers.

9. ***NEVER hand write changes on your resume*** – no matter how minor or insignificant. Handwritten changes ruin the quality of presentation and communicate to a prospective employer that "marginal" work product is acceptable to you. It is not!

10. ***NEVER include negative information about a past employer on your resume*** – even if it is the truth! Your resume is a tool that should be designed to market your qualifications, not describe the difficulties of an employment situation or an unreasonable manager. Leave this sensitive discussion for the interview.

Chapter 4

Tips From The Pros

WRITING WINNING RESUMES

Have you ever sat and stared at a blank piece of paper? You think that you are ready to write your resume, but the words just will not come. Try the following professional "tricks" of the trade.

1. Type your name, address, phone, fax and email.

2. Type in your major headings – Career Summary, Professional Experience, Education and other section titles.

3. Fill in Education, Affiliations, Technical Skills and other information. Generally, this text does not involve writing; just typing, formatting and documenting specific data.

4. Begin writing your job descriptions, starting with your very first career position. The amount of text you include for this job and others from years past will be significantly less than your current and most recent positions. Now, before you know it, you are halfway through your resume. All you have left to write are your few most recent positions and your summary.

5. Write the text for your most recent positions. Spend adequate time and effort on writing these descriptions, be sure to highlight your achievements, and use words and concepts that "sell" your success. As we have discussed, your most recent job descriptions are critical to the quality, caliber and impact of your overall resume presentation.

6. Write your Career Summary last, but do not summarize your career. Rather, highlight qualifications and achievements that are most related to your career objectives.

7. You are finished with writing your resume and ready to edit, proofread and finalize the presentation.

The Resume Writing Process Is Much Easier If You
WRITE FROM THE BOTTOM UP!

DESIGNING WINNING RESUMES
Capture Your Reader's Attention & Sell, Sell, Sell!

The visual presentation of your resume is critical. In order to sell yourself as a professional, you must "look" like a professional. With the advent of word processing, desktop publishing and laser printers, there is no excuse for poor visual presentation. You have the tools at your disposal to make your resume look sharp!

When designing your resume, your goal is to create a document that is conservative in nature yet competitive in visual presentation. By using a unique typestyle, inserting a few lines, or perhaps putting your summary section in a box at the top of your resume, you create a document that is visually distinct, sharper and more professional than other candidates. You get noticed!

Consider the following "tricks of the trade" when designing and producing your resume.

- Use **Bold**, *Italics*, <u>Underlining</u> and CAPITALIZATION to highlight key information. But, be careful not to overdo it. If you highlight too much, nothing will stand out.

- Right justify the text for a "cleaner" appearance. If you are not familiar with right justification, look at the right margin of this book. It is flush to the margin; it is right justified.

- Use high quality paper (24 or 28 lb., 25% or 100% cotton).

- White paper is always sharp, "clean" and attractive. You can also consider ivory, light blue or light gray papers which are distinctive, yet conservative. Stay away from bold colors and presentations that are too non-traditional, unless you are in a "creative" profession.

- A bordered paper may give you even a greater visual advantage. Look carefully at the selection available from your local paper distributor or print shop to see if you can find a paper that is unique. A good example is a light gray paper with a white border around the perimeter or an ivory paper with gold border. The presentation is sharp and distinctive.

- Use matching stationery and envelopes for your cover letters. If you have used a border paper, you may consider using a single color paper to complement and offset your resume presentation.

- Proofread, proofread and then proofread again! Errors are unacceptable. 100% perfection is *always* your goal.

- Leave a lot of white space. Readability of your resume is as important to the success of your job search as is the content. If no one reads it, it does not matter how well written and how well documented your achievements.

- Stay away from long paragraphs of more than 6-7 sentences. Break a long paragraph into two shorter paragraphs or use bullets to enhance "read-ability."

- Use a typestyle that is distinct. More than 85% of all resumes are prepared in Times Roman typestyle. It is neat, conservative and perfectly acceptable. However, there is no competitive distinction. Consider using an alternative typestyle such as Arial, Bookman, Fritz, Garamond, Helvetica, Krone, Omega or Soutane. Review available typestyles on your PC and select one that is aesthetically pleasing.

None of the above suggestions are flamboyant. Your goal is to design and produce an upscale presentation that is sharp yet still conservative. Only search candidates in the graphic arts, design, photography, videography, dance, theatrical or related industries should go beyond conservative and develop a resume that clearly demonstrates their creative talent.

WINNING AT YOUR JOB SEARCH

Winning Is More Than Just A Resume ...
It Is An Integrated Job Search Campaign

Resumes are the core foundation for your job search campaign. They are the center from which all of your other job search activities will flow. Without a strong resume, you cannot even begin the job search process. Devote the time and effort necessary to build a resume that clearly and aggressively "sells" your qualifications, career history, success and achievements. Remember, resume writing is marketing! Let your audience know the value of the product!

Once your resume is complete, you are faced with a new challenge – how to plan and manage a successful job search campaign in a market that is intensely competitive and with limited career opportunities.

The most important concept to remember in job search planning and career marketing is that you have a product to sell – YOU! And, just as with any other product, you want to "advertise" throughout all appropriate sales markets. No one is going to buy the product, if they do not know that it is available. Therefore, you must determine who your market is and how to best reach it.

Several critical factors that will impact how you structure and execute your job search are:

- Geographic limitations (if any) and ability to relocate.
- Type of position you are seeking.
- Type of industry you are targeting.
- Personal "quality of life" decisions.
- Compensation requirements.

Once you have integrated these factors into your search strategy, you want to develop a tactical action plan – an integrated job search marketing plan – that will get your resume into the market and in front of the appropriate audience. Your integrated marketing plan should include some, if not all, of the following job search programs. Consider the value of each of these to your search campaign, based upon your specific goals and objectives.

Job Search Marketing Channels

- ***Networking.*** Tried and true, networking is still your single best marketing channel. Nicely, professionally and with diplomacy, let everyone you know be aware that you are in the market. You never know where the "perfect" lead will come from – a past colleague, a current associate, your banker, your attorney, a member of a professional organization to which you belong, a neighbor, a casual acquaintance – the list is endless.

- ***Internet Resume Posting Sites.*** Over the past two years, thousands of sites have emerged on the Internet where you can post your resume for review by prospective employers and recruiters. In fact, Internet resume postings have forever changed the dynamics of job search by creating an entirely new sales channel. No longer must a company run an advertisement (and get 1000 resumes) or hire a recruiter (and pay $10,000+++ in fees). Instead, they can simply surf the Net. It is easy and convenient, allowing employers to review resumes at their leisure and see, if by chance, their "perfect" candidate is right there.

  The Internet truly has changed job search forever. Regardless of the level of your position, the Internet has become an almost mandatory job search channel. Without it, you are excluding yourself from potential opportunities across virtually *every* industry and profession. Be advised that many sites offer confidential postings for individuals maintaining a "low profile" in their search. For a minimum cost (some are even free), you can take advantage of these new opportunities.

- *Internet Job Postings.* Along with resume posting sites, there are now hundreds of job posting sites on the Internet. If you have the time to devote to this (it can be time-consuming), you may consider reviewing these postings, most of which are appropriate for individuals in the technology industries, or college graduates and young professionals. There are still only a few sites that list management and executive opportunities, but these are expanding at a phenomenal rate.

- *Targeted Direct Mail.* Direct mail campaigns can be a highly successful job search strategy if well-planned, well-designed and well-targeted. Your goal is to identify the organizations that would be most interested in a candidate with your qualifications and contact those firms directly. Contact should be made to the President, CEO or other senior hiring executive, and not to the Human Resources Department. Go straight to a manager who has hiring and decision-making authority.

  Direct mail targets can include companies, recruiters, employment agencies, venture capital firms, investment banking institutions, consulting firms, contractors and others. The more appropriate and customized your targets (based on your industry and job experience), the better the response. Spend the time necessary to develop a well-defined and well-researched target list. It will pay off in your results.

There is an inherent strategic difference between mass mailing and targeted direct mail. The former strategy requires that you mail hundreds if not thousands of resumes, assuming that a few will "stick." Targeted mailings, on the other hand, are well-focused and well-planned, and generally yield much better results for a fraction of the cost.

- *Job Lead Reports.* Job lead reports are a great resource. These subscription-only publications list unadvertised professional, management and executive opportunities, providing you with direct access to high-level confidential search campaigns. They are available as print publications and several can also be accessed via the Internet.

- *Advertisements.* We all hear the old adage that no one gets a job from the newspaper. In many instances, this is true. Yet, there are individuals who have identified top-flight career opportunities from the newspaper and gotten the job! Do not totally dismiss the newspaper as a job search tool. Although it can often be extremely difficult to get an interview (no matter how well prepared your resume and cover letter may be), it does happen and can be well worth the effort.

- **College & Alumni Associations.** No matter how many years ago you may have graduated, most universities will be pleased to assist you with your search campaign. Many have their own online recruitment and resume distribution websites. Others maintain direct relationships with companies. Do not forget this important marketing channel.

Chapter 5

Resumes Can Be Fun!

We have devoted the previous 50 pages to the critical importance of resume writing and its tremendous impact upon the success of your job search. Our discussion has been serious in nature as job search is a serious pursuit that can influence your career for years to come.

But, do resumes always have to be serious? Are there situations where resumes can be fun, entertaining, creative and unique? Review the following examples and see what you think.

JOHN A. SUAREZ

23 B Street
Belleville, Illinois 62221
(618) 555-2554

Happy Valentine's Day!!

OBJECTIVE:

To establish and nurture a meaningful friendship based on mutual respect, trust, similarities, differences, dreams, passion, and the joy of waking up together. In the meantime, will you be my Valentine?

QUALIFIED BY:

Twenty years of humility, close calls, lost love, found love, all nighters, one nighters, could've beens, shouldn't haves, and I'll-never-fall-in-love-agains.

EDUCATION:

Master of Blind Faith, B.B. King College of the Blues, 1992
- ♥ Major: Song and Seduction
- ♥ Thesis: "A Comparison Study of the Long Term Effects of Repeated Exposure to the Music of Eric Clapton and Barry Manilow"

Bachelor of Eligibility, University of Hard Knox, 1991
- ♥ Majors: Music/Psychology
- ♥ Selected Coursework: Basic Principles of Rejection, Role Reversal and Lingerie, Advanced Chemistry, Psychotic Behavior

EXPERIENCE:

- ♥ Longest Relationship: 6.5 years, ended by mutual hatred
- ♥ Shortest Relationship: 8 minutes, ended by her boyfriend
- ♥ Most Recent Relationship: Still processing in therapy

AWARDS:

- ♥ Voted Most Likely to End Up Marrying an Ex-Girlfriend's Daughter
- ♥ President, There's One Born Every Minute Club

REFERENCES:

Will admit to them upon request

NORMAN J. ADAMS

50 ADAMS DRIVE
ROCHESTER, NEW YORK 14618
Phone: 911

CAREER OBJECTIVE

A part-time semi-permanent position in a country-club environment between breakfast and lunch with stock options.

SUMMARY OF QUALIFICATIONS

- Experience in integrated organizational capability as it relates to forming relationships.
- Demonstrated ability in total transitional contingency in planning social events.
- Competent utilizing synchronized incremental options to generate clientele.
- Enjoy professional contacts with people everywhere: can count on running into someone no matter how far from home I roam.

RELATED PROFESSIONAL EXPERIENCE

Breakfast Club Manager   Ongoing
- Select and qualify appropriate restaurants for networking with other members of the non-working community.
- Survey attendees to determine optimum meeting time, location and food preference.
- Prepare one-liners for daily entertainment.
- Educate club members regarding negative qualities of location, food and management.
- Locate and qualify appropriate coupons.
- Spokesperson: Liaise between attendees and restaurant personnel.

Movie Reviewer
- Sit through every new release and conduct a critical analysis to deliver verbally as requested (or not requested.)

World Problem Solver
- Assess daily headlines and make determination as to the appropriate solution.
- Declare pertinent statistics to individuals within hearing-aide distance.

OTHER EXPERIENCE

Prior experience includes owning and operating a successful snow plowing business in Boca Raton, Florida. Hired and scheduled staff. Purchased heavy equipment as needed. Handled on-call emergencies 24/hours/day 365 days/year.

EDUCATION/TRAINING

- Several graduate degrees from various diploma mills. Will forward appropriate selection upon establishment of personal interest.

COMMUNITY INVOLVEMENT

Offer personal opinions as deemed necessary to professionals, residents, and consumers. Function as sidewalk-superintendent for various community projects.

Limited references. (Call ahead to confirm status.)

Gordon P. and Rita K. Taylor
"GORD" & "REET"

▲ Profile ▼

Dedicated, caring parents and life partners… committed to each other and to enjoying life together… hard-working business owners with a strong track record of professional accomplishments… active volunteers recognized for efforts to improve their community and the lives of others.

◄ Key Accomplishments: Joint ►

Interpersonal

◎ For 45 years maintained a successful partnership founded on love and respect and cemented with thoughtfulness and good communication.

☼ Raised 8 children, none of whom has ever been arrested, indicted, jailed or convicted; several with advanced educational degrees; and all of whom are gainfully employed and (mostly) self-supporting.

◎ Never went to bed angry.

☼ Seldom cried over spilt milk.

◎ Provided a haven for numerous grandchildren, welcoming their visits of any length, at any time, for any reason.

Managerial/Executive

☼ Successfully managed large household despite a marriage lacking a "born organizer."

◎ Demonstrated effective time and resource management by dividing certain responsibilities (e.g., worrying) to avoid duplication of effort.

☼ Maximized leadership and teamwork skills and set a standard for community service by volunteering gladly anytime anyone asked for anything.

◎ Creatively realized dream of world travel by encouraging offspring to reside in far-flung locations throughout the United States and Europe.

► Key Accomplishments: Individual ▼

Gordon

☼ Revitalized small-town politics by joining underdog political party and making a lot of noise.

◎ Forty years ahead of his time, anticipated a '90s nationwide trend by participating fully as co-parent (making lunches, giving baths, changing diapers, enforcing rules, and so on) at a time when dads didn't.

☼ Pioneered popular "What, me worry?" slogan later made famous by Alfred E. Newman.

◎ Dispensed wit and wisdom along with medications to thousands of customers, none of whom ever sued (over bad advice *or* bad jokes).

Rita

☼ Despite quiet upbringing, learned to tolerate boisterous game-playing, table-banging, and yelling; earned reputation as "Mrs. Jekyll" for extraordinary ability to switch instantaneously from nice to nasty.

◎ Survived two decades as chief pharmacist for hundreds of retirees; developed and perfected ingenious method of disabling child-safe caps.

☼ Overcame budget limitations to creatively decorate and reconstruct family home. Specialized in decorating with seashells and knocking down walls with an axe.

► Celebrating 45 years of wedded bliss! 1952–1997 ▼

SCOTT W. ZANEY, III

Address: Somewhere in Rochester   Phone: Unlisted

OBJECTIVE
A part time position with full-time pay and benefits.

EMPLOYMENT EXPERIENCE

Blue Moon Inc.   Seems like forever
General Manager
- Responsible for providing lunch-time nourishment to staff.
- Handle corporate perk program: Credited with upgrading office facilities with Cable TV, food drawers, and leading-edge vacuum cleaner.
- Utilize computer system to play sophisticated video games and track employee scores.
- Implement all internal facility appearance functions (vacuum, dust and fluff pillows).
- Recipient of "Employee of the Week" award for remembering to bring in pizza.
- Handle "team building" activities (plan parties, after work socials, etc.)

Burger King   While in school
Waitress
- Serviced "dining room" patrons.

Cholesterol King   While not in school
Donut Stuffer
- Selected fillings for various donuts.
- Poked holes and put appropriate selection and correct level of filling into holes.
- Maintained quality control by ingesting defective products.

New York State Thruway Authority   Sometime in the 70's
Assistant Toll Booth Occupant
- Assisted Toll Booth Operator with greeting motorists and making change.
- Gave directions to entrance ramp, refreshment stand and rest rooms.
- Memorized our exit number (Number 1).

EDUCATION

Monroe County Private Elementary School
Continuing course work toward elementary school diploma.   Ongoing

Tender Care Day Care Center for Unique Children
Graduated with Honors

ACTIVITIES

Greater Rochester Area Smooth Operators Company, Inc.
Treasurer/Creative Bookkeeper
Strategically maintained books to account for money squandered.

Society of Universal Engineers
Attended conventions, seminars, and social functions to look good and meet people on someone else's budget.

PERSONAL

- Date cross-culturally, which qualifies me for international leadership positions.

- Interests include anything that doesn't require energy.

Excellent references available from my mom, my buddies, ~~my girl friend~~.

Alexia Kaye Suarez

59 Crayola Court ● Troy, Illinois 62294 ● (618) 555-1669

objecktive

Applying for a skolarship to attend furst grade at Triad Skool

things I can do

- ✓ Follow directions promptly *(especially when daddy's mad)*
- ✓ Work neatly and carefully *(unless I'm wearing new clothes)*
- ✓ Complete activities promptly *(unless mommy is in a hurry)*
- ✓ Operate computer *(Just Me and My Dad, Treehouse, Kid Pix, Lion King)*
- ✓ Stay on task *(sometimes as long as five minutes)*
- ✓ Sit on chair properly *(I can stand on it, too!)*
- ✓ Not bother other students *(only had time-out once, and it wasn't my fault)*

reading

- ✓ Recite alphabet *(consistently get at least 25 of 26 without the song)*
- ✓ Associate sounds with letters *("c" is for "cookie"...that's good enough for me)*
- ✓ Recognize rhyming words *(fully-trained on Dr. Suess, especially Green Eggs and Ham)*
- ✓ Recognize and name eight basic colors *(nine if you count "Barbie pink")*

math

- ✓ Write numbers 1-10 *(specializing in random sequence)*
- ✓ Count to 100 by 5's *(without starting over more than twice)*
- ✓ Understand concept of more v. less *(the more I whine, the less I get)*

motor skillz

- ✓ Color in one direction and stay in lines *(maintained a 98% in-line rate)*
- ✓ Use scissors and glue correctly *(helped turn the cat into a tiger)*
- ✓ Hold pencil and crayons correctly *(no lost-time accidents)*

ejukashun

Graduated Kindergarten at Baden Elementary, 1996

- ✓ Had the same kindergarten teacher as my mommy
- ✓ My bestest classes were reading and recess

Summer Enrichment Classes, 1996

- ✓ Dance (Tap, Ballet, and Jazz)
- ✓ Swimming Lessons

Chapter 6
KeyWords: Winning Words That Sell!

KEYWORDS

- You talk to a resume professional, recruiter or executive career coach, and each mentions ***KeyWords***.

- You read about the Internet and online job search, and the emphasis is on ***KeyWords***.

- You listen to a CNN news brief about employment trends, and the reporter highlights the importance of ***KeyWords***.

- You attend a job search training and networking seminar, and the focus in on ***KeyWords***.

- You speak to a prospective employer and he inquires if your resume is scannable and includes ***KeyWords.***

- You talk to your fellow job seekers and the discussion focuses on ***KeyWords***.

What Are KeyWords And Where Did They Come From?

No resume book today would be complete without discussing KeyWords and their importance to the quality and strength of your resume, cover letters, broadcast letters, thank you letters, leadership profiles and other job search communications. Today, we hear about KeyWords all the time. You may ask yourself, "What are KeyWords and where did they come from?"

KeyWords are buzz words – the "hot" words associated with a *specific industry, profession or job function* – that clearly and succinctly communicate a *specific message*.

KeyWords were originally defined as nouns only – words such as compensation (for Human Resources), contract negotiations (for Sales), capacity planning (for Manufacturing), corporate litigation (for Law) and systems design (for Information Technology). These KeyWords communicate a specific message:

KeyWord	*Message*
Compensation	Salary, benefits, bonus and incentive planning and administration.
Contract Negotiations	Client presentations, product demonstrations, pricing and contracts.
Corporate Litigation	Defense planning, case presentation and trial proceedings.
Capacity Planning	Personnel, budgets, technologies and resources.
Systems Design	Technology needs assessment, acquisition and implementation.

Just as resumes are the foundation for a successful job search, KeyWords are the foundation for successful resumes. These words allow you to communicate key messages that demonstrate your competencies and qualifications for specific employment opportunities.

Today, the definition of KeyWords has expanded to include what are referred to as *Action Verbs* used to present your qualifications, achievements and results in an "aggressive" style. Action Verbs are common words such as accomplished, championed, generated, led, managed, presented, restructured and transitioned. No longer is a passive approach to resume writing the acceptable norm. Job search success will rely on your ability to "sell" your qualifications, using both KeyWords and Action Verbs to communicate results.

Resumes today, greatly influenced by the tremendous competition in the job search market, require that you present your skills and qualifications in an action-driven style. Your challenge is to demonstrate that you can deliver strong performance. There is no better method in which to accomplish this than with the use of powerful words and phrases that clearly demonstrate your capabilities.

KeyWords are also an important consideration in relation to resume scanning, a rapidly evolving technology that allows companies to quickly review each candidate's qualifications by searching for KeyWords, skills, qualifications and experience. Without the appropriate KeyWords, your resume is likely to get passed over, not noticed.

Use the following sample listing of KeyWords to get you started in developing your own KeyWord list – words specific to your career, experience, industry background and current objectives.

Sample KeyWords By Profession

Profession	*KeyWords*
Accounting	Accounts Payable
	Accounts Receivable
	Financial Analysis & Reporting
	Cost Reduction & Avoidance
	Systems Automation
	General Ledger Accounting
	Internal & External Audit
	Job & Project Costing
	Project Accounting
	Regulatory Compliance
Administration	Office Management
	Administrative Management
	Executive Liaison Affairs
	Meeting Planning & Scheduling
	Project Management
	Office Automation
	Customer Communications
	Document & Records Management
	Efficiency & Productivity Improvement
	Workflow Planning & Prioritization
Association Management	Member Relations
	Board of Director Presentations
	Revenue Centers
	Legislative & Regulatory Affairs
	Vision & Leadership

Constituent Advocacy

Foundation Management

Grassroots Campaign

Industry Relations

Marketing Communications

Banking

Deposit & Lending Operations

Asset & Portfolio Growth

Multi-Site Branch Operations

Consumer & Commercial Credit

Regulatory Filing & Compliance

Debt & Equity Financings

Correspondent Banking

de novo Banking

Merchant Banking

Foreign Exchange

Customer
Service

Customer Loyalty

Customer Retention

Customer Satisfaction

Call Center Operations

Help Desk Operations

Customer Perceived Quality

Service Training & Support

Process Redesign & Simplification

Client Relationship Management

Sales & Marketing Support

Engineering

New Product Development

Technology Design & Engineering

Technical Specifications

Quality & Testing

Product Lifecycle Management
Cross-Functional Design Team
CAD, CAM & CAE
Final Customer Acceptance
Manufacturing Integration
Methods & Standards Design

Finance

Corporate Financial Planning
Treasury & Cash Management
Public & Private Investment
Long-Range Strategic Planning
IPO Road Show Presentations
Corporate Risk Management
Investor Relations
Mergers, Acquisitions & Divestitures
Letter of Credit Transactions
Financial Modeling & Projections

Government

Request for Proposal (RFP)
Contract Award & Administration
Indefinite & Fixed Price Contracts
Competitive Procurement
Inter-Agency Liaison Affairs
Public/Private Partnerships
Regulatory Review & Compliance
Fiscal Year Budgeting
Grant Funding & Administration
Constituent Affairs

**Graduating
Student**

Leadership Capabilities
Oral & Written Communications
Project Research & Presentation

Training, Tutoring & Mentoring

Time Management

Team Building & Camaraderie

Organization & Coordination

Reporting & Presentations

Data Collection & Analysis

PC Proficiency

Health Care

Hospital Administration

Health Care Delivery System

Community Health & Outreach

HMO, PPO & Other Provider Networks

Cost Reduction & Avoidance

Ambulatory, Acute & Chronic Care

Continuity of Care

Case Management

Physician Credentialing

Regulatory Standards

Hospitality

Food & Labor Cost Controls

Multi-Unit Operations Management

Meeting & Special Events Planning

Room Sales & Revenue Growth

Guest Relations & Satisfaction

Contract F&B Operations

Menu Planning & Pricing

Portion Control

Vendor Sourcing & Negotiations

Amenities Program & Service

**Human
Resources**

Benefits & Compensation

Training & Development

Gainsharing & Performance Improvement

Corporate Culture Change

Organizational Development & Effectiveness

Pension Plan Administration

HRIS Technology Design & Implementation

Manpower Planning

Workforce Optimization

Team Building & Team Leadership

Human Services   Community Outreach

Client Advocacy

Program Development & Administration

Budgeting & Fundraising

Counseling & Interpersonal Relations

Caseload Management

Diagnostic Evaluation

Crisis Intervention

Protective Services

Treatment Planning & Follow-Up

Information   Client/Server Architecture

Technology   LAN & WAN Technologies

Object Oriented Design

JAD & RAD Methodologies

Programming Languages & Operating Systems

Applications Development

Systems Interconnectivity

Electronic Commerce

Online Internet Technology

Office Automation

Insurance	Policy Underwriting & Administration
	Sales & Marketing Management
	Premium & Revenue Growth
	Personal & Commercial Lines
	Agency Management
	New Product Introduction
	Multi-Lines Representation
	Risk Management
	Insurance Brokerage
	Regional Sales & Market Management
International Business	New Market Development
	New Product Launch
	Global Sales & Marketing Management
	Multinational Joint Ventures & Partnerships
	Cross-Cultural Negotiations & Liaison Affairs
	Trade & Barter Transactions
	Diplomatic & Cultural Protocol
	Import & Export Operations
	International Financing & Deal Structuring
	Offshore Operations
Investment Finance	Debt & Equity Offerings
	Stock & Investment Portfolio Management
	Public & Private Placements
	Transaction Negotiations
	Asset Divestiture & Liquidation
	Road Show Presentations
	Multi-Party Transactions
	Mergers, Acquisitions & Divestitures
	Receivership & Creditor Reimbursement
	ROI, ROE & ROA Projections

Legal	Intellectual Property
	Corporate Risk Management
	Legal Transactions & Documentation
	Multi-Party Contract Negotiations
	Mergers, Acquisitions & Joint Ventures
	Client Relationship Management
	Corporate Recordkeeping
	Legal Due Diligence
	Legal Advocacy
	Legislative Review & Analysis
Logistics	Multi-Site Distribution Operations
	Warehousing & Facilities Maintenance
	Fleet Acquisition & Management
	Process Simplification & Consolidation
	Multimodal Transportation
	Materials, Purchasing & Inventory
	Logistics Planning & Management
	Asset Management & Disposition
	Productivity & Efficiency Improvement
	Workforce Planning & Optimization
Manufacturing	Capacity Planning & Optimization
	Quality Performance Measurement
	Cellular Manufacturing
	Cost Reduction & Profit Growth
	Materials, Purchasing & Inventory Operations
	Multi-Site Operations Management
	Continuous Process Improvement
	Production Yield Optimization
	Ergonomic Efficiency
	Cycle Time Reduction

Marketing	Market Research & Data Analysis
	Strategic Market Planning
	Competitive Product Positioning
	New Product Introduction
	Multimedia Marketing Communications
	Competitive Market Research
	Global Marketing & Business Development
	New Venture Start-Up
	Cross-Functional Marketing Teams
	Data Collection, Analysis & Reporting
Media	Multimedia Broadcasting
	Programming & Scheduling
	Multimedia Graphics & Presentations
	Public Performance & On-Air Talent
	Transmission Planning & Distribution
	Cable & Satellite Broadcasting
	Press Relations & Briefings
	Creative Design & Production
	Audiovisual & Electronics Technology
	Artistic Representation
Meeting Planning & Events	Planning & Logistics
	Event Scheduling
	Agenda & Guest Speakers
	Contract Negotiations
	Entertainment Selection
	Event Management & Promotion
	Budgeting & Cost Control
	Media Affairs & Corporate Sponsorships
	Advertisements & Communications
	Conference Planning & Management

Military Conversion	Leadership Skills
	Team Building & Mentoring
	Budget & Resource Management
	Inter-Organizational Liaison Affairs
	Commercial & Industrial Applications
	Information Technology
	Project Planning & Management
	Manpower Planning & Optimization
	Budget Control & Administration
	Resource Planning & Logistics
Public Relations	Public Speaking & Presentations
	Wall Street & Investor Communications
	Media Relations & Briefings
	Crisis Communications
	Advertising & Promotional Communications
	Campaign Management
	Creative Services
	Special Events Planning & Promotion
	Press Releases & Investment Reports
	VIP & Shareholder Relations
Purchasing	Worldwide Vendor Sourcing
	Supplier & Contract Negotiations
	Materials Planning & Management
	Inventory Planning & Control
	JIT Purchasing Programs
	Contract Administration
	Cost Savings & Cost Avoidance
	Barter & Trade Operations
	MRO & Capital Equipment Acquisition
	Multi-Site Parts Distribution

Quality	TQM & ISO 9000 Certification
	Supplier Quality Certification
	Quality Test & Measurement
	Standardization & Reporting
	Quality Documentation & Review
	Statistical Process Control
	Quality Training & Performance Improvement
	Materials & Finished Production Inspection
	Failure Mode Effects Analysis (FMEA)
	Malcolm Baldrige
Real Estate	Portfolio Management & Diversification
	Asset Growth & ROI Performance
	Investor Presentations & Funding
	Project Development & Management
	Historic Preservation & Revitalization
	Asset Workout & Recovery
	Investment Valuation
	Competitive Bidding
	Design & Engineering
	Turnkey Construction Project
Research & Science	Research Planning & Management
	Data Collection & Statistical Analysis
	Research Project Management
	Public & Private Funding
	Presentations & Publications
	Foundation & Corporate Sponsorships
	Results Reporting & Analysis
	Multidisciplinary Team Leadership
	Laboratory & Inventory Management
	Testing & Data Analysis

Retail	Multi-Site Store Operations
	Sales & Merchandising
	Inventory Planning & Allocation
	Promotions & Special Events
	Security & Loss Prevention
	Hardgoods & Softgoods
	Point of Sale (POS) Promotions
	Product Management
	Warehousing Operations
	Customer Service & Satisfaction
Sales	Region & Territory Management
	Key Account & National Account Management
	Sales Training & Team Building
	New Product Launch
	Competitive Market Share
	Competitive Product Positioning
	Consultative Selling
	Customer Relationship Management
	Promotions, Incentives & Premiums
	Product Lifecycle Management
Senior Executive	Visionary Leadership
	Strategic Business Planning
	Corporate & Business Development
	Revenue, Profit & Market Share Growth
	World Class Organization
	Best Practices Benchmarking
	Executive Team Building
	Competitive Market Positioning
	Multi-Functional Expertise
	Tactical Planning & Leadership

Sports **& Recreation**	Team & League Management Competitive Leadership Top-Ranked Conference Performance Corporate & Advertiser Sponsorships Special Events Planning & Management Equipment Management Transportation & Accommodations Hotel & Airline Negotiations Press Relations & Coverage Athlete Recruitment
Teaching	Curriculum Design & Development Instructional Materials Classroom Management Teacher Training & Leadership Task Force & Committee Participation Student Teacher Preceptorship Special Events Planning & Management Parent Participation Student Counseling & Crisis Intervention Educational Administration

There are virtually hundreds of KeyWords for each profession and each industry. Carefully consider the KeyWords specific to your past experiences and current objectives, and be sure to appropriately integrate them into your resume and other career marketing materials.

Sample Action Verbs

Use the following action verbs to clearly, succinctly and aggressively present your skills, qualifications, achievements, contributions and competencies. Integrate these words with your KeyWords to create powerful sentences and a top-flight resume.

Accelerate	Build	Construct
Accomplish	Calculate	Consult
Achieve	Capture	Continue
Acquire	Catalog	Contract
Adapt	Champion	Convert
Address	Chart	Coordinate
Advance	Clarify	Correct
Advise	Classify	Counsel
Advocate	Close	Craft
Analyze	Coach	Create
Apply	Collect	Critique
Appoint	Command	Decrease
Arbitrate	Communicate	Define
Architect	Compare	Delegate
Arrange	Compel	Deliver
Ascertain	Compile	Demonstrate
Assemble	Complete	Deploy
Assess	Compute	Design
Assist	Conceive	Detail
Author	Conclude	Detect
Authorize	Conduct	Determine
Brief	Conserve	Develop
Budget	Consolidate	Devise

Direct	Execute	Inspect
Discover	Exhibit	Inspire
Dispense	Expand	Install
Display	Experiment	Institute
Distribute	Export	Integrate
Diversify	Facilitate	Intensify
Divert	Finalize	Interpret
Document	Finance	Interview
Double	Forge	Introduce
Draft	Form	Invent
Drive	Formalize	Inventory
Earn	Formulate	Investigate
Edit	Found	Judge
Educate	Generate	Justify
Effect	Graduate	Launch
Elect	Guide	Lead
Eliminate	Halt	Lecture
Emphasize	Head	License
Enact	Hire	Listen
Encourage	Honor	Locate
Endure	Identify	Maintain
Energize	Illustrate	Manage
Enforce	Imagine	Manipulate
Engineer	Implement	Manufacture
Enhance	Import	Map
Enlist	Improve	Market
Ensure	Improvise	Mastermind
Establish	Increase	Measure
Estimate	Influence	Mediate
Evaluate	Inform	Mentor
Examine	Initiate	Model
Exceed	Innovate	Modify

Monitor	Procure	Reorganize
Motivate	Program	Report
Navigate	Progress	Reposition
Negotiate	Project	Represent
Nominate	Promote	Research
Observe	Propose	Resolve
Obtain	Prospect	Respond
Offer	Provide	Restore
Officiate	Publicize	Restructure
Operate	Purchase	Retrieve
Orchestrate	Qualify	Review
Organize	Question	Revise
Orient	Rate	Revitalize
Originate	Realign	Satisfy
Outsource	Rebuild	Schedule
Overcome	Recapture	Secure
Oversee	Receive	Select
Participate	Recognize	Separate
Perceive	Recommend	Serve
Perfect	Reconcile	Simplify
Perform	Record	Sell
Persuade	Recruit	Solidify
Pilot	Redesign	Solve
Pinpoint	Reduce	Speak
Pioneer	Reengineer	Specify
Plan	Regain	Standardize
Position	Regulate	Stimulate
Predict	Rehabilitate	Streamline
Prepare	Reinforce	Structure
Present	Rejuvenate	Succeed
Preside	Render	Summarize
Process	Renegotiate	Supervise

Supply	Test	Unite
Support	Train	Update
Surpass	Transcribe	Upgrade
Synthesize	Transfer	Use
Systematize	Transform	Utilize
Tabulate	Transition	Verbalize
Target	Translate	Verify
Teach	Troubleshoot	Win
Terminate	Unify	Write

For a more comprehensive listing of KeyWords and Action Verbs, pick up a copy of *1500+ KeyWords for $100,000+ Jobs* (written by Wendy S. Enelow; Impact Publications, 1998).

Chapter 7

160 Winning Resume Samples

REBECCA M. SAMUELSON
2923 Beaver Creek Drive
Milwaukee, Wisconsin 63431

Home (920) 788-0867

Office (920) 343-1282

PROFESSIONAL PROFILE

Accountant / Financial Analyst with 13 years increasingly responsible experience. Combines cross-functional competencies in all phases of general accounting, financial planning and financial reporting. Excellent analytical, negotiations, oral and written communication skills. Decisive, proactive and precise. Proficient with numerous customized accounting systems, Lotus 1-2-3, Excel, Word, Windows, LAN, email and the Internet.

PROFESSIONAL EXPERIENCE

ACCOUNTANT / FINANCIAL ANALYST (1989 to Present)
Bekat & Marshall, L.L.P., Milwaukee, Wisconsin

Recruited to join the accounting and financial management team of a professional services corporation. Challenged to strengthen accounting practices, streamline financial reporting processes and improve the quality/caliber of financial data. Significant responsibilities and achievements include:

Financial Planning, Analysis & Reporting

- Created, interpreted and reported financial information in support of general business operations and long-range strategic planning functions.

- Prepared and presented monthly financial information package to senior management team.

- Developed financial forecasts, projections and analytical tools.

- Compiled financial data for sensitive corporate, legal, credit and general business issues.

General Accounting

- Coordinated month-end closings, prepared monthly analyses of all balance sheet accounts and facilitated the preparation of annual financial statements.

- Managed all accounts payable and accounts receivable functions for completion of month-end financial statements.

- Reconciled revenue accounts to general ledger and subsidiary reports.

- Streamlined and enhanced accounting, reporting and analysis techniques.

Budgeting & Cash Management

- Prepared and managed monthly and annual budgets for operations, overhead expenditures and miscellaneous costs. Administered up to $10 million in annual funds.

- Recommended and implemented improved variance analysis and expense forecasting methods.

- Formulated cash projections, monitored cash flow and implemented cash controls.

Information Technology

- Actively involved in the planning and implementation of expanded PC applications to further automate accounting and financial systems.

- Participated in the selection and coordination of PC systems conversion and upgrade project.

General Business Management

- Project Team Leader for the planning, coordination and management of two corporate relocations. Divested assets and coordinated transition of accounting and financial operations to new HQ locations.

- Trained and supervised professional accounting and accounting/administrative support staff.

ASSOCIATE MANAGER (1987 to 1989)
Accessories, Inc., Milwaukee, Wisconsin

Member of a five-person team leading all regional sales, account management and customer service affairs for this national retail chain. Held additional responsibility for inventory control. Ranked as a top revenue producer.

ACCOUNTING MANAGER (1985 to 1987)
Multimedia Broadcasting, Inc., Green Bay, Wisconsin

Held diversified accounting and financial reporting responsibilities for the corporate headquarters and five operating divisions of this regional television broadcasting corporation. Analyzed and reconciled accounts, prepared journal entries, calculated monthly sales summary, led month-end closing and analysis, and prepared all financial statements.

- Designed a consolidated monthly balance sheet and income statement. Provided senior management with detailed financial information for use in strategic planning and forecasting.

ACCOUNTS RECEIVABLE ADMINISTRATOR (1984 to 1985)
Sytex Corporation, Madison, Wisconsin

Directed the complete accounts receivable function for this collateral management corporation. Responsibility encompassed all billing, credit, collections, inventory control and reporting. Prepared monthly sales and cash receipt reports, account analyses, journal entries, customer credit adjustments and bad debt write-offs. Acquired extensive experience in customer communications and collection negotiations.

EDUCATION

B.A., ACCOUNTING & POLITICAL SCIENCE, 1984
University of Wisconsin at Madison
Dual Major. 3.5 GPA.

CAROLYN MOIRA

15 West End Lane
South Ozone Park, New York 11223

Phone: (718) 222-3456
E-mail: cmoira@aol.com

SUMMARY
- Results-oriented professional with a solid background in accounting and auditing.
- Expertise in financial analysis, financial statements, tax accounting, P&L analysis, and management consulting.
- Advanced user of financial, statistical, spreadsheet, and word processing programs.
- Excellent written and verbal communication skills; Fluent in French and Italian.
- Adept at working under pressure and solving complex problems.

EDUCATION

Bachelor of Science in Accounting, 1996
NEW YORK UNIVERSITY, New York, NY

- Financed education 100%
- Dean's List, 1993 to 1994
- Accounting Society, member, 1992 to 1996
- Soccer Club, President, 1994 to 1996

EMPLOYMENT

1996 to present

Audit Specialist
PRICE ANALYST COMPANY, INC., New York, NY
(Accounting and Consulting firm with more than $2 billion in revenue)
- Conduct audits to assist businesses in making sound financial decisions.
- Serve million dollar companies and organizations in diversified industries:
  - finance
  - health care
  - service
  - retail trades
  - education
  - real estate
  - non-profit
  - investment
- Review client's data, such as audited numbers, balance sheet, income statement, and P&L report to assess financial status.
- Recommend operational changes to reduce client's expenses and improve efficiency.
- Use diplomacy, courtesy, and tact in dealing with staff during audits.
- Confer with attorneys and investment bankers regarding audit results.
- Compile narrative and statistical audit reports that average 25 to 35 pages.
- Receive extensive training on audit policies and procedures.

1992 to 1996

Accounts Manager
METROPOLITAN MEDICAL GROUP, INC., Hempstead, NY
(Medical company with $1 to $1.5 million in sales)
- Maintained accounts receivable, accounts payable, and general ledger.
- Prepared monthly, quarterly, and year-end financial reports.
- Completed bank transactions, reconciliations, and employee payroll.
- Ensured that doctors received payment for services rendered.

1993 to 1996
Tax Season

Tax Assistant
VOLUNTEER INCOME TAX ASSISTANCE, New York, NY
(Volunteer program that assists individuals such as the elderly and students)
- Trained and certified by IRS in tax return preparation.
- Advised individuals on tax law and assisted with preparing returns.

AFFILIATIONS
- National Association of Public Accountants
- American Institute of Certified Public Accountants

COMPUTERS
- Interactive Data Extraction and Analysis (IDEA)
- Field Audit System Technology (FAST)
- Audit Sampling
- Microsoft Excel
- Lotus 1-2-3
- Audit Program Generator
- WordPerfect
- Time Value4 (T value4)
- Minitab
- Microsoft Word
- CaseWare / CaseWin

ELIZABETH S. BARKER

39000 Carrollwood Circle
Tampa, Florida 33600
(813) 000-0000

PROFESSIONAL PROFILE

Corporate Controller with 11-year tenure comprised of unique blending of accounting and information systems experience involving building and managing results-driven financial and administrative operations. Record of progressive advancement reflecting ability to augment fiscal efficiency; maximize operational productivity; and initiate directives producing strong, substantive results. Goal-directed leadership exhibited in devising/instituting corporate policies/controls focused on growth and profitability in both remanufacturing and office environments. Skilled in managing information systems, deploying high-level functional project plans, upgrading/converting computer applications, establishing computer system data integrity, and performing electronic data processing. **Expertise includes:**

➤ **Strategic Business Planning**   ➤ **Automated Accounting Information Systems**
➤ **Operational Needs Assessments**   ➤ **Software Functionality**
➤ **Project Management**   ➤ **Corporate Accounting**

COMPUTER SKILLS

Excel, Word Perfect, Windows 95, Microsoft Office Pro v. 7, Lotus 1-2-3, PICK English/Recall

EMPLOYMENT HISTORY

PROFESSIONAL TEMPORARIES   **Present**
Controller/Senior-level Accounting Consultant
* Contracted to assist companies with enhancing efficiency of automated accounting systems.

COMMUNICATIONS SERVICES, INC.   **1988 - 1997**
Corporate Controller   (1990-1997)
Assistant Controller   (1988-1990)
Reported to President. High-level performance, combined with analytical ability, competent decision-making, effective organizational management and strong problem-solving skills, led to promotion and assuming pivotal role of diverse scope of responsibilities.

MANAGEMENT
* Ensured smooth-running of all daily operations concerning financial, distribution and internal production.
* Developed and instituted corporate policies/operational procedures and negotiated software/hardware contracts with vendors.
* Chaired employee benefits committee re: 401K plan, health care, dental and other insurance programs.
➤ **Increased employee skill sets company-wide by 35%.**

INFORMATION SYSTEMS
* Migrated company from a propriety distribution and accounting software system (on a Honeywell mini-computer) to a Microsoft NT server network with Pentium work stations utilizing Windows 95. Converted to Macola manufacturing, distribution and accounting software packages.
➤ **Pioneered implementation of operational methods to increase productivity and improve customer service.**
➤ **Positioned company to achieve competitive edge via initiating expansion of product lines.**

ACCOUNTING
* Integral role in developing productive corporate financial profiles; prepared annual departmental budgets, monitored employee benefits and pension/profit sharing plans, and managed bank funds between accounts.
* Spearheaded all facets of general ledger, tax, AP, AR, payroll, order entry, invoicing, and customer service responsibilities.

PROFESSIONAL TEMPORARIES   **1986 - 1988**
Accounting Consultant
* Handled special projects requiring accounting expertise.

EDUCATION

B.A. Business Accounting FLORIDA STATE UNIVERSITY (G.P.A. 3.7) (*Worked full time while attending college*)

HELEN M. CARTER
8400 Industrial Parkway
Plain City, Ohio 43064
Office: (614) 555-3123 • Residence: (614) 555-3368

OVERVIEW:

Experience includes **Accounts Payable**, **Payroll**, **Insurance**, and **General Office Administration**. Proficient with Lotus. Self-motivated and detail oriented, possessing the following personal attributes:

- Organize work materials for quick, easy reference.
- Verify information by reviewing, checking or comparing from various sources.
- Select most appropriate solution to problem situations.
- Plan and schedule work activities considering priorities, workload and timelines.

EXPERIENCE:

CENTRAL INSURANCE, Columbus, Ohio   1/82 - Present

Actuarial Support Technician (12/91 - Present)
- Compile annual and quarterly industry surveys for Central and its six subsidiaries.
- Formulate financial information critical in annual statement preparation.
- Prepare quarterly analysis for expenses, commissions, administration fees and reserves.
- Track and maintain complex department reports. Calculate GAAP adjustments.

"Helen works with outstanding diligence. She consistently demonstrates good analytical, compilation, and reconciliation skills as reporting needs change." — Paul Simmons, Senior Group Actuary

Group Actuarial, Dividend Clerk (3/85 - 12/91)
- Calculated dividends for group life and health policies weekly.
- Determined quarterly dividend liability.
- Posted claims, legal and printing expenses.

Technical Clerk, Tax Shelter Products Department (1/82 - 3/85)
- Assigned tedious task of cleaning up three-year backlog of policy paperwork problems. Accomplished task three months ahead of projected goal.
- Processed new and renewal business for agents' commissions.
- Calculated investment factors for six funds.
- Trained temporary and new employees on clerical procedures.

STATE EMPLOYEES RETIREMENT SYSTEM, Columbus, Ohio   1/74 - 12/81

Accounting Department
- Calculated retirement benefits.
- Resolved insurance problems on retired members' accounts and employee plans.
- Performed accounts payable functions, computed and processed office payroll, acted as back-up to investment accountant, posted accounts receivable and helped compile annual statement.

HARRISON CONTROLS, Columbus, Ohio   4/71 - 1/74

Accounts Payable
- Played key role in converting manual accounts payable system over to data processing.
- Posted accounts receivable.

THOMAS BRADLEY, Certified Public Accountant

222 Marcus Street
Jefferson City, Missouri 99999
999/999-9999

PROFILE

Certified Public Accountant with over 13 years' bank related experience. Skilled in analyzing data, performing audits, and examining internal control procedures. Solid background in, and knowledge of, financial analysis. Detail-oriented with strong planning and organizational abilities. Enthusiastic team player. Communicate effectively with colleagues, supervisors, and clients.

PROFESSIONAL EXPERIENCE

Bank Examiner

Real Estate and Banks Department, Jefferson City, Missouri District, 1984 to Present

- Selectively hired to examine state chartered banks ensuring safety and soundness, covering territory of 76 banks in 15 counties
- Work cooperatively with team of seven examiners handling 40+ banks annually conducting on-site examinations/audits
- *Loan Area*: audits include financial, Profit and Loss, and cash flow statements
- *Operations Area*: examine balance sheets, P & L statements, investment portfolios, liquidity, and interest rate sensitivity positions
- *Monitor* internal routines and controls instituting corrective action plans, where necessary
- Prepare audit reports and present recommendations to bank officers/board of directors
- Supervise and develop trainees in regulations, policies, and procedures
- **Accomplishments:**
  - **Promoted** four times in 13 years
  - Youngest Examiner-in-Charge of largest bank in the state
  - Implemented new line sheet as member of Loan Analysis Committee
  - Piloted program for analyzing funds' management involving market, capital market, and liquidity risk

EDUCATION

Bachelor of Science Degree in Business Administration
St. Louis University, St. Louis, Missouri, 1984
Major: **Accounting**

C.P.A. State of Missouri
Chartered Financial Analyst (**CFA**)

Seminars and Workshops:
  Series 7 Training
  Capital Markets
  Vary Bank Related
  Off Balance Sheet Risk Analysis
  Internal Routine and Control
  Numerous other banking topics

REFERENCES

Available on request

KATHRYN WILLIAMSON
115 North Union Boulevard
Colorado Springs, Colorado 80909
719/632-9050

OFFICE MANAGEMENT - OFFICE ADMINISTRATION - CUSTOMER SERVICE

Summary of Qualifications
- Excellent qualifications for Office Management or Office Administrative positions
- Organized, efficient and precise with strong communication and liaison skills
- Skilled in planning and execution of special projects during time-critical environments.
- Decisive and direct, yet flexible in responding to constantly changing assignments
- Unique problem resolution and time-management experience
- Able to coordinate multiple projects and meet deadlines under pressure
- Enthusiastic, creative and willing to assume increased responsibility
- Proven ability to adapt quickly to challenges and changing environments
- Outstanding record of flexibility and adaptability to any assignment

Special Skills
- PC proficient with a wide variety of computer software applications
- Experience with medical terminology
- Progressive experience in office management, scheduling and support services
- Travel arrangement experience

Relevant Skills

OFFICE ADMINISTRATION - OFFICE MANAGEMENT:
- Collecting and recording statistical and confidential information
- Assembling and organizing bulk mailings and marketing materials
- Data entry, with exceptionally fast typing and related Office Administrative activities
- Organization specialist, able to ensure smooth and efficient flow of functions
- Expediting and balancing skills to prioritize time-critical assignments
- Able to independently manage all office administrative activities

CUSTOMER SERVICE:
- Extremely sociable and able to put visitors immediately at ease
- Highly skilled at solving customer relations problems
- Excellent verbal and written communication skills
- Effectively able to communicate with customers, staff and management

CONFIDENTIALITY:
- Experience in handling extremely confidential records
- Held a "Secret" Security clearance

Relevant Professional Experience

DEPARTMENT SECRETARY - HEALTH SCIENCES
Western College of Nursing and Health Sciences, Colorado Springs, Colorado

DEPARTMENT SECRETARY - METRO VICE-NARCOTICS-INTELLIGENCE DIVISION
Manitou Springs Police Department, Manitou Springs, Colorado

DEPARTMENT SECRETARY
Southern Infirmary Medical Center (700 Bed Hospital), Mobile, Alabama

SECRETARY AND ADMINISTRATIVE ASSISTANT - CONFIGURATION MANAGEMENT
Systems Administration Corporation, San Diego, California

REFERENCES AND FURTHER DATA UPON REQUEST

ELIZABETH ROBINSON

806 Riverlawn Drive
Bellevue, Washington 98636
Home: (472) 310-7875   Office: (472) 338-3969

EXECUTIVE SECRETARY / ADMINISTRATIVE MANAGER

Sixteen years' experience planning and directing executive-level administrative affairs and support to Chairmen, Boards of Directors and Executive Management. Combines strong planning, organizational and communication skills with the ability to independently plan and direct high-level business affairs. Trusted advisor, liaison and assistant. Proficient with leading PC applications including word processing and presentation programs. Qualifications include:

- Executive & Board Relations
- Regulatory Reporting & Communications
- Confidential Correspondence & Data
- Special Events & Project Management

- Executive Office Management
- Staff Training & Development
- Federal Property Acquisition & Reporting
- Crisis Communications

PROFESSIONAL EXPERIENCE:

INTERNATIONAL TECHNOLOGY CORPORATION   1991 to Present

Executive Secretary (1995 to Present)
Senior Secretary / Office Manager (1991 to 1995)

Recruited to administration and office management position working with the senior management team of this diversified research venture founded by major U.S. corporations in the high-technology industry. Promoted to Executive Secretary in 1995 as the personal assistant to the Chairman of the Board of Directors and CEO.

Executive Liaison between Chairman/CEO and Executive Management Committee, Business Departments and employees to plan, schedule and facilitate industry and inter-company business functions. Manage confidential correspondence, appointments, meetings, travel and schedule for the Chairman/CEO. Coordinate quarterly shareholders meetings, manage liaison affairs and facilitate print production of shareholder communications.

Special Project Highlights

- Planned, staffed and directed all office management functions for the Chairman/CEO, Senior Vice President and CFO as well as the Executive Vice President and CTO. Provided training and supervision to Executive Department's support staff.
- Spearheaded facility and equipment upgrades in response to the corporation's rapid growth and expansion. Negotiated contracts for the purchase of equipment and supplies.
- Coordinated corporate-wide open house for more than 1000 guests. Managed both internal and external communications, logistics and project management functions.
- Prepared detailed proposals and research documentation for funding of research and product development projects by public and private investors.
- Managed the complete materials acquisition process (e.g., order entry, tracking, receipt, billing, recordkeeping) for $3 million in government purchases.

WASHINGTON DEPARTMENT OF COMMERCE   1990 to 1991

Executive Assistant

High-profile, administrative position directing constituent communications/relations, special events, reporting and administration functions. Planned, scheduled and facilitated a broad range of initiatives, objectives and business functions on behalf of the Director and the Board of Directors.

STUDENT LOAN MARKETING ASSOCIATION   1988 to 1990

Executive Secretary / Assistant Supervisor

Recruited to this national student services organization to coordinate the start-up of an operating facility in Washington. Worked in cooperation with senior management team to facilitate the entire project cycle including construction, facility design/layout, scheduling, budgeting and equipment acquisition. Held concurrent responsibility for establishing operating infrastructure, writing policies and procedures, and recruiting administrative/support personnel. Led a team of 40 and administered a $1.5 million operating budget.

- Played key role in the successful completion of a multi-million dollar construction project.
- Recruited more than 100 personnel responsible for loan origination, project management and customer service.
- Exceeded all corporate standards for productivity, efficiency and operations management.
- Selected by corporate headquarters for special assignment conducting crisis management training at five centers throughout the U.S.

UNITED STATES ARMY   1982 to 1988

Executive Secretary / Stenographer

Fast-track promotion through several increasingly responsible administrative management positions throughout the U.S. and abroad. Advanced based on consistent success in effectively managing high-profile, sensitive military affairs for commanding generals and other top military officers. Received numerous commendations and awards for outstanding performance. Significant projects and achievements:

- Managed confidential correspondence, scheduling and meetings for Judge Advocate. Independently researched, responded to and followed up on requests for legal documentation and reports for a team of 10 attorneys managing 100+ cases per week.
- Planned and directed security, logistics and administrative affairs for foreign dignitaries, congressional leaders and other military officials visiting Korea's demilitarized zone.
- Appointed Special Secretary to Commanding General during field training exercises.
- Selected from a competitive group of candidates for a co-ed, joint military Primary Leadership Development Course. Graduated with distinguished honors.

EDUCATION & PROFESSIONAL TRAINING:

- Graduate of a three-month intensive Army executive administrative, secretarial and stenography training program.
- Attended seminars while continuing with higher education sponsored by universities and professional associations.

DAVID R. WALKER
3546 London Bridge Court
Houston, Texas 77000
(713) 555-9786

OPERATIONS / MANAGEMENT EXECUTIVE

AREAS OF EXPERTISE

Medical Billing Procedures / Laws ♦ Strategic Growth Planning / Development

Automated System Conversions ♦ Personnel Training / Management ♦ Conflict Resolution

Critical Problem Analysis / Resolution ♦ Organizational Reengineering / Revitalization

HIGHLIGHTS OF QUALIFICATIONS

♦ **Proactive Operating Executive** with 15 progressive years of experience and expertise in **Medical Billing**; thoroughly cognizant of medical billing / reimbursement / reporting procedures and laws.

♦ Outstanding **leadership** and **problem-solving** abilities; innate ability to analyze team members and create innovative methods to motivate them to achieve high level of performance / productivity; earn respect and cooperation from staff. Efficiently identify / correct **source** of problems.

♦ Strong computer literacy: AS/400; IBM System 38 and PCs; software applications, including medical billing systems; Internet; E-mail. Executed myriad computer conversions; trained operators on use.

♦ Exceptional **communication** and **interpersonal** skills; easily interact with people of all levels; establish excellent working relationship with team members. Effective **negotiator / motivator**.

♦ Function well under pressure. **Versatile. Innovative. Loyal.** Highly **results-** and **team-oriented**.

PROFESSIONAL EXPERIENCE

POWER MEDICAL BILLING SERVICES
Vice President of Operations

Houston, Texas
January 1986 – Present

♦ Recruited to assist in development and expansion of new company providing computerized billing services to healthcare providers; rapidly progressed from **Billing Supervisor** to **Manager** to **Director** to **Vice President**.

♦ Scope of responsibility encompasses direct supervision of department heads (with staff increasing from 4 to 60+), management of all operations, and extensive problem solving.

♦ Manage all computer and communication functions; **vital participant in IBM System 38 to AS/400 conversion; coordinated client conversions to PMBS billing systems**. Train/supervise operators. Audit billing operations.

♦ **Developed astute marketing strategies** to **accelerate client account base; successfully negotiate contracts** with healthcare providers and managed care companies; **expanded client base** from 7 to more than 100 healthcare providers.

♦ Consult with clients and managed care executives; evaluate physician operations and recommend coding and filing strategies; negotiate pricing and reimbursement fee schedules with managed care executives.

♦ **Significantly improved billing operations** and **increased gross revenues from $400,000 to $3 million**.

PRESBYTERIAN HOSPITAL   Houston, Texas
Manager of Professional Billing Services   May 1982 – December 1985

- Rapidly progressed from **Supervisor of Inpatient Insurance Follow-up** to **Supervisor of Collections** to **Manager of Professional Billing Services** (separate division) responsible for staff of 18 providing billing services to more than 50 physicians.

- **Completely reorganized/reengineered** 6-month-old chaotic department; **streamlined all areas** and **drastically reduced extensive delinquency backlog**.

- **Formulated billing and collection policies and procedures**; trained all employees on operation of system.

- Established and efficiently managed $1+ million operating budget; **reduced expenditures** and **increased profits**.

- **Planned, organized, coordinated, and implemented two major computer system conversions**.

- As **Supervisor of Collections**, supervised 13 Credit Interviews / Collectors; negotiated payment arrangements with patients; resolved complaints.

- As **Supervisor of Inpatient Insurance Follow-up**, directed activities of 8 Collectors; managed $13 million A/R; interacted extensively with insurance carriers regarding claim and payment status.

OHIO FINANCE CORPORATION   Dayton, Ohio
Branch Manager   July 1978 – April 1982

- Began as Manager Trainee; completed intense training program; acquired professional development in Operations Management, Finance, Marketing, and Personnel Management.

- Managed total operations of 1200-account branch providing financial loans and income tax preparation services to clients in highly competitive market.

- **Significantly increased client base / market share** through strategic management practices and perseverance.

- Recruited, trained, and directed all employees, ensuring compliance with stringent rules/regulations.

- Critiqued / verified loan applications; approved/rejected loans; initiated corrective action on delinquent loans.

EDUCATION

WILMINGTON COLLEGE – Wilmington, Ohio
Business Administration

Professional Development Programs in all aspects of **Business Management**
IBA Healthcare Seminars (Medical Billing Laws) (Ongoing)

PROFESSIONAL AFFILIATIONS

Charter Member, INTERNATIONAL BILLING ASSOCIATION

Esteban J. Olmos

8404 East Valley Ranch, #4022
Irving, Texas 75000
(972) 471-5555

International Administrative Director

Extensive experience in planning and directing administrative affairs and providing support to Chairmen, Boards of Directors and Senior Management. Brings strong organization and communication skills, and ability to independently plan and direct high-level business affairs. Delivers strong operating results in productivity and efficiency improvement, cost reduction, technological advancement, and improved communication in a multiethnic environment. Excellent team-building and leadership skills.

Personal Profile:

- Professor, International Commerce, Universidad de Rafael
- Research Study, Jesuit Foundation, Universidad de Rafael
- Extensive travel throughout the United States, Central and South America, Europe, and the Middle East. Comfortable interacting with people of diverse cultures.
- Fluent English and Spanish.

Education:

M.B.A., International Management, Southern Methodist University, Dallas, Texas
B.A., Economics, Southern Methodist University, Dallas, Texas

Professional Experience:

L. L. JACKSON CO. CONSTRUCTORS   1993 to Present
Latin American Headquarters   Guatemala City, Guatemala
$60 million highway construction project

ADMINISTRATIVE DIRECTOR

Charged with start-up and management of project site headquarters. Plan, staff and direct administrative function. Scope of responsibility is diverse and includes human resources, employee relations, accounting and financial reporting, and purchasing. Key in creating a procedure that ensured the accuracy of reports on available resources for the Board of Directors.

- Decreased operating costs by establishing a Purchasing Department to supply and track company resources.
- Upgraded I.S. to current technology.
- All activities conducted in multiethnic environment.

Addendum

Teaching and Research Studies:
Time, Talent and Expertise Donated to University

UNIVERSIDAD de RAFAEL - Guatemala City, Guatemala

Research Study, Jesuit Foundation -1996

Recruited by Dean of Academics to identify potential contributors for university funding among multinational organizations in Germany, Japan and the United States, with operations in Guatemala.

- Built a database containing corporation names, Guatemalan contacts— including their address and telephone number—and foreign contacts.

PROFESSOR, INTERNATIONAL COMMERCE -1995

Graduate course for discussions and problem solving on globalization of commerce.

- Final project: students chose a country, a product and a strategy to successfully penetrate domestic markets. Variables included cultural, historical, political and demographics of targeted markets.

LINDA E. WELL
112 Greendale Street
Willimantic, CT 06226
(860) 456-5555

WORD PROCESSING / DESKTOP PUBLISHING

Broad range of experience and expertise in the word processing/desktop publishing field. Enjoyed designing and exploring the creative process of layout. Recognized for developing and designing the most effective alternatives for completion of training materials. Innovative office support for a staff of 10 trainers. Outstanding background in effectually dealing with customers across the United States.

HIGHLIGHTS OF QUALIFICATIONS

✓ Over 10 years experience with desktop publishing and word processing.
✓ Enthusiastic, creative idea generator; flair for graphic design.
✓ Able to consistently meet deadlines and maintain sense of humor under pressure.
✓ Sharp, resourceful, quick learner; ability to adapt swiftly to a challenge.
✓ Diplomatic, tactful; communicate well with a wide range of personalities.
✓ Thrive on helping clients get desired results.

TECHNICAL SKILLS

❏ Type 70 words per minute
❏ Comprehensive experience with: Microsoft, Word for Windows, Wordperfect, and IBM

WORK HISTORY

Manager
Franco-American Club, Willimantic,CT, 1993-1997
Training Specialist/Desktop Publisher
Travelers Ins. Co., Hartford, CT, 1976-1993

PROFESSIONAL EXPERIENCE

Graphic Design & Layout
❏ Created graphic design and layout of posters, flyers, programs, brochures, and resumes.
❏ Conceived ideas using a variety of media, on a limited budget, for newsletters, programs, manuals, and other publications, activities and events, using graphics, typefaces and unusual layout elements for eye-catching displays.
❏ Designed mass distribution promotional material and business brochures for small-business clients. Captured the right "look" for their individual needs.
❏ Determined and managed the best alternative to getting text materials completed for training managers and consultants, i.e., completed project within department or "contracted" out for completion.
❏ Provided support and training material to the training consultants and training managers.

TRAINING

Desktop Publishing, Travelers Ins.
Microsoft Word, Travelers Ins.
Various Self-Study Programs, Travelers Ins.

CALVIN MANCHESTER, CAE

1234 N. Kingston Highway
Orlando, Florida 32000
(407) 555-1212

CERTIFIED ASSOCIATION EXECUTIVE

Registered Lobbyist

Over seven years executive-level experience in the development, growth and leadership of member-driven, not-for-profit organizations, plus 15 years senior operating and management experience in private industry. Consistently successful in increasing revenues and funding, expanding membership, enhancing member services and developing governance infrastructures focused on current and future trends. Expertise includes:

- Financial / Budgetary Management
- Revenue Raising
- Strategic Planning
- Fundraising / Philanthropic Events
- Public Speaking
- Member Development / Retention
- Public Relations / Affairs
- Educational Programs
- Political / Legislative Advocacy
- Media Relations

PROFESSIONAL EXPERIENCE:

CONSTRUCTION ASSOCIATION OF CENTRAL FLORIDA, Orlando, Florida   1992 to Present

Executive Director / COO

Recruited by Central Florida's leadership while employed at the National Construction Association with full operational and P&L responsibility for this not-for-profit trade association. Hold complete accountability for a $2.0 million budget and all financial affairs, a direct reporting staff of 15, association policy, member development and retention, member services, public relations and communications. As a registered lobbyist, direct the activities of two governmental affairs lobbyists who monitor legislative matters in the Florida State legislature and the 25 municipalities in the association's jurisdiction.

Created a strong proactive member-driven association previously plagued with inconsistent organization, management, declining revenues and rapid turnover.

- Developed and instituted a leadership program, structure and initiatives reflective of today's volunteer environment attracting and encouraging future leaders to participate in the association. Modified the governance structure to ensure continued volunteer commitment.
- Increased cash reserves by over $250,000 through the development of several non-dues revenue programs and development of a multi-year financial business plan.
- Evaluated, expanded and utilized available technology providing for cost-effective and timely communications with members.
- Created and instituted an award-winning educational curriculum providing continuing education opportunities for members while simultaneously serving as a tool to educate members about the association and the services and benefits available.
- Strengthened the association's public image through development and orchestration of community philanthropic events enabling the association to donate $400,000 to various community charities during 1994 and 1995.
- Identified and capitalized upon opportunities to enhance the association's stature and influence in the community through relationship fostering with community groups and partnership building with related industry organizations.
- Authored and implemented a staff performance management system, expanded and updated staff policy manual, and cultivated a dynamic professional team. Conducted leadership training seminars for officers, directors, and committee chairpersons.

PROFESSIONAL EXPERIENCE (Continued):

NATIONAL CONSTRUCTION ASSOCIATION, Washington, DC 1990 to 1992

Regional Services Manager

Regional consultant to local and state construction organizations in the Southwest ranging in size from 20-20,000 member firms with full responsibility for business management, strategic planning, leadership development, governmental affairs, issues management, member services and communications.

- Developed leadership orientation programs for presentation and use by local associations and assisted local associations in identifying, expanding and delivering local member services.
- Personally visited with the leadership of over 100 local and state associations on multiple occasions. Worked with directors to identify positive, creative solutions for various issues. Facilitated strategic planning meetings and was a frequent presenter at state and national leadership conferences.
- Authored a workshop on "Surviving in the 90s".
- Member of a four-man senior executive team responsible for the development of a Local Governance Audit Program.

THE ADAMS BILT COMPANY, Raleigh, NC 1986 to 1989

Director of Development

Responsible for land acquisition (commercial and residential) as well as the development, construction, marketing, sales and financing for the residential division of the company. Recruited and supervised field superintendents and sales staff.

- Developed a successful public relations and marketing campaign to address Realtor attitudes resulting from misrepresentations by contract sales organization at one of the company's communities.
- Established an in-house sales department for the company's new home communities.
- Slashed costs in maintenance expenses of the company's new home communities.
- Led expansion into two new markets.

MANCHESTER BUILDERS OF DURHAM, INC., Durham, NC 1978 to 1985

President / Owner

Founded and built a general contracting business. In spite of a recession and the 20% interest rates of 1980-81, generated revenues of $5.0 million in 1984.

EDUCATION:

B. S. – Mathematics – University of North Carolina

Educational Programs of the American Society of Association Executives (General Association Management, CEO Symposium, Certified Association Executive, Communications)

AWARDS / RECOGNITION:

David Lloyd Award (Presented by NCA-EOC for outstanding performance as an EO)
Presidential Award (Presented by NCA-EOC President for leadership excellence)
Association Excellence Awards presented by NCA-EOC (15 awards in 5 years)
Rainbow Award (Presented by the Adam Walsh Children's Fund)
Community Service Award (Presented by Orange County Convention & Tourist Bureau)
American Society of Association Executives (ASAE) Gold Circle Award

LUKE M. LaMEADOWS
3368 Independence Street
Grove City, Ohio
(614) 555-0105

CAREER SUMMARY

Dynamic 20+ year career in the management, administration, and leadership of trade and professional associations. Demonstrated ability to develop, implement, and oversee innovative marketing and promotional campaigns, which increased overall membership counts, improved member retention rates, increased non-dues revenues, and provided value-added membership benefits. A proactive administrator, recognized for motivational leadership, cohesive team building, and solid results-oriented approaches. Significant achievements in:

- Membership Development/Retention
- Financial Management/Budgeting
- Convention/Trade Show Management
- Written/Verbal Communications
- Continuing Education Programs

- Strategic/Business Planning
- International Relations
- Legislative/Government Relations
- Member/Customer Relations
- Public Awareness/Visibility

Researched and developed three separate hardware/software computer programs for multiple associations which streamlined overall efficiency while reducing bottom-line operating costs.

PROFESSIONAL EXPERIENCE

HARRISON GROUP, Columbus, Ohio   1992 to Present

Chief Executive Officer
Provide management/consulting support services to state, national, and international clients, including trade/professional associations, nonprofit organizations, societies, foundations, and religious groups.

Revenue Growth

- Initiated membership marketing campaign, increasing membership 31%, retention rate 13%.
- Developed member specialties advertising and group insurance programs, increasing new sources of income 14%.
- Developed marketing for annual convention, increasing attendance 46% in first year.
- Established advertising rate structure/marketing campaign, increasing revenues 37%.
- Expanded society into world largest distributor of industry publications, increasing revenues 17%.

Educational Programs

- Doubled continuing education seminars/workshops. Inaugurated foundation to fund educational programs which generated $350,000+ in first year.
- Increased certification exams 49%; refresher course registrants 68%. Secured $1.5 million in government funding for specialized program.
- Developed college course curriculum which received approval by national accrediting board.

Organization/Management

- Initiated first strategic plan/vision, business plan, and fiscal budget.
- Developed new association logo, promoting public awareness and increasing membership.
- Initiated and negotiated signing of professional cooperative agreements with 22 international associations.
- Re-engineered headquarters' operation and staff. Developed staff policies/office procedures. Streamlined operation by restructuring association board and committees.
- Consolidated headquarters' international department and country offices into regional concept, reducing operating costs. Redefined job descriptions; developed strategies and vision focus.

WORLDWIDE EXHIBITORS ASSOCIATION, Miami, Florida   1986 to 1992
Executive Director
Provided leadership to the corporate member trade association, comprised of 1,600 members and 17 chapters, representing companies using trade shows as marketing/promotional medium worldwide. Managed annual budget of $1.7 million. Relocated international headquarters from Chicago to Washington, DC.

Achievements:

- Increased membership base 117%; chapters 110%. Raised growth in trade show exhibit space 150% and increased annual conference attendance 183%. Tripled income to $2.7 million. Increased reserve funds $1.5 million.
- Established Exhibit Industry Education Foundation, producing $550,000+ annually. Orchestrated development of four-year university degree program in exhibit management/design. Developed and coordinated Certified Exhibit Manager (CEM) certification program.
- Served as lobbyist relating to legislative, government, union, and industry relations issues.
- Spearheaded marketing efforts throughout European and Asian expositions representing coalition of 44 US aerospace/defense industry corporations.
- Represented association as a US Presidential Appointee, EXPORT NOW Initiative; member of the US Chamber of Commerce Export Promotion Council; and Coordinator of the US/USSR 1990 Trade Briefing.

OHIO UNIVERSITY, School of Continuing Studies, Athens, Ohio   1982 to 1986
Director, International Conference Center, and Conference Services
Provided overall facility management and coordination of meetings and conventions for this $143 million facility consisting of 35 meeting rooms. Created and developed 50-60 annual professional seminars, conferences, and workshops; directed comprehensive support services to all events.

Achievements:

- Initiated major international advertising/promotional mail campaign and telemarketing effort which doubled projected income in first six months.
- Orchestrated $1.5 million fund-raiser to construct continuing education facility; exceeded goal 7.8%.
- Managed university's downtown campus. Increased/coordinated continuing education programs and professional development conferences 145%.

TRAVEL AGENTS OF AMERICA, INC. (TAA), New York, New York   1980 to 1982
Director, Meetings, Conventions and Trade Shows
Directed logistical details for over 50 annual events. Prepared and administered annual operating budget of $2.7+ million. Coordinated annual International Travel Congress & Trade Show attracting 10,000 delegates, representing 60 countries.

Prior experience in CHAMBER OF COMMERCE MANAGEMENT included preparation of grant application resulting in $6.5 million in federal funds for acquisition/development of waterfront property into public park.

AFFILIATIONS

> American Society of Association Executives (ASAE)
> > Member, Board of Directors (ex-officio), 1991-92
> > Chairman, International Section Council, 1991-92

EDUCATION

> Postgraduate, Institute for Organizational Management of US Chamber of Commerce
> BA, Industrial Relations, University of Georgia

JASON M. VERMETTE

P.O. Box 555
Sometown, NH 55555

Phone: (888) 888-8888
Fax: (222) 222-2222

CAREER PROFILE

Visionary self-starter offering over 20 years' experience educating, motivating and empowering groups to reach organizational goals.   Expert in leading cross-functional teams to action and achievement. Highly successful in identifying, recruiting and developing leaders for state and local action. Skilled contract negotiator for both public and private sectors. Outstanding oral and written communication skills; exceptional organizational skills. Capabilities include:

- Strategic & Mission Planning
- Policy & Procedure Development
- Political & Legislative Affairs
- Member Development

- Volunteer Recruitment
- Community Outreach
- Public Speaking
- Committee Leadership

- Fundraising
- Media Relations
- Financial & Budgetary Affairs
- Special Events Management

PROFESSIONAL EXPERIENCE

CHAIRMAN   1996 to Present
"Voter Registration - Get out the Vote" Campaign   One Town/Second Town, NH
　　Developed draft document and plan to generate community interest and increase participation in state and federal elections. Organized and worked with community groups to establish a planning committee and subcommittees. Selected campaign sponsors and orchestrated fundraising activities. Wrote and distributed media and press releases.   Facilitated meetings and consulted with subcommittees to develop and implement program goals. Analyzed national, state, and local results.

Overall Results
- Exceeded all goals; revitalized community interest, increased registered voter participation to 63%, established open lines of communication between the two towns and bonded $5M for the purpose of public school renovation.

REPRESENTATIVE OF THE GENERAL PRESIDENT   1993 to 1996
United Brotherhood of Carpenters and Joiners of America   Washington, D.C.
　　Guided all field administrative operations. Formulated and implemented organizational policy. Planned, developed and evaluated programs, including promotional materials, brochures, and publications to organize around local and central issues. Worked with state and local union leaders in the research and development of market area surveys, multiple craft project agreements, jobsite and project targeting. Directed negotiations, handled local grievances and arbitrations.

　　Assisted in the development of the C.O.M.E.T. program; served as supervisor and director. Directed the work and implementation of the District Organizing Program for local unions in the Northeast Region. Planned and directed strategies for dealing with the issue of Double-Breasting and the impact that it had on our organizations, membership and contractor base.

Overall Results:
- Rejuvenated community involvement; successfully identified and developed leaders to train union members and integrate the program into their local communities.

PROJECT DIRECTOR, TALLAHASSEE CARPENTERS PROJECT   1992 to 1993
National Resource Staff, United Brothers of Carpenters and Joiners of America   Washington, D.C.
　　Directed a pilot program to explore total workforce organizing concept and to develop practical methods for building a Carpenters local union into an organization with the power to raise overall craft standards. Organized workers in the construction industry. Managed all educational and manpower projects. Oversaw development and guided all technical management functions. Spearheaded the

Project Director, Tallahassee Carpenters Project Cont.

creation and integration of an organizing strategy and program within the local union. Evaluated on-site operations to insure effective implementation of program.

Overall Results
♦ Successfully increased the wages of carpenters an average of $3 per hour within 18 months. Motivated member participation, empowered members to "take charge" and developed leaders for community involvement.

REPRESENTATIVE OF THE PRESIDENT FOR PRIVATE/FEDERAL SHIPYARDS   1983 to 1992
United Brotherhood of Carpenters and Joiners of America   Washington, D.C.
Managed all educational and training projects of the UBC membership employed in federal and private shipyards. Organized and maintained a system to identify, recruit and train local leaders for community and state action. Coordinated national policy and supervised implementation of the General President's directives. Researched and prepared reports for Congressional and affiliate presentation. Negotiated district and local agreements for public and private sectors.

Developed the Pacific Coast District Council of Carpenters to service and train carpenters in California, Oregon and Washington states. Developed organizing strategies; trained local leaders in grievance and arbitration procedures as well as the filing and processing of ULP's for both the public and private sector.

CHIEF STEWARD AND TREASURER, METAL TRADES COUNCIL   1978 to 1983
Portsmouth Naval Shipyard   Portsmouth, NH
Directed budget allocation and reporting functions for District Council finances. Planned and orchestrated biannual convention. Developed and coordinated implementation of the federal naval shipyard legislative agenda. Managed all grievances and arbitrations; trained local leaders in the procedures and in the filing and processing of ULP's. Served as Council trainer for contract negotiations, contract interpretation and Market and Wage Survey techniques.

SHIPWRIGHT JOURNEYMAN   1978 to 1993
Portsmouth Naval Shipyard   Portsmouth, NH

SHIPWRIGHT/CARPENTER APPRENTICE   1974 to 1978
Portsmouth Naval Shipyard   Portsmouth, NH

HELICOPTER COMBAT SUPPORT SQUADRON FIVE   1966 to 1972
United States Navy   Honorably Discharged

EDUCATION AND PROFESSIONAL DEVELOPMENT

♦ C.O.M.E.T. and Teaching Techniques, Training the Trainer Course, UBC and Cornell University, 1993
♦ Leadership Training for Officers and Business Representatives for Construction,
♦ Workforce Organizing, George Meany Center for Labor Studies, 1992 to 1993
♦ Computer Training, Accounting, Desktop Publishing, University of New Hampshire, Division of Continuing Education, 1981 to 1986
♦ Organizing One-on-One, IAM Federal Employee Organizing Program, 1980
♦ Metal Trades Council Officer/Stewards Training Program, Metal Trades Department, Washington, D.C., 1979
♦ Analytic Trouble Shooting Program, Kepner/Tregoe, 1978
♦ Graduate United Brotherhood of Carpenters and Joiners of America, Apprenticeship Program-Carpenter, 1978
♦ Graduate U.S. Navy Apprenticeship, Program-Shipwright, 1978
♦ U.S. Navy Nuclear Power Qualified Worker Program, Public/Private Industry, 1977

ANNETTE J. STOKES

659 Devonshire Drive
Maulberry, KY 46794
(354) 987-3467

CAREER OBJECTIVE

SENIOR VICE-PRESIDENT - COMMERCIAL LENDING

SUMMARY OF QUALIFICATIONS

- 16 years of commercial and residential real estate lending/mortgage banking experience, including origination, underwriting, loan negotiation/structuring, appraising and investment analysis, credit analysis, and closing/administering construction and permanent loans.

- 3 years of loan portfolio and credit administration experience, including asset management and disposition, workouts and restructures, bankruptcies, and foreclosures.

- 3 years of multifamily development management and administration experience encompassing market research and site analysis, financial analysis, development, construction and operations budgeting, and construction contract negotiation.

- Excellent reputation for thorough knowledge of real estate markets, owners and developers in Virginia and the Carolinas.

- Analytical, organized, possessing a strong "numbers" aptitude.

- Solid background and knowledge of real estate appraisal methodology and market research.

PROFESSIONAL EXPERIENCE

AMERICAN BANK & TRUST COMPANY, Maulberry, KY   1976 - Present
Real Estate Lending Officer/Assistant Vice-President
- Originated and administered approximately $140 million in construction and permanent loans, specializing in strip shopping centers, medical and general purpose buildings, office/warehouse facilities, apartments, hotels, and single family residential.

- Implemented new business development activities and strategies, primarily through customer identification and call programs and involvement with industry and professional trade organizations.

- Prepared appraisals and loan submission requests, made verbal and written presentations to loan review and investment committees, and prepared and negotiated loans.

- Structured and assisted with acquisitions of income producing properties approximately $10 million in value.

- Prepared budgets for company-owned real estate and assisted in property management operations.

- Serve as member of Commercial Credit Committee, acting on commercial and industrial loan requests and line-of-credit renewals.

- Directly supervise staff of eight.

Loan Officer/Assistant Vice-President

- Administered a portfolio of loans totaling $40 million in value requiring appraisal review, collections and delinquencies, maturities, loan classification, tax and insurance payments, escrow account analysis, and on-site inspections.

- Administered construction loan portfolio including construction draw requests and inspections.

- Audited loan files and performed loan documentation reviews.

- Assisted General Loan Administration in revising the bank's Income Property Lending Manual.

- Structured and supervised functions of 25 branch employees to ensure maximum efficiency and security.

  — Charged with direction of daily work assignments of tellers, new accounts, clerical, and security personnel.

  — Conducted semi-annual evaluations and salary reviews.

  — Executed frequent internal audits of cash, travelers checks, and bonds.

  — Wrote training outline for execution by Head Teller.

QUEENS INVESTMENT PROPERTIES, Maulberry, KY   1973 - 1976
Real Estate Developer
- Planned and developed 102 unit Deer Crossing Apartments in Jefferson, KY, and 100 unit Deer Crossing Apartments in Flagstone, KY.

  — Responsible for site identification and acquisition, project conceptualization and architectural design, negotiating project financing, development, construction and operating budget administration, leasing, and asset management.

  — Completed project on time and within budget, resulting in bonus through incentive fee clause.

EDUCATION

B.S. Degree in Business Administration
UNIVERSITY OF KENTUCKY, Maulberry, KY

Successful completion of course work in Basic Appraisal Principles, Capitalization Theory and Techniques, Urban Properties, and Investment Analysis.

AFFILIATIONS

Member, National Association of Commercial Lenders
Treasurer, Maulberry Chapter of the Professional Business Women's Association
Board of Directors, Little Life

Excellent References Upon Request
Willing to Relocate

ROBERT T. OTUS

333 Wilshire Drive • Anytown, Georgia 30000 • (999) 999-9999

VICE PRESIDENT, COMMERCIAL CREDIT

SUMMARY OF QUALIFICATIONS

Proven and verifiable success in the banking industry; recognized for substantial contributions in the area of commercial lending, public relations, and business development. Strengths in planning and organization with excellent facility for correlating a wide range of activities. Precise, committed, resourceful.

- Outstanding interpersonal, communication, and leadership skills; ability to unify diverse groups to achieve a common goal.

- Demonstrated ability to analyze complex situations, set priorities, and devise feasible strategies that produce satisfactory solutions.

- Concern for well being of community demonstrated through involvement and leadership roles in Kiwanis, Jaycees, Lions Club, American Cancer Society, United Way, Chamber of Commerce, and Boy Scouts of America.

EXPERIENCE

A BANK IN GEORGIA, Anytown, Georgia   1990 to Present
formerly A Different Bank in Georgia

Vice President, Commercial Lending
- Render seasoned credit judgement to ensure sound financial growth of institution.
- Cultivate and monitor long-standing relationships; routinely assess customers' credentials to ensure a high quality portfolio of loans with high profitability at reasonable risk.
- Structure complex loan agreements, advise and counsel customers, and assure appropriate documentation during life of transaction.
- Effect loyalty, efficiency, and high quality standards among staff through personal example and leadership. Foster exemplary customer service levels.
- Additionally, served as Compliance Officer, 1990 through 1993, and Community Reinvestment Act Officer, 1990 through 1995.

  - *Contributed substantially to institution's growth — from no assets and $6 million in capital to $72 million in assets in 1995; reached nearly $200 million in assets after merger in 1995.*
  - *Generated approximately $4.5 million in new loans in 1994; generated $7.5 million in 1995.*

ROBERT T. OTUS

EXPERIENCE *(Continued)*

NATIONAL BANK, Atlanta, Georgia   1973 to 1990

Manager, New Branch Center 1990
  - Selected to open new branch; successfully facilitated opening.

Manager, Old Branch Center 1987 to 1989
  - Directed all branch activities and supervised 13 employees while focusing on business development, commercial and consumer lending.

      - *Grew loans over 54% and deposits over 19% in the first year.*

Manager, Beginning Banking Center 1982 to 1987
  - Oversaw opening of new branch and all facets of operations and management; met challenging goals of developing and maintaining profitability and stability from early years and through merger transition.

      - *Achieved profit in highly competitive, mature market within 18 months.*
      - *Facilitated Lilburn Center conversion from First Gwinnett to First Atlanta system, 1985.*

Management Trainee to Commercial Lender and Assistant Branch Manager Largest Banking Center 1973 to 1982

EDUCATION

UNIVERSITY OF GEORGIA, Athens, Georgia
Bachelor of Business Administration with *Major in Marketing*

GEORGIA BANKING SCHOOL AT ATHENS, Athens, Georgia
  Graduated second in class of over ninety bankers.
  Distinguished Graduate, 1982

Ongoing education through courses at:
  American Institute of Banking
  C&S National Bank Training School
  A Bank In Georgia Training
  National Bank Training

RICH N. FAMOUS

21196 Real Estate Road, Escondido, California 92026 ● (760) 555-1212

CAREER PROFILE

Confident, competent, and organized Commercial Banking Executive with considerable progressive experience as a Relationship Manager augmented by a formal education and refined by specialized professional training. Accustomed to managing client deposit base of $70+ million and $65+ million in loans developed from 75 client relationships. Specific expertise focuses on companies with annual revenues up to $250 million and on high net worth individuals. Verifiable record of significantly increased responsibilities spanning more than two decades. Accurate, personable, and stable; proven record of performance demonstrated through personal initiative, tenacity, and loyalty. Qualifications include competence in:

- Administration
- Bottom Line Profits
- Business Development
- Client Services
- Commercial Banking

- Credit Underwriting
- Financial Management
- Goal Setting
- Internal Auditing
- Loan Portfolios

- Operations Management
- Private Banking
- Problem Resolution
- Security Procedures
- Staff Development

AREAS OF RESPONSIBILITY

- Administering broad-based client services maximizing cross-selling opportunities; and recognizing, fostering, and expanding business opportunities.

- Developing and managing profitable banking relationships with high net worth clients and small-to-medium size business owners.

- Orchestrating and coordinating new business development activities; selling value-added credit, deposit, and investment services.

- Maintaining credit files and portfolio performance records.

MANAGEMENT EXPERIENCE

FIRST REGIONAL BANK, La Credenza, California - 1987 to present

Senior Vice President and Primary Relationship Officer. 1994 to present.

Vice President and Primary Relationship Officer. 1992 to 1994.

Vice President and Assistant Manager. 1987 to 1992.

(Continued on next page)

ACHIEVEMENTS and CONTRIBUTIONS

- Consistently generated more than $4.5 million in new loans between 1990 and 1994.

- Increased loan and deposit portfolios 75% during 1993 to 1995 by focusing on growth from personal business development activities.

- Consistent record of retaining business, demonstrating leadership, initiative, flexibility and adaptability during management transitions.

- Retained 98% of relationships intact and experienced low loan losses despite an industry-wide shrinkage in 1990 to 1994.

- Created and implemented an effective, reliable in-house internal audit process; trained staff in audit procedures, and consistently achieved highest ratings in regulatory compliance issues.

- Developed broad knowledge in all facets of the banking industry including credit and portfolio management, business development, cross-selling techniques, administration, financial management, and human resources responsibilities.

EDUCATION AND PROFESSIONAL DEVELOPMENT

American College, San Bernardino, California
    Masters of Business Administration
    Bachelor of Business Administration

West Ridge Banking School, Medford, Oregon
    Graduate: Certificated Banking Program

Continuing Education and Professional Development Courses
- Auditing Procedures
- Budgeting & Forecasts
- Credit Issues
- Customer Service
- Documentation
- Personnel Management
- Regulatory Issues
- Strategic Planning
- Sales and Negotiations

Morris Roberts & Associates, San Diego, California
    Iomega Bank Test - Completed 1994

REFERENCES

Appropriate personal and professional references are available.

JANE M. SMITH
2000 North 11th Street
Wisconsin Rapids, Wisconsin 54494
(715) 325-5888

BANKING PROFESSIONAL
Head Teller

A competent and highly motivated banking professional with exceptional training skills. Efficient in streamlining operations and communications. Excellent organizational, analytical, and problem solving skills.

EXPERIENCE

SMITH CREDIT UNION, Pittsville, WI   10/94-Present
Branch Head Teller
Member Services Representative
Loan Representative
Direct and manage a team of approximately ten tellers. Personally train all new branch tellers and participate on a rotating basis as a corporate classroom teller trainer. Scope of responsibility is diverse and includes tellering, scheduling, security, customer service, auditing and balancing teller drawers, balancing the vault, check orders, money ordering, traveler's checks, and machinery maintenance. As a Personal Banker, open new accounts and work up loan papers for Officer's approval.

Accomplishments:
• Developed procedures for cash carryover documentation that *significantly* reduced teller errors.
• Instituted uniform standard procedures for teller tape documentation that increased efficiency and *significantly* reduced teller errors.
• Reinvented the Teller Training manual into a day-to-day reference and training tool.
• Created forms and procedures for recalling work packets that increased corporate/branch efficiency.
• Streamlined the ordering of office supplies; procedures adopted by corporate and other branches.
• Developed log book system for night depository that reduced teller errors .
• Coordinated a weekend move for the Teller Department to a new building. Maintained service through Friday evening and opened Monday morning on time.
• Member of VIP Grand Opening and Branch Grand Opening Committee.

EDUCATION

Bachelor of Science, Business Administration - August 1997
        Private College, Milwaukee, WI

Continuing Professional Development
Teller Essentials Seminar - Action Training Systems
Advanced Tellering Seminar - Colorado Banking Institute
Security Training for Financial Institutions - Mid-State Bank
Insurance Training and Credit Union & Compliance- Smith Insurance Company
ACH & Federal Payments Seminar - Midwest Coalition
Member Service Training and Loan Training - Lakes Credit Union
Notary Public, expires 11/00

Documentation and References Available Upon Request

LAWRENCE W. JOHANSEN
3554 Longmeadow Drive
San Ramon, California 95630

Office (481) 533-4541 x542

Home (481) 877-5631

SENIOR CUSTOMER SERVICE EXECUTIVE

Dynamic management career, building top-performing customer service and order fulfillment organizations. Delivered consistent gains in customer satisfaction and retention through expertise in work process design, measurement, analysis and improvement.

Strong leadership, problem solving and communication skills. Flexible, positive and responsive to change. Master of Arts in Organizational Management.

PROFESSIONAL EXPERIENCE:

PSI INSTITUTE, San Ramon, California   1991 to Present
(Market leader in management training and consulting; subsidiary of Turner Systems.)

Strategic Team Leader - Customer Svc, Fulfillment & Collections (1995 to Present)
Customer Service Manager (1991 to 1995)

Recruited to PSI in 1991 to revitalize the Customer Service organization, improve customer satisfaction and retention, and drive forward a number of innovative performance improvement programs. Led a customer service staff of 20 responsible for material fulfillment and service billings. Managed a $1.5 million annual operating budget.

Promoted to newly-created position as Strategic Process Team Leader in 1995. Challenged to architect and implement improved business processes throughout the Service, Fulfillment and Collections Departments. Currently leading a number of cross-functional process teams working to align operations with client needs and business strategies.

Financial & Performance Gains:

- Increased customer service and shipping accuracy to 99%. Within one year, decreased service and shipping errors by 66.7% and overall order fulfillment errors by 63%.
- Achieved consistent customer service ratings of 6.7 on 7.0 scale.
- Designed and produced a catalog of training materials and services, simplifying order processing and reducing unit cost per catalog from $9.00 to $3.00.
- Resolved long-standing invoicing issues, reducing late payments 25% and credit memos 22%.
- Managed a 20% increase in order volume with existing staff, while continuing to increase order fulfillment accuracy and customer satisfaction.

Operations & Organizational Reengineering:

- Won 1995 **"PSI Quality Cup"** for measurable improvements in customer satisfaction.
- Currently directing the relocation of Customer Service to San Francisco. Managing set-up of existing inbound service function and leading strategic, process and organizational design for first-ever outbound/telemarketing operation.
- Spearheaded the successful transition from in-house to outsourced distribution in cooperation with strategic partner. Project met/exceeded all performance, quality, productivity and cost objectives.
- Established quarterly client focus groups (top 20% of customers) to facilitate communications and ensure that all service processes, measures and customer service levels were aligned with customer expectations.
- Documented and standardized key customer service work processes as corporate-wide benchmark for service, productivity, quality and financial performance.

Technology Gains:

- Led successful implementation of enterprise-wide accounting and order fulfillment software program (Lawson). Brought project from contract through installation and training within a "recordbreaking" six months.
- Championed the development of bar code standards for major vendors, relabeled over 100,000 stock items and improved shipping accuracy by an additional 50%.

INTERFACE COMPUTER, San Diego, California   1989 to 1991

Customer Service Manager

Independently planned, staffed, budgeted and directed Customer Service and Order Administration departments for this $100 million technology solutions provider to domestic and international markets. Trained and supervised a 15-person staff.

- Reengineering procedures to streamline and expedite order processing for $100 million a year in computer systems, software and spare part sales.
- Led a series of cross-functional process improvement teams with ITS, Marketing, Sales, Manufacturing and Engineering. Delivered strong performance gains in quality, productivity and efficiency of operations.
- Expanded relationships with major distributors and VARs nationwide to enhance customer satisfaction.

NOTE: Multi-billion dollar Interface Corporation, (headquartered in Taiwan) acquired Wagner Computer in 1990. Established the corporation's first U.S. customer service and field support organization.

TECHNOLOGY INSTRUMENTS, San Diego, California   1985 to 1989

Sales Support Supervisor (1987 to 1989)
Customer Acceptance Representative (1985 to 1987)

Joined this $30 million technology design and engineering firm as Customer Acceptance Representative, working one-on-one with key accounts to facilitate installation of advanced inspection technologies for large-scale manufacturing. Verified and documented quality and performance of all system operations.

Promoted to Sales Support Supervisor managing all Customer Service and Sales Administration functions. Coordinated system and installation schedules with field support and customer representatives, compiled monthly financial reviews and forecasts, and established procedures to enhance the delivery, quality and performance of service/support. Directed regional and national trade show programs.

EDUCATION:

Master of Arts in Organizational Management	University of Washington	1994
Bachelor of Arts in Social Science	San Diego State University	1986

PSI Training:
- Certified in Strategic Process Management Program
- Facilitating for Results, Team Leadership and Team Effectiveness

References Available Upon Request

Andrew B. Champion

16 Terryville Avenue
Bristol, CT 06010
860-583-7500

Top-producing **Customer Service/Sales** professional. Five years of proven success in building client relationships, increasing customer satisfaction and improving profit margins. Excellent presentation, negotiation and closing skills. Expertise in re-energizing stagnant customer accounts. Strong background in effective management/leadership.

PROFESSIONAL EXPERIENCE

ABC SUPPLY COMPANY, Marietta, GA   1992 - 1997
Customer Service Representative
   Built, established and nurtured customer base, doubling individual activity to over 150 clients; managed inventory encompassing over 4100 line items. Assessed client needs; provided superior products and service to ensure long-term customer satisfaction. Researched technical information to supply high-tech, state-of-the-art products at competitive prices; rebuilt customer confidence and loyalty. Trained new salesmen.

- Earned Employee of the Month awards four times over life of incentive program; received award for Employee of the Year (1993).
- Nurtured key account, increasing annual sales revenues for this client company from $80K to over $400K in just two years.
- Instrumental in building company reputation for quick deliveries: Developed customer follow-up system which increased sales revenues substantially and necessitated purchase of second delivery vehicle.

U.S. MARINE CORPS   1971 - 1992
Aviation Supply Chief
   Achieved supervisory rank after first two years. Directed, trained, evaluated and motivated up to 120 personnel. Full responsibility for ordering, follow-up, delivery and availability of over 40,000 inventory parts. Trained personnel, utilizing highly effective leadership techniques. Created lesson plans; instructed personnel in new procedures and recurrent training.

- Analyzed pilot/aircraft needs; provided parts quickly and efficiently, decreasing "down" time and enhancing operational effectiveness.
- Assessed available stock and determined suitability of replacement parts, researching and verifying safety and effectiveness.
- Earned personal recognition from Commanding General of Desert Storm for consistency in parts supply, enabling pilots to complete 94 consecutive on-time missions.

PROFESSIONAL DEVELOPMENT

   U.S. MARINE CORPS: Numerous motivation, management, leadership and technical courses.

Ellen Stafford

18 Ridge Crossing
O'Fallon, Illinois 62269
(618) 555-9339

Environmental Engineer/Project Manager

Six years experience managing all phases of environmental projects including hazardous waste management, pollution prevention, natural/cultural resources preservation, soil treatment technologies, and air/water quality. Directed numerous remediation investigations and cleanup actions, reducing exposure and liability, cutting costs, and achieving regulatory compliance.

Qualifications include:

Phase I/Phase II - Site Assessment/Remediation
Crisis Management & Emergency Response
Government Liaison/Public Affairs

Wetlands Protection/Mitigation
Project Budgeting and Management
Contract Negotiations

Regulatory Affairs

Extensive knowledge of Superfund requirements and government regulations:
RCRA, CERCLA, SARA, NCP, UST, CWA, OSHA, and NEPA

Project Management Experience

Directed project teams of up to 20 engineers and field personnel. Wrote project investigation, remediation and management plans, prepared budgets, and monitored field operations. Oversaw industrial hygiene standards, occupational safety, health and safety affairs, and permitting. Managed outside liaison affairs with contractors, regulatory agency personnel, and media. Coordinated base closure and property conversion/disposal actions.

Professional Experience

Environmental Engineer/Project Manager, 1994-1996
McGuire Air Force Base, New Jersey

Scoped, initiated, and negotiated remedial investigation/feasibility study project at three former underground storage tank sites. Served as Quality Assurance Evaluator during field work and work plan preparations.

- As Natural and Cultural Resource Manager, finalized basewide wetlands delineation, threatened and endangered species survey, and historical and archaeological inventories.
- Drafted all wetlands permits and associated Pinelands development applications per state law.
- Initiated rapid response (emergency) project resulting in notice of violation avoidance and savings in excess of $850,000. Successfully coordinated work plans with Dept. of Environmental Protection and Pinelands Commission.

Environmental Engineer/Installation Restoration Program Project Manager, 1994
March Air Force Base, California

Identified, analyzed, and formally established IRP objectives to achieve remedial actions/cleanups. Developed estimates, justifications, and facilitated rapid review and subsequent acceptance of planning/design documents by federal, state, and local regulatory parties. Reviewed contractor work for environmental/health/permit compliance.

- Monitored and oversaw extensive contaminated soil and landfill removal actions at four sites.
- Directed contractors during emergency response removal actions in sensitive wetlands and endangered species habitat.
- Coordinated removal actions of underground storage tank removal, landfill excavations and capping, and drum burial site removal.

Professional Experience (cont.)

Environmental Engineer/Installation Restoration Program Project Manager, 1993-1994
Air Force Base Conversion Agency, Norton Air Force Base, California

Provided on-site representation prior to and following base closure. Prepared, implemented, and maintained IRP and Environmental Compliance and programs to abate and limit contamination of the environment and endangerment to public health. Served as spokesperson to public and private entities on the administrative and regulatory requirements under CERCLA, SARA, and RCRA.

- Led all post-closure environmental compliance programs including storm water permits, hazardous waste disposal, RCRA facility closures, and underground storage tank removal.
- Finalized the TCE Groundwater Plume Record of Decision with extensive regulatory input/coordination.
- Accomplished an EPA requested basewide Preliminary Assessment/Site Investigation at 43 areas of concern.
- Authored NEPA documents supporting the lease and transfer of approximately 10 land parcels.
- Provided engineering review on contracts in excess of $4 million.
- Streamlined IRP comprehensive budgeting and billing process.
- Assisted in conversion of the Technical Review Committee to the Restoration Advisory Board.

Environmental Engineer/Remedial Program Manager, 1991-1993
Minot Air Force Base, North Dakota

Represented Minot AFB as the manager of a $5 million restoration program. Implemented remedial investigation at petroleum, oil, and lubricant facility. Completed two landfill site investigations.

- Conducted remedial action quality assurance evaluation of basewide underground storage tank removal, soil cleanup, and RCRA landfill closure.
- Successfully gained regulatory acceptance and closed eight of eleven IRP sites in FY91, the highest total in Strategic Air Command.
- Created and led the original Technical Review Committee and conducted quarterly meetings.

Additional background:

Associate Engineer, City of Merced, California, 1990: Created preliminary design for replacement and expansion of existing sewer system. Completed survey and design on storm drainage, ditches, culverts, and piping.

Transportation Engineer, Georgia Department of Transportation, 1988-1990: Completed department-wide two year training program. Inspected multi-million dollar highway construction. Provided baseline data for environmental impact analyses. Designed a compatible computer program to modernize existing traffic planning program.

Education/Specialized Training

Bachelor of Civil Engineering, Georgia Institute of Technology, Atlanta, Georgia, 1988

- Hazardous Waste Operations and Emergency Response Training (Refresher), 1994/1995/1996
- New Jersey Freshwater Wetlands Permitting, 1995
- Technical Requirements - Site Remediation, 1995
- USAF/EPA Team Approach to Environmental Cleanup and Risk Communication, 1992
- Hazardous Waste Operations and Emergency Response Training, 1992
- Treatment Technologies for Superfund, 1992
- Installation Restoration Program, 1992

Knowledge of Windows '95, Word for Windows, PowerPoint, Excel, WordPerfect, Wang Systems, Computer Aided Design-Intergraph System, GIS Systems, ENVEST, RACER, and ADPM.

KEVIN J. PETERSON
111 W. Lincoln, #222
Merced, California 93888
(715) 325-5888

PROFILE

Civil Engineer with three years of progressively responsible experience in engineering and project management for clients throughout California. Combines excellent technical, analytical and engineering qualifications with demonstrated achievements in acquiring and delivering projects on-time and within budget. Strong leadership, management, communication and problem-solving skills. Qualifications in:

- Proposal Writing
- Project Design & Management
- Estimating, Budgeting and P&L
- Engineering Management
- Client Relationship Management
- Field Management

PROFESSIONAL EXPERIENCE

McKINLEY CONSULTING, INC., Sacramento, CA   June 1994-Present
Project Manager, (August 1995-Present)
Promoted to high profile position managing the Construction Inspection/Materials Testing Division of a five division, four office $5 million corporation. Division responsibilities are diverse and include directing the activities of two engineers and twelve field technicians, writing project proposals and management plans, preparing budgets, acquiring technical resources, conducting field investigations, directing field operations and overall division profit and loss. Project highlights include:

➤ Authored five proposals that secured five bid packages worth $300,000 at the Masonik State Prison. Project came in on-time and with a 30% profit margin and required the management of up to seven field technicians and close to 15 general and sub-contractors.

➤ Wrote proposal and managed $45,000 project for a $11 million school expansion with Merced Unified School District.

➤ Personally writing proposals for and managing $1.5 million in revenues per year; manage on average 95 projects per month.

➤ Proof and sign over 2000 concrete testing reports and 500 steel inspection reports per month.

Civil Engineer, (January 1995-August 1995)
Wrote all proposals for the Construction Inspection/Materials Testing Division and approximately 30% of the Geotechnical Division proposals.
Civil Engineering Intern, (June 1994-January 1995)

EDUCATION

Bachelor of Science, Civil Engineering   December 1994
California University

AFFILIATIONS AND CERTIFICATIONS

Registered Civil Engineer, Pending
ICBO, International Conference of Building Officials - Reinforced Concrete #58580
Engineer-In-Training (EIT)

ERIK K. WILSON

200 Woodside Avenue
Waterford, Colorado 06385

Phone: (860) 316-1702
Email: ewilsk@ines.com

GEOLOGICAL ENGINEER / PETROLEUM EXPLORATION PROFESSIONAL

Talented, resourceful and dedicated, offering a combination of unique professional skills. Proven success in managing projects through field assessment, research and data compilation to proposal preparation and presentation. Excellent technical reporting, oral/written communications and public speaking qualifications. Hands-on use of geological laboratory techniques (e.g., XRD, SEM, Frantz Magnetic Separator). MAC and PC proficient with leading software (e.g., Microsoft Word, Microsoft Excel, AutoCAD, WordPerfect) and industry applications including PERC, HDS and OIL/PDS.

EDUCATION

Candidate for M.S. in Geology, Expected May 1999
B.S. in Geological Engineering, May 1997
COLORADO SCHOOL OF MINES, Waterford, Colorado

Concentration & Special Projects

- Petroleum Geology & Exploration
- Mineral Deposit Geology
- Field & Underground Mine Mapping
- Multi-Disciplinary Petroleum Design

Awards & Affiliations

- Dean's List & Honor Roll
- American Association of Petroleum Geologists
- Association of Geoscience Students
- Bicycling Club & Outdoor Recreation Center

PROFESSIONAL EXPERIENCE

BABCOCK OIL CORPORATION, Denver, Colorado

May 1997 to August 1997

Summer internship participating in several projects with the Major Gas Projects Group of this $1 billion oil and gas corporation. Projects included geologic correlations, analysis of water producing zones, unit tops and well recompletions. Researched well histories and compiled data incorporating well logs, mud logs, correlations, interval depths, perforations, density porosity, water saturation, drilling rate, crossover and gas production rates. Prepared detailed reports, spreadsheets and summaries for use by key personnel in site feasibility, gas production and well lifecycle analysis. Key assignments:

- Prepared a comprehensive spreadsheet of 56 wells throughout Western Colorado to determine recompletion zones above the current producing intervals. Resulted in a bid to recomplete one well with potential to produce more than one million cubic feet of gas per day.
- Compiled field data into an automated spreadsheet application for use by corporate geologists in construction of cross-sections and structure maps. Program provided immediate access to key data and was instrumental in decreasing map production cycles.
- Prepared a 39-page report on the potential impact of excess water production in eight different wells. Report was used as a tool to resolve issues and improve gas production capabilities.

AMERICAN GEOLOGICAL SURVEY, Denver, Colorado

July 1996 to October 1996

Three-month internship with the Central Mineral Resources Team. Worked with lab technicians in the preparation of rock samples for cutting, crushing, magnetic and heavy liquid separation, and microscope observation for use in Lead Isotope Analysis.

BBN EXPLORATION, Boulder, Colorado

March 1996

Provided plotting and mapping services for this regional mineral exploration firm. Transferred mineral data compiled by field geologists into presentation-quality maps for use in future exploration projects.

NICOLE R. HENDERSON

6547 West "H" Street # 123
Washington, D.C. 20223-2536
(202) 891-8747

CAREER PROFILE

Dynamic **Management Professional** with 10+ years experience in the design, engineering and quality improvement of multi-million dollar technology. Combines technical and engineering expertise with strong project management, financial management and resource management skills. **Certified Acquisition Professional**.

Expert in team building to achieve productivity, performance, quality and cost objectives.

PROFESSIONAL EXPERIENCE:

PROJECT ENGINEER   1986 to Present
U.S. Army Systems Command, Washington, D.C.

Fast-track promotion advancing through several increasingly responsible general management positions leading the research, development and production of a $2.8 billion advanced military systems contract. Member of six-person systems engineering team at Army headquarters participating in a joint industry/government project. Key responsibilities include:

Team Leadership

Act as the direct liaison between military personnel, IBM (contractor) and other subcontractors. Coordinate the transfer of information and documentation to and from the contractor, and provide periodic updates to senior military officials to keep them abreast of project status.

Project Management

Guide three multi-functional teams of design, systems engineering, testing and technical support professionals working on specific components of the project. Facilitate cooperation and communication between team members and other project teams to expedite project planning and execution.

Costing & Scheduling

Determine the most cost-effective and technically sound approach to systems development and production. Oversee compliance with contract to ensure all quality, technical specification, scheduling and budgetary requirements are being met.

Quality & Performance Management

Oversee testing and evaluation of system components at military installations throughout the U.S. Identify and resolve issues impacting systems performance, and document proposed modifications for presentation to IBM. Member of Safety Team.

EDUCATION & CERTIFICATIONS:

B.S., Chemical Engineering, 1985
University of New Hampshire

Certificate in Engineering Management, 1992
The American University

Acquisition Professional in Systems Planning, Research, Development & Engineering, 1996
U.S. Army Systems Command

TIMOTHY HANKS

57 Canden Drive • Hamden, Massachusetts 01288 • (555) 676-9089

ENGINEERING & PROJECT MANAGEMENT:

An experienced engineering professional with a successful career leading the design and development of sophisticated products for diverse industries and markets. Analytical, technical and engineering expertise combines with achievements in cost reductions, quality improvement and project management. Strengths:

- **Extensive qualifications in staff training and leadership, resource management, project planning and management, and documentation.**
- **Proficient in all aspects of electro-mechanical design from requirements definition and analysis through conceptual design, drawings and customer presentations.**
- **Effective customer, vendor and inter-departmental liaison with outstanding troubleshooting, problem solving, relationship management, and negotiation skills.**
- **Thoroughly versed in commercial and MIL specifications, CAD and other applications; DOD secret clearance.**

PROFESSIONAL EXPERIENCE & ACCOMPLISHMENTS:

THOMPSON CORPORATION, Hamden, Massachusetts   (1987-Present)
Project Leader
Advanced Mechanical Designer

Promoted to oversee design and development of multi-million dollar electro-mechanical and mechanical projects. Create conceptual and detail designs, delivering presentations in senior management and customer design reviews. Recruit, train and lead engineering and drafting teams. Establish and maintain all documentation standards. Source, select and negotiate with vendors.

- **Selected as project engineer to spearhead $35 million program, delivered ahead of schedule and well within budget.**
- **Led project team in concept development and design of new product line generating $20 million in annual sales.**
- **Saved $1.2 million in annual production costs through implementation of continuous improvement initiatives.**
- **Discovered and rectified critical design flaw, preventing costly, catastrophic system failure of product.**
- **Created and instituted CAD standards and trained engineering staff company-wide.**
- **Instrumental in engineering department's efforts in achievement of ISO 9001 certification.**

PIERSON CORPORATION, Fullerton, California   (1985-1987)
Senior Engineering Designer

Developed and designed electro-mechanical consoles for multi-billion dollar global corporation. Trained and delegated project assignments to technical staff.

- **Selected as 1 of 3 top designers in division to lead project team in development of high-priority product line.**
- **Developed design methods for CAD system, incorporated in division-wide staff training.**

JOHNSON CORPORATION, Anaheim, California   (1983-1985)
Associate Engineer

Coordinated design, development and manufacturing of precision dental instruments for $10 million industry leader. Tested and evaluated all new products. Supervised drafting and toolmaking staff.

- **Developed new instrument at half the cost of previous models without compromising quality standards.**
- **Redesigned x-ray machine with expanded application capabilities which generated $500,000 in sales.**

MORELAND COMPANY, Fullerton, California   (1980-1983)
Mechanical Designer

Designed mechanical assemblies, tooling and molded plastic parts for $100 million international manufacturer of latches and fasteners.

- **Contributed to diversification of product line and boosted sales by developing new fasteners for electrical assemblies.**
- **Designed tooling which expanded production capacity by 25% while reducing costs 10%.**

COMPUTER CAPABILITIES:

MS-DOS
Windows NT and 95
MicroStation Modeler
AutoCAD
Computervision Personal Designer
Microsoft Office Suite

EDUCATION:

FULLERTON COLLEGE, Fullerton, California
Associate of Arts

Additional Training:

ANSI Y14.5M - 1982 ... ASME Y14.5M - 1994
MicroStation Modeler ... AutoCAD
TQM/Continuous Improvement
Project Management ... Team Building

AFFILIATIONS:

American Society of Mechanical Engineers

KIRK STRATHMORE

243 Main Street West, Ann Arbor, Michigan 48103 • (313) 555-0000

PERSONAL PROFILE

Organized, efficient, and achievement-oriented professional with diverse experience enhanced by a formal education in Environmental Science and refined by specific expertise in Geographical Information Systems (GIS) applications. Strong work ethic reinforced by a positive team player attitude and excellent interpersonal skills. Accurate, focused, and methodical self-starter with quick learning abilities. Gifted with an innate ability to promptly handle multiple tasks and projects simultaneously.

PROFESSIONAL EXPERIENCE

TYLER & ASSOCIATES, Ann Arbor, Michigan, - 1991 to present

Senior Staff Analyst reporting to the Vice President of a consulting agency specializing in Site Location Research. Coordinate, train, and develop Staff Research Assistants. Train and orient new Analysts in field evaluations, forecasting and techniques. Develop sales forecasts and analyses using automated systems and a variety of quantitative methods including analog and gravity models. Assist in developing customer profiles and databases. Utilize various Geographical Information Systems (GIS) including Arc/Info and Mapinfo and their practical applications in market research. Conduct market analyses, screenings, and strategies including multiple or single site and in-fill opportunities for destination-based retailers.

- Evaluated redeployment and market-entry strategies for supermarket clients by developing gravity based market models, sales forecasts, and projections.

- Developed excellent reputation for knowledge, skills, and abilities in the GIS environment.

Research Assistant and **Technician** reporting to the Vice President of the Statistical Department. Primary responsibilities included: utilizing various desktop database programs, researching accurate and up-to-date census data, demographics, business, consumer, industrial, and specialized data. Analyzed data using GIS system applications and produced various maps to be employed in large and small market strategies.

- Key participant in creating a unique GIS multiple use database capable of producing singular, targeted, and variable information.

- Promoted to Analyst position based upon superior knowledge, skills, and abilities.

DEPARTMENT OF NATURAL RESOURCES, Lansing, Michigan, - 1988 to 1991

GIS Technician in the Land and Water Management Division working with Michigan Resource Information Systems (MIRIS). Utilized Intergraph work stations and their GIS capabilities in the UNIX environment generating PAX plots and displays of physical and geographical features. Manipulated environmental data for projects. Created State Forest Compartment Maps (FCM) for the Forest Management Division. Digitized Intermediate School Districts (ISDs) boundaries. Created borders and legends and produced map sets for the State.

- Promoted to GIS Technician position based upon skills and abilities.

Hydrologic Technician (Intern) in the Hydrologic Studies Unit. Accurately delineated water sheds, input hydrologic data into various layers by use of Intergraph microstation software. Applied technical knowledge in resource management. Interpreted aerial and infrared photos as well as soil conservation service county soil surveys to ensure topological accuracy. Performed field evaluations including stream flow measurements, field inspections, and elevational surveys.

EDUCATION

Eastern Michigan University, Ypsilanti, Michigan - 1988
Bachelor of Science - Major: Environmental Science

MATTHEW J. COOKE

3426 South Main Street
Billings, WA 55555

Phone/Fax: (888) 888-8888
E-mail: cooke@email.com

PROFILE

Peak-performing **Senior Project Manager / Controls Engineer** with extensive experience and a verifiable record of achievement in delivering strong and sustainable financial gains and cost reductions. Combines exceptional technical, analytical, and engineering qualifications with outstanding business development, project planning, and project management skills. Expertise includes demonstrated technical leadership in facility and production systems design, systems development and integration, and PLC and PC applications software programming. Highly self-motivated with superb interpersonal and communication skills. Willing and able to travel.

PROFESSIONAL EXPERIENCE

MANUFACTURING CONTROL SYSTEMS ENGINEER
Under contract to XXX

1997 - Present
Lebanon, KS

Recruited to increase production capabilities at the Lebanon City manufacturing plant. Design and integrate PC and PLC manufacturing tools control software. Direct manufacturing tool installation, integration and commissioning on production lines. Full responsibility for process system integration and manufacturing tools control hardware/software upgrade designs (A-B PLC 2s/3s/5s and SLC 5/04s on Intranet).

- Redesigned, retrofitted, and commissioned production assembly equipment for the automation of disassembly capabilities on rear strut subassembly systems; measurably improved safety by eliminating the dangerous hand disassembly method.
- Developed and implemented new methods for processing chrome wheels; increased profits 1% on each automobile and enabled the plant to meet expanded production goals.
- Redesigned and initiated the use of new rapid fluid fill methods as a key component of a project to allow 10% expansion of daily production.
- Overall results: Increased profits and revenue generation 10% on redesigned system upgrades while concurrently improving personnel equipment safety.

GENERAL MANAGER/PROJECT MANAGER
Consulting, Inc.

1996 - 1997
Simmons, WA

Directed sales, marketing, customer service and contract performance for consultant and engineering projects at this firm specializing in project management and systems applications development. Designed and implemented customized business software designed for efficient account processing. Supervised activities of 5 staff.

- Created, published and orchestrated a five-year program plan for a $100M underwater storage complex; saved $1M in operating costs during the first year of implementation.
- Generated Independent Cost Estimates and Critical Analyses using MCACES; reduced client's annual expenses 13%.
- Pioneered and led innovative marketing and sales programs; increased sales of technical support contracts $150,000 within the first 6-months of operation.
- Designed and programmed an engineering database retrieval program using MS Access, ADT, and Visual Basic.

PROJECT MANAGER/CONTROLS ENGINEER 1994 - 1996
Engineering Corp. *Richville, WA*

Generated acceptance test procedures, published system documentation, and performed systems turnover on assigned design and build projects. Directed up to 30 personnel in the performance of field projects.

- Administered systems engineering subcontracts on an emerging environmental technology contract; increased sales $1M+ within the first year.
- Drove $14M in contract sales through various proposal and project management activities.
- Conceived and developed hardware and software systems utilized in the deployment of 9 hazardous waste pumping stations for use in remote locations.
- Integrated and programmed multiple Allen-Bradley SLC 5/03 PLC's.

GENERAL MANAGER/PROJECT MANAGER 1990 - 1994
Roberts Environmental & Energy Services *Simmons, WA*

Full P&L responsibility for this start-up office. Established an environmental engineering client base and expanded office to 12 professionals. Supervised 30 engineers and technicians in the performance of environmental field projects.

- Grew contract sales to more than $1M annually.
- Created and led a Facility Effluent Monitoring Plan to comply with EPA requirements for a $1Billion TSD facility.
- Developed testing and transportation methodology for the first use of medical isotope gadolinium in the treatment of osteoporosis.

OPERATIONS MANAGER/PROJECT MANAGER 1987 - 1990
United Laboratory Inc. *Simmons, WA*

Guided the efforts of engineers and technicians in the materials research laboratory. Executed facility upgrades and process systems automation. Utilized Primavera to perform project plan generation, costing, and reporting. Directly supervised 15 professional engineers and technicians; oversaw project management activities of over 30 engineers and scientists.

- Developed and implemented strategic marketing plan to promote research capabilities; expanded research contract sales $15M.
- Oversaw the design and integration of motor controllers, PLC's, and examination systems to mainframe computers.
- Led the design and upgrade of a large multi-zone differential pressure HVAC system used in the safe containment of hazardous wastes in a large materials research facility.

EDUCATION AND TRAINING

B.S., PHYSICS, Some State College

Power Plant Engineering School, Some Engineering Laboratory, Falls River, XX
Continuing Education, Some State University, Tri-Cities, XX
Project Management Professional Certification (In-Progress)

TECHNOLOGY SKILLS

LANGUAGES: Basic, Visual Basic, Assembly, Fortran
OPERATING SYSTEMS: Windows 3.11, Windows 95, DOS 6.22, UNIX, Macintosh 7.0+
SOFTWARE: MS Access & ADT, Netscape, MSIE, MCACES, Primavera, Timeline, MS Office, Lotus Notes, AutoCAD 13, MS Project
PLC PROGRAMMING: Allen Bradley PLC's and SLC's, Gould Modicon, Texas Instruments, General Electric

MARY P. JANE, CPA

One Crystal River, Suite R, Jakarta, New York 87965
(555) 398-7653 • (800) 234-6789 pager

PROFILE	
	• **Over 15 years comprehensive financial and management experience** including financial planning, capital budgeting, forecasting, and accounting. Record for improving business processes and systems through analysis and benchmarking activities. Core competencies:

- strategic corporate planning
- quarterly & year-end reporting
- debt & equity management
- corporate tax planning & preparation
- employee benefits administration
- payroll administration
- corporate tax compliance
- cost & managerial accounting
- financial statement disclosures
- review of internal control processes

- financial analysis
- cash flow
- asset allocation
- internal audit
- shareholder relations
- corporate treasury
- credit & collections
- lease/contract negotiations
- cost reduction/avoidance
- budget preparation

- **Led audit engagements for:** retail, manufacturing, fund entities, professional services, government subsidized agencies. Proficient in reviewing the design of internal financial control and administrative systems.

SELECTED ACHIEVEMENTS

STEELE, BRAKEN, & NORRIS, Inc., Jakarta, New York
Financial Controller (1987-present)

- **Directed financial and accounting functions for commercial real estate development operation** with annual revenues exceeding $52 million staffed with 400 employees.

- **Advanced company's profit performance through a variety of measures including:**

- strategic planning
- managerial financial forecasting
- capital funding & expenditure
- internal / external reporting

- financial analysis
- cash management
- tax planning & preparation
- business plan development

- **Streamlined and enhanced the Corporate budgeting process** and made it the cornerstone upon which the Company's operations are measured.

- **Obtained outside lines of financing** for operating and capital leases to fund operational cash needs and equipment purchases.

- **Introduced a new integrated cost accounting system** which automated a diversity of accounting, analysis, and reporting systems. Installed and set-up all modules required by accounting. **Developed end-user procedures and conducted training programs** on system application.

- **Reengineered all key business processes for accounts payable and receivable functions** which streamlined and automated documentation requirements.

DELOITTE & TOUCHE: **Certified Public Account & Business Consultant** (prior to 1987)

EDUCATION	
	• **Master of Science - Business Administration (Major: Accounting)**
	• **Bachelor of Science - Business Administration (Major: Accounting)** New York State University, Winnsantak, New York (both degrees)
	• **Certified Public Accountant**

AFFILIATIONS	
	• New York Society of Certified Public Accountants
	• American Institute of CPAs
	• Contractor's Financial Management Association

COMPUTERS	
	• Open Systems Accounting Software - most accounting software packages as auditor - Windows 97 - MS Office 97 - Word - Excel - Lotus Programs - Internet - Intranet.

RICKIE NELSEN

9 Maurie Lane, Encinitas, California 92052 • (760) 555-2222

CAREER PROFILE

Considerable experience in the design, development, implementation, evaluation, and management of comprehensive corporate accounting, budgeting, financial reporting, financial modeling, tax, and MIS systems. Consistent success in linking accounting with general operations to provide hands-on financial leadership for strategic planning, sales and marketing, purchasing, inventory, production, and distribution. Delivered strong and sustainable revenue gains. Equally effective in capturing cost reductions through process redesign and performance management.

PROFESSIONAL EXPERIENCE

SILVERGRAPHICS, INC., Vista, California - 1988 to present

CONTROLLER reporting to the Chief Financial Officer. Functional authority includes direct supervision of the accounting department staff; a financial analyst, a senior accountant, and four accountants. Primary responsibilities include completion of monthly statistical and financial reports, payroll preparation, monitoring of department budgets; budgeting, forecasting, cash management, investments, audits, reconciliations, tax preparation, insurance benefits, workers' compensation, and 401K administration. Collateral duties include all management aspects of HR activities.

- Effectively incorporated necessary procedural adjustments as the company grew from $1.75 to $50+ million in sales volume.

- Successfully guided the company through its first Price, Waterhouse audit (Due Diligence) leading to a leveraged buy-out by Pinnacle Partners of Boston.

- Increased investment monies by using a cash management system, determining daily cash needs, and investing the rest in securities.

- Oversaw implementation and development of a multi-user computer environment and trained the entire accounting staff in proper utilization.

- Established and implemented the first near-term and long-range company budgets; implemented a forecasting and strategic planning process.

GUNNEA, WILSON, & TITTERING, San Marcos, California - 1981 to 1988

STAFF ACCOUNTANT reporting to the Senior Partner. Engaged in routine accounting activities for a CPA firm. Applied principles of accounting to analyze financial information and prepare financial reports. Compiled and

(Continued on next page)

PROFESSIONAL EXPERIENCE *(Continued)*

analyzed financial information to prepare entries to accounts documenting business transactions. Analyzed financial information detailing assets, liabilities, and capital, and prepared balance sheets, profit and loss statements, and other reports to summarize current and projected financial positions.

- Established Cash Management functions, Credit Policies and Procedures; trained entire accounting staff.

- Developed and implemented appropriate internal Policies and Procedures; brought all accounting and payroll functions in-house.

- Authored and implemented a Policy and Procedures manual providing standardized controls and increasing department efficiency by 50%+.

- Developed excellent reputation for organizational skills and accuracy.

LUMBER PLUS, Encinitas, California - 1980 to 1981

ESTIMATE PROCESSOR reporting to the Manager of the Accounting Department. Processed estimates for general and specific contractors.

- Negotiated contracts for national travel resulting in significant savings.

- Noted for ability to quickly and accurately process estimates.

EDUCATION

PALOMAR COLLEGE, San Marcos, California
Undergraduate Studies - Major: Accounting - GPA: 4.0

Company Sponsored Professional Development Seminars, Workshops, and Courses

- A/R and A/P
- Budgeting
- Collections
- Cost Controls
- Financial Reports
- General Ledger
- Inventory Management
- Payroll
- Strategic Planning

COMPUTER TECHNOLOGY

- Solomon Accounting Systems Applications and Timberline Payroll Software
- Microsoft Excel, MS-Windows 95 and NT, MS-Office 97 Pro, PowerPoint, Access, Word
- ADP Payroll Software and Report Design Software

Appropriate personal and professional references are available

WILLIAM P. DALY, CPA

1503 Winding Road
Charleston, WV 34554

Home (304) 956-8168
Office (304) 641-8658

SENIOR FINANCIAL EXECUTIVE

*Strategic Business & Financial Planning / General Accounting / Corporate Banking & Lending
Acquisition & Divestiture Management / Investment Management / Corporate Tax / MIS Technology*

Over 10 years of senior-level Corporate Finance experience for turnaround and high-growth corporations. Combines strategic and tactical financial expertise with strong qualifications in general management, human resources and transaction structuring/negotiations. Excellent leadership, team building and business development skills. CPA. Member of American Society of Certified Public Accountants and Texas Society of Certified Public Accountants.

Delivered strong and sustainable financial gains in highly-competitive business markets nationwide through expertise in cost reduction, process redesign, revenue growth and profit improvement.

PROFESSIONAL EXPERIENCE:

Corporate Controller   1994 to Present
BUILT-RIGHT, INC., Charleston, West Virginia
($300 million publicly traded diversified specialty maintenance, engineering and construction firm)

Recruited to a three-person senior management team to plan and orchestrate an aggressive reorganization of the entire corporation, introduce state-of-the-art financial and operational management systems, and reduce escalating overhead costs significantly impacting the bottom-line. Scope of management responsibility spans both the corporate and divisional level including three operating companies and 25+ subsidiary business units throughout the U.S.

Personally direct all financial planning, accounting, payroll, tax, consolidated financial reporting, shareholder/board relations, legal and administration affairs. Hold additional management oversight for acquisitions/divestitures, audit, MIS and other special operational projects. Direct a team of six managers and 21 staff personnel.

Operating Achievements

- Championed the introduction of a fully-integrated, real-time project accounting computer system to consolidate four separate stand-alone operating environments. Managed the one-year $2 million project to completion on time and within budget.

- Facilitated the transition of accounting and administrative personnel following a major acquisition. Eliminated duplicate functions, reduced headcount and delivered $600,000 in annual savings.

- Implemented Oracle Project Accounting and Field Accounting systems for a $100 million subsidiary operation. Successfully completed two major turnaround maintenance projects valued at $35 million.

Financial Achievements

- Structured/negotiated the $100 million acquisition of Fischer Associates. Secured a $35 million commercial letter of credit and won an $83 million international contract that was in jeopardy due to lack of funding. Subsequently reduced tax exposure by $2.5 million and reduced project tax rate by 10%.

- Researched, analyzed and prepared risk assessment of all company investments. Identified several activities that did not meet the corporations current requirements and captured $12 million in write-offs.

- Played a key role in negotiating a 42% increase in the company's capital line of credit.

Assistant Corporate Controller   1990 to 1994
APPLIED LOGISTICS, Memphis, Tennessee
($500 million publicly traded diversified engineering/construction firm and independent power company)

Senior Manager with full responsibility for the complete finance, accounting and audit functions for the corporation and several subsidiary operations. Led a team of six including three Controllers, Director of Accounting, Government Compliance Manager and Payroll Manager responsible for financial planning/analysis, SEC reporting, shareholder relations, payroll, government affairs, accounting and administration.

Worked directly with senior management team on a broad range of corporate initiatives including the structuring of global joint venture agreements, several divestitures of non-performing operations, a corporate-wide cost reduction program and a major systems conversion.

Operating Achievements

- Managed the complete assessment of all core operating functions and identified key areas for consolidation. Eliminated duplicate functions, streamlined operations and reduced headcount by 169 resulting in a $7.6 million annual cost savings.

- Facilitated the transition from in-house payroll systems to outsourced payroll processing company (ADP), decreasing payroll budget by 50%.

- Championed the introduction of advanced networking and PC technologies throughout the organization. Converted a costly IBM 3090 mainframe to IBM RS6000 on a UNIX-based operating environment. Managed the entire project cycle from planning through selection and implementation within six months.

- Evaluated purchasers, managed due diligence, evaluated proposals and divested a $15 million operating subsidiary. Negotiated transactions with four separate purchasers and delivered $2.5 million in cash.

Financial Achievements

- Played a key role in the development of an international joint venture with Dieldendorf GmbH, to further develop a $15million toll road privatization project in California. The partnership generated $2.5 million in cash and a long-term commitment from Cofiroute to share future projects.

- Facilitated due diligence and determined purchase price for divestiture of insurance business unit. Evaluated prospective buyers and negotiated sale for $8.9 million.

- Researched, selected and implemented new stock option tracking software to improve long-term incentive compensation plans. Significantly improved the accuracy and speed of information.

- Led all accounting, finance and reporting functions for Technology Resources, a $20 million partially owned subsidiary of Applied Logistics. Held concurrent responsibility for preparation of a Proxy distributed in conjunction with a $10 million financing transaction and Form S-3 to register four million common shares.

Senior Accountant / Audit Manager   1985 to 1990
DELOITTE & TOUCHE, Charleston, West Virginia

Fast-track advancement with this preeminent public accounting firm. Promoted to Audit Manager one year ahead of peers based upon success in client relations and leadership. Provided accounting expertise to major public and private companies nationwide including the preparation of quarterly/annual reports, registration statements, secondary offerings, and other financial research and documentation.

- Led 25+ engagements in the oil & gas, petrochemical, manufacturing and entertainment industries.

- Appointed Corporate Instructor leading national training programs for senior accountants and clients.

EDUCATION & CERTIFICATIONS:

BBA (Accounting), UNIVERSITY OF CHARLESTON, 1985
Certified Public Accountant, State of West Virginia, 1986

GREGORY C. ANDREWS, CPA

CHIEF FINANCIAL OFFICER

Seasoned, versatile leader with broad background in **financial, treasury, and operations management**. CPA and CFO experience in a variety of settings, including automotive, industrial, and public.

Expertise includes:

- → Timely Financial Reporting
- → Strategic Planning
- → Contract Negotiations
- → Tax Planning
- → Human Resources

- → Cost and Pricing Analysis
- → Merger Analysis
- → Property Purchase and Sale
- → Multi-entity, Multi-location
- → Policies and Procedures

Strong record of generating cost savings through effective financial and operations management. Troubleshooter and proven problem-solver. Able to balance and evaluate fast-changing priorities. Willing to travel.

PROFESSIONAL EXPERIENCE

Management Auditor & Consultant WORLDWIDE AUTOMOTIVE, INC., Detroit, Michigan
(Remanufacturer, Distributor, Big 3/Tier I) 1995-Present

- Made *critical* recommendations in the areas of cost accounting and reporting, computer applications, human resources, insurance, and general management and operations philosophies.
- Instrumental in analyzing and preparing a win-win offer for a competitor's business.

Director & Treasurer HENDERSON FORD SALES, INC., Novi, Michigan
(Auto Dealer, Auto Rental) 1985-1995

- Directed a broad-based reorganization of all financial and organizational aspects of multi-location company. Managed all accounting functions. Supervised staff of 40 and facilities in multiple entities.
- Turned company – which had accumulated $2,000,000 loss – into a substantial profit-maker. Generated over $250,000 tax savings over original return by national CPA firm. Saved $600,000 in taxes upon sale.
- Reduced reporting time by over 50%, while improving statement accuracy. Reduced auditors adjustments 80% to tax-related entries.
- Designed collection procedures and worked individually with problem customers to reduce bad debts from 5% to 2/3% of sales. Designed and implemented cost accounting within a general accounting computer system.

Continued...

1423 River Road • Grosse Pointe, Michigan 48236 • (313) 555-0987

GREGORY C. ANDREWS, CPA

EXPERIENCE
(Continued from page 1)

Consultant VARIOUS COMPANIES 1983-1985
(Auto dealers, restaurants, legal defense, and prior employers)

- Assisted in purchase of businesses and supervised installation of accounting systems for a restaurant and a used car operation.
- Handled business affairs of Henderson Ford holdings upon sale.
- Developed special multi-year audit and report to defense law firm in groundbreaking lawsuit by multiple entities against CPA firm.

Controller HAMPTON INDUSTRIES, INC., Detroit, Michigan 1980-1983
(Patented machine tool designer and manufacturer)

- Assisted with the allocation of $5M annually for a manufacturing company with 50% overseas sales.
- Recruited to assist with downsizing as world financial environment declined. Developed staff reduction and cost control programs to rebuild organization's internal structure.
- Established first in-house financial reporting and tax capability.

Prior Employment

- Secretary-Treasurer and Director of W. A. Riley's various businesses, Southgate Michigan.
- Internal Audit Manager, Construction, for Canton Corporation, Southfield, Michigan.
- Accounting Supervisor, City of Trenton, Michigan, Utilities Division.

CREDENTIALS

State of Michigan, Certified Public Accountant.

Continuing Education through Michigan Association of CPA's and Other Organizations:
- 146 CPE hours, split approx. 50/50 between public accounting applications and private company applications. Includes Compressed MBA in Accounting course.
- Continuing education includes frequent seminars, workshops, and conferences, in addition to on-going review of business and professional literature.

UNIVERSITY OF MICHIGAN, Ann Arbor, Michigan
- Business courses with emphasis on Management, Finance and Accounting.

Member, Michigan Association of CPA's; American Institute of CPA's

1423 River Road • Grosse Pointe, Michigan 48236 • (313) 555-0987

Robert Golden, CPA

158 Buffalo Avenue
Staten Island, New York 10312
(718) 492-7880

Summary of Qualifications

Broad-based experience as a Controller in-service oriented environments. Expertise in the following areas:

Financial Reporting	Employee Benefits	Retirement Plans
Supervisory Management	Budgetary Control	Forecasting
Banking Relations	Business Software	Management Team

Profile

Known as a results-oriented problem solver.......ability to interface with professionals on all levels and advise managers regarding various methods of cost reductions in each department.......monitor cash flow and financial investments for the company.

Experience

North Shore Medical Group, Staten Island, NY
Controller   1980-Present

North Shore Medical Group is an HMO with 400 employees and annual revenues of $35 million. Report to the Medical Director (President). Responsible for all financial reporting and retirement plans. Retirement plans are currently valued at $20 million. Manage a staff of eight accounting personnel in the Finance Department. Advise at all Shareholder, Board of Directors and Finance Committee meetings. Pension Plan Trustee. Duties include financial statement preparation for internal and external reporting, budgeting, forecasting, pension and welfare benefits, payroll, personnel records and insurance. Coordinate external audit. Involved in all computer hardware and software decisions. Negotiate with vendors regarding various software systems, contracts, and price reductions.

- Computerized general ledger and accounts payable systems saving 1.5 employees ($50,000 per year).
- Spearheaded efforts to completely revamp company profit sharing/401K plan resulting in 15% increase in earnings per year for all participants ($2.4 million) and larger annual contributions for all participants. These included executive and higher paid employees.
- Organized company 401K plan and set administrative guide lines.
- Instrumental in negotiating with major source of revenue for an annual increase of $5 million.

Noble Lynch International, New York, NY
Assistant Controller   1975-1980

Nobel Lynch International is the twentieth largest insurance broker in the United States, with offices in various cities as well as Israel and Bermuda. Reported to the Controller and supervised a staff of three accounting personnel. Responsibilities included consolidating financial reporting and consolidating federal and other states' corporate tax returns. Coordinated external audit, internal audit. Served as liaison with audit of branches. Responsible for special projects and analyses for management.

Diversified CPA Firm Experience   Prior to 1975

Personal

Bachelor of Business Administration, Brooklyn College, City University of New York.
Treasurer of the New York State Society of CPA's, Brooklyn Chapter. Editor of the chapter Newsletter.
Computer skills include Lotus 123, Word, Access and Macola Accounting Software.

CHARLES TINSLEY

168 Jason Terrace, #21-01 Jason Tower • Singapore 458556
(65) 432-1234

SENIOR FINANCE EXECUTIVE

Corporate Finance Executive with nine years experience leading the financial management of multinational worldclass organizations. Combines strong analytical skills and creative thinking to deliver strong and sustainable financial gains and expense reductions in highly-competitive business markets globally. PC Proficient. MBA in Finance. Expertise includes:

- Strategic Business & Financial Planning
- Treasury & Banking
- US & Foreign Tax Planning & Compliance
- International Trade Finance & Credit

- Acquisitions / Joint Ventures / LBOs
- Equity & Debt Financing
- Customs Import / Export
- ESOP / 401K Plans

PROFESSIONAL EXPERIENCE

FALCON TECHNOLOGY INC., Singapore   April 1996 to Present

A multinational Fortune 500 worldclass manufacturer/distributor with global annual sales of $1.2 billion.

Regional Controller / Director of Finance - Asia

Senior Finance executive responsible for strategic planning, management and control of monetary funds and operating profit, budget and financial accounting, tax and legal accountability. Manage a team of 5 In-Country and Joint Venture Controllers/Finance Managers, 15 support staff and a $15 million operating budget. Liaison between US corporate executive management and all 8 Asia locations. Report to International President.

- Currently providing expertise in leading Falcon Asia's financial management strategies to support 1997's 50% growth to $25 million, and additional 20% growth projections for 1998.

Finance Director for Falcon International's new business development throughout Asia with responsibility for strategic planning and development of full business plans for Falcon Power Systems joint venture pursuits in Korea, India, China, Thailand, Malaysia and Indonesia.

- Coordinated financing requirements, performed market study reviews and assisted with start-up phases of two new joint ventures (Korea and India) in 1997 generating $20 million in sales.
- Leading and guiding development of four new joint ventures in 1998.

HEWLETT-PACKARD, Singapore   1995 to 1996

Director of Finance, Accounting & Treasury

Recruited as interim Director with responsibility for the creation and implementation of an $81 million budget tracking system for each of HP Singapore's ASEAN countries. Interacted with Finance Head of each region and reported to Vice President of Finance.

LEVI STRAUSS CORPORATION, San Francisco, California   1988 to 1995

$1.5 billion multinational designer/distributor with offices located in 20+ countries.

Director of Finance, Tax, Import & Export / Assistant Corporate Treasurer & Secretary

Financial Director for this $300 million San Francisco-based business unit with full responsibility for a $10 million budget. Held direct responsibility for finance, treasury/banking, tax/credit, customs import/export, international trade finance, debt/equity, intercompany pricing strategies and regulatory compliance. Provided technical and administrative support for Human Resources and worldwide trademark licensing subsidiary. Managed a direct reporting staff of 5 and line staff of 45. Interacted with CEOs and COOs.

- Reengineered financial operations and instituted technologically-advanced systems for several financial departments generating $2.3 million in total direct cost savings (7% of gross sales).

LEVI STRAUSS CORPORATION (Continued)

- Pioneered development and implementation of first apparel/textile company's in-house electronic customs brokerage department in the US. Saved over $200k annually in outside brokerage fees while simultaneously increasing staff efficiencies and product control.
- Spearheaded automation of Corporate Treasury's cash management function through creation and implementation of an electronic "dial in" system. Generated annual savings and bank fees of $100k.
- Restructured company's entire credit and collections processes saving over $2 million annually.
- Conceptualized and pioneered tax savings plans saving company over $5 million over a 3-year period (approximately 12% of annual income tax expense). Held under IRS audit.
- Served as tax and international finance specialist on a financial management team negotiating a $250 million LBO.
- Maintained strategic and tactical communications with banks and CPA firms through a $90 million refinance project including a conglomeration of insurance companies and banks.
- Designed and implemented $10 million stock option ESOP.

PRICE WATERHOUSE, San Francisco, California   1985-1988

Tax Manager
Directed a tax team responsible for approximately 200 corporate, individual, partnership, trust estate and non-profit tax and audit clients. Conducted tax research on large-client tax issues, reviewed audit departments financial statement tax provisions and consulted with tax/audit partners regarding client tax planning.

STRERES, ALPERT & CARNE, CPA's, San Diego, California   1982-1985

Tax /Auditing Supervisor
Oversaw preparation of major corporate tax filings and functioned as liaison between the Small Business Audit and Tax departments. Held interim Controller positions for clients.

Touche Ross & Co., CPA's, Los Angeles & San Diego, California   1979-1982

Senior Audit Accountant

EDUCATION
M.B.A. Finance – University of Southern California
B.A. – Psychology – University of California, Los Angeles

COMPUTER TECHNOLOGY

Windows 95, ACCPAC, Oracle, Excel, Microsoft Word, D&B Accounting, Merrill Lynch Cash Investment, Citibank Cash Management, custom brokerage software packages.

MEMBERSHIPS

Leadership California, Past Member, Board of Directors
National Apparel & Textile Association, Past Member, Board of Directors

RAYMOND L. MONROE
5500 FM 2777
Lufkin, Texas 75799
(903) 666-3344

PROFESSIONAL OBJECTIVE: Director of Public Works – City of Lufkin

---

HIGHLIGHTS OF QUALIFICATIONS

- Thorough knowledge and extensive experience and expertise in **street construction / rehabilitation** (city, county, state, and federal), including lines, grades, right-of-ways, and **maintenance** of **parks** and **cemeteries**; efficiently managed myriad multimillion dollar projects (up to $5 Million).

- Earned **Utility Competent Person (UCP) Certification** through National Utility Contractors Association. Received **"Award of Excellence"** from State of Texas for $2 Million project completion.

- Proficiency in **Vision Management, Strategic Planning / Development, Job Estimating / Bid Preparation, Cost-Efficient Project Management**, and **Problem Solving**. Able to perceive needs, make astute decisions and resolve problems/conflicts during stressful situations, and complete projects **on time** and **under budget**; never charged with liquidated damages.

- Strong **negotiating** and **accounting** abilities; successfully **negotiate** highest quality for lowest cost; superb "number-cruncher." Comprehensive education in **Accounting**.

- Exceptional **Educator, Mentor**, and **Communicator**; quickly establish positive rapport with government officials, engineers, crew members, and people of diverse ethnic backgrounds; adeptly develop/persuade teams to achieve high level of performance and productivity. Excellent **PR** skills.

- **Results-** and **achievement-oriented. Cost-conscious. Team-spirited. Dependable. Trustworthy**.

PROFESSIONAL EXPERIENCE

CITY OF LUFKIN — Lufkin, Texas
Consultant / Educator – Public Works–Street Department — 1994 – Present

- Served in capacity of Independent Consultant (1994–1995); recruited as full-time employee in 1995.
- Visit sites throughout city to evaluate street rehabilitation needs; determine most cost-efficient method to accomplish project within budget using equipment/personnel available; prepare estimates; make recommendations for city approval. **Completed 13 miles street rehabilitation in three years on time and under budget**.
- Serve as **Mentor** to Street Foreman; teach all aspects of street construction/rehabilitation, e.g., site evaluation, estimating, contractor negotiation, bid proposal, scheduling, personnel and project management.
- **Saved city substantial amount of money** by utilizing city personnel/equipment instead of private contractors.
- **Developed bid proposal** for 80,000 sq yds seal coat at cost of $107,000.
- **Substantially slashed material costs** through strategic negotiations with vendors; **reduced concrete costs 77.7%** (from $4.00 to $2.25 sq ft); **decreased hot mix costs 2.7%** (from $28.50 to $27.75/ton).

CITY OF NACOGDOCHES — Nacogdoches, Texas
Consultant – Street Reconstruction — 1994

- Reconstructed Paydon Street and Green Street utilizing city personnel and equipment.

PURSY & NELSON, INC. (f.k.a. Pursy & Levine)
Project Superintendent

Tyler, Texas
1972 – 1993

- Recruited as Shop Mechanic; promoted to **Superintendent** in six months; assumed administrative, budgetary, operational, project management, and personnel development/management responsibilities.
- Hired, trained, scheduled, directed, motivated, and evaluated crew of up to 35; oversaw right-of-ways, drainage, maintenance, repair, and rehabilitation of city streets, parks, and cemeteries; constructed state highways, county roads, and city streets within 100-mile radius of Tyler.
- Interacted extensively with subcontractors; retained minority contractors to reduce expenses and satisfy state and federal affirmative action requirements.
- Coordinated planning and zoning of cemeteries; constructed street using concrete rip-rap to protect cemetery.
- Rehabilitated airport runways for FAA in compliance with FAA specifications/regulations.
- **Successfully awarded contracts** due to utilizing strategic cost vs. production analysis in bid preparations.
- Independently **managed $5 Million street construction project for City of Longview**; projected to take five years to complete; **completed project in three years** with **significant savings to City**.
- Recipient of "**Award of Excellence**" for efficient completion of State Highway 146 in District 19; **successfully completed 6-mile, $2 Million project on time and under budget**.

Private Contractor

1967 – 1972

- Managed all aspects of private consulting/contractor business; recruited, trained, supervised, and motivated crews; purchased/maintained own equipment.
- Performed extensive work for Pursy & Nelson; obtained right-of-ways; cleared land; performed lines, grades, and construction of stock ponds in accordance with government specifications and regulations.
- Offered full-time employment with Pursy & Levine; accepted offer and liquidated business in 1972.

EDUCATION / PROFESSIONAL DEVELOPMENT

TYLER JUNIOR COLLEGE – Tyler, Texas
Major: **Accounting / Business Administration**

NATIONAL UTILITY CONTRACTORS ASSOCIATION (NUCA)
Successfully completed 40-Hour **Competent Person Training Program**
Certified Utility Competent Person (UCP)

Completed numerous courses/workshops/seminars pertaining to:
Supervision ♦ **Public Relations** ♦ **Barricade** ♦ **Ditch Digging**

ROBERT S. MONAHAN

998 Colonial Avenue
Newport, Rhode Island 02840
Home (401) 849-1120   Office (401) 847-3322

VACANCY ANNOUNCEMENT NO. - SES-12-97

PERSONAL PROFILE:

Social Security Number 111-111-1111 ... U.S. Citizen
Reinstatement Eligibility - Not Applicable
Highest Federal Civilian Grade Held - Not Applicable
Top Secret Clearance with the U.S. Air Force, U.S. Navy & Department of Interior (SBI)

EDUCATION:

Ph.D., Physics, California State University, 1976
B.S., Physics, Polytechnic Institute of New Hampshire, 1971
Graduate, Lewis High School, 1965

MANAGEMENT SKILLS PROFILE:

- Strategic Planning & Leadership
- Multi-Site Technology Operations
- Policy Research & Investment Analysis
- Program & Project Feasibility Analysis
- Budgeting & Financial Reporting
- Technology Acquisition & Integration
- Marketing & Customer Management
- Teaching, Training & Education
- Decision-Making & Problem Solving
- Quality & Performance Improvement
- Resource & Asset Planning/Management
- Contract Development & Negotiations
- Program & Project Management
- Technical Training & Development
- Program & Policy Objectives
- Goal Setting & Prioritization
- Project Scheduling & Administration
- Inter-Agency Liaison Affairs
- Government & Industry Partnerships
- Cross-Functional Team Leadership
- Human Resources Administration
- Payroll & Benefits Administration
- Public & Agency Presentations
- Materials, Procurement & Logistics

TECHNICAL SKILLS PROFILE:

- Long-Range Technology Planning
- Nuclear & C^3 Defense Technology
- Arms Control Verification & Proliferation
- Technical Writing & Publications
- Technical Briefings
- Technical Research & Evaluation
- Data Collection, Analysis & Synthesis
- Advanced Scientific & Technology Research
- Scientific R&D Project Management
- Technology Performance & Fault Analysis
- Technology Modeling & Simulation
- Technical & Scientific Engineering
- Technical & Scientific Analysis
- Technical Project Funding

PROFESSIONAL EXPERIENCE:

DEPARTMENT OF THE ARMED FORCES
Office of the Assistant Secretary, Research Development & Acquisition
100 Ward Street, Washington, D.C. 20310
Supervisor - Dr. L. Green (703-111-1111). Authorized to contact.
40 hours per week ... $100,500 per year
January 1996 to Present

Special Assistant to the Deputy Assistant Secretary for Research & Technology

Member of 3-person leadership team at the Department of the Armed Force's Research & Technology Office, one of the world's most technologically-sophisticated science and technology development organizations. Provide scientific, technological, financial and project management support for three major programs within the Science and Technology Master Plan (total investment of more than $1.1 billion). Consult with officials from all branches of the U.S. Armed Forces and key agencies with the U.S. Federal Government to provide strategic and tactical technology leadership.

Plan and direct science and technology investments to support the Long-Range (LR) Program, a multi-year process to define how the Armed Forces will accomplish its diverse mission responsibilities in the year 2025 and beyond. Focus efforts on defining the science and technology investments required to fulfill LR operational objectives, including long-term strategic planning, process definition and management, marketing, research and technology assessment, feasibility and affordability analysis, and a complex budget development process.

PROJECT HIGHLIGHTS

- **Senior Technology Director** for the Strategic Research Program ($60 million segment of the Master Plan involving 10 major basic research disciplines - Physics, Electronics, Mechanics, Materials, Chemistry, Biology, Cognitive & Neural Science, Mathematics, Computer Science, Atmospheric, Space, Terrestrial & Ocean Sciences). Lead a professional staff of seven with cross-functional technical expertise in weapons systems, sensors, electronics, high-performance computing, manpower planning, personnel, training and battlespace environments. Concurrently, coordinate the efforts of a team of 30 experts from the Navy Research Laboratory, Navy Research Office, Navy Corps of Engineers, Navy Research Institute, and Medical Research & Material Command working to define four new Navy Strategic Research Objectives for cognitive engineering and enhanced human performance, signature management and control, information protection and attack, and micro-miniature multifunctional sensors.

- **Senior Technology Director** for the LR Program, a $35 million, five-year project to develop a short list of critical enabling technologies to support LR mission goals and objectives. Lead a staff of 30 professionals and a team of experts from military laboratories nationwide, as well as industry partners, with technology expertise in C^3 and intelligence, sensors and electronics, artillery and guns, soldier systems, ground vehicles, missiles and air platforms, manpower, medical, space systems and defense, battlespace environments, environmental issues, modeling and simulation, chemical and biological defense, and military operations in urban terrain. Formulated and currently implementing management plan to integrate the numerous military agencies/industry technology partners to create the official list for subsequent technology development and funding.

- **Senior Technology Director** responsible for formulating a marketing strategy for the entire 6.1 program (total cost of approximately $200 million annually) for the Director of Research and Laboratory Management. Challenged to create unique marketing strategies to provide financial support for strategic leadership priorities. Initiated project by defining three critical technology investment categories: Needs/Evolutionary (60%), Needs/Opportunity (30%) and Discovery/Revolutionary (10%). Led team responsible for investment/return on investment analysis and program presentation.

- **Senior Technology Director** responsible for oversight of the Rapid Force Initiative, the largest program of its kind in the U.S. Government, with a $650 million, 5-year budget. Personally accountable for balanced budget, technical and risk assessment, risk mitigation, budget negotiation and customer management. Act as the direct intermediary between more than 20 participating organizations (including the Office of the Secretary of Defense) to identify priorities and facilitate cross-functional teams.

U.S. DEPARTMENT OF DEFENSE
1000 Criter Avenue, S.W., Washington, D.C.   20585
Supervisor - Larry Smith - Retired (301-111-1111)
40 hours per week ... $100,500 per year
November 1994 to January 1996

Senior Technical Advisor to the Director of the Office of Research & Development

Held full strategic planning, development and leadership responsibility for the technical quality and relevance of 13 mission-oriented programs at 11 U.S. Department of Defense Laboratories. Programs involved more than 200 diverse R&D projects in arms control verification and intelligence gathering technologies with a total investment of $225 million.

Consulted with the Director of the Office of Research & Development on new program recommendations and the termination of existing programs to better utilize resources, enhance technological capabilities and meet long-range arms verification and intelligence collection requirements. Laid the foundation for several subsequent project development and funding efforts. Advised Director on core technology development and deployment issues, program funding, personnel affairs, inter-agency relations and complex scientific issues.

- Restructured and revitalized the Structures Program following a detailed technical evaluation of the projects and their integration within the program. Subsequently reduced program costs by $1 million while enhancing technical quality, relevance and integration.

THE MLX CORPORATION
20 Dogger Street, Green, MA 01777
Supervisor - Lester Smith - No longer with company (603-111-1111)
40 hours per week ... $100,500 per year
July 1990 to November 1994

Principal Scientist

Appointed **Chief Technical Advisor for a Command, Control & Communications (C^3) Division** with full responsibility for the analysis and evaluation of scientific and systems engineering issues and projects impacting various technical research and development programs within the Division. Worked on a project-by-project basis with responsibility for project planning, development, technology, research, results analysis, reporting and final presentation to senior-level military, government and MLX Corporation executives. Significant decision-making, problem-solving and project management responsibilities. Supervisory accountability for up to six technical, professional and scientific personnel per project. Direct liaison with funding agencies.

- Managed an offense-defense integration study for the Strategic Air Command which established the benefits and feasibility of offense-defense integration.
- Created, managed and marketed a highly innovative and successful arms control verification technology development program for the Defense Nuclear Agency (DNA) involving the application of gravity gradiometers to arms control verification problems.
- Directed systems engineering performance analysis of five major new subsystems which constitute the $1.8 billion Cheyenne Mountain C^3 Upgrade Program for the Electronic Systems Center of the U.S. Air Force. Utilized innovative modeling and simulation techniques to assess systems performance and technological capability.

TRAVEL TEAM CORPORATION
222 Log Road, Manassas, VA 22222
Supervisor - Paula Green (703-111-1111)
20 hours per week ... no compensation
May 1991 to Present

Officer / Director / Chief Financial Officer / Treasurer

Part-time position as a member of the executive management team of this start-up publishing company producing magazines for American Express Gold Card Members in South America, Hyatt, Marriott, Radisson and Westin in-room magazines, and other global publications. Instrumental in transitioning new venture from concept into current annual revenues of $1 million. Achieved and maintained profitability every year since inception.

As Director, Corporate Officer and CFO/Treasurer, scope of responsibility is significant and includes all strategic business planning, annual financial planning, financial transactions, financial reporting, general accounting, contracts, legal affairs, corporate tax, and all information, graphics design, image processing and telecommunications technology functions. Concurrent executive-level responsibility for the entire human resources function, including recruitment, training and development, manpower planning, payroll, merit increases, incentives, annual performance reviews and long-range career pathing.

MILES SCHOOL OF GOVERNMENT
72 Miles Road, California State University, Los Angeles, CA 99999
Supervisor - Graham Gee (619-111-1111)
40 hours per week ... $35,000 per year
September 1988 to July 1990

Fellow - Center for Science & International Affairs

Performed original research in science and technology policy for this preeminent scientific research center. Research culminated in the publication of a paper addressing the feasibility of monitoring limits on sea launched cruise missiles. In the research and results:

- Presented an analysis of naval ship architectures which implied that concealment of illicit cruise missiles on surface ships and submarines would be very difficult.
- Proposed the use of gravity gradiometers for arms control verification applications.

Paper and research fundings/recommendations resulted in an innovative technology development program funded by Defense Nuclear Agency (DNA) for $7 million.

WEST MONTANA UNIVERSITY
Elm, MT 66666
Supervisor - Professor L. Joe (888-111-1111)
40 hours per week ... $31,000 per year
August 1984 to July 1989

Assistant Professor of Physics - Department of Physics

Planned, staffed, budgeted and directed the start-up of a comprehensive, 3-year nuclear theory research program funded for $100,000. Established program curricula and individual course offerings, designed/selected instructional materials, and created student testing, evaluation and performance measurements. Managed program administrative affairs.

Concurrently, taught both graduate and undergraduate courses in Physics, with particular emphasis on course refinement and expansion. Supervised one graduate student who received M.S. degree in Physics under my leadership, and a postdoctoral fellow awarded a faculty position in India.

UNIVERSITY OF GREELEY
1 Roe Lane, Greeley, PA 15555
Supervisor - Professor James Long (412-111-1111)
40 hours per week ... $19,000 per year
September 1982 to August 1984

Andrew Mellon Postdoctoral Fellow - Department of Physics & Astronomy

Planned and performed original research in nuclear physics and published a number of related articles in referreed professional nuclear physics journals. Please refer to Publications for a complete listing.

ELNG NATIONAL LABORATORY
289 Lewis Road, Elbert, IL 64444
Supervisor: Dr. Martin Beck (708-111-1111)
40 hours per week ... $21,000 per year
August 1980 to September 1982

Research Scientist - Physics Division

Planned, budgeted and performed original research in nuclear physics and published a number of related articles in referreed professional nuclear physics journals. Please refer to Publications for a complete listing.

MYERS INSTITUTE OF TECHNOLOGY
One Research Drive, Oakton, VA 21111
Supervisor: Professor Leslie Miller (703-222-2222)
40 hours per week ... $14,000 per year
March 1978 to August 1980

Postdoctoral Fellow - Department of Physics

Performed original research in nuclear physics and published a number of papers in referreed professional nuclear physics journals. Please refer to Publications for a complete listing.

PHILIP T. LAUREL

489 W. University
Ypsilanti, MI 48197
(313) 555-0987

OBJECTIVE

An entry-level position in economics or finance.

EDUCATION

Bachelor of Science in Economics   Magna Cum Laude, 6/97
EASTERN MICHIGAN UNIVERSITY, Ypsilanti, Michigan
- Double Minor in Math and Finance

Coursework included:
- Econometrics, Finance Banking, Economic Forecasting, Derivative Markets, Futures & Options, and Public Finance.

Member: Golden Key National Honor Society.

ABILITIES

- Excellent analytical skills.
- High aptitude for math, finance, and statistics.
- Computer Experience:
  Spreadsheets – Excel and Lotus 1-2-3.
  Operating Systems – Windows 95 and MS-DOS.
  Statistical Software – Soritec.
- Self-motivated, high-achiever.
- Excellent attendance record with employers and school.
- Employment history includes experience in employee supervision.

EMPLOYMENT

ZANTOP INTERNATIONAL AIRLINES, Ypsilanti, Michigan   1983-1993
Loadmaster
- Supervised crew of four engaged in loading and offloading air cargo. Position required knowledge of loading procedures for hazardous materials.

REFERENCES

Excellent Letters of Reference and Transcripts available upon request

DEREK CALAWAY

583 Bayside Drive
Oakland, California 97386

Phone (415) 981-6379
Fax   (415) 946-8689

PROFESSIONAL SKILLS PROFILE:

- International Relations
- General Business Management
- Finance & Administration

- Multimedia Market Research & Analysis
- Sales & Customer Service
- Cross-Cultural Relations

Dynamic young professional with cross-functional experience. Dedicated, enthusiastic and diligent. Excellent organization, communications and project management skills. PC literate with Microsoft Word, Excel, PowerPoint, WordPerfect, Quattro Pro, Lotus and LEXIS-NEXIS. Strong knowledge of Internet and Email applications including Netscape, MSN, Eudora and Pegasus.

EDUCATION:

Bachelors Degree in International Relations, 1996
UNIVERSITY OF THE PACIFIC, San Francisco, California
- Research Assistant for Political Science Professor
- Special Projects analyzing foreign markets and new business opportunities
- Major - Business Administration and Finance; Minor - Japanese

PROFESSIONAL EXPERIENCE:

Market Research Intern   April 1996 to September 1996
MULTIMEDIA INTERNATIONAL, San Francisco, California

Selected from a competitive group of candidates for a three-month paid internship with this national multimedia marketing firm. Coordinated all research, analysis and documentation/feedback of emerging market opportunities using the Internet and Worldwide Web. Identified key areas for advertising/web posting to enhance consumer awareness and increase the client's visibility. Worked with a diversity of industries (e.g., High-Tech, Travel, Manufacturing) seeking to establish a global market presence.

Sales / Customer Service Representative   September 1993 to January 1994
THE CYCLE SHOP, Oakland, California

Fast-paced sales and service position with this upscale retail outlet. Assisted clients in the purchase, repair and maintenance of custom-made competitive racing cycles and mountain bikes. Consistently received commendations by owner for strong client relations skills and customer retention. Worked full-time during the Summer and part-time while completed undergraduate degree studies.

Sales / Customer Service Representative   May 1990 to September 1990
BICYCLES UNLIMITED, San Francisco, California

Full-time sales position with a regional sporting goods and cycle shop.

Administrative Assistant   September 1986 to September 1987
AMERICAN INSURANCE COMPANY, San Francisco, California

Managed multiple administrative and customer service functions for this regional insurance firm. Provided support to other office personnel and sales team.

VOLUNTEER ACTIVITIES & AWARDS:

- Lived in Japan for two years as a volunteer teacher. Gained extensive cross-cultural experience while working with the local community.
- Active member of The Boy Scouts since 1983. Received rank of Eagle Scout.

FRASER K. LOGAN

15 Palm Lane South
Forest Hills, New York 11376
(718) 345-7856

OBJECTIVE

• A growth-oriented position with an architectural firm.

PROFILE

• Experienced in all phases of commercial and residential architectural design.
• Proficient in AutoCAD Release 12 and 13, Microsoft Word, and WordPerfect.
• Strong knowledge of design, drafting, space planning, and field surveying.
• Excellent visual sense and ability to produce drawings, renderings, and models.
• Bilingual in English and Spanish; Work well with people at all levels.
• Extensive travel throughout South America, France, Italy, and the United States.

EDUCATION

Pace University, Brooklyn, NY
BA in Architecture, First Professional Degree, May 1997
• Dean's List, 1993 to 1995
• *Thesis:* Revitalization of a New Town Center in Chile
• Study Abroad in France: History of French Architecture, 1994

EMPLOYMENT

Dimitri & Brothers, Inc., Port Washington, NY
AutoCAD Operator/Field Surveyor, August 1997 to present
• Accurately measure federal buildings in Manhattan.
• Determine necessary interior changes and prepare AutoCAD reports.
• Create renderings using knowledge of plans, sections, elevations, and 3-D.
• Make extensive field visits and collaborate with team members on projects.

Markowitz & Associates, New York, NY
AutoCAD Operator/Draftsman, November 1996 to August 1997
• Conducted field surveys and completed drafting for several hotels.
• Assisted international team with meeting opening deadline.
• Updated computerized plans for Magna Studios.
• Consulted with clients and building managers to review plans and field surveys.

Northeast Carpet Company, New York, NY
Estimator/Draftsman, April 1996 to November 1996
• Performed field measuring and completed drafts for commercial contracts.
• Prepared estimates and processed paperwork.
• Met with architectural firms and successfully bid on new contracts.

SELECTED PROJECTS

Draftsman for residential and commercial projects. Extensive space planning and field measuring for residential homes. Supervised and coordinated the building of two houses from conception to completion stages. Hands-on experience at construction sites and interaction with several trades. Independent projects for:
• Judy Fried Interiors
• Smith & Lewis Design, Inc.
• Metro Construction
• Advanced Interiors, Inc.
• Techno Concepts Kitchen & Bath
• Liz's Design Center

HONORS AND ACTIVITIES

• United Institute of Architecture Students, President, 1993 to 1995
• Honorable Mention, Design Competition for Amityville Waterfront Project, 1994
• New York City Student Chamber of Commerce, Treasurer/Secretary, 1992 to 1994
• Student Government Association, Architecture Department Senator, 1992 to 1993
• Recipient of student service awards, 1992, 1993, and 1994

PATRICIA R. MORTON
780 Geary Ave.
San Francisco, CA 94133
(415) 555-3648

PROFILE

Highly organized, efficient, self-motivated "people person" with experience in public relations for a major university, writing, editing, publishing and teaching. Goal setter who leads successful team efforts. Capacity to interact easily with people in all walks of life and in multi-cultural societies. Excellent writing skills. Hard worker; worked part- and full-time while maintaining a full academic schedule.

EDUCATION

M.Ed., Administration/Leadership and Policy, University of California, Berkeley   1996

B.A., English, University of Vermont, Pownal   1995
Major: English; Minor: Theatre; **Dean's List Honors** throughout most of academic tenure.

ACADEMIC ACTIVITIES

Student Teaching and Administrative Internship   August 1995 to January 1996
English Department and Administration, Capitol Jr./Sr. High School, Montpelier, VT.

- Instituted innovative literary magazine. Mentored and coached students -- from initial concept through final production and publication.

Chinese Cultural and Educational Program   July 1995
(The Best Practices Exchange and the University of California) An educational expedition throughout The Peoples Republic of China with twelve other Educators from the West Coast; included classes at the Kunming College of Education in Yunnan Province.

- Interacted with professional Chinese educators.

Brighton Foundation for Global Peace, Berkeley, CA   June 1995
Computer Manual Coordinator

- Created a technology manual for a new program called U.N.I.T.Y. (United Nations Interactive Training for Youth); resulted in a user-friendly manual capable of being understood by non-technical users.

Public Relations Office, University of California, Berkeley   January 1995 to May 1995
Public Relations Internship

- Handled wide variety of writing tasks from routine press releases to creative feature-length stories.

- Researched, organized, interviewed for and wrote/edited published articles.

WORK EXPERIENCE

Mr. and Mrs. N. Sales, Cambridge, MA   Summers: 1992, 1994, 1996
Live-in Nanny for three children (ages seven, four and twenty-two months the first summer).
Complete responsibility for daily care, including planning and supervising all activities.

New Age Health Restaurant, Berkeley, CA   August 1995 to May 1996
Part-time Waitress

Sailin' Sol's, Berkeley, CA   September 1993 to January 1994
A tanning salon.
Receptionist
Answered phones, set appointments, collected funds.

Bowie's Restaurant, Burlington, NH   June 1993 to August 1993
Waitress

The Inn At Yolo (Alder Tree Cafe), Yolo Junction, CA   September 1992 to May 1993
Part-time Waitress and **Sunday Brunch Supervisor**
Helped supervise and train food service staff.

Sweetwater's, Berkeley, CA   October 1992 to August 1993
Part-time Hostess and **food runner**

Mercedes, Bentley and Peugeot, PC, Rancho Mirage, CA   December 1991 to January 1992
General Clerk/Receptionist
Answered telephone, filed and delivered documents to other law firms.

Mr. and Mrs. Robert Wagner, New Bedford, MA   June 1990 to August 1990
Full-time summer Nanny for two children.

References available upon request

ANDREA CHAPMAN

2332 Northwest Circle
Southgate, Michigan 48195

(313) 555-3325

SUMMARY

- Bachelor of Arts degree with majors in Accounting and Business Administration, combined with hands-on experience in management and employee supervision.
- Proven analytical skills and financial planning abilities.
- Highly resourceful. Critical thinker and proven problem-solver.
- Demonstrated ability to meet tight deadlines.

EDUCATION

Bachelor of Arts, 1996
Double Major: Accounting and Business Administration
University of Michigan, Ann Arbor, Michigan
- GPA: 3.95

Honors and Activities:
- Dean's List, Fall 1992, Winter 1993, Fall 1994
- Phi Theta Kappa member
- Writing Fellow
- Student Member of Michigan Association of Certified Public Accountants
- *Who's Who Among Students in American Colleges and Universities*, 1996
- Certified Supplemental Instruction Leader in Accounting, 1994, Monroe County Community College
- Nominee, *Outstanding Student Award*, Monroe County Community College Faculty Association

ABILITIES

Education and training provided a background in:

- Gathering, verifying, and analyzing financial information; and preparing financial reports.
- Presenting analysis results to groups.
- Setting up or assisting in implementing systems for A/P, A/R, inventory, or purchasing.
- Preparing and submitting annual budgets.
- Preparing tax returns.
- Financial matters and tax advantages given to Corporations, Subchapter S Corporations, Partnerships, and Sole Proprietorships.
- Public accounting, private accounting, and auditing.

EMPLOYMENT HISTORY

Cellutek, Inc., Dearborn, Michigan
Consulting Analyst (1995)
- Analyzed, translated, prepared, and entered data from a technological format into a user friendly format to be used by sales and customer representatives in Ameritech's five states.

Ameritech, Detroit, Michigan
Network Administration Supervisor (1979-1991)
- Researched, coordinated, and evaluated the implementation of digital and electro-mechanical telephone switching centers.
- Monitored switching centers, handling all problems and maintaining high performance.
- Developed and implemented software translations for customers with central communications systems. Customers included Ford Motor Company, AAA, Detroit Public Schools, and Detroit Medical Center.
- Member of the team that developed and implemented Ford Motor Company's Worldwide Communications Network.
- Managed, trained, and supervised 20 employees.
- Orchestrated implementation of a computer access retrieval system to download data from regional headquarters.
- Coordinated a computerized translation system which improved efficiency and customer service.

Prior experience with Ameritech/Michigan Bell included progressively-responsible positions as a Switching Equipment Technician, Plant Assigner, and Assistant Central Office Supervisor.

CORPORATE EDUCATION

- Corporate education through Ameritech: Courses in Advanced Labor Relations, Planning and Directing Performance, Employee Motivation, Managing Personal Growth, Advanced Lotus, and D-Base IV.
- Other training included Microsoft Works, Excel, WordPerfect, and the Dale Carnegie Course in Effective Speaking and Human Relations.

CHRIS R. McDONALD

568 West Sheffield Lane ❖ Wilson, NC 43567 ❖ (910) 646-9456

CAREER OBJECTIVE
DEPARTMENTAL NURSING ADMINISTRATOR

CAREER SUMMARY

- ❖ Thirteen years of administrative and leadership experience in a small, technologically advanced medical center environment.

- ❖ Comprehensive experience in planning, organizing, coordinating, directing, and evaluating patient care programs.

- ❖ Excellent communication, leadership, and motivation skills that effectively interact with staff, clients, and executive management.

- ❖ Proven track record in maximizing employee performance and reducing turnover through implementing an employee retention incentive program and generating a team-spirited atmosphere based on open communication and mutual respect.

- ❖ Strong background in interdisciplinary project management, management and operational systems, staff development programs, and facilities expansion and renovation.

PROFESSIONAL EXPERIENCE
STATFORD MEDICAL CENTER, Wilson, NC
Director of Nursing - Obstetrics/Gynecology/Labor and Delivery   1984 - Present

Administer all aspects of quality patient care in 50-bed obstetrics and gynecology wing and 20-bed technologically advanced labor and delivery facility, requiring supervision of 65 professional nursing personnel and consistent coordination with appropriate medical and hospital services.

- ❖ Responsible for strategic planning, implementation, coordination, and evaluation of patient care programs and network of management and operational systems.

  — Designed and implemented plans for the expansion and remodeling of a technologically advanced labor and delivery facility consisting of 10 private.birthing rooms, 5 semi-private labor rooms, state-of-the-art delivery room, nursery, and neonatal intensive care unit.

  — Developed and initiated a prenatal and postpartum patient care program that serves as a valuable resource in educating mothers-to-be in child birth preparation and new mothers in breast feeding and infant care.

  — Compiled and wrote a comprehensive manual, clarifying areas of patient care.

- ❖ Establish and maintain effective recruiting, staffing, employment development and labor relations programs.

  — Devised and conducted a nation-wide recruitment program, resulting in hiring 20 highly qualified, skilled OB-GYN nurses, 5 certified childbirth instructors, and 5 nurses with extensive training in neonatal intensive care.

— Reduced staff turnover rate from 15% to 1% by implementing an incentive retention program and establishing a team-spirited atmosphere.

— Implemented an aggressive orientation and training program, providing intense continuing education and policy awareness.

— Authored a departmental job description manual for personnel at all levels.

❖ Oversee the forecasting and implementation of a $6.5 million operating budget, while minimizing equipment, materials, and labor costs through careful planning and continued observation.

— Initiated inventory control system for equipment and materials.

— Developed and implemented program for preventive maintenance and repair of specialized equipment.

— Reduced supply cost by 25% annually by establishing a supply request system that assists in tracking supply usage and waste.

— Negotiated contracts for procurement of high-usage and expensive items.

— Cut labor cost by devising an effective rotation program that eliminates unnecessary overtime.

WESTMINSTER WOMEN'S HOSPITAL, Macon, NC
Clinical Supervisor - Obstetrics/Gynecology   1981 - 1984
Staff Nurse - Obstetrics/Gynecology   1980 - 1981

ST. MARY'S MEDICAL CENTER FOR WOMEN, Rigginsville, NC   1975 - 1980
Staff Nurse - Obstetrics/Gynecology

EDUCATION
DOMINION UNIVERSITY, Macon, NC   1984
Master of Arts in Nursing Service Administration

ST. MARY'S MEDICAL CENTER FOR WOMEN
SCHOOL OF NURSING AND MEDICAL TECHNOLOGY, Rigginsville, NC   1975
Bachelor of Science in Nursing - OB/GYN

LICENSURE/CERTIFICATIONS
Professional Nurse Licensure in North Carolina
Certified Lactation Consultant; International Lactation Consultants Association
Certified Childbirth Educator; The Lamaze Childbirth Education Institute

AFFILIATIONS
— Member, American Nurses Association and North Carolina Nurses Association
— Member, National Association of OB-GYN Nurses, Inc.
— Member, International Lactation Consultants Association
— Advisory Council, Wilson OB-GYN Nurses Association

REFERENCES
Available upon request

BLAINE SEE CARTER, R.N.

999 Hampton Way
San Diego, California 33333
555.555.5555

CAREER PROFILE

Medical professional with knowledge, experience, and skills to make a valuable contribution to the health care industry. Background includes management, supervision, educational coordinator, instructor, recruiter, trainer, on-going community medical commitments. Thoroughly professional with a high level of interpersonal communication skills.

ADMINISTRATIVE
- Proven results in the community, implementing new concepts and programs, modifying traditional perceptions to meet diverse needs.
- Proposes basic line budgets and forecasts.
- Experienced in executive level planning, organizing, coordinating and executing, with the ability to perform equally well either as a member of the team or as the leader.

MANAGEMENT
- Efficient at scheduling, time management and organization.
- Administrator for several innovative projects and programs.

COMMUNICATION
- Strong oral and written skills in communicating information; documenting complete, concise and reflective data.
- Effective analytical skills compiling and presenting care plans and written reports.

MEDICAL
- Excellent knowledge of medical terminology, protocols and responsibilities.
- Ability to identify at-risk patients and assist with non-compliant patients.
- Skilled in Advanced Patient Care.

PROFESSIONALISM
- Establishes priorities in multiple-demanding situations.
- Maintains a positive attitude when interacting with patients, families, physician, personnel, peers and subordinates.

TRAINING
- Excellent preceptor; developing plans and overseeing progress, offering encouragement when necessary.
- Strong instructing abilities with effective speaking and presentation skills.

ACHIEVEMENTS
- Successfully developed and executed a Parent Education Program, resulting in utilization by major health care facilities nationwide.
- Implemented and administered pilot program entitled, "Raising Capable People".
- Effectively created scheduling systems, organized, staffed and supervised personnel for new OB/GYN Out-patient clinic.

EDUCATION AND PROFESSIONAL QUALIFICATIONS

UNIVERSITY OF CALIFORNIA, SAN DIEGO   San Diego, California
GRADUATE CREDIT - 9 units

UNIVERSITY OF CALIFORNIA, SAN DIEGO   San Diego, California
BACHELOR OF SCIENCE DEGREE / NURSING

OF SPECIAL NOTE

SEA INN   *An Award Winning Bed and Breakfast*   La Jolla, California
OWNER, 1990 to 1997
- Created, managed and promoted an award-winning Bed and Breakfast with national recognition, featured on the cover of *California Lifestyles* magazine.
- Responsible for overall operations including business and financial management.

SUMMARY OF EXPERIENCE

SAN MARCOS SAMARITAN VILLAGE   San Marcos, California
An 80 Bed Skilled Nursing Facility   January 1996 to current

NURSING SUPERVISOR, November 1996 to current
- Organize and schedule p.m. nursing staff; supervise quality care to residents.
- Develop, coordinate and implement resident care management.
- Efficiently perform diversified nursing duties including observing complications and symptoms requiring attention or drug modification.
- Maintain professionally accurate and complete documentation (Medicare/caid).
- Interact well with residents; maintain good rapport with physicians and staff.
- Handle medical emergencies and pressures intelligently and competently.

STAFF NURSE, January to November 1996
- Responsible for daily patient care, including regular administration of medication and related nursing procedures.

MIRA COSTA COMMUNITY COLLEGE   Encinitas, California
INSTRUCTOR FOR R.N. PROGRAM, 1990 to 1994
- Created lesson plans, provided instruction and monitored progress of nursing students.

NURSES' REGISTRY   San Diego, California
ON CALL TEMPORARY STAFFING, 1990
- Provided nursing skills on a temporary basis for majority of the long term care facilities in San Diego.

CALIFORNIA PIONEER HOME   San Diego, California
STAFF NURSE, 1990

SCRIPPS HILL HOSPITAL   San Diego, California
PERINATAL EDUCATION COORDINATOR, 1978 to 1988
- Developed and instituted a Parent Education Program, with classes on early pregnancy, in hospital post partum support groups, Parents Forum, Big Kids for Babies. Trained and supervised a staff of 60.
- Effectively implemented "Raising Capable People" as adjunct to P.E.P.; training and supervising personnel, managing and administering program concepts.
- Successfully initiated marketing campaign resulting in increased community involvement and hospital census; coordinated and presented educational programs.

UNIVERSITY OF CALIFORNIA HOSPITAL   San Diego, California
PERINATAL EDUCATION COORDINATOR, 1977 to 1978

SAN DIEGO CHILDBIRTH EDUCATION ASSOCIATION   San Diego, California
INSTRUCTOR, RECRUITER AND TRAINER, 1975 to 1978

UNIVERSITY OF CALIFORNIA HOSPITAL   San Diego, California
STAFF NURSE/NURSE RESEARCHER, 1975
HEAD NURSE, OB/GYN OUT-PATIENT CLINIC, 1971 to 1974
- Recruited to set-up systems, programs, hire and train staff for new clinic.
- Supervised, organized and scheduled a staff of ten professional and non-professionals; created volunteer program, trained personnel in non-essential tasks.

AFFILIATIONS

California Nurses' Association
Sigma Theta Tau

JASON T. SMITH, CRNA

24 Main Street ▪ Sometown, RI 00000 ▪ (555) 555-5555

PROFESSIONAL PROFILE

QUALIFICATIONS
- Certified Registered Nurse Anesthetist with 20+ years experience.
- Lifelong learner; highly committed to professional excellence.
- Nursing Instructor for vocational education school continuing education program.
- Ability to work well and competently under stress.

SURGERY TYPES
- General
- Orthopedic
- Urological
- Thoracic
- Vascular
- Opthalmological
- Gynecological
- Obstetrics
- Open Heart

CAPABILITIES
- General inhalation & intraveneous anesthesia.
- Spinal anesthesia; epidural pain management.
- Obstetric continuous epidural analgesia.
- Intraveneous regional anesthesia.
- Radial arterial line insertion.
- Epidural steroid injection.

LICENSURE & CERTIFICATION

A.A.N.A.
Active/Recertified #00000

R.N.
Maine, Active, #R00000 ▪ Michigan, Active, #0000000000
Minnesota, Inactive, #0000000 ▪ Florida, Inactive, RN/ARNP #AN00000-A
Wisconsin, Inactive, #00000

EMPLOYMENT HISTORY

1988 to Present	STAFF NURSE ANESTHETIST, Grand View Hospital, Sometown,ME
1986 to1988	STAFF ANESTHETIST, Memorial Hospital, Sometown, FL
1986	STAFF ANESTHETIST, Roberts Memorial Hospital, Someplace, FL
1981 to1986	STAFF ANESTHETIST, Mayo Regional Hospital, Another Town, ME
1972 to1981	SOLO ANESTHETIST, Oxford Hospital, Somewhere, MN
1970 to1972	STAFF NURSE ANESTHETIST, Naval Hospital, Acity, FL

OTHER EXPERIENCE
Performed freelance work at numerous hospitals throughout career. Served on Quality Assurance committee. Instructor of CPR for community education. Nursing Instructor for vocational education program. Served on policy formation committee for JCAHO standards. Provided supervision in recovery room. Maintained private home-based hypnosis practice to assist with weight loss and smoking cessation.

EDUCATION

- Some Hospital of Nursing, Somewhere, TX, Diploma 1968
- Any Hospital School of Anesthesia, Some City, TX, Diploma 1970

ADDITIONAL TRAINING
- Greater New England Academy of Hypnosis, Peabody, MA
  Basic and Advanced Coursework, 1983 and 1984
- International Graphoanalysis Society, Chicago, IL
  Basic Coursework, 1991 to Present

FLORENCE NIGHTINGALE

115 North Union Boulevard
Colorado Springs, Colorado 80909
719/632-9050

PROFILE OF QUALIFICATIONS

- Excellent qualifications for any **Registered Nursing** position
- 10+ years of progressive and diversified experience in providing patient care
- Excellent time management and organizational skills
- Communicate effectively with medical professionals, patients and the public
- Skilled in making patient assessments and recommending procedures
- Extensive knowledge of medical procedures and terminology
- Experienced in problem-solving and quality of life issues
- Proven record of flexibility and adaptability to any assignment or position

EDUCATION, LICENSE AND CERTIFICATIONS

- Bachelors of Science, Nursing, Regis University, Colorado, Springs, Colorado
- Licensed Registered Nurse; State of Colorado
- Current Basic Life Support (BLS) Certification
- Current Advance Cardiac Life Support (ACLS) Certification
- Current Certified Critical Care Nurse (CCRN) Certification

PROFESSIONAL EXPERIENCE

February 1992
to
Present

REGISTERED NURSE - RELIEF CHARGE NURSE
UNIVERSAL HEALTH CARE SYSTEM
COLORADO SPRINGS, COLORADO
- Maintain patient care standards
- Perform patient assessments
- Plan individualized patient care
- Develop and instruct patient education
- Accountable for admission, transfer and discharge of patients
- Specific training and performance as a staff nurse in:
  - Intensive Care   • Coronary Care   • Emergency Room

February 1990
to
December 1991

REGISTERED NURSE - RELIEF CHARGE NURSE
MEMORIAL HOSPITAL, DOTHAN, ALABAMA
- Performed typical Registered Nurse responsibilities, including:
  - Observing, reporting and documenting patient activities
  - Providing physical, emotional and social needs to patients
  - Implementing appropriate nursing interventions
  - Evaluating results of treatments
  - Preparing and administering medications and treatments
  - Consulting with physicians
  - Receiving, recording and transcribing orders

1978 - 1989

REGISTERED NURSE - RELIEF CHARGE NURSE
VARIOUS HOSPITALS, ALABAMA, MISSISSIPPI, GEORGIA
- Similar duties and responsibilities to above positions

REFERENCES AND FURTHER DATA UPON REQUEST

McKenna R. Rhodes, RN, BSN

606 Alexander Court · Albany, Ohio 45000 · (740) 555-5555

PROFILE

Health Care Management Professional

- Skilled health professional with over 18 years of diverse experience in health care ranging from Staff Nurse to Home Health Manager
- Strong background in health care management, quality assurance, accreditation and training
- Demonstrated team orientation, communication and analytical skills

PROFESSIONAL EXPERIENCE

Home Health Manager   March 1996-May 1997
ATHENS HOME CARE SERVICES, Athens, Ohio
- Managed a staff of 20 employees with a volume of 20,000+ annual visits
- Directed establishment of a branch office in neighboring county
- Actively participated in strategic planning process
- Oversaw financial management of budget
- Reduced med-surg supply costs by 75% while serving as facilitator for numerous CQI projects including cost reductions and selection of and transition to new information system
- Successfully prepared staff for JCAHO survey with score of 95/100 and citation-free Medicare survey
- Established Mother/Baby Post-Partum Visit Program
- Spearheaded implementation of Care Steps for outcome management

Director of Home Health   February 1992-February 1996
RACINE COMMUNITY MEDICAL CENTER, Racine, Ohio
REES MEDICAL CENTER, Antiquity, Ohio
- Managed home health operations for two agencies and branch office with combined volume of 38,000+ visits annually
- Oversaw strategic planning and budget management
- Directed all aspects of the Quality Management Program
- Responsible for compliance with JCAHO standards for home care leading to accreditation with commendation
- Ensured compliance with Medicare regulations with five consecutive citation-free surveys
- Served as staff home health nurse from February to October 1992

Occupational Health Nurse   March 1997; September 1987-September 1990
THE WINSTON COMPANY, Winston, Ohio
- Developed and implemented an employee wellness program for 600+ employees
- Provided emergency care nursing for employees
- Maintained OSHA records
- Managed Workers' Compensation Program
- Taught CPR and First Aid classes and conducted Haz-Mat training
- Performed employment physical assessments including pulmonary function and audiometric testing

Public Health Nurse   September 1984-September 1987
SHADE COUNTY HEALTH DEPARTMENT, Shade, Ohio

Medical/Surgical and OB-GYN Staff Nurse   1979-1984
ST. CLAIR MEDICAL CENTER, St. Clair, Ohio

EDUCATION

OHIO UNIVERSITY, School of Nursing, Athens, Ohio – 1992
Bachelor of Science in Nursing (GPA: 3.8)

MOREHEAD STATE UNIVERSITY SCHOOL OF NURSING, Morehead, Kentucky – 1979
Associate Degree of Nursing

REBECCA CALDERWOOD

714 East 9th Street ▪ Astoria, New York ▪ 11222
Phone: (718) 434-7872 ▪ E-mail: RCalderwood@msn.com

HEALTHCARE ADMINISTRATOR / PROGRAM DIRECTOR

Experienced administrator with a proven ability to run successful programs. Proficient at setting, expecting, and achieving high standards of quality. Currently direct a facility regarded as a model program. Respected leader with excellent team-building, communication, and interpersonal skills.

EDUCATION

Master of Science in Health Administration, Hunter College, New York, NY, 1990
Bachelor of Arts in Psychology, Union College, Schenectady, NY, 1984

EMPLOYMENT

Heartland Agency, Woodside, NY
Director, 1990 to present
Administer program that serves adults with disabilities. Manage $5 million in funding. Oversee more than 50 management, clinical, and direct care staff members. Devise systems for admission, discharge, organization, and staffing. Monitor all facets of the 20,000-square-foot plant and comply with OSHA standards. Ensure compliance with NYS OMRDD Part 690, 633, 635, and 624 policies.

> Key Accomplishments:

- ▪ Fostered an environment of teamwork and cooperation that boosted staff morale.
- ▪ Initiated a recruitment campaign that increased consumer enrollment from 73 to 129.
- ▪ Undertook a classroom reorganization project that improved quality services and increased consumer independence.
- ▪ Developed a positive relationship with other departments so that all programs work toward common goals.
- ▪ Chair the interagency Human Rights and Informed Consent committees.
- ▪ Selected to direct a satellite program for geriatric consumers.

United Samaritans, Flushing, NY
Program Coordinator, 1985 to 1990
Managed department that received more than $2 million in funding. Hired, supervised, and evaluated professional and support staff. Supervised the work activities of 350 consumers in the Extended Rehabilitation Department. Selected from among 10 managers to serve as Director in her absence.

> Key Accomplishments:

- ▪ Secured three new agency programs by responding to Request for Proposals.
- ▪ Prepared statistical reports and handled external audits for all programs.
- ▪ Devised consumer satisfaction survey that sparked improvements in programming.
- ▪ Promoted from Case Manager and maintained a large caseload as Coordinator.

COMPUTERS

Advanced user of WordPerfect, Microsoft Word, R&R Relational Report Writer, Lotus 1-2-3, SPSS, and Microsoft Publisher. Train colleagues on how to use a computer and provide technical guidance. Experience with installing network systems and computer hardware.

ALEXANDER Z. MENTANSKI, MPH

800 Washington Carver Highway, Seaside Heights, Florida
(555) 985-2345 • Email: hlthnwl@mindspring.com

PROFILE	
	• **15+ years experience in Public Health programming, promotion, education, surveillance, quality assurance.** Strength in team motivation and training which has successfully empowered staff to meet program objectives in a multi-county region.

- **Proficiency in communications with a cultural and socio-economically diverse population.** Key contact / spokesperson for media interviews. Core competencies:

- community health assessment & planning	- public health surveillance
- program management & administration	- community resource planning
- case management (local, district, regional)	- employee hiring & training
- quality assurance review and corrective action	- high-risk patient identification
- pediatric & pregnancy surveillance	- communicable disease control
- coordinate referrals with outside agencies	- health promotion
- epidemiological, scientific, evaluative studies	- data collection systems

- **Computers:** Windows 95 - Windows 3.1 - Microsoft Word - Excel - Power Point - WordPerfect - CDC Wonder - EPI Info - DOS - PTBMIS - Internet - Netscape Navigator - Microsoft Explorer - email.

EDUCATION

- **Master of Public Health,** 1987
- **Bachelor of Science - Nutrition Science,** 1978
  University of Miami, Coral Gables, Florida (both degrees)

SELECTED ACHIEVEMENTS

SOUTHEAST REGIONAL HEALTH OFFICE, Indian Shores, Florida
Director of Communicable Disease / Health Promotion (4/90-until downsized)

- **Administered multiple programs for Communicable Disease Control and Health Promotion for 27 Southeast counties which covered diverse responsibilities:**

- program evaluation, planning, development	- needs assessment
- resource allocation (budgets / personnel)	- administrative management
- disease surveillance reporting system	- statistical analyses / reporting
- sentinel physician reporting system	- staff compliance
- employee training & performance evaluation	- resource utilization
- task force participation (local / regional)	- administrative management

- Dedicated extensive time and energy in **conducting ongoing analyses to evaluate the efficiency, quality, and productivity of Department.** Designed numerous process improvement procedures and communications systems resulting in:

  - Indian Shores becoming the first rural region to completely capture communicable disease and rabies data and generate surveillance reports.
  - over 750 physicians, laboratory personnel, and health departments in 23 counties receiving real-time information on communicable disease incidences.
  - the formation of a "sentinel physicians" alliance throughout the 27 county region which increased physicians reporting of communicable diseases by 200%.

AIDS Surveillance Representative (4/87-4/90)

- **Achieved a regional interview rate of 95% on new HIV patients (a 300% increase over state wide average).** Designed a new surveillance methodology which involved physician consent.
- **Served on several key task forces:**
  - Member: AIDS Centers of Excellence Subcommittee which developed eligibility criteria for designation as a Center of Excellence
  - Epidemiologist: Regional HIV Community Planning Group
  - Member: Consortium of Public Health Advisors, East Coast Chapter

Disease Intervention Specialist (2/86-4/87)

SELECTED ACHIEVEMENTS (continued)

SMITH COUNTY HEALTH DEPARTMENT, Jacksonville, Florida
Nutritionist / Nutrition Education Coordinator (2/79-2/86)

- **Planned, organized, and evaluated nutritional component of county wide health services.** Prepared statistical reports based on findings and available sources.
- Performed nutritional assessments, certification, and health education for HealthWatch Outreach Program which served a caseload of **1,930 patients.**
- **Awarded Commissioner's Distinguished Service Award** for program leadership in HealthWatch Outreach Campaign resulting in a 55% caseload increase in first year of project's initiation.
- **Directed the effectiveness of regional and community health care services** and programming which involved project leadership in:
  - public health surveillance / assessment
  - Nutritional Quality Assurance
  - public health problems & risk evaluation
  - community public health education
  - health issue prioritization & intervention
  - cholesterol screening
  - statistical data compilation
  - public awareness presentations
  - state task force participation
  - professional staff training
- **Communicated via media (print / broadcast) and public forums on health care:**
  - heart disease & coronary wellness
  - weight management & myths
  - food purchasing & budgeting for well care
  - cholesterol & nutrition link
  - healthy food preparation
  - lifestyle changes for wellness

FIELD TRAINING
- Epidemiology in Action: Centers for Disease Control (CDC) (two week course in Atlanta)
- Introduction to Sexually-Transmitted Disease Intervention: CDC (two week course)
- Vaccine Preventable Diseases: CDC
- Continuous Quality Improvement
- Completed: State of Tennessee Supervisor Training
- Interaction Management

AFFILIATIONS
- Florida Public Health Association
- President (two years): Association for Practitioners in Infection Control (APIC) the local chapter of national organization

Susan B. Stephens, M.D.

1255 West Shore Avenue
Lunenburg, MA 01246
Available for Relocation

Voice Mail: 508-582-0000
Facsimile: 508-583-1000
Email: susan@mit.edu

QUALIFICATIONS

PHYSICIAN EXECUTIVE qualified for senior-level management opportunities where strengths in strategic planning, development, and visionary leadership will promote high-growth business ventures. Highlights:

⇒ **Market-Driven Executive** -- Initiated business re-engineering in a 38-physician practice to address the emerging commercialization of medicine in early 1990's; cut costs through innovative cost-containment programs; brought consensus among divergent interests during transition to market-focused paradigm.

⇒ **Academic Qualifications** -- Harvard Executive MBA graduate with management and financial skills backed by clinical competence of 15+ years of practice as a board-certified internist and anesthesiologist. Substantial experience in emergency services, aeromedical evacuation, and special operations.

⇒ **International Orientation** -- Advanced the accessibility of health care in third world nations through commitment to international healthcare organizations (eight trips to Malaysia, Korea, and India as team chief and service as program director for an overseas teaching hospital).

⇒ **White House Fellowship** -- Regional finalist among highly competitive candidate list of 800; sought to address global health care issues (special project: development of counter-strategies for medical terrorism).

PROFESSIONAL EXPERIENCE

HEALTHCARE MANAGEMENT   Partner, Medical Consultants, Boston, MA   1/93-Pres.
                            Partner, Medical Group, Boston, MA   1/90-12/93

Provide executive leadership as managing partner of physician group generating $18 million in annual revenue. Lead through hands-on involvement in financial affairs, professional/support staff administration, service planning, patient care, quality improvement, peer review, and credentialing. Well-versed in managed-care operations and negotiation of managed care/capitation contracts. Provide comprehensive anesthesia services and internal medicine consultations for Boston Memorial and other locations.

Accomplishments:

➢ Led practice through successful transition to thrive in a managed-care environment utilizing new market-driven, community-oriented patient care model.
➢ Delivered significant savings through development of operational enhancements and strategic alliances.
➢ Consultant for critical start-up of innovative home pain management therapy service.
➢ Resolved sensitive physician relations issues on Medical Staff Quality Council for 300-bed hospital.
➢ Mentored new physicians, helping to grow practice by 30%.
➢ Researched and implemented computerized digital technology for cellular, paging, and voice mail services.

OPERATIONS MANAGEMENT   Chief of Medicine, Virginia Military Organization   1989-Pres.

Plan and direct medical services to ensure health and combat readiness of 72 aircrew and over 1,500 ground personnel. Liaison between flying squadron and medical services. Participate regularly in flying missions including active duty deployments and mission qualification in RF4-C, a supersonic fighter aircraft. Directly supervise 25 officers and enlisted personnel. Additionally accountable for public health and safety, bio-environmental engineering, and occupational health issues.

◆ continued ◆

Accomplishments:

➤ Selected for fast-track promotion to rank of Major and Lt. Colonel.
➤ Designed and implemented innovative flying safety and emergency medical training programs.
➤ Recipient of two Air Force Achievement Medals, Air Force Outstanding Unit Award, Armed Forces Reserve Medal, and National Defense Service Medal.
➤ Authored 100-pg guide to human factors and physiological stress in flying advanced fighter aircraft, providing flight surgeon support for the zero mishap record during transition to F-16 aircraft.
➤ Formerly served as Chief of Clinical Services; Commander for Squadron Medical Element; and General Medical Officer.

Prior Experience:

➤ Clinical Faculty, Department of Internal Medicine, Boston Medical Center   1980-1982
➤ Attending Physician, Emergency Dept., New Bedford County Medical Center   1979-1980
➤ Medical Director, Medical Clinic   1978-1979

EDUCATION

M.B.A., Management -- Harvard School of Graduate Business   1994-1996
Residency in Anesthesiology -- Boston Medical Center, Boston, MA   1983-1986
Residency in Internal Medicine -- Boston Medical Center, Boston, MA   1979-1981
M.D. -- San Francisco State University School of Medicine, San Francisco, CA   1978
B.S. Degree, Biology (cum laude) -- Arizona State University, Tempe   1973

CERTIFICATION, LICENSURE

Diplomate -- National Board of Medical Examiners
Diplomate -- American Board of Internal Medicine
Diplomate -- American Board of Anesthesiology
Flight Surgeon -- USAF School of Aerospace Medicine
Medical Licensure -- Massachusetts, Arizona, New York

AFFILIATIONS

American College of Physician Executives
Aerospace Medical Association
American Society of Pathologists
Massachusetts Society of Pathologists
Undersea and Hyperbaric Medical Society
American Medical Association

PROFESSIONAL APPOINTMENTS

Utilization Review Committee -- Boston Medical Center
Medical Staff Quality Council -- Boston Medical Center
Chair, Department of Pathology -- Children's Hospital
District Director and Board of Directors -- Massachusetts Society of Pathologists

ADDITIONAL DATA

Commercial Pilot
Concert Violinist
Conversant in Spanish, French, and Italian

ALICE M. BROWN

11 Old Town Road • Summerville, Georgia 30000 • (770) 979-9999

MEDICAL LABORATORY TECHNICIAN
Hematology / Chemistries / Drug Testing / Blood Gases / Urinalysis
Coagulation / Blood Banking / Phlebotomy / Parasitology
with focus in Microbiology

SUMMARY OF QUALIFICATIONS

Proven and verifiable record of consistent achievement and professional growth in the field of medical technology with expertise in microbiology. Recognized for *"outstanding performance"* and administration of *"excellently organized and proficient bacteriology section."* Analytical, detail-oriented, organized, accurate, flexible, and committed.

Certified Medical Laboratory Technician
Certified Technologist in Microbiology
Georgia Department of Human Resources

Certified Laboratory Scientist in Microbiology
National Certification Agency

Certified Clinical Laboratory Assistant
ASCP

Experienced with multiple test procedures:

Urinalysis	Chemistries	Mono Spot
Toxicology	Coagulation	RPR
Therapeutic Drug	Blood Banking	Serum and Urine Pregnancy
Blood Gases	Hematology	Parasitology
Phlebotomy	Sickle Cell	TB Processing

EXPERIENCE

SUMMERVILLE HOSPITAL, Summerville, Georgia   1982 to Present

Clinical Laboratory Scientist in Microbiology Department
Medical Laboratory Technician (simultaneous assignment)
- Composed and compiled Microbiology Procedures Manual for origination of Microbiology Department at Summerville Hospital. Maintain updated manual.
- Manage all day-to-day operations including inventory control and acquisition of testing identification systems.
- Inoculate and evaluate plates for significance. Identify pathogens (anaerobes and aerobes); perform sensitivity testing when necessary.
- Perform Medical Laboratory Technician responsibilities regularly in various departments of the lab.
- Adhere to all CLIA guidelines and procedures to ensure quality control is maintained.

EXPERIENCE *(Continued)*

WINTER CITY MEDICAL CENTER, Seasonal, Georgia   1972 to 1981
      formerly Autumn General Hospital
  Staff Technologist, Microbiology Department, 1977 to 1981
  Certified Laboratory Assistant, 1972 to 1977

AUTUMN GENERAL HOSPITAL, Seasonal, Georgia   1971 to 1972
  Certified Laboratory Assistant, 1971 to 1972
  Laboratory Aide, 1971 (Part-time)

AFFILIATION

American Society of Clinical Pathologists (ASCP)

EDUCATION

SUMMERVILLE COMMUNITY COLLEGE, Summerville, Georgia
  Associate's Degree in Science, 1975

  Medical Laboratory Assistant Diploma, 1972

1234 Twisty Hill Road
Somewhere, AZ 85555
Voice: 555.555.5555
Fax: 555.555.4444

ANNE EXAMPLE, R. D. H.

PROFILE

➤ Registered Dental Hygienist with excellent credentials and more than twenty years experience
➤ Flexible. Fit in well with many types of office environments
➤ Dedicated professional with compassionate and caring attitude
➤ Skilled in working with a variety of people and all age levels
➤ Committed to excellence in job performance
➤ Display willingness to develop continually evolving skills to maximum efficiency
➤ Utilize solid organizational, work and time management skills
➤ Enthusiastic, highly-motivated and resourceful
➤ Excellent oral and written communication skills
➤ Team player

PROFESSIONAL ACHIEVEMENTS

➤ Invented device to assist in diagnosis and treatment of oral pathogens (U.S. Patent Pending)
➤ Proficient in the diagnosis and prognosis, follow-up and overall management of periodontal disease with root planing and curettage technique
➤ Creates and implements programs for individual oral hygiene.
➤ Skilled at intra-oral periodontal camera. PSR charting utilizes job specific computer software
➤ Trained to implement Nitrous Oxide sedation
➤ Promotes total oral health including microbiological research into tongue and throat organisms
➤ Provides education and OHI on proper usage of tools for maximum oral health in accordance with patients' needs and capabilities

CLINICAL EMPLOYMENT SUMMARY

1997 to present	Dr. Mark Nagao	Somewhere, AZ
1995 to 1997	Dr. Richard Nelg	Anywhere, AZ
1995 to present	Dr. Michael Cleary (On call)	Somewhere, AZ
	Registered Hygenist Service	There, AZ
1992 to 1994	Dr. Ralph Sperliner	Masillon, OH
1991 to 1994	Dr. Doug Rolf	Wooster, OH
1990 to 1991	Dr. Craig Beth	Anywhere, AZ
	Dr. Philip Lester	Anywhere, AZ
	Dr. Ralph Werner, Periodontist	Anywhere, AZ
1985 to 1989	Dr. Richard Avery	Somewhere, AZ
	Dr. Michael Smythe	Somewhere, AZ
1983 to 1985	Northern Dental Health Center	Somewhere, AZ
1980 to 1983	Independent Contracting and Temporary Services	Anchorage, AK

EDUCATION

ANYWHERE COLLEGE OF DENTAL HYGIENE, 1975   Anywhere, AZ

CERTIFICATIONS AND LICENSURE

Council of National Board of Dental Examiners
Arizona State Dental Board
Local Anesthesia Certification

PROFESSIONAL AFFILIATIONS

American Dental Hygienist Association
Arizona Dental Hygiene Association
Central Arizona Hygiene Association
The Western Society of Periodontology

ANIBAL ROMEO

95 Smith Avenue
Mount Kisco, NY 10549
(914) 241-1998

SOUS CHEF

Specializing in American Fine-Dining Cuisine
Dynamic, Results-Oriented & Team Spirited

Over ten years of professional cooking and kitchen management experience.   Exemplify leadership qualities and professionalism, backed by a consistent, verifiable record of achievement.

SUMMARY OF QUALIFICATIONS

- ✓ Extensive experience in large scale restaurant and catering operations.
- ✓ Comprehensive training in all phases of culinary preparation.
- ✓ Strong front of the house and back of the house expertise.
- ✓ Dedication to professionalism and quality, while keeping an eye on costs.
- ✓ Excellent mastery of classic culinary techniques, emphasizing French and American cuisine.
- ✓ Demonstrated capacity in preparing a wide variety of beef, fish, poultry, and vegetable dishes.

AREAS OF EXPERTISE

- ◆ Demonstrated track record in having meals completed and served, as per specification, on time.
- ◆ Expertise in maximizing kitchen productivity and staff performance.
- ◆ Proven ability to "assemble staffing teams" that work to optimal levels, improving performance of the team effort.
- ◆ Possess strong purchasing and negotiation skills. Reconcile restaurant bookings with inventory-on-hand, to make appropriate purchases and obtain higher quality produce.

RAVE REVIEWS

- ◆ ... "It is not easy to match such refined cuisine with comparable desserts, but *Pastry Chef Anibal Romeo does so with great flair*."   Gannett Suburban Newspapers: Dining Out
- ◆ ... "Pastry Chef Anibal Romeo does Crabtree's proud ..."   Travelhost
- ◆ ... *"Anibal Romeo, the pastry chef, is a Merlin of his art. We've succumbed to his wizadry"*... The New York Times: Dining Out
- ◆ Recognized by management and guests alike, for producing a dessert that "*one develops an appreciation for the craftsmanship and artistry.*"

PROFESSIONAL TRAINING

INTERNATIONAL PASTRY ARTS, ELMSFORD, NY

Hotel and Restaurant Desserts taught by Albert Kumin (former White House chef)	1990
Customizing the Contemporary Dessert taught by Mike McCary	1988
Culinary Skills Development taught by Mike McCary	1988

EXPERIENCE
May 1987 -
Present

CRABTREE'S KITTLE HOUSE, Chappaqua, NY

Pastry Chef / Garde Manger for this four star establishment grossing $4 million per year.

- ◆ Coordinate banquets of up to 400 guests.
- ◆ Supervise preparation of all desserts; oversee all cold foods.
- ◆ Expedite and maintain a smooth, quick line, providing excellent training to assistants.
- ◆ Authorize purchasing of goods to maximize profitability and minimize wastage.
- ◆ Commended for changing Alsatian Cheese Cake recipe, receiving repeat requests and maintaining place on menu for over three years.
- ◆ Have become a highly valued authority in other areas and am counted on to provide input to future changes.
- ◆ As *Sous Chef* assist Chef in preparing vegetable, poultry, fish and beef dishes.

REFERENCES   Excellent References Will Be Furnished Upon Request

Chris Allen Dotson

1212 Central Place, Melbourne, Florida 32939   (407) 555-1212

The Passion

Established with the purpose of breathing new life
and creativity into culinary arts and hospitality.

The Imagination

As an artist, I have a belief in symphony of flavors, colors, textures,
and progressive styles.

The Expression

Focus on harmony between vision and target market by understanding guest
needs and desires. Utilize leadership techniques including Communication, Neuro
Linguistic Programming, Time Management, Team Building, and Conflict Resolution.
Ability to budget food and labor cost, perform menu design and layout, and
implement various organizational skills.

The Experience

- Over 18 years of experience in Culinary Arts and Hospitality.
- Extensive background including client consultation, demographics, food and labor costs, menu design, contracts, coordination with rental companies, bakers, hiring of staff, advertising, marketing, sales, food preparation, and display.
- Teaching experience as Assistant to European Chef for 30 to 45 students in Advanced Cooking. Also taught culinary class at Byron Park and performed culinary demonstrations for Classic Catering at various Napa Vineyards.
- Specialize in unique and creative dessert preparation.
- Extensive wine knowledge and wine appreciation courses.
- Ability to prepare and design a vast array of cuisines and specialty dishes.
- Experience in nutrition, dietary needs, kitchen safety and sanitation.

The Destiny

Welcome to experiencing new destinations, cultures, and cuisines.
Extensive background of domestic travel. Willing to relocate or travel
when opportunity arises.

The Achievement

- Collaboratively owned and operated Creative Palate, a catering company which received various write ups in newspapers including Contra Costa Times, The San Francisco Chronicle, and Examiner Social Scene, and also in Diablo Magazine.
- Donated 5% of annual profits to AIDS Project of Contra Costa.
- Chef de Cuisine for Diablo Arabian Association, Heartnite, and Casino Night for AIDS Project of Contra Costa. This included recruiting, food, linen, equipment, and volunteers, and organizing charity functions.
- Catered Wine Country Weddings, Hot Air Balloon rides, Army Nursing Association, Holy Names College, and Yale University Speaker functions, California School Employee Association and California Mosquito Abatement.
- Provided cooking and display assistance for AT&T Golf Tournament.
- Received $1000 Scholarship from San Francisco City College, 1988 to 1989.
- Honorary Member, Alpha Gamma Sigma, California Community Colleges.
- Member, San Francisco Food Professional Society, 1996.

The Education

Nutrition in Food Service-American Culinary Federation, San Ramon, CA, 05/91
Hotel and Restaurant Management-Diablo Valley College, Pleasant Hill, CA, 06/90
Accounting & Data Processing Certificates-Heald Business College, Walnut Creek, CA, 08/86
Cooking-Hiram G. Andrew Center, Johnstown, PA, 04/81
Food Service Certificate-Mahoning County Joint Vocational School, Canfield, OH, 05/79

The Work History

A.M. Sous Chef - Holiday Inn Oceanfront, Indialantic, FL, 06/95 to Present
Executive Chef/Owner - Creative Palate, Walnut Creek, CA, 04/93 to 01/94
Chef - Byron Park, Walnut Creek, CA, 06/92 to 03/93
Dietary Cook - Manor Care, Inc., Walnut Creek, CA, 05/92 to 05/93
Chef - Classic Catering, Pleasant Hill, CA, 06/89 to 02/92
Chef (AT&T Golf Tournament) - Pebble Beach Lodge, Pebble Beach, CA, 01/90 to 02/90
Teacher Assistant, Adv. Cook/220 - Diablo Valley College, Pleasant Hill, CA, 08/89 to 12/89
Lead Breakfast/Lunch Cook - Hilton Hotel, Concord, CA, 11/88 to 06/89
Line Cook - Mel's The Original, Walnut Creek, CA, 08/87 to 09/88
Kitchen/Dining Room Manager - Papa Charlies-Geno's, Concord, CA, 07/85 to 04/86

Jason Brunetti
23 Hillside Drive
Flemington, New Jersey 08822
(609) 934-8441

Summary

Increasing responsibilities in **Food Service Management.** My background includes training and practical applications in the following:

Food Preparation and Production.....Menu Development....Supervisory Management ....Human Resources.....Budgetary Responsibilities.....Profit and Loss.....Inventory Control.....Catering Supervision.....Merchandising.....Sales Building.......Customer Relations and Follow up Financial Reporting.....Accounts Receivable.....Forecasting.....Corporate Programs .....Quality Control.....Proper Food Sanitation Practices....Computers.

Experience

FOOD SERVICE MANAGER
Harvard's, Plainfield, New Jersey   **1991-Present**

The company was formerly known as Classic Food Service. It was bought by Harvard's in 1993. I was consistently promoted throughout the takeovers to larger facilities with more supervisory responsibilities.

- Responsible for a 1,200 person restaurant facility in Somerville, New Jersey, at the Tower Center, corporate headquarters for Federal Atlantic Bank and Highland Securities.

- Instrumental in obtaining Lucent Technologies as our company's largest client in New Jersey. Lucent Technologies switched from a competitor after 30 years. I personally set up and implemented the tour of our Somerville facility. Harvard's was awarded two new facilities with an estimated $3.5 million in sales.

- Supervise one chef, one sous chef, two food service attendants, one utility employee and two cashiers.

- Manage the daily operations of breakfast and lunch for corporate employees. Menu encompasses fresh fruit salad, bagel bar with ten different types of spreads, breakfast to order, and fresh-baked goods. Monitor quality control and time management. Increased repeat clientele through the use of quality control methods and interesting, creative menus.

- Prepare one entree, a grilled special, an upscale deli special, and a healthy offering. (low calorie, low fat). Offer display/cooking pasta bars. Forecast customer trends and plan accordingly. Create point of sales merchandise displays; work with corporate programs and branding concepts.

- Consistently exceed bottom-line profits every year. Monitor sales, customer accounts, and check averages. Administer billing with outside catering functions. Responsible for collections and balancing account invoices.

- Direct catering for up to 500 people. Duties include supervising staff, planning and pricing menus and working with corporate clients. Instrumental in facilitating excellent customer relations to fulfill all clients demands.

FOOD SERVICE MANAGER
Classic Food Service (1992-1993)

- Responsible for an 800-person restaurant facility at the corporate headquarters of Metropolitan Life Insurance and Metro Securities. The office park was located in Parsippany, New Jersey.

- Stabilize the client relationships. Previously, the facility had five managers within one year. Maintained a subsidized location while reporting profits over and above corporate goals.

- Introduced a new signage program to brighten up the facility and direct the flow of customers to key stations.

CHEF MANAGER
Classic Food Service (1991-1992)

- Responsible for a 400 person restaurant facility at the Forrestal Center, located in the Route 1 Princeton Corridor, West Windsor, New Jersey.

- Featured in an article in *Restaurant News* with regards complimenting the quality of our food and the diversity of our menu.

- Planned a theme catering luncheon for 1,500 people. Gained initial experience in catering production.

SOUS CHEF
Diamond Lilly's (1990-1991)

- Prepared breakfast and lunch for 400 people at the Forrestal Center, on Route 1, in the Princeton Corridor. Responsible for purchasing food and supplies and practicing proper sanitation procedures.

- Promoted to manager with only one year of experience in the company. Gained experience in human resourses, accounting, and general food service management.

Additional Employment

CHEF
Enzo's Italian Restaurant   1985-1990

- Prepared dinners and specialty dishes from scratch. Learned advanced cooking skills. Responsible for quality and portion control. Purchased food and kitchen supplies.

Foreign Language

- Working knowledge of Spanish

Certifications

- Certified through the National Restaurant Association
- Certified SERVSAFE Food Protection Manager

Continuing Professional Development

- Train the Trainer; Front Line Leadership; AIDS in the Workplace

DONALD BASS
92 Belcher Road • New City, New Jersey 07022
(908) 555-5555

HOSPITALITY / FOOD SERVICE MANAGEMENT

Value Offered:
- Increase sales utilizing both innovative and common-sense marketing strategies.
- Target and cultivate emerging markets while expanding existing client base.
- Effectively motivate staff to achieve sales objectives by improving performance and customer satisfaction levels.

High-performance, proactive management professional with expertise in process and productivity improvement, administration, human resources, training and development and creative business channeling. Excellent team building and interpersonal relations skills.

PROFESSIONAL EXPERIENCE

Sales Representative / Sales Supervisor (1992 - present)
MASTER WINES AND LIQUORS, Gap, PA
(Currently the largest full-service wholesale liquor and wine distributor in Pennsylvania, supplying restaurants, bars/pubs, packaged goods stores and service organizations. Recruited to develop and maintain long-term account relationships in northern Pennsylvania territory. Supervised staff of 15 account representatives serving entire state.)
- Increased sales from $325,000 to over $1 million in 2½ years.
- Identify, secure and maintain key accounts in a highly competitive market.
- Maintain high level of customer satisfaction utilizing focused conflict resolution methods.
- Perform comparative account analyses to meet or exceed established sales quotas.
- Develop and implement directed marketing programs for targeted products.

Manager (1988 - 1992)
MACINTIRE'S SALOON, Long Valley, NJ
(Directed the daily operations of a neighborhood pub/restaurant including hiring, training and scheduling staff; ordering food, liquor and supplies; financial/accounting responsibility; inventory/portion control.)
- Jumpstarted weekend-only profitability to develop seven-night-a-week thriving business, through well planned and executed creative promotional techniques.
- Designed and implemented successful performance-based incentive programs resulting in increased customer satisfaction and 20% increase in revenue within 1 month.
- Introduced innovative menu revisions delivering increased sales and profitability.

EDUCATION

Bachelor of Science, Leisure Services Management (1973)
EAST STROUDSBURG UNIVERSITY, East Stroudsburg, PA

MATTHEW LANDREW

123 Hotel Circle
Convention City, Arizona 55555

Voice: 555.555.5555
Data: 555.555.5555

PROFILE

Proven record in executive, operations, and program management, staff supervision, customer service, marketing and sales. Extensive hands-on experience in virtually every area from maintenance to human resources to front desk. Progressed through the ranks to management positions and principal in entrepreneurial endeavor.

HOSPITALITY

- Twelve years industry experience.
- Responsible for daily audit, balancing of all revenue outlets, track expenditures within budgeted guidelines.
- Provides daily and monthly profit reports.
- Maintains accurate postings of guests' room charges, taxes and incidental charges.

MANAGEMENT AND ADMINISTRATION

- Effectively plans projects, assesses tasks involved, makes manpower assignments, and provides scheduling, training and assistance.
- Strong interpersonal skills are evident in the ability to interface with customers, colleagues and vendors.
- Supervised up to 60 hospitality personnel in all aspects of motel operations.
- Manages accounts payable, receivables, collections and payroll.
- Tracks expenditures within budgeted guidelines. Provides daily and monthly reports to owners.

MAINTENANCE AND TROUBLESHOOTING

- Ability to evaluate and troubleshoot utilizing problem solving capabilities.
- Knowledge of operating procedures and equipment to accomplish repairs quickly and efficiently.
- Performs quality assurance inspections of rooms, common areas and grounds. Ensures all facilities were safe, clean and well maintained.

CUSTOMER SERVICE AND SALES

- Develops rapport and builds relationships with customers through attention to detail in defining needs and providing service and solutions.
- Coordinates corporate and group reservations, accommodations and conference rooms.

CAREER EXPERIENCE

MANAGER, 77 rooms	Mountain View, Convention City, AZ	1996 to current
PRINCIPAL (1/3 interest), 43 rooms	Shilo Inn, Anywhere, AZ	1994 to 1996
MANAGER, 103 rooms	Double Tree, Somewhere, AZ	1993 to 1994
MANAGER, 77 rooms	Comfort Inn, Desert, AZ	1991 to 1993
PRINCIPAL (1/3 interest), 78 rooms	Econolodge, Durango, CO	1990 to 1991
MANAGER, 24 rooms	Rodeway Inn, Somewhere, AZ	1989 to 1990
MANAGER, 24 rooms	Sleep Inn, Desert, AZ	1987 to 1989
MANAGER, 24 rooms	Twiggs Motel, Somewhere, AZ	1985 to 1987

AFFILIATIONS

Convention City Chamber of Commerce
Asian-American Hotel-Motel Association

PROFESSIONAL DEVELOPMENT

Seminars and Training Sessions in Hotel, Motel Management, Business Practices and Customer Service sponsored by Econolodge and Comfort Inns, among others

MANAGEMENT   HOSPITALITY   OPERATIONS

SUSAN CHINSANTHAL, CHA

529 Beacon Avenue -- Naples, New York 10021
(212) 234-2356

HOTEL / RESORT MANAGEMENT

Management Development ♦ Sales & Marketing ♦ Operations ♦ Public Relations ♦ Corporate Image Development

Corporate Policy Development ♦ Guest Services ♦ Advertising & Promotions ♦ Key Account Management ♦ Event Planning

Certified Hotel Administrator with distinguished career in the profitable management of multi-million dollar hotel operations. Successful background in research and development of new venture properties. Equally competent in impacting bottom-line profit performance of existing operations through efficiency improvements, service enhancements and cost reductions. Persuasive promoter, motivator, negotiator and closer.

PROFESSIONAL EXPERIENCE

GENERAL MANAGER / V.P., RESEARCH & DEVELOPMENT -- Beverly Place, New York, New York (1984-Present)

Manage profit performance of 4-diamond, 200-room hotel with convention facilities and full-service restaurant. Supervise department directors for reservations, housekeeping, maintenance, catering, banquet and restaurant operations with total staff of 120. Indirectly responsible for Director of Sales and sales team for related properties. Promoted from Catering Manager to General Manager in just two years.

Management / Operations:

- ♦ Quadrupled gross room revenues from $1.1 million to $4.6 million.
- ♦ Profoundly impacted net operating profit, with an increase from 13.7% to 40.5%.
- ♦ Initiated departmental budgeting and expense controls (subsequently implemented company-wide).
- ♦ Awarded "Best of the Region" from New York Restaurant Association for hotel, restaurant and banquet facilities.

Public Relations / Promotions:

- ♦ Established hotel as leading corporate, convention and visitor's hotel through image enhancement and new market development.
- ♦ Collaborated with Sales and Marketing on development of marketing plan that achieved $5 million in total room and F&B revenues.
- ♦ Built largest frequent traveler program and longest average guest stay among area hotels.
- ♦ Developed concept for gala ball to benefit American Heart Assoc., now a prestigious event which kicks-off annual telethon locally.

Image Development:

- ♦ Promoted ideology of "a hotel built for guests, not staff."
- ♦ Renovated property including accountability for design concept and construction management of $650,000 project.
- ♦ Directed the research and development of company's profitable new limited service property.

Human Resources Development / Training:

- ♦ Brought leadership and cohesion to operation in need of improved interdepartmental communications and employee morale.
- ♦ Implemented team building program which reduced housekeeping and front desk turnover 27%.
- ♦ Trained department managers in budget process, operations and guest services.

DIRECTOR OF MARKETING -- Miami Chamber of Commerce (1983-1984)

Organized conference featuring prominent keynote speaker (Vice President George Bush). Coordinated annual Economic Development Summit.

EDUCATION, AFFILIATIONS

CERTIFIED HOTEL ADMINISTRATOR -- Educational Institute of the American Hotel/Motel Association

BACHELOR OF ARTS DEGREE, LIBERAL ARTS -- University of Florida, Miami

American Business Women's Association; State Hospitality Association; Hotel/Motel Association (past Vice President); Chamber of Commerce; Lions Club (Vice President); State Restaurant Association; Soroptimists; Toastmasters International

MARK SHUSTER
1072 Whipple Lane • Milpitas CA 95000
(408) 555-5555

Highly motivated self-starter with strengths in:
- *Business development* • *Marketing/sales* • *Customer retention* • *Staff training/development*

QUALIFICATIONS:
- Six years of successful experience involving development, retention and re-establishment of positive customer relationships in a competitive industry.
- Team-building, leadership and motivational abilities; goal-oriented attitude.
- Proven interpersonal, organization/planning and problem-solving skills.
- Effective performance under pressure; strong decision-making and multi-task capabilities.

ACCOMPLISHMENT HIGHLIGHTS:
- Successfully turned around 3 poorly performing locations; increased profit at latest unit from -2.4% to 13.1% within 6 months by setting up "partnerships" with health clubs, delivering samples to local businesses, and utilizing other business development/marketing techniques.
- Built operating income at one location from 2.6% to 18.6% and increased sales 12.5%.
- Hired, recruited and trained 50 managers in 1996; developed management training program to support 150% growth.
- Earned multiple awards: Top Shoppers scores, 1996; Manager of the Year, 1994; Pioneer Manager (1 of 3 managers awarded 10,000 shares of stock).

EXPERIENCE:

Luna Restaurants, Inc., Mountain View, CA   1991-Present
CORPORATE TRAINER/GENERAL MANAGER (1995-Present)
Overall responsibility for P&L/profitability of locations supervised, employee recruitment/training, sales/marketing activities, and customer service.
- Track employee turnover in conjunction with training program to identify reasons for losing employees and determine appropriate corrective actions.
- Created materials for training program, including manuals, tests and tracking forms.
- Supervised 3 training managers and training units (1996-1997).

RESTAURANT MANAGER (1993-1995)
- Maintained P&L responsibility, including reconciliation and cost controls.
- Hired, trained and supervised restaurant staff to ensure outstanding customer service.
- Opened 3 restaurant locations as manager, which included coordinating with general contracting firm to facilitate arrangements and ordering all initial supplies/inventory.

ASSISTANT MANAGER (1991-1993)
- Operated unit during manager's absence; trained and supervised staff.
- Opened/closed unit and managed cash handling, inventory, ordering and receiving functions.
- Joined company when it had only 1 restaurant location and participated actively in expanding business to 52 locations.

EDUCATION/PROFESSIONAL DEVELOPMENT:
- Associate of Arts in Business, De Anza College, Cupertino, CA, 1991
- Dale Carnegie Management Courses: selected from 14 managers to attend

EDWARD C. SHARP
433 Campton, Bloomfield Hills, Michigan 48302 • (313) 555-3412

HUMAN RESOURCES EXECUTIVE

Manufacturing . . .Multi-Facility Operations . . .Union & Non Union Workforces

Senior-level HR executive with a strong record of achievement with Fortune 500 manufacturers. Expert in implementing Human Resources policies that deliver bottom-line results. Established first-time HR policies following start-ups and mergers. Chief spokesperson for numerous labor agreements. Established greenfield non-union operating unit. High-energy internal consultant who understands relationship between employee relations and profits. Master's degree in Human Resources Development.

- Preventive Labor Relations Strategies
- Team Building
- ISO / QS 9000
- Organizational Development
- Training
- HRIS Technology
- Strategic Planning

- Risk Management
- Compensation / Benefits
- Merger Reorganization
- Recruitment
- Motivating / Managing Performance
- OSHA - Safety
- Negotiation

RECENT ACCOMPLISHMENTS

- Introduced employee financial incentives that improved productivity, reduced absenteeism, and resulted in a 15% increase in gross profits.

- Designed and implemented an innovative job certification and pay-for-skills system to support JIT synchronous manufacturing, Continuous Improvement, Employee Involvement, and Team Building management philosophies. Replaced an outdated piece-rate system and autocratic style of management.

- Led company to readiness for ISO/QS 9001 certification nine months ahead of projected schedule. Served as lead internal auditor, management representative, and author of the company's quality procedures. Developed problem-solving technique based on ISO.

- Successfully obtained $239,000 in state training funds for 1997 and 1998.

- Key player in contract negotiations resulting in wage increases of less than 4% on a four-year average. Experience includes negotiation with Teamsters, UAW, and AFL-CIO. Successful in maintaining non-union environment at all non-unionized facilities.

- Reduced turnover for entry-level positions from 67% to 30% within first two years as HR Director by training front-line supervisors in problem-solving and decision-making.

- No EEO or OSHA complaints in the last four years as HR Director. Resolved numerous unresolved discrimination charges from previous management.

- Reduced costs of salary and benefits by $240,000 by consolidating functions following a merger.

- Redesigned medical benefits plan, which reduced costs by more than $100,000 while maintaining existing level of benefits. The plan also reduced employee's costs while increasing flexibility.

EXPERIENCE

Director of Human Resources   INDUSTRIAL STEEL, INC., Detroit, Michigan   1993-Present
Steel manufacturer with 1200 employees and six plants nationwide.

Recruited to direct the start-up of a complete HR function in conjunction with change of management. Manage Human Resources and Quality Assurance departments. Spearheaded transition from autocratic management style to team concept. Key member of senior management team developing strategic plan and policies for a privately-held company with multiple facilities in the U.S. Implemented new programs in training, Organizational Development, compensation, benefits, and employee relations. Leader in ISO Certification.

Director of Human Resources   PARKMAN BROTHERS, Livonia, Michigan   1988-1993
650 employee, multi-plant manufacturer of automotive components.

Directed all Human Resource functions. Member of Divisional Board of Directors and Strategic Planning Team. Relocated company to a new facility in the Southeast and screened all-new workforce. Implemented team concept philosophy.

Personnel Director   HARRISON FOODS, Chicago, Illinois   1984-1988

Recruited for start-up of a new facility in Chicago. Successfully negotiated many challenging union contracts while maintaining full production capacity.

Human Resources Manager   A.B HANFORD, Troy, Michigan   1982-1984

Developed a successful minority hiring program. Defeated union organization drive. Instituted Human Resources policies, procedures, and compensation systems.

EDUCATION

Master of Human Resources Development   ADRIAN COLLEGE, Adrian, Michigan

B.S., Human Resources / Industrial Relations   UNIVERSITY OF DETROIT, Detroit, Michigan

Institute of Labor and Industrial Relations   UNIVERSITY OF MICHIGAN, Ann Arbor, Michigan

Applied Management and Technology Center   WAYNE STATE UNIVERSITY, Detroit, Michigan

MISC. PROFESSIONAL ACTIVITIES

Public Speaking: Speak to local high schools on Career Day;
and make presentations to the Wayne County Chamber of Commerce.

Member of Adrian College "Goals 2000" Committee.

Languages: Speak fluent French.

GEORGE M. DURST

3165 Coral Palm Way   **[H] (305) 555-3781**
Miami Shores, FL 33158   **[W] (305) 555-6987**

HIGH-IMPACT HUMAN RESOURCES EXECUTIVE
Market-driven • Benchmarking Generalist • International Entrepreneur
M & A • Joint Ventures • Outsourcing • Manufacturing • Utilities • Consumer Goods

Energetic and highly experienced U.S. and Latin American innovator with extensive experience in offshore and start-up environments. A creator, strategic analyst and implementer of leading-edge policies and interventions. In-depth command of multilingual/multicultural environments. Able to conceive and achieve regional commercial development programs. Highly regarded Adjunct Professor in university MIBA Program. Special expertise in:

➢ Compensation/Bonus Plans	➢ Executive Recruiting, Selection & Coaching
➢ Benefits Administration	➢ Organizational/Process Consulting
➢ Quality Improvement (TQM)	➢ Succession Planning/Repatriation
➢ Management & Administration	➢ Training, Development & Delivery
➢ Third Party Distribution Systems	➢ Psychometric Testing, Assessment

Added expertise in: Organizational Development, Team Building, Performance Management, 360° Feedback, and High Potential/Leadership Development & Cross-Training.

PROFESSIONAL HISTORY

INTERNATIONAL BEVERAGE, INC., Miami, FL   1995 - Present
Subsidiary of **Harp PLC**, London FTSE-listed manufacturer & distributor of branded spirits, with sales of US$6.7B (e.g., Crown Royal, Gordon's, Slivovits, Dewars, variety of single malts, Bourbons, rum, etc.).

Organization Development Manager (Executive), Latin America
Oversee Executive/Management development and training, performance management, regional manpower strategy and recruiting, succession planning, internal resourcing, international transfers and placements, organizational consulting at regional level and direction of H.R. staff for in-market operating companies. Present quarterly reports on regional HR strategies and implementation.

> ➢ Developed and implemented sales and marketing training for Latin America that generated an annual increase of 10% in trading profits for the region.

> ➢ Created and effected a university-based Management Development program that built a consistent corporate culture.

> ➢ Recruited expatriate marketing and sales directors for the Mexican, Uruguayan and Brazilian markets and a key account manager for parallel trade channels.

> ➢ Developed HR policies and foundation in Uruguay that backed joint venture formation; created HR policies for corporate mergers for impacted Latin American businesses.

DOW CHEMICAL COMPANY, Cape Coral, FL   1990 - 1995
A $4.9B specialty chemical company listed on the NYSE.

Training Manager, Latin American Region
Directed the company's organizational effectiveness function in Latin America, including training and development. Implemented and maintained best-in-class training and development capabilities for the region.

> ➢ Increased sales by 50% over two years while maintaining costs at 1994 levels; facilitated the executive re-engineering team; restructured sales and distribution functions, and reduced plant staffing levels based on world-wide best practices formula.

> Introduced an integrated Performance Management program with a revised incentive-based compensation system, to produce a performance-driven evaluation system that tied compensation to team performance.

> Introduced 360° Leadership Feedback instruments for executives, managers and first line leaders, that effected a corporate culture change driven by newly-defined leadership competencies and roles.

> Identified, selected and assessed candidates for Fast Track Development program for regional marketing managers and commercial managers that increased pool availability of trained candidates for key manager positions.

WISCONSIN ELECTRIC AND POWER COMPANY, Green Bay, WI   1981 - 1990
NYSE-listed, 11,000 employee major US utility with other diversified holdings; owned by Columbia Power.

Manager of Quality and Productivity   1986-1990
Served as quality team facilitator, working with TQM teams from executive to plant floor levels to conduct Organizational Development intervention.

> Supervised 250 teams and generated total savings of approximately $350MM.

Director of Training and Development   1982-1986
Managed 15, a $1.2MM budget, project scheduling and operation of staff development activities.

Organizational Development Consultant   1981-1982
Conducted organizational analyses; designed functional layout for General Books/Accounts Payable/Financial Forecasting Departments.

UNIVERSITY OF WEST VIRGINIA, Lanark, WV   1979 - 1981

Associate Professor, Business and Government, General Faculty
Supervised staffing/supervision of instructors in statewide non-credit training programs. Headed training programs, workshops and seminars for business, industry, government and non-profit organizations.

MANAGEMENT CONSULTANT, Charlotte, North Carolina   1976 - 1979
Consulted in training and organizational development to textile machinery manufacturers, tool and die companies, textile manufacturers, hospitals and chemical manufacturers throughout North and South Carolina and Georgia.

CASTRO ASSOCIATES, Houston, Texas   1974 - 1976
Market Research Analyst

COLORADO TECHNOLOGICAL UNIVERSITY, Durango, Colorado   1970 - 1974
Assistant Professor of Modern Languages

EDUCATION

MBA, International Management, University of Dallas, Irving, TX   1976

University of Hamburg, West Germany
    Ph.D., French and Spanish   1970

    MA, Philosophy of Education   1967

    BA, Liberal Arts   1965

LANGUAGE PROFICIENCY

Fluent in: English, Spanish, German (native), French

Competency in: Portuguese, Italian

Stephanie N. Thornton

P.O. Box 45689   ❧   Oak Ridge, CA 23599   ❧   (609) 554-5655

OBJECTIVE

HOTEL MANAGEMENT — HUMAN RESOURCES

HIGHLIGHTS OF QUALIFICATIONS

More than 17 years of experience in management and personnel recruitment . . . Excellent organization and time management skills . . . Outstanding communication, interpersonal and public relations skills . . . Ability to function well in a progressive environment under stressful conditions . . . Highly self-motivated with innovative ideas and concepts for increasing employee morale and improving communications . . . Demonstrated ability to work effectively and congenially with employees at diverse levels . . . Results-oriented individual with the capacity to take on added responsibility . . . Computer operation to include Windows 95 and corporate software packages . . . Payroll . . . Budgeting . . . Marketing . . . Public Relations . . . Purchasing . . . Quality Control.

PROFESSIONAL EXPERIENCE

AMERICANA HOTELS, INC, Oak Ridge, CA   1980 - Present

Personnel Manager

Implement comprehensive knowledge of recruitment, screening and interviewing techniques in hiring quality management and operations personnel for corporation consisting of 36 hotels and 1,200 employees throughout California.

❖ Responsible for interviewing, hiring and terminating all management personnel.
❖ Plan and conduct training classes and seminars for operations and management staff.
❖ Develop and maintain personnel and management manuals, setting forth policies and procedures for all facets of corporation.
❖ Interpret and oversee implementation of all personnel policies; control administration of comprehensive employee benefit programs.
❖ Maintain EEO guidelines and ensure compliance with federal and state regulations.
❖ Implemented electronic processing of credit cards, saving the company approximately $500,000 over a period of one year.
❖ Incorporate creative motivation, excellent communication skills, problem solving abilities and team building concepts in developing cost effective measures and promoting quality operations.
❖ Extensive knowledge of OSHA regulations and compliance laws for hotel operations.
❖ Work directly with bookkeeping, payroll and customer service departments in the performance of daily operations.
❖ Plan and oversee the set up of new hotels to include working with contractors, scheduling on-site clean up and set up of furniture, hiring and training staff and supervising grand opening events.
❖ Honored as Employee of the Year 1985, 1989 and 1995.

Regional Manager

Ensured quality operations for six hotels in regional territory through direct supervision of management staff and implementation of corporate policies and procedures.

❖ Hired, trained and oversaw the performance of management staff.
❖ Worked with managers in properly training hotel personnel.
❖ Coordinated all remodeling and repairs.
❖ Performed evaluations on management staff and made recommendations to upper management.

EDUCATION

CALIFORNIA SCHOOL OF BUSINESS DEVELOPMENT, Falling Rock, CA
B.S. In Business Management

WILLIAM R. COPP

(904) 789-9996 • 1395 Voltaire Street • Deltona, Florida 32725

HUMAN RESOURCES / TRAINING & DEVELOPMENT PROFESSIONAL

- Talented HR Professional with excellent qualifications in the development and management of multi-discipline HR functions and affairs throughout large divisions worldwide.
- Excellent qualifications in personnel training, development and leadership programs.
- Consistently successful in the development of core efficiency initiatives to drive organizational change and performance improvements.
- Extremely successful in facilitating cooperative relationships among employees and supervisors.

QUALIFICATIONS SUMMARY

Human Resources Management
- Senior level management positions directing and leading HR operations through a direct reporting staff of 5 division managers and line staff of 19,000 HR employees.
- Manage strategic planning, logistics, and operations for a multicultural workforce worldwide.
- Strong administration skills in all HR generalist affairs including recruitment, selection, long-term manpower planning, benefits, claims administration, and employee services.

Organizational Development and Leadership
- Spearheaded organizational development initiatives incorporating quality of work-life improvements, participative leadership, employee empowerment, and process reengineering.
- Pioneered innovative change management programs focused on core efficiency and productivity improvements. Redefined staffing levels and logistics to increase efficiencies.
- Developed HR policies and procedures and authored comprehensive manuals at all levels.
- Authored articles for publication in organization-wide communication vehicles.

Staffing / Recruitment Management
- Analyzed, prepared and presented personnel forecasts to project long-term and immediate workforce demands.
- Led a massive workforce reengineering initiative to reassign and reclassify 8,000 employees within 2½ years.
- Managed recruitment, selection, placement, and training processes.
- Counseled managers in employee relations, performance management, appraisal process and disciplinary procedures within regulatory guidelines.

Compensation / Benefits Management
- Developed policy and directed administration of compensation and benefits programs through departmental supervisors.
- Oversaw and monitored bonus incentive and advancement programs.
- Created a competency-based performance analysis and appraisal system to identify top performers and facilitate fair progressive career movement.

Employee Relations / Services
- Improved and expanded employee relations initiatives through in-house Employee Assistance Programs and counseling programs.
- Managed expatriatiation, employee relocation, and travel logistics for employees and families.

170

Labor Relations Management

- Executed investigation and timely response into Congressional and Presidential inquiries providing interpretation of governmental laws and procedures.
- Wrote directives advising departmental managers of company policy regarding EEO, compensation and employee benefits. Effectively presented information to top management and public groups.

Training Programs / Management

- Directed an entire Educational Center, a staff of 9 faculty members and all educational programs for more than 750 students annually.
- Coordinated a curriculum consisting of Management Principles, Effective Communications Skills, Sexual Harassment, Total Quality Management and Leadership Training.
- Led development and implementation of in-house training programs within 10 individual business units for more than 350 employees. Developed and administered a $900,000 budget.

Public Relations

- Spoke to numerous corporate management groups, industry advisory boards, business groups, civic and community organizations regarding all phases of HR affairs.
- Developed and conducted numerous training programs, total quality management programs, leadership counseling, employee relations, and communications skills for corporations.

EMPLOYMENT HISTORY

UNITED STATES AIR FORCE – 1972 to 1997
Senior Master Sergeant, E8

TECHNOLOGY SKILLS

Experienced in utilization of mainframe-based HRIS
PC Literate in standard software applications

EDUCATION

Bachelor Of Science – Psychology Major / Education Minor – 1984
NORTHWESTERN PACIFIC UNIVERSITY

U.S. Air Force Courses (Relevant):	
Total Quality Management, 1993	USAF NCO Academy, 1983
Sexual Harassment, 1992	Career Advisor for the entire USAF, 1981
Deputy Director, 1991	USAF Leadership, 1976
USAF Senior NCO Academy, 1990	Technical Instructor, 1974
	Personnel Administration, 1972

RELEVANT AWARDS

Senior NCO of the Year, 1995	Commandant of the Year, 1989, 1990
Personnel Specialist, 1972, 1973, 1983	Instructor of the Year, 1974 to 1978
Career Advisor of the Year, 1981	

VOLUNTEER WORK / FUNDRAISERS

Red Cross, Muscular Dystrophy, Habitat for Humanity

Archie Bunker

704 Hauser Street • Indianapolis, Indiana 46220
(313) 555-1991 (office) • (313) 555-1992 (home) • (313) 555-1993 (fax)

Senior Organizational Effectiveness Executive
Multi-Industry Experience...Fortune 200 Companies...International Consulting

Demonstrated expertise in managing all aspects of large-scale organizational change. Especially skilled at developing powerful business strategies and aligning organizations, business processes, and HR functions to deliver world class standards of productivity, efficiency, and quality. Solid record of fast-track advancement in building high value-added organizational development and training functions that deliver tangible and measurable business results. Well-versed in leading-edge technologies that promote corporate growth, profitability and sustained organizational competitiveness.

Expertise includes conducting and managing:

Strategic Planning	Staff/Management Training	Team Development
Capability Assessment	Process Reengineering	Performance Measurement
Organization Redesign	Total Quality Management	Diversity

Career Highlights

ELI LILLY AND COMPANY, Indianapolis, Indiana   1995 to Present
(Global research-based pharmaceutical company with 29,000 employees in 156 countries and $7.3 billion in revenue)

Director of Organizational Effectiveness
Recruited to provide global leadership for a comprehensive corporate transformation process, requiring the integration of four different improvement groups into an effective consulting organization focused on strategic bottom-line performance. Manage a 30-person department with a $4 million operating budget. Report to Executive Director of HR.

- Co-created with the Strategic Planning Group, the company's first strategic planning and integrated change process, monitored by balanced scorecard measures.
- Co-authored with CEO the company's first-ever value statement, used as foundation for senior management training and implementation plans to bolster commitment of new value-based culture aligned to strategy.
- Oversaw, coordinated, and evaluated consulting activity for major process redesign projects:
  ⇒ Reduced product development cycle by more than 30%.
  ⇒ Redesigned the largest supply chain to reduce costs by $120 million.
  ⇒ Realigned sales/marketing processes contributing to the most successful new drug campaign in pharmaceutical history.
- Lead consultant to initial transition assessment of a $4 billion acquisition. Consultant to new president on complete restructuring, governance system setup, and executive teambuilding that stabilized and redirected critical acquisition.
- Strategically realigned and managed major corporate change efforts in the areas of TQM/Baldridge Assessments, Employee Attitude Surveys, Performance Management Systems, 360-degree Management Assessment, and Diversity.

AMOCO CORPORATION, Chicago, Illinois   1988 to 1995
(International natural gas and petroleum refining company with 41,000 employees and $33 billion in revenue)

Practice Area Leader for Organizational Capability, Architecture, and Assessment (1994 to 1995)
Directed the development of a new strategic organizational analysis process. Served as primary partner to the Strategic Planning Group to build a corporate-wide integrated planning system and consulting approach.

- Designed, documented, and trained internal consultants to facilitate the application of a consistent strategy format tied directly to corporate decisions.
- Facilitated multiple organizational capability assessments and action planing sessions with senior management.

AMOCO CORPORATION (cont.)
Manager of Organizational Development and Learning Systems (1992 to 1994)

Orchestrated the worldwide organizational development and training functions for a 14,000-employee exploration and production division. Managed multiple departments with a budget of $11.8 million. Partnered with Strategic Planning Group to direct full-scale, integrated change efforts in alignment with strategic objectives. Reported to the Vice President of HR. Third promotion in four years.

- Successfully implemented four reengineered business processes that saved $250 million annually.
- Redesigned executive management and committee processes that enhanced strategic thinking and decision making.
- Established processes that translated organization capabilities to competency profiles. Aligned strategic staffing, training, and performance management processes to ensure competency acquisition.
- Achieved "best-in-class" levels of organizational effectiveness survey results through successful implementation of major change efforts. Results increased an average of 25%.
- Created and implemented a learning organization strategy and served as corporate liaison to Peter Senge's Organizational Learning Center at MIT. Instituted company-wide high performance team building process.

Lead Organization Effectiveness Consultant (1990 to 1992)
Senior Organization Effectiveness Consultant (1989 to 1990)
Senior Corporate Training and Development Consultant (1988 to 1989)

Promoted twice in two years to build start-up organizational effectiveness and training capability. Consulted to senior management by designing and facilitating high-leverage change processes that enhance organizational effectiveness. Designed and implemented first organizational effectiveness survey; an employee involvement process; recognition and reward processes; performance management processes; and a career development process.

THE SIGNATURE GROUP, Schaumburg, Illinois   1985 to 1988
(Insurance and direct-market product company with 4,000 employees and profits of $78 million; subsidiary of Montgomery Ward)

Director of Service Quality and Training (1987 to 1988)
Corporate Training and Organization Development Manager (1986 to 1987)
Manager of Management Development (1985 to 1986)

Promoted rapidly to increasingly responsible departmental management positions with emphasis on implementing a comprehensive customer service strategy using improved training and staffing processes, management development, and redesigned business operations.

Additional experience (1976 to 1985): Directed campus activities and student union operations at three universities (Northwestern University, Mercer University, and University of Iowa). Provided OD consulting and held adjunct faculty positions teaching organizational and leadership development.

Professional Memberships

Organizational Development Network...Strategic Leadership Forum...World Future Society...The Human Resource Planning Society...Organizational Development Institute......American Society for Training and Development

Education

Advanced Degree, Organization Development/HR Management, Columbia University, New York, NY (1995)
Master of Arts Degree, College Student Personnel/Business Management, University of Iowa, Iowa City (1980)
Bachelor of Science Degree, Psychology, University of Iowa, Iowa City (1976)

YVONNE VAN TANGO

34 Camino Verde, Fallbrook, California 92028 • (760) 555-2345

PERSONAL PROFILE

Organized, accurate, detail-oriented Human Resources Professional with substantial, diverse experience enhanced by a formal education and refined by specialized, industry-related training. Computer literate in a wide variety of accounting, word processing, and spreadsheet applications. Superb interpersonal and communications skills; adept listener. Positive attitude, personable demeanor, and professional image. Bilingual: Spanish. Qualifications include knowledge, skills, and abilities in:

- Accuracy & Detail
- Administration
- Human Resources

- Organizational
- Problem Analysis
- Staff Coordination

- Task Management
- Time-management
- Troubleshooting

RELEVANT PROFESSIONAL EXPERIENCE

TN-Network, Cardiff-by-the Sea, California - 1993 to present

Human Resources and Administration Manager reporting to the Chief Operating Officer. Functional authority includes direct, daily supervision of a 7 person staff engaged in all facets of human resources management activities. Primary duties focus on and include interviewing, screening, and orienting new hires with company benefits, policies and procedures; implementing terminations; and conducting exit interviews. Collateral duties involve overseeing the preparation of the company payroll for 350+ personnel.

- Streamlined the new hire process reducing time lost in the "pipe line" by 28%.

- Created checklists and forms increasing accuracy, eliminating redundancies, providing accountability, ensuring uniformity, and improving audit reliability.

- Increased efficiency 45% by reorganizing the Human Resources Department.

- Implemented an effective open door policy that resulted in increased efficiency and problem resolution by improving accessibility to management for employees.

- Created and implemented an employee manual and handbook.

- Researched, analyzed, and recommended acquisition of ADP software to increase efficiency and reduce costs.

Cassidy Construction, Inc., Visalia, California -1990 to 1993

Staff Accountant reporting to the Controller. Functional responsibilities included payroll, quarterly taxes, workers' compensation, job costing and bank reconciliations. Ancillary duties included A/R, and A/P. Collaterial duties involved direct liaison with subcontractors, vendors and superintendents.

(Continued on next page)

PRIOR PROFESSIONAL EXPERIENCE

Pacific Coast Mechanical, Wildomar, California - 1988 to 1990

Assistant Controller reporting to the Controller. Functional responsibilities included A/P, A/R, payroll, quarterly taxes, worker's compensation, job costing, general ledger, deposits, and bank reconciliations. Additional duties involved direct supervision of 4 office personnel. Ancillary duties included dealing with subcontractors, vendors and superintendents.

Encinitas Tile, Encinitas, California - 1987 to 1988

Accounting Supervisor reporting to the President. Functional responsibilities included managing the computerized accounting department. Duties involved A/P, A/R, payroll, billing, collections, taxes, worker's compensation, auditing, budgeting and financial forecasts.

EDUCATION AND PROFESSIONAL DEVELOPMENT

University of California, San Bernardino, California - 1994

Bachelor of Arts in Sociology

- President, Association of Latin American Students (ALAS)

Palomar College, San Marcos, California - 1992

Associate of Arts in General Studies

- Vice-President, Associated Student Body (ASB)

Bolero Associates, Irvine, California - 1997

Graduate: Certificated Continuous Improvement Process (CIP) Course

University of Arizona (Satellite Campus), San Diego, California - 1996

Certificated Human Resources Manager Program - Graduate

Mira Costa Community College, Oceanside, California - 1990

Undergraduate Studies - Emphasis in Accounting

REFERENCES

Appropriate personal and professional references are available.

DREW KENNEDY, Ph.D.

318 Amarillo Lane
Reed, Iowa 50312
(888) 555-1212

*"Our young people have enough critics...
what they need are more role models."*

CAREER PROFILE

- Vision-driven leader with extensive experience as a lecturer, counselor, researcher, and public speaker in the direction of educational, cultural, community, business, and public relations activities throughout the United States and abroad.

- Strategic/financial planning expertise under stringent budgetary controls.

- Proven ability to establish rapport with people of all backgrounds and socio-economic levels.

AREAS OF EXPERTISE

Program Effectiveness and Evaluation
Operations and Fiscal Management
Continuous Quality Improvement
Quality Control/Risk Management
Fundraising and Grant Writing
Project Development and Management
Staff Training and Development
Problem Identification, Analysis and Resolution

AWARDS AND RECOGNITIONS

Iowa County Opportunity Council
Meritorius Human Service Award, 1993

Quincy-Princeton College
Humanitarian Award, 1991

Iowa Alcohol and Drug Abuse Association **Administrator of the Year Award,** 1990

"Drew Kennedy Day," Proclamation presented by John Smith, Mayor, City of Reed, 1990

CAREER EXPERIENCE

**Founder and Chief Executive Officer
Center for Addiction Assistance
1974-1995 (Retired)**

Performance Established the first substance abuse treatment center in Iowa County. Guided the expansion of the agency as it grew to over 23 clinic sites in Iowa, Zion, and Madison Counties, encompassing the Fourth Judicial Circuit.

Responsibilities Operated from a budget of over $6 million, the agency employed over 200 professional and support staff who intervened in the cases of nearly 2,000 substance abuse involved adults, youths, and their families annually. Services included prevention and education programs, outpatient services, adult residential programs, four adolescent residential programs, criminal justice intervention through the Street Crime Options Program (SCO), drug testing, and professional training.

Duties included the overall administration of all program components:

- Implemented policy and program actions as assigned by the Board of Directors; kept the Board informed and made recommendations concerning activities, progress and problems of the agency.

- Assessed need for public information, community education, and referral services including target communities and populations, extent of need, and current availability of services to meet needs.

- Planned for programs, staffing, physical resources, and funding to meet assessed needs within policy guidelines established by the Board; developed short-term and long-term agency plans and assured annual update of plans based on changing needs and progress toward objectives.

- Developed, managed, and controlled the agency's fiscal resources to assure that funding was sufficient to meet service needs and that funds were used efficiently to provide effective services.

- Recruited, hired, trained, and evaluated staff.

- Established and maintained positive working relationships with community groups, service agencies, government agencies, and other relevant groups.

- Assured that there was an ongoing Quality Assurance and Risk Management Program, set up to objectively and systematically monitor and evaluate quality and appropriateness of patient care services, pursue opportunities to improve patient care, and identify and resolve problems.

Key Accomplishments Built the program from ground zero to one of the most internationally recognized models for chemical substance abuse treatment. Opened first juvenile prison facility in Iowa. Facilitated the first AIDS education/training seminar in Iowa.

EDUCATION

PhD—Counseling Psychology
Iowa College, 1992
Cedar Rapids, Iowa
Graduated Summa Cum Laude

ThM—Theology
Dubuque Baptist Theological
Seminary, 1972
Dubuque, Iowa

BS—Psychology
Rockfield State University, 1969
Rockfield, Illinois

PROFESSIONAL LICENSES AND CERTIFICATIONS

Licensed Pastoral Counselor, 1992
Licensed Temperament Therapist, 1992
Achieved *Expert Witness* ranking in the
    area of chemical substance abuse by
    the Iowa State Attorney's Office.

Former Certifications Held:
National Certified Addiction Counselor
Cert. Criminal Justice Addiction Prof.

PROFESSIONAL AFFILIATIONS

National Christian Counseling Assoc.

Formerly Affiliated With:
Institute for Rational Emotive Therapy
Amer. Mental Health Counselors Assoc.
Amer. Assoc. for Couns. and Develop.
Iowa Alcohol and Drug Abuse Assoc.
Iowa Anthropological Society

CIVIC INVOLVEMENT

Iowa County Citizens Task Force
    for Children

Governor Jim Greene's Vision 2000
    Committee on Criminal Justice and
    Human Service Needs for the New
    Millenium

Advisor to State House of Represent-
    atives on Juvenile Justice Reform

TEACHING EXPERIENCE

Quincy-Princeton College - Quincy, Iowa
    Sociology Department
Central Iowa Human Services Centers Training Seminars
    Ethics, Confidentiality, Mediation, and Anger Management
Iowa City College - Des Moines, Iowa
    Counseling the Resistant Patient
    AIDS: Challenge of the Eighties
Quincy Community College - Quincy, Iowa
    What To Do When Your Patient Is An Addict
National Christian Counseling Association - Dublin, Iowa
    The Utilization of the Local Addiction Treatment Centers to the
    Private Practitioner
Dublin County Community College - Dublin, Iowa
    Treatment and Care of the Addictive Patient
St. Joseph College - St. Joseph, Iowa
    Effective Law Enforcement Techniques: Dealing With the
    Addictive Personality
University of Southern Iowa - South Park, Iowa
    Management by Objectives

ADDITIONAL TRAINING/EDUCATION

*Anger, Alcoholism, and Addiction: Treating Anger in a Chemical
    Dependency Setting (Individuals, Couples and Families)* by
    Ronald T. Potter-Efron.

Rational Emotive Therapy (RET), 40 hours, by Albert Ellis, Ph.D.,
    founder of the Rational Emotive Therapy Institute.

Rational Behavior Therapy (RBT), 50 hours, as innovated by
    Maxie C. Maultsby, Jr., M.D., Medical Director, Psychiatric
    Medical School, Howard University, Washington, DC.

Intensive Group Therapy, 32 hours, by Terrance Gorskie, inter-
    nationally reknowned group therapy innovator. University of
    Iowa, Iowa School of Addiction Studies.

Marriage and Family Therapy 'Til Divorce Do Us Part, Karl
    Menninger, M.D., Menninger Clinic, Kansas City, Kansas.

Reality Therapy, 10 hours, William Glasser, M.D., Atlanta,
    Georgia.

Schools Without Grades, 8 hours, William Glasser, M.D., Atlanta,
    Georgia.

*Continuous Quality Improvement (CQI) rather than Quality
    Assurance (QA), a New and More Effective Quality Control,*
    Iowa Mental Health Conference, Des Moines, Iowa.

*"Our young people have enough critics...
what they need are more role models."*

PROGRAM DESCRIPTION

Iowa County Human Services Centers, a private, not-for-profit organization dedicated to serving the substance abuse and related social service needs of the Northeastern Iowa community.

Since 1974, the agency has grown from one adult outpatient program serving the Iowa County area to a multi-service organization with over a dozen locations serving adults and adolescents and their families from Iowa, Zion, and Madison Counties. The agency employs over 200 professional and support staff members who provide a comprehensive scope of services ranging from community-based prevention and education programs to adult and adolescent residential treatment centers. The program's components include:

- Prevention Services
- Central Intake
- Street Crime Options (SCO)
- Urinalysis Testing
- Outpatient Services (Dixon, Peoria, Princeton, Quincy, Danville, Cherokee, Ames, and Clarinda)
- Juvenile Assessment Unit
- Intensive Overlay Programs (Iowa Halfway House, Iowa County Probation and Restitution Center, Iowa Correctional Institute)
- Adult Residential Treatment Center
- Juvenile Residential Treatment Center
- Wilderness-Based Programs
- Drug-Free Workplace Assistance
- Speakers Bureau
- Bilingual Services
- Professional Training
- Ropes Challenge Course
- Maritime Institute
- Vocational Training Center

Iowa County Human Services Centers
A Component of the Center for Addiction Assistance

Administrative Services
Central Intake & Assessment
Outpatient Treatment Center
Drug Testing
Ropes Challenge Course
Employee Assistance Program
1300 Queensland Drive, Suite #200
Dublin, Iowa 05212

Street Crime Options (SCO) and Iowa County
Outpatient Treatment Center
1543 Main Street
Zion, Iowa 05342

Street Crime Options (SCO)
Post Office Box 15,346
Smithfield, Iowa 05349

Representative Gaylord Stringfield Outpatient Treatment Center
54 North Lakeshore Drive
Dublin, Iowa 05216

Dublin Probation Restitution Center
1549 Queensland Drive
Dublin, Iowa 05212

Friendship Village Juvenile Residential Treatment Center
2398 Peoria Way
Wellston, Iowa 05978

Adult Residential Treatment Center
3256 South Lemon Street
Danville, Iowa 05436

Iowa County Halfway House
4232 Pine Avenue
Clarinda, Iowa 05278

Zion Hills Outpatient Treatment Center
87 Mulberry Lane
Zion Hills, Iowa 05963

Ames Wooden Boat School and Vocational Center
1254 Stuttgard Avenue
Ames, Iowa 05128

Sandy Berkowski

P.O. Box 39
Okawville, Illinois 62271
(618) 555-3394

Seeking a position as a
Mental Health Technician / Case Worker

Experienced with
Developmentally Disabled / Mentally Retarded
Elderly / Chronically Mentally Ill

Related Background

OAK CREEK MENTAL HEALTH CENTER, Cahokia, Illinois, Feb. - May 1997
(partial hospitalization program currently undergoing downsizing and restructuring)

Mental Health Technician: Worked with schizophrenics, chronic depressives, bipolar disorders, chronically mentally ill, and developmentally disabled adults as part of a multi-disciplinary team. Participated in five daily therapy sessions, observing affect/behavior/response as member of the treatment planning team. Documented benefits of treatment and discussed future interventions. ***Earned outstanding performance-related comments from staff and superiors.***

Job Skills:

Therapy Facilitation	Documentation
Medicaid/Medicare Administration	Admissions
Treatment Planning/Reviewing	Observation/Treatment Issues
Patient Relations	Community Resources
Confidentiality Laws/Patient Rights	CPR Certified

Self-Management Skills:

Time Management	Oral/Written Communication
Organization	Project Management
Decision-making	Continuous Learning
Working under Stress	Independent/Self-Motivated

Education

KEYSTONE COLLEGE, Lenon, Illinois
Bachelor of Arts Degree in Psychology

Additional Experience

While staying home to raise a family, owned and operated a successful mail order craft company featuring 28 patented product designs and patterns. Also held store management positions for two fast-food restaurants. Formerly licensed in food handling and insurance sales.

References Available Upon Request

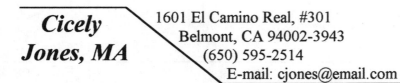

Cicely Jones, MA

1601 El Camino Real, #301
Belmont, CA 94002-3943
(650) 595-2514
E-mail: cjones@email.com

HIGHLIGHTS OF QUALIFICATIONS

- Enthusiastically motivated to inspire and support others.
- Able to communicate ideas effectively through writing and speaking.
- Exceptionally resourceful, well organized and flexible.
- Able to generate innovative ideas while maintaining focus and intent.
- Works efficiently independently and as a cooperative team member.
- Fifteen years experience educating and counseling individuals, groups and families.

PROFESSIONAL EXPERIENCE

Program Development

- Recruited, organized and implemented activity programs working with an all volunteer staff for Singles population. Managed budget, program costs, purchases and allocation. Wrote Singles newsletters, flyers and press releases. Contacted, organized and negotiated fees for speakers. Liaison with community center management staff and board. Conducted meetings, held elections and supported fundraising functions for the center.

- Directed Senior lunch and activities programs with an all volunteer staff. Recruited volunteers, worked with vendors, encouraged participation and attended to special needs of the population. Kept records and accounting for the program.

- Developed and taught Stress Management and Self-Esteem classes and seminars for HMO Medical Centers, The Health Plan of the Bay Area, Santa Clara County Mental Health Association, Family Survival Project, Battered Women's Center, Sales and Marketing Executives, schools and small businesses.

- Created and produced *FULL FIGURED GIRL,* the first all-day conference in the Bay Area for full-figured women. Included 16 workshops, a catered luncheon, fashion show and vendors. Coordinated with an all volunteer staff.

- Created and taught weekly movement class and support group for large women, at community center and HMO Medical Centers.

- Designed *DON'T WORRY, BE HAPPY,* a workshop for Wellness Day event, focusing on humor, music, art, play and meditation.

Organizational and Administrative Expertise

- Telemarketing Representative. Conducted research and surveys for software company.
- Coordinator for interviewing and hiring of prospective personnel for computer software firm.
- Coordinator for worldwide HP3000 software computer conventions in Bay Area, United Kingdom, Scotland and the Netherlands. Directed all aspects of trade shows including: advertising, travel, booth setup and preparation for speakers.

EMPLOYMENT HISTORY

1983-97   Health Educator and Counselor. Palo Alto and Redwood City, CA
1990-94   Health Educator and Instructor. Great Shape!
          HMO Medical Centers, Redwood City & Santa Clara, CA
1990-92   Health Educator and Instructor. Health Skills At Work. HMO Medical Centers.
1988-90   Singles & Assistant Seniors Director. Senior Center, Palo Alto, CA
1985-87   Instructor. Adult Learning Center, Palo Alto, CA
1983-85   Telemarketing and Personnel Assistant. ABC, Palo Alto, CA

EDUCATION AND CREDENTIALS

Degrees

M.A., Health Education and Counseling, Small University, CA
M.A., Rhetoric, (Writing and Communications) State University, CA
B.A., English, State University, NY

Credentials

Language Arts and Literature Community College Credential - Life
Student Personnel Worker, Community College Credential - Life
Adult Education Credential

Special Training

Yoga Teacher Training
Therapeutic Imagery Professional Training

MICHAEL GRAHAM

1408 Crosby Court ♦ Staten Island, New York ♦ 12456
Phone: (718) 222-7672 ♦ E-mail: mgraham@msn.com

Social Services/Youth Program Administrator with seven years of successful management experience. Committed to developing and running programs that help out-of-school youths achieve success. Extensive experience coordinating GED Preparation, Job Training, Computer Instruction, Career Counseling, Recreational, and After-School programs for 14- to 21-year-old youths. Proven strength in:

- Staff Supervision and Training
- Vocational Guidance
- Maintaining Auditory Compliance
- Curriculum Development
- Community Outreach
- Job Development
- Workshop Presentations
- Generating Referrals
- Program Marketing

Respected leader, motivator, and role-model. Excellent interpersonal relations with youths, parents, schools, colleagues, businesses, and community groups. Computer literate in Windows and MS-DOS operating systems.

EXPERIENCE

YOUTH ADVANTAGE, INC.   New York, NY

Program Director, 1990 to present

Oversee educational and recreational program that serves 50 to 120 out-of-school youths each year. Train, supervise, and evaluate eight counselors and teachers. Liaise with community groups and local employers to develop opportunities for participants. Coordinate After-School Program and act as Site Director for Summer Youth Employment Program. Travel throughout East Coast presenting workshops on youth development. Create promotional materials and attract new participants. Conduct extensive follow-up after program completion.

- 1997 and 1996: Recognized for being among top 5 community-based programs.
- Commended by Community Board 14, East Village Community Conference, Manhattan School to Career Project, and New York Medical Center.
- Consistently achieve positive internal and external audit results.
- Secured a $75,000 grant increase at a time of severe youth program funding cuts.
- Turned a high staff turnover rate into a high staff retention rate.
- Developed hundreds of private-sector job opportunities for participants.
- Currently developing Real Estate and Entrepreneurial programs.

Youth Counselor, 1989 to 1990

Devised curricula and taught Career Education and GED Preparation classes. Handled paperwork for 120 participants. Assisted troubled youths with building self-esteem and formulating realistic goals. Encouraged family members to take an active role in their children's development and progress.

- Effectively conducted educational and counseling sessions, reflected in a high number of successful completions.
- Leadership, dedication, and teamwork earned promotion to Program Director.

ATHLETICS

Basketball Player, 1980 to 1989   San Juan, Puerto Rico
Played Division I basketball and coached 9- to 12-year-old children.

COMPUTERS

♦ Proficient user of WordPerfect and Microsoft Word
♦ Knowledge of Microsoft Access and PowerPoint

EDUCATION

HUNTER COLLEGE   New York, NY

B.S. in Community Mental Health, 1980

PAMELA M. DAWSON
13222 Vista Bay Drive
Tampa, Florida 33624
(813) 000-0000

PROFESSIONAL PROFILE

- **Broad spectrum of counseling, teaching and management expertise** that integrates guidance skills, career accomplishments, and academic credentials with lifelong interest for helping others achieve personal/professional goals.

- **Diverse scope of qualifications** encompassing more than nine years of spearheading and devising comprehensive counseling programs; four years of career/academic counseling; and a prolific background in directing administrative operations.

- **Competent facilitator with keen analytical ability**; adept in needs assessments, program efficacy, problem-solving, executing counseling agendas, and creating instructional materials.

- **Self-directed and highly motivated**; successfully acclimate to new professional roles. Able to respond effectively to demanding situations, provide visionary leadership, and follow through with diligence and competence.

- **Articulate communicator,** experienced in working one-on-one or with large groups.

EDUCATION

TRI-COUNTY UNIVERSITY - Tampa, FL

A.B.D., Curriculum and Instruction   Expected completion 1998
Emphasis - Educational Foundations and Counselor Education

TAMPA UNIVERSITY - Tampa, FL
M.B.A.   1985

TRI-COUNTY UNIVERSITY - Tampa, FL
M.A., Guidance and Counseling   1973

ST. MARY'S DOMINICAN COLLEGE - New Orleans, LA
B.S. Major: Biology / Minor: Chemistry   1970

Ph.D. INTERNSHIP PROGRAM

- Taught Introduction to Guidance Process (Fall, 1991; Summer, 1994)

- Supervised Master's in Counselor Education practicum students (1991)

- 162 counseling hours at Catholic Social Services, Lake, FL (1/91-8/91)
  Counseled women from diverse backgrounds and social sectors. Gained experience in:

Assessment Diagnosis (related to issues such as)
Crisis Intervention . . . Family/Child Adjustment . . . Depression . . . Destructive Relationships . . . Mental Health . . . Adolescent Issues

Treatment
Developed plans consistent with needs of individuals, provided educational resources and served as a liaison linking individuals with applicable auxiliary community services.

Individual/Group Counseling
Furnished guidance and emotional support concurrently with building a working rapport; evaluated needs, strengths and weaknesses; exercised resourcefulness and flexibility plus identified coping mechanisms.

PAMELA M. DAWSON

EXPERIENCE

TRI-COUNTY UNIVERSITY - Sarasota Campus, FL   **1982 - Present**
Dynamic record of consistent achievements and goal-directed motivation led to progressive promotions to visible, leadership positions. Exhibited astute skills in guidance counseling, program development, and organizational management that contributed to augmenting academic, student and computer lab services for a regional campus with a student population of 1100.

Assistant Dean Academic Services (January 1996 - Present)
Preside over scholastic components and departmental cost parameters of Academic Support Services. Direct the development, implementation and administration of academic programs in Arts and Sciences, Business and Education; interpret and recommend administrative policies/procedures for instructional/student services. Key areas administered include: Campus Management, Instructional Services, Student Services and Distance Learning.

Director for Academic Support Services (May 1991 - January 1996)
Associate Director for Student Services (June 1989 - May 1991)
Acting Associate Director for Student Services (October 1987 - June 1989)
Advancement paralleled growth of start-up initiatives to maximize the operational efficiency of all related student service functions. Results-driven attitude combined with realignment of administrative emphasis led to promotion in 1991 and managing academic service areas. Promoted to Assistant Dean in 1996.

Advisor / Pre-professional Sciences Office, College of Natural Sciences (July 1982 - October 1987)
Charged with interviewing, screening and documenting credentials of students applying for admission to health-related professional schools; wrote evaluations; conducted career counseling; developed curriculum planning and scheduling for up to 1,100 students annually; performed orientation of new students; represented the College of Natural Sciences at public speaking engagements; and updated brochures and printed materials.

ACADEMY OF ST. JOHN - Tampa, FL   **1971 - 1982**
Director of Guidance (1972- 1982)
Physical Science Teacher (1971-1972)
Conceptualized and implemented a unique, comprehensive guidance program for 400 secondary students that initiated a successful pilot program for peer counseling. Conducted one-on-one student counseling pertaining to curriculum, career and personal concerns. Selected and administered standardized testing program, interpreted test data, and analyzed statistical reports.

➤**During tenure, 100% of Academy's graduates were admitted to college and scholarship awards increased by 50%.**
➤**Pioneered establishment of peer counseling group among select group of high school students and conducted all training.**
➤**Assisted three other private high schools in coordinating an annual college night program.**

MEMBERSHIPS

Tampa Campus	Sarasota Campus
Associate Deans Council	Administrative and Academic Councils
Student Affairs Leadership Team	Education Advisory Council
Council on Academic Advising	Senior Citizen Advisory Group
HIV Committee	

Academic Advising Association (NACADA)

CONFERENCE PRESENTATIONS
(Co-presenter with Dr. Ellen Kendal on the following topics)

16th Annual Lilly Conference on College Teaching - **"Feminist Pedagogy Across the Curriculum: Beyond the Women Studies Wall"**
15th Annual Lilly Conference on College Teaching - **"In Search of Relationship"**

AWARDS

Recipient of Grant-in-Aid Award - Spring 1995

MARGARET J. THOMAS

66 Main Street • Sometown, NH 09786 • (555) 555-5555

CAREER OVERVIEW

Dedicated professional with over 20 years of progressive experience working with the elderly population and their families. Deeply committed to enriching the lives of others; recognized for sensitivity to the needs of clients and for ability to effectively balance professionalism with empathy. Work well under pressure and deadlines. Qualifications include outstanding leadership and supervisory skills, extensive administrative experience and comprehensive knowledge of social services. Specific capabilities include:

- Crisis Intervention
- Long & Short-Term Counseling
- Group Facilitation
- Treatment Planning
- Needs Assessment Interviewing

- Multi-Disciplinary Team Leadership
- Staff Development
- Human Resources
- Volunteer Recruitment

- Policy & Procedure Development
- Operations Management
- Public Relations & Networking
- Special Events & Activity Coordination

HIGHLIGHTS OF EXPERIENCE

Supervision & Administration

- Coordinate in-house and inter-agency case planning for extended medical care in a 108 bed facility; direct daily functions in accordance with federal, state and local guidelines and standards.
- Developed a patient information packet with information regarding patient rights and responsibilities, operating policies and procedures, and activity schedules; formalized the admission process.
- Plan and conduct numerous in-service, OJT and orientation programs to increase professional abilities of staff. Recognized for outstanding teaching style and for developing trainings that are informal yet educational and enlightening.
- Develop and implement policies and procedures to assure the highest degree of quality of care for residents and to facilitate rapport and teamwork among departments.
- Recruit, interview and hire personnel; supervise and consult with seven department directors concerning the operation of their departments. Counsel, discipline and terminate employment when necessary.
- Streamlined and formalized the hiring and orientation process; provide and oversee the facility orientation program and developed an information packet new employees.
- Assist in the development of annual operating budget and resource allocation; oversee accounts payable.
- Conduct, compile, analyze and present results of comprehensive quality assurance and resident satisfaction surveys.
- Co-facilitate 15 member in-house ethics committee, serve on the medical records and safety committees; assist in the implementation of safety issues.

Counseling & Treatment Planning

- Provide crisis intervention and long term counseling for individuals and families dealing with stress of illness, disability and life transition.
- Design and implement numerous activities and programs to enrich the lives of patients and guide them toward their highest physiological and psychological abilities.
- Facilitate weekly support groups designed to address emotional and spiritual needs as well as educate on issues of patient rights and responsibilities.

Interviewing & Needs Assessment

- Conduct in-depth personal assessments dealing with financial transactions, estate planning and financial assistance.
- Identify patient's emotional needs during the pre-admission and throughout the admission process; assist the elderly population in using community resources and support them in dealing with issues of aging.
- Work as a member of a multi-disciplinary team to aid in case planning and to address the social and emotional needs of patients.

Community Services & Resource Development

- Key participant in the formation of two private retirement homes designed to accommodate a small number of independent elderly individuals desiring a shared lifestyle. Established criteria and guidelines, coordinated services with local hospitals, conducted needs-assessment interviews with prospective residents and planned recreational activities.
- Compiled and maintain a comprehensive collection of up-to-date information regarding community social service resources for patients and their families.
- Develop and maintain relationships with community organizations, churches, senior citizen groups, schools and local businesses; built a comprehensive network of resources.
- Author and design a public relations newsletter currently distributed to over 400 families, physicians and home health agencies.

EMPLOYMENT HISTORY

SUNNYBROOK MANOR, SOME CITY, NH, **1976** TO PRESENT
Associate Administrator (1996 - Present)
Administrator in Training (1995 - 1996)
Director of Social Services Admissions (1980 - 1995)
Activity Coordinator (1978 - 1980)
Secretary to Director of Nursing (1977 - 1978)
Certified Nursing Assistant (1976 - 1977)

EDUCATION & PROFESSIONAL ACTIVITIES

B.S., HUMAN SERVICES (1985) State College, Some City, NH
Certified Nursing Home Administrator - License #8888

Additional Training

Medicare & the Changing Health Environment • Managed Care - The Medicare Perspective
Maximizing the Medicare Pilot Program • Psychoactive Drugs & Effects on the Elderly
TQM and the Survey Process • How to Start Your Own Ethics Committee
OSHA's Long Term Care Initiative • Employment / Labor Law
Tapping the Innovator in You • Legal Aspects of Managed Care
Elder Abuse/Domestic Violence • Grassroots and Long Term Care
Ethical Issues in Long Term Care • Quality and How to Pay For It

Associations

Chairperson, CNA Craft Committee, Adult Learning Center
Member, County Coalition to Prevent Elder Abuse Committee
Member, New Hampshire Health Care Ethics Committee
Voting Member, American College of Health Care Administrators

MICHAEL P. WALLACE
225 Winter View Place
Overland Park, Kansas 60551
(601) 239-7987

STATEMENT OF QUALIFICATIONS

❖ Experience in program design/direction, presentation and training; educated in leadership, administration, management, and human relations to provide high quality, effective, relevant training and development opportunities to increase productivity, improve customer satisfaction and minimize cost

❖ Specialize in organizational management and personnel development with knowledge of instructional technology, design, and adult learning principles

❖ Expertise in behavioral objectives, learning theory, listening skills, questioning techniques, lecturing, demonstration and discussion leading, generating enthusiasm and motivation

❖ Testing and validating techniques, analyzing problem areas in course effectiveness, recommending and implementing solutions, modifying course curriculum

❖ Defining, developing and scheduling program requirements for comprehensive educational and community programs with effective follow-through techniques to ensure objectives

❖ Speaking publicly, conceptualizing and presenting seminars

❖ Communication Skills: Effectively relating to and interacting positively with individuals at all levels, diplomatic, listens actively

❖ Personal Qualities: Energetic. Resourceful. Facilitator. Idea Generator. Empowering Leader. Problem Resolution.

Certification/Professional Designation

Competence, Credibility, Capability (CCC) Certified

EXPERIENCE AND ACCOMPLIISHMENTS

1996 - Present   US SPRINT/UNITED   Overland Park, KS
                  EDUCATIONAL CONSULTANT/TRAINER
- Trained Sprint employees in various management professional and educational courses nation wide to improved capability and skills, motivate employees to perform quality work in the most cost effective manner.

Accomplishments:
➢ Designed and developed curriculum and materials for the Vendor Conference 1997.
➢ Recognized for superior course delivery performance through customer surveys.
➢ Redesigned and improved course curriculum in diversity.
➢ Certified in: Value and Diversity; Managing Diversity; Negotiation Skills; Interviewing Skills; Basic Project Management; Link Performance Management; Guiding Performance; Working Together; Decision Making and Problem Solving; Seven Habits of Highly Effective People

EXPERIENCE AND ACCOMPLIISHMENTS

1985 - 1996 KANSAS CITY, MISSOURI POLICE DEPARTMENT Kansas City, MO
SERGEANT - *Robbery Unit*
- Supervised operations, monitoring incoming offenses, assigning cases to detectives, disseminating daily reports, and reviewing cases to be presented for prosecution.
- Supervised/evaluated detectives.

Accomplishments:
➢ Headed the Kansas City Task Force on Crime, resulting in arrest of three criminal suspects involved in a kidnapping/car jacking.
➢ Developed a computer system to log and monitor crimes in the metropolitan area, resulting in strategic crime patterns.
➢ Developed curriculum and taught diversity classes for all officers training.
➢ Lectured to out-of-state officers on "Diversity Awareness".

DETECTIVE - *Burglary Unit* (1987-1990)
Accomplishments: ➢ Developed strategic plans for crime patterns.

POLICE OFFICER (1985-1987)

1979 - 1985 METROPOLITAN COMMUNITY COLLEGE DISTRICT Kansas City, MO
PIONEER COMMUNITY COLLEGE
COMMUNITY SERVICES SPECIALIST - COORDINATOR
- Coordinated activities and needs of the community to assure effective relationship; evaluating new/existing educational programs, designing credit/non-credit courses and developing site classes, seminars and workshops for businesses, agencies and targeted populations with a $100,000+ budget.
- Selected, supervised, and evaluated staff and instructors.
- Assisted in and developed proposals/grants, identifying potential funding sources.

Accomplishments: ➢ Developed, supervised, and operated the following activities:

ENGLISH AS A SECOND LANGUAGE: Provided instruction to Indochinese refugees at the Don Bosco Community Center.

ISSUES IN FOSTERING: Designed course to assist current and prospective foster parents in acquiring necessary skills and understanding the responsibility of foster parenting.

WAYNE MINOR HOUSING PROJECT: Training program for residential women in coping with crisis situations, budgeting, nutrition and gaining self-reliance. "Survival Skills for the Urban Women"

BASIC SUPERVISION AND JANITORIAL MAINTENANCE TRAINING: Provided basic supervision and janitorial maintenance training for the supervisors and maintenance employees of the Kansas City Housing Authority.

HEALTH ACTIVATION PROGRAMS FOR SENIOR CITIZENS: Developed two health activation programs for senior citizens with Mid-American Regional Council (MARC) to insure wellness as opposed to medical treatment of illness.

EDUCATION

University of Missouri   **Master of Arts in Higher Education Administration** - May 1996
Kansas City, Missouri   Emphasis: Leadership and Administration

Graduate Assistant - Dr. Elizabeth Noble, 1995
Research assistant in the Linda Mood concept of linguistic studies

Internship: Dr. Elizabeth Noble, Upward Bound Program, UMKC, 1996
Longitudinal study for retention of low income and minority students.

Mid-American Nazarene College   **Bachelor of Arts** - December 1994
Olathe, Kansas   Major: Management and Human Relations

Continued Professional Development
US Sprint/United
- CCC Certification   January 1997

PUBLICATIONS

Payton-Watkins, Minnie. "The Effects of Institutionalization on First Time Juvenile Offenders", <u>Wilson and Smith Publishing Co</u>., 1994.

PERSONAL DATA

Language: Working knowledge of French.

REFERENCES

Virginia Cobbs   Home: (816) 765-2693
9811 Hardesty   Teacher
Kansas City, Missouri 64131   Kansas City, Missouri School District

Doris Ashley, President   Office: (816) 444-4435
LàNail Institute
7500 Troost
Kansas City, Missouri 64132

Darrell Fortè   Office: (816) 235-5100
Sergeant, Homicide Unit
Kansas City Missouri Police Department
1125 Locust
Kansas City, Missouri 64106

Reggie Stanley
5 Tiosa Lane • Dallas, Texas 75230 • (972) 555-3772

Data Center Operations / Voice & Data Communications
Information Technology / Project Management / Strategic and Operational Planning

Dynamic technical manager with exceptional track record for reengineering data center, desktop, and networks to improve asset performance, operational efficiencies and expense reduction. Strong international networking and telecommunications background with a solid history for delivering outstanding customer service. Proven ability to build and manage creative, highly energized, focused teams.

Management Experience

Networking Strategy & Direction	Acquisition/Integration (Voice/Data)
Contract Negotiations	Workload Planning
Budgeting and Administration	Human Resources
Training and Support Planning	Vendor Relations

Technical Expertise

Nortel PBX's	Cisco Routers
Cabletron Hubs	Frame Relay
T1, DS-3, OC-3, ISDN	Cat 5 Cable Plant
VMS, NT, Unix, Novell	MS Office, MS Mail

Professional Highlights

MARY KAY COSMETICS, INC. *($1.2 billion annual revenues)*, Dallas, Texas, 1993 - Present

Group Manager, Global Operations (1996 - Present)
Global Voice & Data Communications (1994 - Present)
International LAN Deployment (1993 - Present)
(Hired to manage technical teams responsible for the replacement of obsolete systems in 15 international subsidiaries with new LAN & WAN technology. Led the organization through a series of upgrades to capitalize on emerging technologies and application enhancements. Expanded job duties to include concurrent responsibility for Global Voice & Data Communications and Operations. Currently managing a staff of 48 and an annual operating/capital budget of $15.2 million.)

Network Enhancements and Upgrades

- Renegotiated contract with primary telecommunications provider reducing operating expenses $1.9 million over three years for long distance, frame relay, and clear line fees.

- Negotiated five-year, $800,000 contract to provide OC-3 (Sonnet) service within the Dallas metroplex, networking 11 sites with redundant paths to primary and secondary long haul carriers. Provided solid option for minimizing network outages while maximizing options to modify and enhance the network.

- Managed the daily operations of an 11 node Nortel PBX network. The network consisted of one Option 81, five Option 61's and five Option 11's all networked via ISDN supporting 2,700 users and 300 agents.

- Directed the design, implementation, and operation of a frame relay network with nodes in Hong Kong, London, Switzerland, Russia and Texas.

- Directed the installation of a voice and data network in Moscow and St. Petersburg, Russia utilizing fiber and microwave technologies. Negotiated 3-year contract, installation expenses and recurring cost.

190

Professional Highlights (cont.)

MARY KAY COSMETICS, INC. *($1.2 billion annual revenues)*, Dallas, Texas, 1993 - Present

Group Manager, Global Operations (1996 - Present)
Global Voice & Data Communications (1994 - Present)
International LAN Deployment (1993 - Present)

Technology Infrastructure
- Project managed diverse team responsible for the design and installation of technology infrastructure for 600,000 square foot corporate headquarters including 10,000 square foot computer and operations center, 3,000 voice and data outlets with fiber backbone, redundant telecommunications access paths, redundant power facilities with generator backup.

- Built and directed team responsible for providing design, implementation, configuration, tuning and administration support for DEC Alpha Cluster (8400's), 45 NT , 4 Unix, and 17 Novell servers.

Corporate Relocation
- Directed a 36-member team responsible for the relocation of the corporate data center (Alpha Cluster), voice services (Nortel Option 81), data services (15 domestic sites), and 1,000 end users to the new corporate office. Completed the relocation of the data center in less than 18 hours with no unplanned interruption to the business.

International Systems Implementation
- Managed the implementation and support of Novell LAN's in 15 countries including China, Japan, Russia, Switzerland, and United Kingdom. Accountable for vendor relations, legal and financial issues.

BLOCKBUSTER ENTERTAINMENT, INC. *($4 billion annual revenues)*, Dallas, Texas, 1986-1993

System Management
- Responsible for DEC VAX Cluster system tuning, layered product installation and support, performance tuning, end user administration

Store System Support
- 1,000 stores, equipment configuration, ordering systems from vendor for all stores, responsible for in store technology installation and support.

Additional experience: Vaughan Nowlen & Associates, Applications Programmer (1983 to 1986)

Education

Southwest Texas State University, San Marcos, Texas 1983
Bachelor of Business Administration/ Computer Information Systems

References Available Upon Request

PAUL V. ZIELMAN

12212 North Wind Drive
Rye, New York   10189

Home (914) 977-8112
Office (212) 236-7929

TELECOMMUNICATIONS INDUSTRY EXECUTIVE

General Management, New Business Development & Advanced Technology Networks
Corporate Development, Change Management & Business Process Reengineering
Start-Up, Turnaround & High-Growth Operations

PROFESSIONAL EXPERIENCE

NORTHTEL COMMUNICATIONS   1989 to Present

Dynamic management career with one of the nation's largest and most technologically advanced telecommunications providers. Combines expertise in strategic planning, organizational development and change management with strong qualifications in identifying and capitalizing upon emerging opportunities to drive revenue/ profit growth and market expansion. Extensive experience in creating and leading complex, cross-functional operating and service teams.

Instrumental in positioning Northtel as a high-tech customer-driven network solutions provider. Played a key role in the creation of an innovative operating environment to support the research, development and delivery of advanced communications, technologies and services.

DIRECTOR OF REGIONAL NETWORK OPERATIONS (1994 to Present)
SERVICE, MAINTENANCE & NETWORKING

Senior Operations Manager spearheading a corporate-wide reengineering effort. Challenged to streamline all core operations, build new infrastructure and create a customer-driven, regionally focused organization. Given full autonomy for strategic planning, budgeting, profitability, new business development, technology innovation and customer support. Manage up to 800 personnel through 12 direct reports and administer $50 million annual operating budget.

Hold concurrent responsibility for Northtel Regional Operations with emphasis on:

Broadband Services	Project & Service Management
Customer Service	Special Services, Provisioning & Maintenance
Unbundling / Interlata Transport Services	Circuit Engineering
Network Modernization	Plant Inventory Assignments

Corporate Development & Business Process Reengineering

- Created corporate model and standard operating procedures adopted throughout the Northtel Organization. Program has served as a guideline for other leading telecommunications companies worldwide.
- Consolidated 20+ facilities throughout the Eastern U.S. into four primary locations with focus on key account development, turnkey network solutions and emerging market opportunities.
- Standardized all operating functions, process flows, methods and procedures, systems and internal controls to achieve higher service levels and increase profitability.

Operations & Facilities Management

- Built new operating infrastructure to streamline operations, eliminate duplicate functions and integrate processes into team-based concept. Delivered $2 million in annual operating savings.
- Directed a three-year $10 million construction project to design and build a multi-site operations center. Completed project $1 million under budget and six months ahead of schedule.
- Recruited a top-flight management team from both internal and external resources to launch network service operations.
- Integrated multiple work disciplines, and created high-performance teams.

Key Account Management & Customer Service

- Built Major Customer and Special Services Centers providing single points of contact based on specific customer market segments. Currently manage 1200 commercial accounts across diverse industries delivering $1 billion in revenues.
- Conceived and implemented innovative project and service management concept for major commercial accounts. Captured accounts throughout the banking, financial services, healthcare, government, university other telecommunication carriers and Internet service providers.

Advanced Networks & Technologies

- Championed the introduction of LAN, intranet and advanced PC technologies into the customer service organization. Achieved a two-year advantage over competition, and significant improvements in quality, accuracy and delivery of services.
- Created new Video Maintenance Center to capitalize upon emerging opportunities in the Video Dial Tone market (e.g., distance learning, pay-per-view). Led process from prototyping through test marketing.
- Established operations for Unbundled/Interlata Transport Services due to changes in federal regulations.

DIRECTOR OF OPERATIONS / CORPORATE REENGINEERING TASK FORCE (1991 to 1994)

Promoted with full responsibility for the New York Metro Area and 150 personnel in four distinct organizations. Analyzed all core operating functions and identified key areas to reduce costs, improve services and generate new revenue streams.

- Conceived and implemented a team-based approach for customer service operations. Realized 25% increase in productivity and efficiency. Model was subsequently adopted as the corporate standard throughout the organization.
- Recognized throughout the industry for innovation and business process reengineering. Subject of numerous articles and publications including a complete chapter in "Reengineer the Corporation", Hammer & Champy, CSE Index.
- Presented with "Spirit of Excellence Award" for outstanding performance. Personally recognized at 1993 Chairman's Conference for commitment to customer service.
- Instrumental in reducing access intervals in New York Metro Area for HICAP and DDS service following 15% decrease in market share. Achieved significant competitive advantage and won back 10% market share in 6 months.

OPERATIONS MANAGER - SPECIAL SERVICES (1989 to 1994)

Led all planning, budgeting, management and delivery of customized telecommunications services for key accounts throughout the Northeast Region. Held concurrent responsibility as the Service Liaison managing exclusive account relationships with the U.S. government, foreign dignitaries and multinational news media. Member of numerous corporate task forces leading quality improvement, organization/technology analysis and systems administration.

- Spearheaded start-up of Northtel's "Showcase" operation providing customer-driven voice, data and communications solutions. Managed $8 million capital acquisition of state-of-the-art technologies.
- Completed several assignments at the Capitol including US/USSR Summit, Presidential Inaugurations and other special events requiring sophisticated communications systems.
- Led the installation and maintenance of large PBX systems, voice, data, radio, audio and visual services for major government clients including the White House and Secret Service.

EARLY NORTHTEL EXPERIENCE   1978 to 1988

Fast-track promotion through a series of increasingly responsible technical and management positions. Gained extensive experience in all aspects of planning, scheduling, installation and maintenance. Supervised up to 20 field technicians servicing the Northeast Region.

EDUCATION

MBA, **System Theory & Cybernetics**, New York University, 1991
BA - Business Administration/Computer Applications, SUNY- Stonebrook, 1989

JAMES STARTER

222 W. Hitting Lane • Los Angeles, California 90001

310 555-7890
Pager: 310 555-9433

INFORMATION TECHNOLOGIES / VOICE AND DATA COMMUNICATIONS
DATA CENTER OPERATIONS / SYSTEMS PROGRAMMER
SOFTWARE DEVELOPER / INVENTOR

Creative and results-driven expert in the design, development, and delivery of cost effective, high-performance technology solutions to meet challenging business and multimedia demands. Extensive qualifications in all facets of project life cycle development from initial feasibility analysis and conceptual design through documentation, implementation, user training, quality review, and enhancement. Solid technical and musical training, and customer service skills. Effective communicator with developers and senior management. Extensive knowledge of video/audio recorders and enhanced CD. Worked with over 60 Fortune 500 companies. Basic conversational Spanish.

Experience applicable to diverse industries, markets, and opportunities.

PATENTS

U.S. Patent 4,520,710	Drum and Cymbals Pedals Assembly
U.S. Patent 4,640,176	Quick Disconnect Retainer for a Detachable Drumstick Head
U.S. Patent 4,640,177	Drumsticks or Mallets with Para-Hemispheroidal Heads and Their Assembly

SYSTEMS

- Heavy design and programming experience with

Windows	OOP	Visual BASIC
Solaris	HTML	FORTRAN
UNIX	Java	Turbo PASCAL
DOS	C++, C	COBOL

  and various scripting languages such as shell, batch, JPL, as well as major application packages (e.g. Microsoft Excel, Word, PowerPoint, Project, Access and several others).
- Telecommunications, modems, packet switching equipment, major LAN software (e.g. NT, Sun workstations, controllers, interfaces).
- Various typesetting and graphics packages (e.g. FileMaker Pro, X-Press, Pagemaker, Photoshop, Draw, HP Graphics, AutoCAD, and many others).

PROFESSIONAL EXPERIENCE

MOP, INC., Los Angeles, CA   1996 - 1997
Consultant

Led a user-interface portion of state-of-the-art global banking software project through R&D cycle to develop application-specific systems capable of meeting current and long-range information management requirements. Participated in cross-functional project teams and team meetings. Performed task- and task-flow analysis on Citibank transactions to identify core components and patterns of use, as well as needs assessment on Citibank transaction suite to identify natural functionality clusters.

Assisted in the development of sophisticated GUI across multiple delivery platforms, with a high degree of interactivity utilizing multimedia. Researched and analyzed the project to be completed and collaborated with developers to render this global ATM product more flexible and user friendly. Acted as liaison with 8 translators and assisted them in resolving unforeseen difficulties.

LEONARD PRODUCTIONS, Anywhere, CA   1996
Consultant
> Designed lighting system and assisted in construction of production office for D.E.VA Productions' commercial rehearsal studio.

NEW COMMUNICATIONS, INC., Anytown, CA   1995
Data Manager
> Managed data entry personnel and rightsized large database operation. Implemented improved backup system and procedures. Entailed extensive debugging and multiple software and hardware revisions/changes and close working relationship with senior management. Trained staff in use of GUI.

TR, Los Angeles, CA   1995
Software Developer
> **Designed, proved, and delivered ahead of schedule** a new electronic newsletter, a management tutorial/preview, and phased-rollout options, using MS Excel 5.0 and Visual Basic. **Recognized by Microsoft** for using innovative and useful techniques (contract project).

SERVICE WORLDWIDE, Los Angeles, CA   1995
MIS Assistant Director (Temporary)
> Appointed to handle 100 networked stations. Repaired printers and trained users. Successful disaster recovery of approximately 400 MB of critical, highly valuable data on damaged SCSI-based writable optical disk.

UCLA CAPITAL PROJECTS, UCLA, Los Angeles, CA   1994
Budget Analyst
> Prepared Capital Improvement Budgets (ranging from $10,000 to $240M) and related proposals and charts for presentation to various state and federal agencies. Streamlined computer processes for project initiation. Consulted with managing architects on utilization of office systems and simple yet cost effective improvements. Improved invoice payment method and relationships with key departments. Simultaneously took on full workload of transferred co-worker. Exposure to advanced use of AutoCAD and 3-D rendering programs by experts at UCLA.

Various Management Consulting and Administrative Assistant positions   1992 - 1993
> Seamlessly implemented solutions while performing administrative duties. Developed, formatted, and rewrote various sensitive documents and spreadsheets using multifarious software on Macintosh and IBM equipment on networks and stand-alone systems.

Consultant (Self employed)   1991 - 1992
> Miscellaneous projects, including broadcast equipment repair, and audio and video production. Also hosted and co-hosted radio programs on two 100,000-watt FM stations, served as announcer and producer on numerous radio spots, and directed 30 min. video.

Specialist with Temporary Agency, Kansas City, MO   Prior to 1991
President, Corporation, Kansas City, MO
> Established and operated business primarily involved in R&D and manufacturing of percussion musical instrument products, including all phases of product design, line and contracted operations and marketing strategies. **3 U.S. Patents awarded** for revolutionary percussion actuator products.

EDUCATION
Courses in Music, Computer Science, Math, and Phonetics, University of Missouri, Kansas City, Completed 12-module AT&T course in C Programming Language

WILLIAM R. SCHULTZ

79 Lucent Lane
Forksville, Virginia 22940-0079   Email: WillSz@net.com

(540) 555-1716
Fax: (540) 555-3128

PROFILE

Highly experienced, client-oriented software development, programming and project manager. Accomplished leader, capable of building motivated and productive teams. Significant software engineering analysis expertise including software design. Project management experience for both government and industry includes RFP preparation, review and performance, subcontractor supervision and administration. Flexible and focused, with unique analytical problem-solving ability. Excellent verbal and written communications skills. P&L responsibilities. Exceptional knowledge of and expertise in hardware, software and applications for defense and industry.

PROFESSIONAL EXPERIENCE

MENTOR BUSINESS SYSTEMS, Atlanta, GA   1995 - Present
World-class professional services company providing IT strategy, systems development and integration.

Project Consultant and Senior Technical Project Lead
Developed work and staffing plans, critical path schedules, process flow diagrams, technical requirements, information models, conceptual designs, and network provisioning impact studies for the Network Stabilization & Support System re-engineering activity of BellSouth Information Technology. Led preparation of the formal RFP for the project, participated in review and summary of responses from vendors and performed "life cost" analysis to help determine resulting strategic network funding needs. Identified and recruited project team consultants.

  • Prepared reengineering Project Plan adopted by BellSouth.

NYNEX COMMUNICATIONS RESEARCH (NYCoRE), Aliquippa, PA   1989 - 1994
A 6,200 employee, $1B national telecommunications software, technology, consulting and research organization.

Integrated Services Account Manager and Senior Analyst
Studied network and related software products before purchase by regional telephone company clients. Determined clients' procurement support needs by developing detailed work plan proposals, schedules and budgets. Coordinated work activities handled by NYCoRE. Served as Account Manager to Nation-Com Services, XBR Corporation, and US East Communications. Responsible for $13.4MM revenue stream.

  • Received XBR Corp. "Team Achievement Award" for developing an electronic mail system between NYCoRE and Southwestern Bell - for which no other employee has ever qualified.

  • Received a corporate award for developing and implementing a tracking and budget reporting system for a new NYCoRE product line.

CONSOLIDATED DATA SYSTEMS, Anoka, MN   1987 - 1989
Global data systems software/service company with 2,100 employees and $500MM annual sales.

Engineering Project Manager
Developed Phase I of the F-14D "Tomcat" fighter OS software under subcontract by Grumman Aerospace. Managed a 40-member team of software design, code development, and test professionals under DoD-STD-1679A. Responsible for $6.5MM cost budget.

  • Decreased actual project work time by 10%; introduced Yourdon/DeMarco measurement techniques to track the project and uncover and correct conflicting processes. Completed project 5% under budget.

  • Introduced PC-based project management software to reduce reporting time for status reports to management from one week to less than one day.

196

Senior Software Engineer and Software Product Assurance Manager for the Ada Language System/Navy (ALS/N) development. Prepared the ALS/N Software Configuration Management Plan, Quality Assurance Plan, and Reliability, Maintainability and Availability Plan under DoD-STD-2167. Implemented plans and coordinated Software Quality Assurance and Software Con-figuration Management activities for Control Data and subcontractors: TRW in McLean, VA and SYSCON in Washington, DC. Managed a five-member project-wide support team stationed in Atlanta, Minneapolis, Washington, and San Diego.

GENERAL DYNAMICS SUBMARINE DIVISION, Portsmouth, RI   1985 - 1987
A $10 billion international high technology company producing/serving commercial and defense electronics, engineering and construction, aviation and major appliances.

Senior Software Engineer/Group Leader
Embedded, real-time software designer and Group Leader for the Submarine Advanced Combat System (SubACS) multipurpose console developed under subcontract for IBM Federal Systems, Manassas, VA. Prepared a design specification for the High Density Digital Recorder (HDDR) using Ada/PDL on a Digital Equipment VAX 11/780. Managed a five-member group of software designers to develop the fault detection/location and performance monitoring design specification for SubACS console software and data collection subsystems.

AMOCO CORPORATION, Elizabeth, NJ   1983 - 1985
Worldwide petroleum refining and marketing company operating 27 refineries that produce 5.4MM bbls. of crude oil/day and $1.3 billion annual earnings$_{(1995)}$.

Information Systems Analyst
Maintained and enhanced the Investment Technology Data Management System used by AMOCO Research and Engineering to analyze engineering costs and capital requirements for refineries worldwide.

GENERAL ELECTRIC COMPANY, Daytona Beach, FL   1979 - 1983
Global, $70 billion electronics, aircraft engine, appliances, capital services, lighting, medical systems, broadcasting, services and technology company.

Lead Engineering Programmer/Analyst
Designed/developed the Chrysler XM-1 Tank Simulator image database under contract for the U.S. Army. Designed/implemented physical and logical database for the Compuscene 2000 video processor.

SCHULTZ CONSULTING, Washington, DC   1977 - 1979
Designed and implemented a telecommunications link to the MERLYN financial database to download data to a microcomputer for equities technical analysis for Merrill-Lynch.
Principal

SOUTHERN TIER TELEPHONE COMPANY, Birmingham, AL   1973 - 1977
An international communications holding company with $25 billion in assets and 83,000 employees.

Data Systems Programmer Analyst
Supervised the Rate Master System, Third Number, Credit Card Validation System and the Rate Refund System. Analyst for in-house time sharing applications support group. Assisted in the transfer of engineering applications. Provided technical support, developed and instructed courses in both elementary and advanced FORTRAN applications development to employees.

U.S. ARMY, SP/7 Electronic Maintenance Chief, Honorable Discharge   1968 - 1973

EDUCATION AND TRAINING

MIT Summer Professional Program, The Sloan School, Operations Research   1993
MS, Computer Science, Florida Institute of Technology   1980
BS, Mathematics and Chemistry, University of Alabama at Tuscaloosa   1974

ROBERT BYRNES
1919 SHADY GROVE ROAD
IRVING, TEXAS 75000
(972) 793-5555

UNIX SYSTEMS ADMINISTRATOR/COMPUTER OPERATOR
System Availability / Resource Security / Workload Control / User Training

Innovative and talented computer professional with an impressive record of achievement in technical and systems support. Able to develop procedures to streamline and improve daily operations. Strong communication skills: comfortable interacting at all levels from the Pentagon to co-workers and trainees.

HARDWARE: AT&T 3B2/600G ■ GTSI 433DX/B ■ KG-84 Crypto Equipment
SOFTWARE: AT&T Unix System V ■ CAS-B CAD ■ Windows 3.1 ■ Windows 95
MS Office ■ MS Office Pro 95 ■ Harvard Graphics ■ Power Point
Corell Draw ■ Paintbrush

PROFESSIONAL EXPERIENCE

UNITED STATES AIR FORCE - Lackland Air Force Base Annex   San Antonio, Texas
76th Munitions Squadron
MUNITIONS CONTROLLER/UNIX COMPUTER SYSTEMS ADMINISTRATOR   7/95 TO PRESENT

Designated as **Systems Administrator/Systems Security Operator**. Control all operational programs on AT&T Unix System V. Diverse responsibilities include access control, resource authorizations and permissions, system maintenance and updates, peripheral hardware installation and configuration, performance monitoring, user account audit, system backup and recovery, and user support.

- Maintain mission-critical computer resource in support of Air Force Operations.
- Customized system's user interface to provide improved workflow, reduce time-on-task and enhance system security.
- Identified potential system failures by running built-in diagnostic routines.
- Coordinated with Field Engineers to correct equipment malfunctions.
- Scheduled and performed preventive maintenance.
- Established on-the-job training program to educate users in the correct, efficient use of the computer system and mission-critical software programs.
- Controlled the movement of munitions and insured assets were properly tracked, maintained and delivered.

EDUCATION

ASSOCIATE IN COMPUTER SCIENCE
San Antonio College - San Antonio, Texas

P. C. MODEM

115 North Union Boulevard
Colorado Springs, Colorado 80909
719/632-9050

SUMMARY OF QUALIFICATIONS

- Uniquely well qualified for positions as a **Computer Operator**
- Extensive experience with Mainframe and PC environments
- Operating systems experience includes MS-DOS, Windows, Novell and UNIX
- Application experience with Microsoft products, E-mail and Broadcast FAX
- Knowledgeable with computer aided telephone interviewing (CATI)
- Computer language proficiency includes Assembly, C++ and FORTRAN
- Versed in Computer assisted management
- Extensive experience with technical information storage and retrieval
- Experience with setting up computer systems to solve identified problems
- Computer literate with word processing, data management and spreadsheets
- Managed a large mainframe system support local and remote users
- Implemented system management disciplines including disaster recovery

EDUCATION

Master of Science, Computer Sciences, Knox College, Galesburg, IL

COMPUTER OPERATOR EXPERIENCE

March 1993
to
Present

COMPUTER OPERATOR - NIGHT SHIFT
REHABILITATION HOSPITAL, PUEBLO, COLORADO
- Operate four AS400 Systems at two physical sites
- Responsible for all PC Network Backups
- Maintain multiple LAN/WAN communication systems with 450 stations
- Monitor interfaces between Hospital Lab, Radiology and support systems

September 1990
to
February 1993

COMPUTER OPERATOR - NIGHT SHIFT
POINT LOMA FEDERAL CREDIT UNION, SAN DIEGO, CALIFORNIA
- Operated combined console for multiple inter-dependent systems
- Monitored the operations of ten to thirty systems and 1,000+ jobs per night
- Responsible for exception reporting and follow-up

February 1985
to
August 1990

ASSISTANT DATA PROCESSING COORDINATOR
FIDELITY FEDERAL SAVINGS, CAÑON CITY, COLORADO
- Contact person between all users and data processing:
    - Responsible for all problem resolution
    - Scheduled and prioritized special report requests
    - Computer Inventory Supply Manager
- Complete data processing management for five subordinate companies
* Responsible for Accounts Payable check processing
- Wrote DCL procedures

REFERENCES AND FURTHER DATA UPON REQUEST

STEPHEN RUSSELL

21 N. Stonewood Boulevard
Lake Mary, Florida

Voice: (407) 331-0916
E-mail: bhss@n-jcenter.com

TECHNICAL REPRESENTATIVE / SYSTEMS MANAGER

Dynamic, creative and results-driven professional successful in building state-of-the-art electronic and conventional pre-press and printing systems for start-up, emerging and Fortune 500 companies. Over 16 years progressive experience in introducing leading edge technologies, systems and processes to create technically-advanced, cost-efficient and top performing operations. Accomplished technical representative skilled in customer support, troubleshooting, problem resolution and business development.
Brief summary of technological expertise includes:

Hardware:	Macintosh, PCs, and Scitex
Operating Systems:	Windows 95 and Windows 3.1, DOS, UNIX
Network Systems:	WANs (ISDN, PRI, BRI), LANs Internet
Peripherals:	Scanners, Film Processors, Analog and Digital Proofing Systems, Imagers, CD-ROMs, Magneto Optical Drives, DAT, Backup/Storage Systems
Applications:	Quarkxpress, Pagemaker, Photoshop/Illustration, Macromedia Freehand, Corel Draw, PDF, Pagemill, Suitcase, Streamline, Alphatronix, Kudo and a multitude of Internet, productivity and troubleshooting applications.

PROFESSIONAL EXPERIENCE:

STRANG COMMUNICATIONS, Lake Mary, Florida   1996 to Present

Systems Manager
Management and technology executive responsible for creating, developing and managing state-of-the-art electronic and conventional pre-press production systems for this $3 million company. Full accountability for overall strategy for technology acquisition and integration, process automation, MIS functions, Internet communications, sales support functions, quality control, vendor selection and negotiation, scheduling, administration, safety, human resources, training and support, and daily operations.

- Provide technical expertise for sales presentations capturing numerous new accounts.
- Troubleshoot and advise customers on technical problems achieving maximum system utilization and digital production quality.
- Created and developed additional revenue streams through emerging multimedia technologies including CD-ROMs, electronic cataloging (PDF) and image databases.
- Redesigned Macintosh and Scitex areas and transitioned work flow from Scitex to Macintosh platform without any interruption of services.
- Increased quality control through installation of a Kodak DCP 9000 proofer.

CROSBY DIGITAL SERVICES, Orlando, Florida   1994 to 1996
Member of Crosby Digital Group, a Division of Crosby Corporation

Systems Manager
Directed all phases of electronic and conventional operations and advanced technology systems for the West Coast pre-press division of this Fortune 500 Company with multiple divisions throughout the U.S. Researched, evaluated, coordinated and managed expansion into emerging technology (i.e. T-1 and Internet), high-speed communications, equipment fields and networks. Conducted Scitex PS/2 and Star upgrades, training and phone support for employees and other Banta sites. Managed a staff of 18 employees and customer service representatives.

- Work with major accounts ($500k-$1.5 million) on-site regarding technical support, equipment installation, work flow patterns and pricing structures creating service focus.
- Generated a 425% increase in revenues within 13 months for this 5-month old division.
- Restructured and redesigned Macintosh/Scitex departments for increased efficiencies.

PROFESSIONAL EXPERIENCE (Continued):

REPROGRAPHIC SERVICES, Orlando, Florida   1992 to 1994

Electronic Pre-Press Coordinator / Production Manager
Recruited to lead, direct and manage start-up operations for this new business unit. Directed all electronic and conventional operations. Responsible for all equipment acquisition, work flow communication systems, Macintosh and Scitex transitions, quality control systems, technical training, operations and personnel functions.
- Consulted with customers and led them through technical transition and optimal use of CEPS systems to support company's rapid growth and market penetration.

DAYTONA COLOR GRAPHICS, Daytona, Florida   1991 to 1992

Plant Manager
Directed all offset printing and trade shop operations for this $2 million company through a direct reporting staff of 10-15 employees. Managed quality control, customer service/support programs, personnel functions, estimating and pricing, trouble shooting/resolution, equipment selection, purchasing and maintenance programs.
- Restructured and reengineered plant operations resulting in increased efficiency and productivity to support company's high growth initiatives.

SALTZMAN GRAPHICS, Memphis, Tennessee   1987-1991

Assistant Production Manager / Journeyman 4-Color Stripper
Assistant manager with responsibility for quality control, 4- and 5-color production, estimating and scheduling, raw- and press-color printing, equipment maintenance and a direct reporting staff of 15-20 craftsmen for this $8 million company.
- Ensured accuracy and quality control standards throughout all phases of production and printing to maintain and enhance high-quality standards.

COMMUNIQUE, Tupelo, Mississippi   1982 to 1987

Pre-Press Supervisor (1984 to 1987)
Promoted rapidly to management position with responsibility for daily production, scheduling and quality control for this $5 million company.
- Developed and instituted infrastructures for new plate filing system to support high-volume, quick-turnaround business.

EDUCATION:

Bachelor of Arts – Communication – University of Central Florida, Orlando, Florida

PROFESSIONAL DEVELOPMENT:

PC Troubleshooting Hardware Seminar (2-day), Fort Wayne, Indiana
Macintosh Troubleshooting Hardware Seminar (2-day), Fort Wayne, Indiana
Seybold Conference – February & September 1995 & 1996
Scitex Graphic Arts Users Association – 1993, 1994, 1995 Annual Conventions
Western Virginia Quality Council – 1993 "Embracing Excellence" Symposium and
    1994 "Quality in the Next Century" Symposium
Star PS, Scitex (2-week intensive course), Chicago, Illinois
Star PS, Dolev 200, I/O Whisper, Graphic Production Services (1-week course)
X-Rite Understanding Densitometry Seminar, Richmond, Virginia
Graphic Arts Technical Foundation, Pittsburgh, Pennsylvania

David L. Washington

3304 Windover Drive
Kansas City, MO 63221
(616) 548-5421

CAREER PROFILE

Dynamic management professional spearheading high-growth insurance sales with expertise in captive insurance and program establishment/expansion; property/ casualty; group/executive life products; loss sensitive programs; and complex workers' compensation sales/service with international exposure.

- ❖ Organizational, strategic and tactical leadership in marketing and sales
- ❖ Agent recruitment and training
- ❖ New product development/launch and administration
- ❖ Language: Working knowledge in Spanish.

Professional Designation
Certified Insurance Counselor
Missouri Resident License; Multiple Non-resident License

BACKGROUND AND EXPERIENCE

NATIONAL INTERSTATE   February 1995 - Present
Kansas City, Missouri
NATIONAL ACCOUNT MANAGER/CAPTIVE SALES
Manage an offshore captive insurance company, representing casualty insurance coverage to members/ stockholders.
- ➤ Founded a new insurance company which is owned by its members to provide insurance for their own risks. Customized coverage, established policies/procedures, designed forms, and negotiated out-sources.
- ➤ Grew new membership premiums $1.6 million since October 1996.

FEDERATED INSURANCE COMPANY   1991 - 1995
Freeport, Illinois
MARKETING REPRESENTATIVE
Marketed specialized property/casualty and group/executive life products to trade group members.
- ➤ "President's Council Award" (1994) ranking 2nd in state for total production.
- ➤ Ranked #1 regionally in life sales (1993) by creating a new application for product.

GLENDALE AGENCY, INC.   1986 - 1991
Denver, Colorado
MARKETING MANAGER/ACCOUNT EXECUTIVE
Represented commercial property/casualty accounts with an emphasis on loss sensitive programs and complex workers' compensation sales/service with international exposure.
- ➤ Selected to manage a satellite office, supervising a staff of 5+ with a 30% positive turnaround within one year.

HARTFORD INSURANCE   1981 - 1985
Shawnee Mission, Kansas
MARKETING REPRESENTATIVE

EDUCATIONAL BACKGROUND

Calvin College   **Bachelor of Arts** - 1981
Grand Rapids, Michigan   Business Administration
   Internship: Stewart Wrightson Brokers, London, England (Lloyd's of London), 1978
   Foreign Exchange: Seville, Spain, 1980/81

Continued Professional Development
- Certified Risk Manager (CRM)   1997
- Life Underwriting Training Council (3 of 4 parts)   1995

PRESENTATIONS AND PUBLIC SPEAKING

Airport Ground Transportation Association, Tampa, Florida
   Guest Speaker: "Alternate Risk Management", Tampa, Florida   1997
   Guest Speaker: "Alternate Risk Management", Denver, Colorado   1996

National Motorcoach Network, Salt Lake City, Utah
   Guest Speaker: "Insurance Alternatives"   1997

Federated Insurance Company, Chicago, Illinois
   Guest Speaker: "Estate Planning for Privately Owned Businesses "   1994

Colorado League of Municipalities, Denver, Colorado
   Guest Speaker: "Workers' Compensation Risk Management"   1990

OTHER SIGNIFICANT ENDEAVORS

Advisor   TRAX Insurance, LTD   1996
            Grand Cayman Island based captive insurance company

MEMBERSHIPS AND AFFILIATIONS

Professional Insurance Agents   (PIA)

JAMES M. CAMPBELL
1111 Orchard Avenue
Wisconsin Rapids, Wisconsin 54494
(715) 325-5888

INSURANCE PROFESSIONAL

Over thirteen years of insurance experience within the SIC organization. Proven ability to meet the needs of our members/customers for insurance products. Extensive customer service and general management skills coupled with outstanding presentation and communication skills. Proven abilities in the following areas:

Team Building	General Management	Sales Leadership
Customer Relations	Business Development	Coaching/Counseling
Business Management	Volunteer Management	Marketing

EXPERIENCE

STATE INSURANCE CORPORATION (SIC), Wisconsin Rapids, WI
District Representative - Registered Representative, Stevens Point (1984-Present)
Sell/market a full-line of insurance and investment services to area churches to assist them in securing and maintaining a high quality of life. Conduct seminars on numerous financial issues to various church groups.

Accomplishments:
- Reactivated several branches including the chartering of a completely new branch.
- Member of Executive Committee.
- NBA National Benefit Award Recipient, 11 years.
- NSA National Sales Award, 11 years.

TELEPHONE COMPANY, Rhinelander and Sturgeon Bay, WI
Service Technician (1968-1984)

EDUCATION/CERTIFICATION/LICENSING

The American College for CLU/CHFC Studies, 1996-Present
IC - Insurance Counselor
LUTC - Life Underwriter Training Counselor Graduate
LUTCF Life Underwriter Training Counselor Fellow

Securities Registered Representative

Dale Carnegie, 1992
Management Development Course -Sierra Technical College, 1975
Various Courses through Telephone Company
Graduate - Eau Claire High School, Eau Claire, WI

PROFESSIONAL AFFILIATIONS

National Association of Life Underwriters (NALU) - Member
National Association of Securities Dealers (NASD) - Member

PROFESSIONAL AFFILIATIONS, CONT.

Wisconisn Rapids Association of Life Underwriters (WRALU) - Member
National Association of Insurance Counselor (NAIC) - Member

VOLUNTEER ACTIVITIES

Good People Church, Wisconsin Rapids, WI
- Board of Directors, 1997
- Expansion Committee Member
- Congregation President - 1996 & 1983
    • Undertook and directed a $800,000 building and remodeling campaign from
      initial financing through completion.
- Director of Evangelism, 1996
- Stewardship Chairman, 1996 & 1983
- Sunday School Superintendent, 140 students

NICHOLAS V. WERNOTT

3532 Lakeside Drive
St. Paul, Minnesota 55025
Phone/Fax: (612) 332-8741

INTERNATIONAL BUSINESS DEVELOPMENT EXECUTIVE

Sales & Marketing Leadership / Global Account Management / Multi-Channel Distribution Management
Industrial & Construction Machinery & Equipment

Dynamic management career, building and leading international business development initiatives worldwide. Combines expertise in strategic and tactical sales planning, field sales management and key account negotiations with strong technical and engineering qualifications. Excellent general management, budgeting, staffing, organizational and project management skills. Fluent English and Dutch. Conversational German.

Delivered strong and sustainable revenue growth through success in
multinational customer development, management and competitive retention.

PROFESSIONAL EXPERIENCE:

International Sales Manager   1995 to Present
HUGO EQUIPMENT, INC., St. Paul, Minnesota
(High-growth horizontal directional drill & related equipment manufacturer)

Challenge: To accelerate international market expansion for this high-growth, U.S. heavy equipment manufacturer.

Results:

- Built International sales from $500,000 in 1995 to $3+ million in 1996.
- Expanded market presence throughout Australia, New Zealand, Malaysia, Hong Kong, Eastern & Western Europe, and Latin America.
- Created an international dealer/distributor network worldwide.

International Sales Manager   1992 to 1994
GLOBAL EQUIPMENT MANUFACTURING, Cedar Rapids, Iowa
(Privately-held, high-growth heavy equipment engineering & manufacturing company)

Challenge: To provide strategic and tactical sales leadership in developing international market opportunities and expanding revenue streams.

Results:

- Developed and directed major dealer organizations worldwide in Australia, New Zealand, China, Japan, Korea, Hong Kong and Singapore. Personally negotiated large dollar direct sales opportunities in the U.S., Europe, Saudi Arabia and Thailand, including a $2.6 million contract against worldwide competition.
- Transitioned Australian dealer network from loss to profitability, established dealer finance program and increased sales to $2.7 million in just one year.
- Established and led $4.2 million dealer network in China.
- Increased Pac Rim sales from $2.1 million to $3.3 million (59%) in first year.
- Pioneered equipment modifications and enhancements to meet complex customer specifications. Provided technical leadership to design and engineering teams.

Sales Representative / Sales Engineer   1988 to 1992
MIDWEST MACHINERY COMPANY, Portsmouth, Ohio
(Privately-owned John Deere dealer/distributor)

Challenge: To accelerate revenue growth throughout both established and emerging customer markets.

Results:

- Provided strong and decisive leadership in sales, marketing and account management to enhance the value and retention of 400+ customer accounts.
- Led the start-up of a U.S. niche market and grew revenues to $1.5 million in two years.
- Managed seven major turnkey plant projects from initial customer consultation through complex sales negotiations to full-scale turnkey start-up.
- Innovated unique barter transactions between manufacturer and supplier, increasing sales $940,000 annually through non-traditional revenue streams.
- Won 9 out of 10 bids presented to the U.S. Department of Transportation.

Sales Representative / Branch Manager   1984 to 1988
AGRICULTURAL EQUIPMENT SUPPLY, LTD., Brisbane, Australia
(Privately-owned John Deere dealer/distributor)

Challenge: Revitalize market presence throughout Australia and drive long-term growth.

Results:

- Revitalized customer relations, renegotiated key contracts and maintained market share despite economic downturn. Achieved/surpassed all revenue goals.
- Initiated and won $1.6 million sale in flat economy and against major competition.
- Increased productivity 30% while providing high level of customer service and technical product support.
- Managed and enhanced the value of 300+ customer relationships.

Product Support Sales Representative   1977 to 1984
LAUDRUP B.V., Amsterdam, The Netherlands
(Privately-owned John Deere dealer/distributor)

Challenge: To build a top-performing regional sales territory throughout The Netherlands' key commercial, industrial and government markets.

Results:

- Built and managed the most successful sales region in the country. Increased customer base from 130 to 300+ accounts, increased market share from 45% to 75% and improved revenue performance 35% (at significantly better than average profit margins).
- Introduced an equipment exchange program that generated $1.3 million in high profit revenues and significantly improved customer retention/resale.
- Created area management program adopted throughout Europe, then implemented worldwide.

EDUCATION:

BBA Degree (Top 5%), Institute of Automotive Business, Driebergen, The Netherlands, 1970
Engineering Graduate, Central Technical School, Breukelen, The Netherlands
Professional Development: 70+ seminars on Sales, Marketing, Management & Customer Service

Timothy McConnell

33c, Kings Court
3 Truman Road
Hong Kong

Telephone 852-2970-6080   e-mail tpconnell@ibm.net   Fax 852-2970-6081

International Sales / Sales Management

➤ A proven performer with consistently strong sales achievements both in individual sales and through leadership of a sales/distributor force.

STRENGTHS

- Developing and implementing strategic business plans to fulfill long-range objectives.
- Working productively with people of different cultures in a challenging and competitive business environment.
- Assimilating and communicating technical information.
- Directing a distributor sales staff to achieve goals by focusing on the development and implementation of individual strategies carefully tailored for each key account.
- Gaining the support and cooperation of sales staff, customers, and professional colleagues though effective leadership techniques.

Professional Experience

MEDI-QUIP INTERNATIONAL, INC.   1988-Present

➤ **International Territory Manager — Australasia** (1993-Present)

Manage the highest dollar volume distributor territory in the International Department, directing sales of medical equipment and disposables to hospitals and cardiologists in the Pacific Rim, Indian Subcontinent, Australia, and New Zealand.

Oversee 14 distributors in 16 countries, each with unique business customs and sales styles. Appropriately assess, adapt to, and sell in these highly diverse cultures, some demanding an efficient, businesslike approach while others require more intensive relationship-building.

Assist distributors with strategic planning, organization, and direction of their sales efforts toward the achievement of personal, regional and corporate goals. Organize and conduct regional sales and product training meetings, focusing on customer service and account follow-up.

Train hospital staff cardiologists, anesthesiologists, and intensive care physicians in equipment use.

KEY ACCOMPLISHMENTS AND AWARDS

- Hired and trained 6 new distributors; grew sales in their countries from zero to more than US$1.2 million.
- Led territory to exponential sales growth (694% in 4 years), from flat sales at US$1.6 million to US$11.1 million in 4 years.
- Inducted into "Medi-Quip Master" Club, an award reserved for only 1 or 2 international managers a year (May 1997) — honored for overachieving sales objectives for the last 3 years.

➤ **International Territory Manager — South America and Far East** (1992-1993)

Focused first-year efforts on the management of a sales and distributor sales/product training force in 8 South and Central American countries.

KEY ACCOMPLISHMENTS

- Added 3 distributors in Mexico, Brazil, and Argentina who achieved sales growth from US$400K to US$1.1 million within first year.
- Stepped into an interim position and, within a few months, achieved outstanding sales results — attributable to hard work, thorough planning, and comprehensive application of sound sales strategies. Sales activity justified the hiring of a full-time South American territory manager and enabled sole concentration on activities in the Far East.

Professional Experience

MEDI-QUIP INTERNATIONAL, INC. (continued)

➤ **Medical Sales Specialist — St. Louis, Missouri** (1988-1992)

Managed the highest volume territory in the Midwest region (#5 nationally), selling critical care devices to hospital departments including surgery, anesthesia, intensive care and emergency care. Provided clinical training to hospital staff on all products.

KEY ACCOMPLISHMENTS AND AWARDS

- Expanded customer base by 25% in major teaching hospitals.
- Developed territory sales from a base of US$800K to US$4.1 million.
- One of 2 winners of the 1990 and 1991 Medi-Quip Circle of Excellence Sales Award.

THE MENNEN COMPANY   1986-1988

➤ **Key Accounts Manager — St. Louis, Missouri** (1988)

Managed sales to major Midwestern retail accounts.

- Increased sales 45% over the previous year.

➤ **Territory Sales Manager — Columbus, Ohio** (1986-1988)

Marketed Mennen products to large regional corporate accounts.

- Achieved annual sales increases of 25%-30%.
- Increased market share in each account by 25%-35%.
- One of 5 entries into the 1987 Green Blazer Council for overall increase in sales volume.

C.B. SMITH COMPANY   1985-1986

➤ **Sales Representative — Columbus, Ohio**

Interacted with established retail accounts and evaluated new customer opportunities for a variety of food and non-food items.

Education

Bachelor of Arts degree, Business Administration, 1985
THE OHIO STATE UNIVERSITY, Columbus, Ohio

SALES TRAINING

- Medi-Quip International Sales School, 1988
- The Mennen Company Sales School, 1986

Additional Information

Date of Birth	September 12, 1961
Citizenship	U.S.
Marital Status	Single
Computer Skills	Proficient in a variety of business applications including Microsoft Word and Excel, Internet research and communication.
Language	Beginning intensive course in Mandarin Chinese, Summer 1997.

No restrictions on travel or relocation worldwide for the right opportunity.

ROBERT J. ASHER

Playa Del Rey, California
310.555.5555

PROFILE
Results-driven executive manager with expertise in global operations,
distribution, international letters of credit, collections, and cross-cultural film technologies.
Strong international and domestic experience.

SELECTED ACHIEVEMENTS AND QUALIFICATIONS

ADMINISTRATIVE AND ACCOUNT MANAGEMENT
- Successfully directed the International Distribution for the 900 title Noiro Pictures library
- Direct responsibility for the promotional and broadcast delivery of 2200 titles in the libraries of: NOMOLOS, LANAC+ (Paris), SACIS (Rome), Dino de Laurentis, OCLORAC, and Active Entertainment, serving over 220 North American and worldwide TV markets
- Operated as the distribution Account Executive for Mira Records and Callé Int'l. (Sidney), primarily servicing Noiro Pictures
- Secured contract approval for deal memos, processed license agreements and amendments, contract collections and account receivables, including opening and negotiating letters of credit
- Apprised sales and acquisition's departments on current and future projects
- Ability to develop rapport and build relationships with customers and clients through attention to detail in defining needs and providing service and solutions to meet those needs
- Excellent management and leadership skills resulting in top employee performance
- Strong emphasis on cost containment, production and distribution control
- Experienced and effective with collections procedures
- Maintained current status reports between sales, production and distribution departments

FILM, PUBLICITY, AND BROADCAST MATERIAL DISTRIBUTION
- Organized post-production and distribution departments; master tape acquisition and production
- Responsible for setting and releasing titles based upon rights availability, and maintenance of world-wide bicycling (tapes) schedule
- Liaison with publicity, post-production and distribution in fulfilling client requirements.
- Demonstrated expertise in comprehensive sound, film, music and effects, dubbing and laboratory requirements, and computerized post-production systems
- Strong background in International post-production standards and distribution requirements for both major foreign and overseas English language markets

Technical Skills - expertise with: D-1-SONY DVR2000; D-2-SONY DVR18/28; DIGIBETA-SONY DVW500/P; 1"-SONY BVH 2000; AMPEX VPR6; Betacam-SONY BVW 75/P

PROFESSIONAL EXPERIENCE

DIRECTOR - International Distribution	*NOMOLOS INTERNATIONAL*, Hollywood, CA	1995 to present
DIRECTOR - International Distribution	*NOIRO PICTURES INTERNATIONAL*, Century City, CA	1992 to 1995
DISTRIBUTION MANAGER	*ACME EXPRESS INTERNATIONAL*, Inglewood, CA	1991 to 1992
DIRECTOR - Licensing and Operations	*EXPORT TRADE GROUP*, Long Beach, CA	1988 to 1991
OPERATIONS MANAGER	*ATLAS, INCORPORATED*, Los Angeles, CA	1987 to 1988
LAW CLERK, DEPT. OF JUSTICE	*U.S. ATTORNEYS OFFICE*, San Francisco, CA	1983 to 1986

EDUCATION

UNIVERSITY OF CALIFORNIA LOS ANGELES   Westwood, CA
    GRADUATE STUDIES   Film, Television and Video program
STANFORD UNIVERSITY   San Francisco, CA
    GRADUATE PROGRAM   Pacific Rim International Business
STANFORD UNIVERSITY   San Francisco, CA
    BACHELOR OF SCIENCE - DOUBLE MAJOR International Affairs and Asian History
        Minor: International Business

AARON M. SHEA

325 Iron Lane
Norwich, Connecticut 06360

Home (203) 849-3165   Fax (203) 849-3027

INVESTMENT INDUSTRY EXECUTIVE

Proprietary Trader / Fixed Income Trader / Hedge Fund Trader / Portfolio Manager
Expertise in Financial Futures & Options on Financial Futures
Extensive Qualifications in Mortgage-Backed Securities & Government Bonds

Talented and successful Trading Professional with 15+ years Wall Street experience. Combines cross-functional expertise in complex investment strategy and execution with a strong record of performance in risk management, yield improvement and profitability. Excellent market knowledge and crisis management skills. PC literate.

PROFESSIONAL EXPERIENCE:

BANK OF NEW YORK, New York, New York   1986 to 1997
($10 billion diversified global financial institution)

Assistant Vice President (1988 to 1997)
Senior Bond Proprietary Trader (1986 to 1988)

Senior Trader responsible for identifying, analyzing, evaluating and capturing trading opportunities in the financial futures and options on financial futures markets. Monitored and tracked interest rates and spreads in the fixed income markets. Purchased swaps, caps, floors and corridors to protect against unusual and/or unexpected changes in interest rates.

In addition, directed the purchasing of U.S. Treasury securities to meet banking and Federal Reserve regulatory requirements and to ensure adequate margins for trading financial futures and options on financial futures.

- Generated an average $1.5 million profit over four consecutive years (1992-96) trading financial futures and options on financial futures.

- Traded short and intermediate term U.S. Government securities during first year with the institution. Generated profit of $650,000.

Assigned concurrent responsibility in 1988 for developing and executing investment management and yield enhancement strategies for a $500 million hedged mortgage-backed portfolio (spread of $5 million to $7.5 million annually).

- Arranged mortgage financing by soliciting bids from primary dealers, resulting in an annual finance savings of $500,000 (equivalent to 10 basis points).

- Introduced yield enhancing strategies by selling options, puts and calls, generating additional income of $2 million annually for six consecutive years (equivalent to 40 basis points).

DAVIS BISHOP, INC., New York, New York   1982 to 1986

Trader - Retail Government Bond Department

Managed the Retail Government Bond Department, including training and technical/financial leadership to a staff of four traders. Actively participated as a market maker servicing the company's retail and mini-institutional system with bids and offerings on U.S. Government Treasury bills, notes and bonds, Federal Agency securities, and trades with other Federal Reserve Bank of New York primary Government bond dealers.

Concurrently, planned and directed Davis Bishop's nationwide CD program. Evaluated market and recommended weekly rates on primary CD's for 32 issuing institutions. Managed a staff of two traders providing bids and offerings on secondary market CD's and supported National Retail Sales Manager in marketing CD products to the 480 Davis Bishop and Regent Financial Service Center offices nationwide.

- Consistently generated yields in the top percentage of the nationwide industry.

CONNECTICUT TRANSCORP, INC., Hartford, Connecticut   1979 to 1982

Government & Federal Agency Bond Trader

Formulated and executed investment trading strategy for both Government and Federal agency bonds, notes and other fixed income investments.

- Generated $400,000 in average annual profit for three consecutive years.

- Developed the institution's first-ever program for financial futures arbitrage and balance sheet hedging, generating an additional $600,000 in annual profit.

TIMOTHY E. CONNOLLY & CO., New York, New York   1976 to 1979

Government Bond Trader

Traded intermediate and long-term U.S. Government Treasury notes and bonds.

BANK OF ATLANTIC, New York, New York   1973 to 1976

Sales Associate

Sold/marketed government bonds, Treasury notes and bonds, and money market investments to institutional accounts throughout New England and the Middle Atlantic region. Strong production record.

- Graduate of intensive 6-month training program in Bank Investment Securities Division. Completed rotations in Operations, Portfolio Management, Research and Trading.

EDUCATION:

B.S., Management, University of Connecticut, Storrs, Connecticut, 1971
Minors in English & Psychology

THOMAS C. MARTIN

436 Declaration Street, Apt. 315
San Diego, California 93209
Residence: (415) 367-7788   Email: tcmartin@ijt.net

EXPERIENCED FINANCE PROFESSIONAL
Investment & Business Valuation / Strategic & Operational Planning / Marketing & Business Development
Financial & Statistical Analysis / Financial Advisory Services / Capital Market Financings
Darden MBA - Top 4% of Graduating Class

PROFESSIONAL EXPERIENCE:

BOYD WHITE & CO., San Diego, California   1996 to 1997
Vice President - Investment Banking (1997)
Associate - Investment Banking (1996 to 1997)

- Key member of new business development team marketing financial advisory/capital market services to corporate clients throughout the transportation, retail/distribution and natural resource industries.
- Developed/refined client business plans, prepared industry overviews and wrote offering memoranda to market companies to potential buyers and raise capital in both the public and private markets.
- Managed due diligence, supervised drafting sessions, and structured over $600 million in transactions (e.g., equity, high-yield, convertible debt and private placement offerings; company spin-off).
- Recruited, trained and directed a team of four financial analysts.

JOHNSON & BELL CORPORATION, New York, New York   1994 to 1996
Associate - Investment Banking

- Instrumental in the successful planning and leadership of Johnson & Bell's expanded market coverage in the automotive parts, airline and air cargo, and oil and gas industries.
- Identified acquisition candidates and developed business profiles to facilitate discussions with potential strategic and financial buyers.
- Prepared valuations of corporate clients and potential acquisitions using comparable public market multiples, historical acquisition multiples and discounted cash flows. Developed proposals on relative costs of equity, debt and convertible securities financings.
- Advised clients and structured/negotiated over $1 billion in acquisition, divestiture, IPO and high-yield transactions. Guided corporate clients in development of shareholder rights plans.

PHILLIPS & FRANKLIN, INC., San Francisco, California   1992 to 1994
Associate - Management Consulting

- Planned and directed high-profile management consulting engagements across diverse industries and market sectors. Provided expertise in strategic planning, corporate finance, marketing and operations.
- Advised major industrial equipment manufacturer on current valuation and business potential of 15 non-core subsidiaries as part of a strategic portfolio review resulting in the $180 million divestiture of several business lines.
- Developed distribution and marketing strategy for petroleum refinery and service operations.
- Created an enhanced market segmentation strategy and analyzed the profitability of specific segments to refocus a major commercial bank's core marketing strategy.
- Evaluated cost savings and regulatory impact of combining two power-line maintenance divisions for a major electric utility.

LINCOLN SERVICES, INC., San Francisco, California — 1989 to 1990
General Manager

- Full P&L responsibility for the operation and subsequent divestiture of family-owned road construction machinery company. Determined divestiture strategy, identified buyers, and profitably sold 40 tons of steel beams and 4,000+ parts inventory.
- Continue to manage seven commercial rental units (20,000+ sq. ft.) and several oil-producing properties, including lease negotiations with tenants ranging from Fortune 500 companies to sole proprietorships.

FIRST VALLEY BANK, San Francisco, California — 1987 to 1990
Financial Consultant (1990)

- Recruited back to First Valley in April 1990 to lead a cross-functional team of more senior professionals in developing a statistical model to predict profitability of new branch operations which outperformed all existing qualitative techniques.
- Created database of demographic and competitive data for over 300 branches throughout California.
- Isolated the importance of key factors in determining branch profitability using various statistical techniques (e.g., regression, factor analysis, clustering).
- Developed business cases for capital expenditures which generated $1.5 million in annual cost savings.

Corporate Finance Associate - Global Banking (1988 to 1989)

- Developed database of existing bank clients and current product usage to identify and exploit opportunities to cross-sell non-traditional financing techniques.
- Created commercial paper and medium-term note financing proposals to offer clients lower borrowing rates than traditional bank lines.
- Promoted as the only non-MBA Associate in department.

Market Planning Analyst - Marketing & Planning (1987 to 1988)

- Prepared competitive analyses for Board of Directors on the California banking industry and provided analytical support to product managers on market trends, competitor pricing and product introduction.
- Devised creative financial model to assess the costs and benefits of a $2.6 million sales incentive program, a key contribution to the plan's approval by the Board of Directors.
- Recipient of quarterly award as #1 performer in division of 60 professionals.

EDUCATION:

THE DARDEN SCHOOL / UNIVERSITY OF VIRGINIA, Charlottesville, Virginia
MBA - Concentration in Finance - May 1992
- Jefferson Scholar - Top 4% of Graduating Class
- Managing Editor - *The Darden Journal*

OCCIDENTAL COLLEGE, Los Angeles, California
BA - Double Majors in Economics & Biology - *Phi Beta Kappa* - June 1987
- Wall Street Journal Award - Graduated #1 in Economics Department
- Published in *Biological Bulletin* - Electron Microscopy Research

Academic Exchange Programs in Bangkok, Thailand and Cairo, Egypt.

Herbert S. Grant

93 Half Acre Road
Piscataway, New Jersey 08854
732-679-4958

Summary of Qualifications

Increasing responsibilities in areas including:

- Consultative Sales
- Commercial and Investment Banking
- Trade Execution

- Account Development
- Economic Forecasting
- Business Management

Experience

Financial Trading

ARTHUR WALLACE, INC., Senior Foreign Exchange Broker   1991-Present
New York, New York

As a Senior Broker on the USD/DM desk, responsible for establishing and maintaining major accounts in the United States, Canada and Europe. Manage account relationships with both Commercial and Investment Banks. Advise clients regarding market activity, trends, and expectations in North America and Europe. Market and develop new business and negotiate brokerage agreements on behalf of the firm. Execute trades for clients that generate approximately $1.25 million in annualized revenues for the firm.

Report directly to the Managing Director of Foreign Exchange. Participate in decisions regarding all aspects of the firm including Human Resources, Marketing, and Communication Systems. Chosen to manage the firms spot risk exposure. Train junior brokers and assist them in promoting business. Expanded institutional client base of international and domestic banks and/or financial institutions.

THOMAS & FINCH, INC., Foreign Exchange Broker   1989-1991
New York, New York

Employed as a Broker on the USD/DM desk. Served as a liaison between New York, London and Dusseldorf branch offices. Involved in the buying and selling of Foreign Currencies including spots, forwards, and arbitrage in all major currencies.

International/Maritime

OVERSEAS TERMINALS, INC., Marine Superintendent   1987-1989
Port Elizabeth, New Jersey

In charge of 75-100 union personnel. Responsible for the loading operations of the entire terminal.

ACME TANKERS, INC., Third Mate   1983-1987
St. Louis, Missouri

As an Officer of the ship, navigated the vessel in the Caribbean and International waters. Directed 25-30 crew members. Involved in the loading and discharging of cargo in port.

Education

Massachusetts Maritime Academy, BS in Marine Transportation, June 1983
Minor: Business Management   Deans List

United States Coast Guard, Licensed Third Mate/Unlimited/Radar Endorsement

Current Certification: First Aid and CPR.

JEFFREY E. SUTER, ESQUIRE

41 Arden Hill
Cowher, Pennsylvania 36104
Home (412) 951-9937   Office (412) 930-8281

SENIOR CORPORATE LEGAL AND REGULATORY EXECUTIVE
Multinational and Non-Profit Organizations in Health Care, Pharmaceuticals and Biotechnology

Senior Executive with expertise in legal and regulatory affairs. Comprehensive knowledge of FDA regulatory issues: field enforcement, inspections, 483 responses, litigation, compliance, and drug, device and diagnostic product submissions. Familiar with a wide range of other governmental policy-making/regulatory entities including EPA, OSHA, EEOC, NIOSH, FTC, and FCC. Highly effective at gaining top-down management and regulatory support for quality assurance programs. Legal/Management strengths include:

- Team Development and Leadership
- Process Reengineering
- Mergers/Acquisitions
- Human Resources

- Strategic Planning
- Policy Development
- Intellectual Property Licensing
- Litigation Management

PROFESSIONAL EXPERIENCE

UNITED BIOMEDICAL FOUNDATION, Washington, D.C.   1994 to 1997
($1 billion biomedical services organization)

Vice President, Regulatory Policy

Chief Regulatory Officer and member of Executive Steering Committee leading the organization through a period of accelerated change and reorganization. Retained by Board of Governors to plan and orchestrate a wide range of FDA liaison, regulatory compliance, strategic planning and reengineering processes.

- Contributed to strong financial results:
  - Developed a board-approved strategy to resolve key FDA issues in 1993 Consent Decree, including a detailed plan to reverse the previous year's loss of $118 million within 14 months.
  - Introduced internal Consent Decree reporting process that saved $1.5 million in outside legal fees.
  - Directed task force reengineering recall S.O.P.'s, resulting in annual savings of $2 million.
  - Spearheaded the amendment of FDA pre-market approval requirements for blood-banking software, eliminating a potential redundant systems expense of $40 million.

- Created environment for, implemented and facilitated FDA acceptance of Quality Assurance program.

- Significantly reduced FDA review time for approximately 600 FDA submissions.

NORTHWEST PHARMACEUTICALS, INC., Seattle, Washington   1991 to 1993
(Publicly-held biotechnology company specializing in CNS drugs)

Vice President/General Counsel

Chief Legal Officer and member of 5-person Senior Management Team with responsibility for strategic planning, business development and management of all legal, human resources and intellectual property functions. Provided expert legal counsel during a period of fast-track growth and expansion.

- Forged strategic alliances with 13 major pharmaceutical partners to facilitate public offering, including multinational firms, NIH and other academic institutions.

- Oversaw NDA submissions process for breakthrough CNS drug (dexfenfloramine).

- Successfully settled EEO litigation and claims, and DEA claim of employee misuse of controlled substances, without adverse stock price impact.

- Pioneered development of the corporation's first-ever Quality Assurance Program.

- Initiated employee awareness program to prevent illegal securities trading.

HEALTHCARE PRODUCTS INTERNATIONAL , New York, New York   1982 to 1991
(NYSE healthcare products manufacturer)

Vice President - Legal and Regulatory Affairs (1988 to 1991)

Chief Legal Officer and member of Operating Committee, reporting directly to the President. Reengineered the healthcare business by creating two separate, integrated business units to enhance customer focus.

Deputy General Counsel (1986 to 1988)

Directed general corporate, trademark, FDA and environmental law. Managed staff of 20. Structured, negotiated and closed legal contracts for 11 acquisitions and divestitures valued at more than $550 million.

Senior Counsel (1982 to 1986)

Point-man in negotiations with the Department of Justice to position Healthcare as a viable business and suitable buyer to gain approval for the purchase of a $220 million pharmaceutical firm.

EARLY PROFESSIONAL CAREER:

Regulatory Attorney, UpJohn Corporation, New York, New York   1978 to 1982
(NYSE pharmaceutical, healthcare and consumer products manufacturer)

General Counsel of Subsidiary, Henderson Pharmaceuticals, Inc., Princeton, New Jersey   1976 to 1978
(Multinational pharmaceutical manufacturer)

Associate, Maxwell, Samuelson & Mitchell, New York, New York   1974 to 1976
(Corporate law firm with heavy FDA practice)

EDUCATION

Juris Doctor, University of Pennsylvania Law School, Philadelphia, Pennsylvania
Bachelor of Arts, Duke University, Durham, North Carolina

ADMISSIONS AND ASSOCIATIONS

Admitted to the practice of law in all courts in New York, New Jersey and Michigan
Admitted to the U.S. Supreme Court
American Bar Association
Former Chair; Law and American Youth Committee ... Former Secretary, Young Lawyers Section
Licensing Executives Society
Regulatory Affairs Professional Society

JOHN P. COSWELL

Office: (212) 395-0097   297 Cedar Woods   Goldens Bridge, NY 10526   Home: (914) 232-1998

SENIOR BUSINESS TRANSACTIONS ATTORNEY
Telecommunications & Technology Law / Negotiation Team Management / Project Management
Proposals and Contracts with Fortune 500 Accounts / Dispute Resolution / Compliance Programs

Twenty-three year highly productive career providing strategic legal counsel and transactional expertise. Skilled negotiator, mediator and executive advisor. Provide sound business counseling expertise to all levels of management and officers. Seasoned Project Manager with strong leadership skills and qualifications in team building. Expertise in: Telecommunications and Technology Law, Software & Hardware Contracts; Project Management; Direct Sales, Sales Channel, Marketing and Network Operation Support; Dispute Resolution and Litigation; Compliance, Audits, Internal Practices, Training Courses; and Regulatory Matters. Proven ability to independently handle significant responsibilities based on in-depth knowledge of the law and broad experience:

- Two years as Project Manager on key business task forces.
- Five years of technology law representing software developers in software development, computer and licensing contracts.
- Eight years representing sales force in complex telecommunications, equipment and service contracts.
- Six years of successful dispute resolution,litigation management and litigation.
- Two years experience in State Regulatory matters.

Provided the strategic and tactical actions that delivered millions of dollars in revenue gains and cost savings to clients.

PROFESSIONAL EXPERIENCE

NYNEX CORPORATION, New York, NY   December 1981 - Present
Corporate Counsel

Management Experience
- Serve as *Project Manager* on the Company's significant complex telecommunications proposals and sales contracts.
- As *Contracts Manager* - Divestiture, managed six attorneys in the implementation of numerous agreements necessary *to split $8.5 B of network assets* during the AT&T divestiture.
- As *Project Manager* -Profit Improvement Program, achieved significant earnings improvement through managing six NYNEX personnel and coordinating efforts of Coopers & Lybrand in a seven month program to improve profitability of a NYNEX subsidiary by real estate consolidations, layoffs, and improved warehouse and billing systems.
- As *Project Manager* for Accounts Receivable Task Force, *orchestrated the collection of $10M* (10% of annual revenue of the subsidiary) while managing ten staff during this six month project.
- Provided counsel and *directed all implementation tasks* flowing from NYNEX's acquisition of Southern New England Telephone Company's customer premises equipment accounts.
- Oversaw selection, hiring and managing of outside counsel and associated budget for Business Law group, resulting in *reduction of outside counsel bills by 20%* over a five year period.

Direct Sales, Sales Channel, Marketing and Network Operation Support
- Serve as Counsel to Telephone Company's sales force providing expertise on the terms of sale of complex telecommunications systems, including advice on regulated tariff services and unregulated network integration offerings.
- Serve as Counsel for all NYNEX's legal needs in the marketing and operations functions for Project FLAG (Fiberoptic Link Around the Globe). Provide legal services to all levels of senior executives and management including corporate governance functions. Drafted and *negotiated Sales/Marketing Agreement yielding $80M* in commissions to NYNEX; *drafted and negotiated Project Management Agreement yielding $40M* in revenue; review of marketing literature; insurance and other operations advice; litigation and dispute resolution responsibilities.
- As *lead attorney*, *oversaw all Divestiture Contracts with AT&T relating to split of $8.5B* of network assets. Drafted seventeen primary agreements, including Billing Agreement *yielding $100M* in revenue to NYNEX.
- Provided counsel to Mobile Telephone Company on all aspects of its cellular telephone business. Drafted and negotiated a wide variety of sales, marketing, reseller, operations and software licensing agreements in addition to trademark licensing advice.
- Provided expertise on all aspects of telecommunications, customer premises, and personal computer equipment requirements of Fortune 500 accounts. Extensive experience in negotiating and drafting of customer, vendor, manufacturer, subcontractor and equipment leasing agreements.
- Advise on all aspects of contracts with the Federal, New York State and Massachusetts governments.

NYNEX CORPORATION *continued*

Technology Law, Software and Hardware Contracts
- Served as *lead attorney* for Telephone Company division which developed and processed one of the first NYNEX post-divestiture patents, a coin auditor counting device *resulting in savings* of *millions* of dollars in the pay phone market.
- As lead attorney, drafted and negotiated a $35M software development and license contract with the Port Authority of NY/NJ Airports and with Dallas/Fort Worth Airport for parking lot revenue control software system.
- Serving as lead attorney and *principal negotiator*, *generated profits of $9M* through agreements for disposition by sale of three software companies sold at $20M, $5M, and $4M.
- As co-counsel, successfully defended NYNEX in a patent infringement case *avoiding exposure of $3M*.
- Negotiated and drafted development license with the Federal Government in a software development venture with the U.S. Federal Highway Administration.
- Played significant role in developing international software distribution channel including software licensing and distribution agreements with customers and distributors in the U.K., Spain, Israel, New Zealand, Australia, Malaysia, and Japan.

Dispute Resolution and Litigation
- As *lead attorney*, *negotiated* Operator Services Contract dispute with AT&T resulting in *$20M settlement* for NYNEX Telephone Companies, *significantly improving earnings*.
- Managed numerous disputes with AT&T relating to the Divestiture including successful defense and negotiation arising from split of customer equipment and inside wire assets, *avoiding a $15M exposure*.
- Litigated average caseload (1982 and 1985) of 125 cases, primarily commercial, contract, and business tort cases.
- *Manage*, on average each year, dozens of customer and vendor disputes, claims, and litigation, using a variety of *alternative dispute resolution methods*.

Compliance, Audits, Internal Practices, Training Courses, Corporate Governance
- Developed, managed, and implemented NYNEX's *Plan for Compliance with Federal and State laws* in government contracting. Drafted Compliance Plan, developed and offered training courses and conducted compliance audits.
- Conducted antitrust *compliance audit* in several NYNEX subsidiaries.
- Developed, drafted and implemented *Subcontractor Procedures Plan* in NYNEX's telecommunications equipment subsidiary.
- Developed, drafted and implemented *Purchasing Practices and Controls* in NYNEX's international subsidiary.
- Developed, drafted, and implemented *Contracting Practices* in NYNEX's computer and software subsidiaries.
- Regularly conduct "How To Contract" seminars with Sales, Purchasing, and Network Operations Managers.
- Performed Secretary/Assistant Secretary, Corporate Governance functions for six subsidiaries.

Regulatory Matters
- Served as co-counsel in two rate increase cases for NYNEX- Vermont preparing discovery, temporary rates brief, rate design brief and affiliated interests investigation and brief.
- Served as counsel to regulatory/marketing staffs on various tariff filings and new product trials.

BROWN, PRIFTI, LEIGHTON & COHEN, Boston, MA   1975 - 1981
Associate
- Engaged in general practice including civil litigation; general corporate; commercial and real estate transactions.
- Primary practice consisted of civil litigation including six jury trials and fifty jury waived trials in State Court and U.S. District Court of Massachusetts.

SWARTZ & SWARTZ, Boston, MA   1974 - 1975
Associate
- Engaged in hazardous products liability and personal injury practice representing plaintiffs.
- Handled all aspects of pleadings, discovery and motion practice in U.S. District Court.
- Handled three jury-waived and two master's trials in State Court.

EDUCATION

BOSTON COLLEGE LAW SCHOOL
Juris Doctor   June 1973
- *Ranked 23 of 275*
- *Honors Scholarship* 2 of 3 years
- Served on Law Review, 2nd year
- Legal Aid Service, 2nd and 3rd years

BOSTON COLLEGE
Bachelor of Arts: History   June 1969
- *Graduated Cum Laude*
- Member: Public Speaking and Debating Team

PROFESSIONAL AFFILIATIONS
- American Bar Association
- Corporate Bar Association (Westchester- Fairfield)

ADMISSION TO PRACTICE
- New York State (12/18/87)
- Massachusetts (6/10/74)
- U.S. District Court for the District of Massachusetts (10/27/74)

CONTINUING LEGAL EDUCATION
- Federal Government Contracting (1992; 1994;1996)
- Software Licensing & Technology Law (1990; 1992; 1994)
- Multi Media & Technology Law (1993)
- International Joint Ventures (1992)
- Negotiation Workshops (1993; 1995)
- Compliance / Federal Sentencing (1993)
- Antitrust Developments (1992; 1994; 1996)

LAURA J. STEVENS
6543 Rivermont Terrace
Baltimore, Maryland 21244-1293

Residence: 410-998-3321   Email: ljstvns@edtrjs.com

CORPORATE COUNSEL
Corporate Law / Litigation / Transactions / HR Law / Risk Management / Intellectual Property
General Business Management / Multi-Site Operations / Corporate Strategic Planning
Participative & Results-Driven Leadership Style. Keen Negotiating & Problem-Solving Skills.

PROFESSIONAL EXPERIENCE:

MITCHELL FOODSERVICE COMPANY, Baltimore, Maryland   1997 to Present
(Diversified foodservice distributor with $1.7 billion in sales, 4000 employees & 13 U.S. locations)

Assistant General Counsel

Manage corporate legal affairs in intellectual property, information systems, employment and labor issues, contracts, product liability, construction/real estate and collections. Advise senior management and outside counsel on litigation and dispute resolution. *Retained on temporary assignment through Special Counsel.*

PEAKLAND INSURANCE CORPORATION   1992 to 1997
Baltimore, Maryland / New York, New York
($45 million in annual revenue, 220 employees and operations in the U.S., Canada, U.K. & Ireland)

Senior Counsel - Litigation & Domestic Transactions (1996 to 1997)
Associate General Counsel (1995 to 1996)
Senior Attorney (1992 to 1995)

Advanced through a series of increasingly responsible corporate legal positions to final promotion as Senior Counsel with full General Counsel responsibilities for company-wide litigation and domestic transactions. Reported to the company President and General Counsel of Pomerance Corporation (parent company). Member of Senior Management Team since 1995.

Rapidly gained the confidence of the senior management team and key personnel in Operations, Marketing, Credit, Finance and Human Resources. Provided hands-on legal support in finance, operations, contracts, employment and labor, regulatory affairs, risk management, anti-trust, credit, loan workouts and general corporate legal affairs.

Organizational & Transactional Leadership

- Revitalized the corporate collections organization, implemented structured business and legal processes, and provided hands-on leadership in litigation and account dispute resolution. In first three years, reduced pending lawsuits by 66%, decreased total outside counsel fees by 70% and recovered $4.4 million in outstanding debt.
- Structured and documented two asset securitization facilities ($495 million), a proposed joint venture, a proposed loan purchase agreement ($30+ million), and numerous operating agreements with insurance companies, brokers and agents.
- Provided legal advice during start-up of company operations in Ireland and the U.K.
- Advised and assisted operations management team in policy development, budgeting, process redesign, cost reduction, real estate leasing and contract negotiations.

Notable Legal Cases, Litigation & Regulatory Affairs

- Lead Counsel in *Shraeder Plan Committee v. Peakland Insurance Corporation*, 200 B.R. 665 (Bankr. N.D. Ill. 1992). Won judicial opinion that overcame unfavorable case law concerning application of preferential transfer law to a premium finance transaction.
- Led recovery and resolution of $5.4 million fraud, *Peakland Insurance Corporation v. United Trucking Association, Inc. et al.*, 765 F. Supp. 621 (W.D. Kentucky 1993).
- Prepared and presented position paper for the Association of Finance Companies regarding proposed revisions to Article 7 of Commercial Code.

MACALLISTER & O'BRIAN, Dallas, Texas   1989 to 1992

Associate - Commercial Litigation (1989 to 1992) / **Associate - Corporate Law** (1989)

Represented business owners and corporations in general commercial and contract litigation, acquisitions and general corporate legal affairs. Represented secured creditors, trustees and receivers in bankruptcy matters involving various bankruptcy issues (e.g., plan confirmation, property of estate, DIP financing, preferential transfer, fraudulent transfer, non-dischargeability, filing ancillary to a foreign proceeding).

Previous Legal Experience (1987 to 1988):

Law Clerk / Summer Associate - MaCallister & O'Brian
Summer Associate - Marchand, Brown, Shaw & Miner
Law Clerk - Shafner & Glen

- Legal research and drafting positions in general tax and tax litigation, securities and broker-dealer law, commercial and contract litigation, ERISA, and corporate litigation and transactions law (e.g., acquisitions, IPOs, bankruptcy).

Previous Professional Experience (1980 to 1986) in the Information Technology and Financial Services industries in a series of increasingly responsible non-legal positions. Experience in financial planning, business planning, organizational design, computerized financial systems, and corporate marketing/customer relationship management. Positions:

Senior Financial Analyst - Campbell & Rice (1986)
Financial Planner - Ewing Financial Services (1984 to 1985)
Technical Writer - Laird Research Corporation (1983)
Business Consultant - Taylor Data Corporation (1980 to 1982)

EDUCATION:

J.D. Degree   *Summa Cum Laude*   South Texas College of Law - Houston

Law Review, Note & Comment Editor, Powell, Burke & Marsh Award for Distinguished Service; Order of the Lytae; American Jurisprudence Award, Secured Transactions & Taxation of Business Organizations; First Prize, Ethan Richards Memorial Competition.

M.S. Degree   GPA - 3.9   University of Wisconsin - Madison
B.S. Degree   GPA - 3.2   Cornell University - Ithaca

Admitted to practice in Maryland and Texas.

PUBLICATIONS: Listing Available Upon Request
AFFILIATION: American Corporate Counsel Association

MARY H. FORREST

78 Magnolia Way
Arlington, Virginia 22209
Phone: (202) 876-1286   Email: forr5@mail.jtd.net

PROFESSIONAL PROFILE:

Attorney with a unique professional career with global legal and business expertise in Intellectual Property, International Trade, Unfair Competition, Marketing, Business Development, and Public/Private Partnerships and Alliances. Created the marketing and business development strategies to drive forward innovative projects, programs and cooperative public/private sector ventures. Expert knowledge of the legal, political and cultural issues of emerging business markets throughout Eastern Europe. Legal expert, team builder, driver and catalyst for change, growth and expansion. Familiar with legal and business issues impacting Internet content providers.

PROFESSIONAL EXPERIENCE:

INTERNATIONAL MUSIC INDUSTRY (IMI)   1992 to 1997
Only worldwide professional association for the music and entertainment industry. 1400 members in 75 countries.

> **Regional Director - Central & Eastern Europe** - Budapest, Hungary (1993 to 1997)
> **Legal Advisor - IMI Hungary** - Budapest, Hungary (1992 to 1993)

Recruited to plan and lead the start-up of IMI's first office in Hungary (then the #1 phonographic piracy center in the world). Organized widespread support throughout the industry, regional governments and the buying public to control piracy and reduce its dramatic economic impact. Promoted to Regional Director within first year with full responsibility for leading IMI's operations in Hungary, Russia, Estonia, Latvia, Lithuania, Poland, Czech and Slovak Republics, Bulgaria, Romania, Croatia, Slovenia, and Ukraine. Earned recognition as the regional expert with significant industry and political influence.

Pioneering Efforts in Intellectual Property and International Trade:

- Led successful initiatives to establish modern intellectual property laws (copyright, trademark, unfair competition), criminal laws and customs measures throughout Eastern Europe. Built the legislative and enforcement infrastructure to protect businesses entering these emerging markets and assisted in the introduction of first intellectual property legislation in six of the region's countries.

- Advised worldwide industry representatives on legal issues regarding business relationships in specific countries in Eastern Europe and the European Union.

- Launched IMI's first public awareness campaign specifically designed to bring industry issues "to the public." Directed press campaigns, regularly appeared on radio and television, and lectured at professional meetings, conferences and symposia. Designed and produced multimedia marketing communications.

- Orchestrated one of the IMI's most successful anti-piracy campaigns and reduced the piracy rate in Hungary from 95% in 1992 to 20% in 1996.

- Lectured on intellectual property at the U.S. Trade Office and Federal Legal Center in Washington, D.C. Briefed U.S. embassies, U.S. Trade Representatives and the U.S. Department of State on legislative developments and key regional issues.

INTERNATIONAL MUSIC INDUSTRY (*Continued*):

- Consulted with Global Entertainment Organization (GEO) in Geneva to provide regional governments with model laws and draft legislation. Lectured at numerous GEO seminars.

- Appointed to numerous legislative and parliamentary committees to guide legal debates, provide legal analyses and develop legislative proposals on competition, trade and intellectual property issues.

Managing New Ventures, Existing Operations & Industry Relations:

- Led the successful start-up of IMI regional offices in both Hungary and Moscow. Led growth of regional operations from approximately 20 to more than 100 member companies and expansion of music market in Hungary from $15 million in 1992 to $135 million in 1996. Managed a $2 million annual operating budget.

- Appointed by the European Committee to administer the European Union's MARE Program (an industry-wide initiative to build the legislative infrastructure for 14 participating nations).

- Led joint public/private sector initiatives worldwide, including programs between foreign governments and the U.S. on bilateral trade agreements.

- Chaired IMI's regional business review committee (regional executives of major multinational corporations: BMG, EMI, PolyGram, Sony, Warner, and MCA) and IMI's legal/enforcement committee for industry groups in Austria, Switzerland, Hungary, Germany, Poland, Russia, and the Czech and Slovak Republics.

- Appointed to the European Regional Board of Directors and numerous other corporate legal and business committees.

U.S. TRADE OFFICE - Washington, D.C. 1988 to 1992

Examiner - Music Section

Analyzed trademark submissions for protectable content. Researched and wrote articles on trademark law and enforcement practices in the music, entertainment, computer and advanced technology industries.

Early Professional Career (1982 to 1988) in the Insurance (New Colony Life), Banking/Financial Services (Commercial Bank of New York) and Radio Broadcasting industries.

EDUCATION:

J.D. - George Mason University - Fairfax, Virginia - 1991
M.A./B.A. - Musicology - Plankawicz University - Geneva, Switzerland, 1981
B.A. - Classical Guitar - Tombarka School of Music - Budapest, Hungary, 1976

Visiting Researcher - Institute for Intellectual Property - Munich, Germany, 1997

PERSONAL PROFILE: U.S. Citizen. Fluent Hungarian and Russian. Member of Washington, D.C. Bar.

GEOFFREY STARLING
1510 Los Viejos, Rainbow, California 92028
Residence: 760 555-3456 • Office: 760 555-3457

ATTORNEY AT LAW

PROFESSIONAL EXPERIENCE

LAW OFFICE OF GEOFFREY STARLING, Rainbow, California
Attorney-at-Law, 1992 to present
Solo practitioner with a diversified case load of real estate transactions and litigation; business transactions and litigation; corporate and partnership matters; estate planning; probate, bankruptcy; and mortgage foreclosures.

STEPHEN B. WILSON & ASSOCIATES, San Diego, California
Associate Attorney, 1988 to 1992
Real estate transactions and litigation; business transactions and litigation; corporate and partnership matters; estate planning; bankruptcy; homeowner associations.

ROBINSON & ASSOCIATES, San Bernardino, California
Associate Attorney, 1987-1988
Real estate transactions and litigation; business transactions and litigation; corporate and partnership matters; estate planning; bankruptcy; homeowner associations.

SMITH, SMYTH, SMITHE, & ROBINSON, Temecula, California
Associate Attorney, 1984 to 1987
Real estate transactions and litigation; business transactions and litigation; corporate and partnership matters; estate planning; bankruptcy; personal injury.

S. LYLE ROBERTSON & ASSOCIATES, Temecula, California
Associate Attorney, 1983-1984
Real estate transactions and litigation; business transactions and litigation; corporate and partnership matters; estate planning.

EDUCATION

UNIVERSITY OF SAN DIEGO SCHOOL OF LAW, San Diego, California
Juris Doctor, 1982
- Phi Delta Phi International Law Fraternity

CALIFORNIA STATE UNIVERSITY, San Marcos, California
Bachelor of Arts - Major: Political Science - GPA: 4.0 - Summa Cum Laude

PAST AND PRESENT AFFILIATIONS

Member, State Bar of Arizona
Member, State Bar of California
Member, American Bar Association
Member, Orange County Bar Association
Member, Riverside County Bar Association
Member, San Diego County Bar Association

ADMISSIONS

Arizona and California State Courts

Federal Courts:
    Southern District of California
    Central District of California
    District of Arizona

Judge Pro Tempore:
    Rainbow Municipal Court
    San Marcos Municipal Court

Arbitrator:
    San Marcos Municipal Court

TIMOTHY C. MEYER

6547 Kennedy Drive • Augusta, AR 87654
Phone: (555) 666-6666 • Fax: (555) 444-4444 • Email: meyer@email.com

OVERVIEW

Well qualified and highly motivated professional seeking a position as **legal assistant/paralegal**. Particular interest in criminal and family law. B.S. degree in Paralegal Studies from an ABA approved program; published writer with extensive additional education and experience in English. Worldwide traveler with exceptional intercultural awareness and sensitivity. Recognized for...

> Commitment and reliability
> Strong written and oral communication skills
> Outstanding research capabilities

> Excellent organizational and analytical skills
> Thoroughness and attention to detail
> Exceptional interpersonal abilities

HIGHLIGHTS OF EXPERIENCE

Research, Writing & Communication Skills: Researched, wrote and published a listening textbook for the university level student. Provided editing support for two textbooks on the topics of academic vocabulary and academic reading practice. Researched and evaluated innovative teaching methods; developed curriculum, presented lectures and instructed students in Japan, Saudi Arabia and Costa Rica on the topics of reading, writing, speaking and listening to English. Counseled and advised students on personal and career issues and on setting and obtaining academic objectives.

Management/Project Coordination: Conceived and founded the English Language School in Japan; researched competitors, negotiated facilities, recruited faculty. Developed, designed and implemented curricula based on students' needs. Developed and integrated student work-study programs within the community. Designed materials and organized classes for the Test of English for International Communication (TOEIC). Supervised and critiqued EFL teacher-training methodology of 70 teachers. Developed curriculum for new Pre-Business program; researched textbooks, videos and cassette tapes, organized class schedules.

Legal Experience / Client Contact: Completed a full-time internship at the York County Prison. Interviewed new inmates regarding their crimes; prepared and presented reports to the county Public Defender. Interacted extensively with the District Attorney. Observed legal proceedings at the court house. Reviewed docket, performed research and compiled reports on various criminal cases; recognized by Public Defender, advisor and judge for thoroughness and attention to detail. Skilled in the use of Legal-West Law and Legal-Lexis/Nexis.

EMPLOYMENT HISTORY

1997 - Present	**Computer Assisted Instruction Coordinator**, Some State University, Augusta, AR
1995 - 1997	**Lecturer**, Some University of Petroleums & Minerals, Dharan, Saudi Arabia
1994 - 1995	**Instructor**, Saudi Aramco, Dhahran, Saudi Arabia
1994	**Instructor**, Centro Cultural Norte Americano Language School, San Jose, Costa Rica
1992 - 1993	**Owner/Instructor**, English Language School, Kanuma, Japan
1991 - 1993	**Instructor**, College of Academics and Business, Kanuma, Japan
1990 - 1991	**Instructor**, Language Scool, Ochinomizu, Japan
1989 - 1990	**Teacher**, ASA English Conversion School, Shinjuku, Japan

EDUCATION

Master of Arts, Teaching - Concentration: English to Speakers of Other Languages
School for International Training, Nissen, ME (1996)
Bachelor of Science, Paralegal Studies (ABA Approved) - Minor: English
University of Someplace, Dover, MS (1988)
Associate of Applied Science, Drafting and Design Technology
Community College, Dover, MS (1986)

President (1987-1988) Vice-President (1986 - 1987), Paralegal Society, University of Someplace

STEVEN MINEO

10 Bronson Court ● Scotch Plains, New Jersey 07076
(908) 555-5555

DIRECTOR OF OPERATIONS — FOOD DISTRIBUTION / TRANSPORTATION
Strategic Business Planning...Team Building and Development
Effective Cost Reduction and Containment Programs

Value Offered:
- Innovative problem-solver, successfully restructuring inefficiencies to enhance bottom line considerations.
- Building positive relationships and streamlining business processes resulting in improved safety levels and significant cost reduction.
- Proven labor union/teamster negotiating and relations qualifications, including several years as high-profile union representative.

Dynamic management career leading high-volume distribution functions and transitioning corporation through mergers, facility closings, relocation and reorganization. Strong general management qualifications in P&L planning (budgeting, forecasting, cost analysis), organizational reengineering and employee incentive programs. Team-oriented leadership style with excellent interpersonal skills.

PROFESSIONAL EXPERIENCE:
DELVIN DAIRY, Plainfield, NJ
FRESHVIEW FARMS, Tuxedo Park, NY (purchased by Delvin in 1987)   1974 - present
Fast-track promotion through increasingly responsible positions directing distribution functions for dairy processing plant and separate depot facility delivering 1 million gallons of product per week to over 7,000 accounts across the entire eastern seaboard. Customers include a full range of consumers, from retail outlets to restaurants and institutions. Currently direct staff of 275 drivers and garage personnel with 4 managerial direct reports. Previously General Manager of entire fluid milk operation, including processing, packaging, loading and distribution.

Achievements:
- Established route reengineering project forecast to cut delivery costs by $4 million.
  RESULT: Actual savings delivered - $6 million.
- Streamlined and restructured order entry department.
  RESULT: Eliminated 12 positions over 2 years, securing $500,000 in payroll savings.
- Created and organized annual "truck rodeo" event promoting driver safety.
  RESULT: 35% reduction in trucking accidents within 3 months of debut.
- Introduced weekly reporting system to track delivery "vital signs".
  RESULT: Effectively isolate and resolve potential problems.
- Restructured distribution process from stagnating 6-day operation to 5-day turnaround.
  RESULT: Ongoing profit realized within 1 month.
- Heavy ongoing interface with sales department developing marketing strategies.
- Designed purchase product/backhold program to reduce shipping expense.
- Developed and implemented raw milk loss monitoring procedures achieving acceptable level of milk loss.

Career Path:
Director of Operations, Delvin, Farmingdale, NY/Plainfield, NJ (1992 - present)
Distribution Manager, Delvin, Farmingdale, NY (1990 - 1992)
General Manager, Delvin, Sayville, NY (1988 - 1990)
Distribution Manager, Delvin, Sayville, NY (1987 - 1988)
Assistant Sales Manager, Freshview Farms, Tuxedo Park, NY (1984 - 1987)
Driver / Packager / Processor / Loader, Freshview Farms, Tuxedo Park, NY (1974 - 1984)

DAVID CUSHMAN

57 New Parcel Drive   Penfield, NY 14526

716-777-7777 (Office)

716-555-5555 (Home)

QUALIFICATIONS SUMMARY

Offering over 10 years of successful experience in all aspects of **warehouse and transportation management**.
- Competent in assessing and implementing overall operations to achieve corporate objectives.
- Computer skills include Oracle, MS Word, Excel and internal shipping & order entry systems in a windows-based environment

WORK EXPERIENCE

1987-Present   **Lighthouse Corporation**, Rochester, NY
Warehouse Transportation Supervisor

Transportation
- Responsible for all corporate materials movement ($9M of air freight and $15M in ground transportation) for this Fortune 500 Company.
- Source and select carriers. Negotiate rates, terms and conditions. Ensure compliance with contracts.

Inventory Control
- Work collaboratively with programmer to modify and upgrade Oracle inventory management software. Oversee training for staff on all levels including management.
- Generate inventory reports.

Personnel Management
- Develop and manage a staff of 10 responsible for coordinating customer orders and ensuring accuracy with order requirements.
- Determine personnel requirements. Interview, hire and train. Evaluate performance.

Purchasing
- Responsible for the purchase of $45M of raw material inventory. Communicate with Engineering and Manufacturing personnel. Evaluate requirements. Select vendors and negotiate contracts, optimizing cost, quality and service.

Budget
- Plan and administrate capital and operating budget. Track and report variances. Audit and approve bills for payment.

Project Management
- Manage designated projects involving distribution needs at corporate level.
- Identify and implement process improvements to reduce operating expenses, and increase efficiency.

Highlights
- Developed entire department from ground floor.
- Oversaw transition from manual to computerized inventory control system. Evaluated inventory control needs. Made recommendations for the development of in-house order-entry system. Set up installation.
- Developed a PC-based shipping system to interface with internal order-entry system.

1986   **Monroe County Office Supply**, Rochester, NY
Warehouse Manager

EDUCATION / PROFESSIONAL DEVELOPMENT

Rochester Institute of Technology (Continuing Education), Rochester, NY
1993   **Traffic Management, Managing Personnel, TQM**

Rochester Institute of Technology, Rochester, NY
1982   **B.S. in Administration**

References available upon request.

PATRICK LECHTINSEN

#2633 Yongsan Vista
23332 Seoul, Korea
Phone/Fax 82-232-646-6664

GLOBAL LOGISTICS EXECUTIVE

International Logistics Management Responsibility
80,000 Distribution Outlets - 70 Cities - PRC, Hong Kong and Macao

International Business Executive with a record of performance in development and profitable management of international logistics and distribution operations. Cross-functional expertise in new business ventures, marketing/business development, key account management, accounting/finance, training and team building. Determined, decisive and pragmatic with strong leadership and problem solving skills.

- Fluent in English & Scandinavian. Semi-fluent in Mandarin, French & German. Danish Citizen.
- Guest Speaker, International Management Conferences. Proficient in Microsoft Office Suite.

PROFESSIONAL EXPERIENCE:

EUROPE/ASIA CONNECTION (EAC), Copenhagen, Denmark   1990 to Present

Fast-track promotion throughout career with this $2.5 billion, 100-year-old, Danish-owned distribution company. Held increasingly responsible logistics management positions in the corporation's Far Eastern operations.

Director - EAC Logistics Asia - Korea (1992 to Present)

Promoted to Senior Operating Executive with full P&L responsibility for the strategic planning, development, start-up and subsequent management of EAC's first Korea logistics and distribution operation. Full P&L responsibility for all operations.

Created what is now the widest controlled distribution system in Hong Kong, Japan and Korea, covering 70+ cities and 80,000 outlets throughout the region. Established business infrastructure, designed all logistics and distribution systems, developed accounting and financial systems, implemented PC technology and automated business processes, and spearheaded regional marketing and business development initiatives.

- Built new venture from start-up to 200 employees and $300 million in annual volume within four years. Year 2000 projections forecast $1.5 billion in annualized volume, $180 million in assets and 3000+ employees.
- Surpassed first year revenue objectives by 10% and profit goals by 5%.
- Negotiated exclusive logistics agreements with Johnson & Johnson, Lego, Mars, Melitta, Philips, Smuckers, Unilever, VO5 and other leading multinational companies. Developed contracts with in-country manufacturing facilities for distribution of products throughout Asia-Pacific.
- Established packing workshops with 150 co-packers throughout the country, adding to EAC's logistics and distribution capacity. Designed intermodal transportation network and a complete transportation management program.
- Championed development and implementation of PC network and other IS technologies for logistics management, sales, marketing, customer management and accounting/finance applications.
- Designed comprehensive inventory planning and supply management schedules for all 80,000 distribution centers and depots throughout Korea, Japan and Hong Kong.

Marketing Systems Coordinator - The Europe/Asia Connection - Bangkok (1991 to 1992)

Promoted to $50 million Bangkok operation to spearhead a reorganization of the company's marketing, logistics, distribution and customer service functions. Challenged to redesign business processes and accelerate revenue, profit and market growth.

- Instrumental in building 1992 revenue volume by $10+ million. Improved profitability 10% and positioned for long-term market growth.

- Introduced EDI technology and other performance improvement programs that increased efficiency 25% and improved price controls.

- Created a key account relationship management team, new sales management process and other service-driven initiatives to strengthen customer loyalty and retention. Member of sales team that closed contracts with Danone, Melitta, Unicharm and other multinational companies.

Project Manager - The Europe/Asia Connection - Philippines (1990 to 1991)

Recruited to EAC to provide economic, financial and analytical direction for a proposed manufacturing acquisition. Within six months, promoted to Project Manager to establish a Philippine-based shipping agency.

Authored business plan and transportation/distribution plan. Developed budgets and accounting systems, created business infrastructure and staffed new organization. Transitioned operations to Managing Director.

UNIVERSITY OF COPEHAGEN, Copenhagen, Denmark   1989

Assistant Lecturer

Taught Accounting, Investment Theory and Cost Analysis to bachelor degree seeking students.

EDI CREDIT, Copenhagen, Denmark   1987 to 1989

Economist

Member of this large Danish mortgage company's acquisition team, researching and facilitating acquisitions nationwide. Concurrent responsibility for detailed real estate market analysis and reporting.

MOBILE OIL CORPORATION, Copenhagen, Denmark   1986

Accounting Assistant

Six-month professional position in Mobile's Copenhagen-based field operation.

EDUCATION:

UNIVERSITY OF COPENHAGEN, Denmark
Master of Economics, 1990
Bachelor of Economics, 1987

United Nations Intern, Summer 1990
The only Danish student and one of only 80 graduate students worldwide selected for three-month internship with the United Nations in New York. Participated in several global economic research and reporting projects.

JEFFREY T. HARTMAN
16561 North Oak Place
Cleveland, Ohio 44809

Residence (330) 295-3913   Office (330) 295-0012 x522

SENIOR MANUFACTURING & PLANT OPERATIONS EXECUTIVE
Specialty Industrial Products, Components & Equipment Manufacturing

Solutions-Driven Manufacturing Manager with 20+ years experience leading high-quality production operations.

- Manufacturing & Production Planning
- Manufacturing & Facilities Engineering
- Cellular Manufacturing Operations
- Materials Management, MRP II & Inventory Control
- ISO 9000 & Quality Management
- Manufacturing & Information Technology

- Capital & Operating Budgets
- Project Planning & Management
- Cost Improvement & Avoidance
- Team Building & Team Leadership
- Union Contract Negotiations
- Performance Planning & Improvement

PROFESSIONAL EXPERIENCE:

SCHWIMMER INDUSTRIES, INC.   1986 to Present

Operations Manager - Cleveland Fan, Inc. - Cleveland, Ohio (1995 to Present)
(*Acquired by King Management Group in 1997*)

Senior Operating Executive with full responsibility for the planning, staffing, technology, assets and management of all production for this $31 million manufacturer of industrial axial and centrifugal fans. Challenged to orchestrate an aggressive reengineering of the manufacturing support operation (machining, foundry, welding, assembly, quality, staffing), reduce costs, streamline production and improve bottom-line profitability. Lead a team of 98 (including 61 direct reports). Manage a $23.5 million annual operating budget.

- Achieved/surpassed all performance objectives:
    - -- Reduced manufacturing cycle time from 10-13 weeks to 8-10 weeks.
    - -- Improved on-time deliveries 15% through formal work scheduling processes.
    - -- Developed capital plan, rationalized assembly processes and reduced annual costs $365,000.
    - -- Restructured teams and reduced annual labor costs 8%.

- Successfully managed union contract negotiations and eliminated individual incentive program, saving over $100,000 annually. Co-authored rewrite of labor contract, reduced from 62 to 20 pages, and improved flexibility in workforce management.

- Established first-ever monthly sales and operations planning sessions to review forecasts and bookings, engineering and manufacturing capacity requirements, and P&L projections. Developed spreadsheets to support departmental budget planning and administration.

- Currently orchestrating selection and implementation of enterprise resource planning solutions.

Director of Operations/Project Manager - Harris Corporation - Boston, Massachusetts (1987 to 1995)

Senior Manufacturing Executive directing all production operations for this $28 million paper winder manufacturer. Scope of responsibility was significant and included the entire manufacturing operation, fabrication, machining, assembly, materials management, quality and production yield. Directed a staff of 105 and managed a $6.5 million annual operating budget.

- Drove a series of successful productivity, quality and operating improvement programs:
    - -- Increased on-time parts delivery from 69% to 87% while reducing lead times 22%.
    - -- Improved on-time customer order shipments from 22% to 90% within first year.
    - -- Reduced inventories 14% and improved inventory turns 35%.
    - -- Implemented CAM and Distributed Numerical Control for a 25% gain in machine utilization.

Director of Operations/Project Manager - Harris Corporation - *CONTINUED:*

- Planned and directed over $1.5 million in capital improvement and equipment/technology projects, including construction of a 10,000 sq. ft. assembly bay ($650,000 project).

- Designed and implemented a LAN-based job tracking system for customer orders.

- Established in-house machine operator training program to compensate for the shortage of skilled machinists to meet production requirements.

NOTE: Transferred from Massachusetts to Wisconsin manufacturing facility in 1995 to co-manage a $17 million paper machine rebuild project critical to the plant's production capabilities. Redefined project scope, reassigned personnel and brought project in on-time and within budget.

CARTER CORPORATION - Buffalo, New York   1979 to 1987

Manager of Manufacturing Engineering (1986 to 1987)
Director of Machining & Manufacturing Engineering (1986)
Superintendent of Manufacturing Engineering (1983 to 1986)
Superintendent of Inventory Control, Warehousing & Transportation (1982 to 1983)
Superintendent of Production Control (1979 to 1982)

Fast-track promotion throughout eight-year management career with this $90 million manufacturer of gear cutting machine tools. Managed successfully through a period of downsizing, reorganization and business redesign to reduce operating costs and improve bottom-line profitability.

- Led the entire manufacturing engineering function with 105 employees and a $7.5 million annual operating budget. Directed process and manufacturing design engineering, part programming, industrial and facilities engineering, and industrial maintenance programs. Delivered over $500,000 in annual cost savings through process redesign and performance improvement.

- Directed 11 production departments and toolroom with total workforce of 285 employees. Improved order schedule completion by 25% and throughput by 35%.

- Developed and implemented a long range resource requirements plan for capital equipment, subcontracting and facility consolidation to support cost reduction goals. Increased machine utilization 30% and provided implemented foundation for introduction of manufacturing cells.

- Created production standards and increased average labor efficiency from 70% to 83%.

- Consulted with U.K. facility to analyze and resolve critical production issues.

- Led a series of information technology projects to enhance internal automation and systems capabilities (e.g., customer order entry, inventory forecasting, production planning). Designed technology to support planning/development of offshore manufacturing facility.

EDUCATION:

Bachelor of Technology in Computer Science, Rochester Institute of Technology, 1976
American Production & Inventory Control Society (APICS) Certification, 1984

References Provided Upon Request

JULIUS ESPERANZA

109 Mountain Drive ▪ Howell, New Jersey 07731
(609) 555-5555

VALUE OFFERED:

High-performance, customer-driven MANUFACTURING SUPERVISOR/FOREMAN with 20 years experience in industrial processes, maintenance and installations for diverse market and industry demands. Strong technical and mechanical ability in welding and electrical applications combined with superior organizational and strategic planning skills. Equally strong performer in both independent and team settings. Recognized for focused attention to detail, consistently reducing costs by completing projects well before deadline.

- **Metals** - Welding; sheet metal fabrications; alloys/super alloys; plumbing
- **Electric** - Safety control and motor wiring; safety upgrades; air processing and circulation equipment; vacuum pumps, diffusion pumps, water pumps, cooling towers and swamp coolers; hydraulics; pneumatics; process grinding equipment
- **Plastics** - PVC, PET, styrenes and RPET; package design, development and manufacture; custom thermoforming; structural seals; DC controls, PLC's; RF sealing

Black Seal License / OSHA and MSHA Safety Training / Blueprint Interpretation

PROFESSIONAL EXPERIENCE:

Field Service Engineer, CORDELL INDUSTRIES, Walden, NY (1995-1997)
$5 million manufacturer, installer and servicer of industrial process equipment (ovens, furnaces, incinerators, paint spray booths) for food and health care industries, utilities, and automobile manufacturers. Completed on-site electrical installations wiring natural gas equipment and installing paint spray booths. Performed sheet metal fabrications and safety upgrades. In-depth insurance code, EPA and federal/state agency regulatory knowledge.
- Evaluated specifications and applications, working closely with engineers to perfect design and installation. Reduced installation time factor by 22% within first 3 months.

Plant Engineer / Plant Manager / Maintenance Mechanic
PACKAGE DEVELOPMENT COMPANY, INC., Rockford, PA (1989-1995)
Fast-track promotion through a series of increasingly responsible positions with a multi-million dollar manufacturer of custom thermoforms and packaging. Clients included Revlon, Maybelline, Mennen and Hartz-Mountain. Scope of responsibilities included production, maintenance, tooling set-ups, concept and design work, machinery modifications, die repair, polishing, and fabrication. Supervised staff of up to 30 laborers, machinists and computer drafts people.
- Directed and completed entire packaging process, from initial concept and design to prototype development, production and follow-up. Achieved 15% cost reduction in development process within first six months as Plant Manager.

Previous Professional Experience included independent home improvement contractor, talcum powder mill mechanic and masonry block plant foreman.

EDUCATION:

RUTGERS UNIVERSITY, New Brunswick, NJ
Completed 2 years toward **Bachelor of Arts, Environmental Sciences** (1979)

JOHN PAUL JONES
10 Wilmont Avenue
Bloomington, Illinois 99999

999/222-9999 (home)
999/222-1888 (office)
Buyer@aol.com

QUALIFICATIONS

15 years' experience of proven ability to identify, qualify, and obtain sources of recyclable materials. Demonstration of effective negotiation skills. Profitable coordination of freight, inventory, and production scheduling.

PROFESSIONAL EXPERIENCE

XYZ Corporation, 1976 to Present

Plastics Recycling Representative, Specialty Products, Bloomington, Illinois, 1981 to Present
- Conceive and implement strategies and quality management for sourcing recyclable materials for blown film manufacturing plants, servicing up to five plants
- Oversee pricing and inventory of recyclable materials
- Source up to 40 million pounds each calendar year
- Work closely with marketing and manufacturing on planning and realization of post consumer recycling program
- Participated in redesign of program resulting in reduction of department manpower by 50%
- Contributed up to $4 million in 1995 in cost savings of 4% of division profit plan
- Consistently received outstanding appraisals

Marketing Representative for Institutional Sales, Detroit, Michigan, 1980-1981
- Sold institutional packaging to distributors routinely meeting quota
- Successfully revitalized dormant sales territory reestablishing distributor networks

Quality Control Manager for Manufactured Goods and
Supervisor of Sourcing for Recyclables, Bloomington, Illinois, 1978-1980
- Administered total quality program for all manufacturing and supervised five personnel
- Designed and administered sourcing program for polystyrene recyclable materials

Manufacturing Supervisor, Chicago, Illinois, 1977-1978
- Met or exceeded manufacturing goals set by department motivating 40 hourly employees to achieve maximum productivity

Warehouse Supervisor, Chicago, Illinois, 1976-1977
- Supervised 15 employees in 7 day a week/24 hour a day operation
- Effectively managed warehousing, loading, and shipping of all finished goods to customers in a timely manner

United States Marine Corps, **Rifle Platoon Commander**, Vietnam and Brooklyn, New York
Led up to 150 soldiers in combat situations
Honorable Discharge; Purple Heart and Bronze Star with Combat V

EDUCATION

University of Notre Dame, Notre Dame, Indiana
Bachelor of Arts Degree

Keller Graduate School of Management, Chicago, Illinois
15 hours of accounting, marketing, and statistics courses

REFERENCES

Available upon request

JAMES VINCENT
2816 North Carroll Street
Oakwood, Kansas 66022
(883) 109-9829

PLANT MANAGER / PRODUCTION MANAGER / OPERATIONS MANAGER
Start-Up, Turnaround & High-Growth Manufacturing Operations

Dynamic management career with consistent contributions to increased production, quality, performance and profitability through expertise in:

- Production Planning & Scheduling
- Distribution & Logistics
- Purchasing & Materials Management
- Vendor Negotiations & Quality
- Traffic & Transportation

- Quality Control Management
- Process Redesign & Reengineering
- Facilities Design & Construction
- Human Resources Leadership
- Capital Investment & Development

Strong and decisive operations leader with excellent analytical, organizational, team building and planning skills. Strong background in government relations, environmental compliance and customer management.

PROFESSIONAL EXPERIENCE:

PLANT MANAGER / PRODUCTION MANAGER   1977 to Present

Recruited in 1977 by Michael Washington, an established entrepreneur and principal in several manufacturing facilities nationwide. Over the next 19 years, promoted rapidly through a series of increasingly responsible production and plant management positions in more than 12 different manufacturing companies in the Eastern and Midwestern U.S.

Specialized in the management of start-up manufacturing operations and the turn-around/reengineering of non-performing business units. Delivered strong and sustainable gains in productivity, quality and profitability by introducing leading edge production management, facilities management, staffing, training and performance improvement programs.

Directed production operations for facilities distributing to major food manufacturers nationwide. Client base included Stouffer, Nestle, Sysco, Lipton and RJR Nabisco.

Productivity & Financial Achievements

- Delivered a 33% increase in plant production yield and 40% reduction in annual labor costs at Barnesville Farms in Marlboro, Maryland. Instrumental in positioning Barnesville as one of the nation's largest and most profitable precooked bacon manufacturing facilities.

New Venture Start-Up

- Brought new manufacturing operation in Oakwood, Kansas from concept through design, staffing and production development start-up to current full-scale operation with projections for 200+ employees and over $40 million in annual revenue.

Turnaround Management

- Assumed full operating management responsibility for North Atlantic Spice Company, a production plant with low production yields, virtually no quality organization and a stagnant management team. Within one year, improved productivity by more than 10%, increased capacity 12% and reduced labor costs 20%.

Facilities Development & Capital Improvement

- Planned, staffed and directed more than $10 million in capital investment over the past 17 years. Directed more than 20 new facilities construction, facilities renovation and expansion, and equipment acquisition programs.

Human Resources Management

- Trained and directed teams of up to 150 production employees and supervisors. Managed staffing, scheduling, skills training, safety training and performance reviews. Introduced innovative team building and participative management programs. Managed within both union and non-union facilities.

Training & Development

- Served as the Production Operations and Plant Management "Trainer" providing on-site leadership in production, planning, staffing, facilities management, quality, operations, distribution and logistics to newly-hired supervisory and management personnel. Guided changes in operating management and orientation of new management teams.

Career Progression:

Barnesville Farms, Inc., Oakwood, Kansas (1995 to Present)
Swanson Foods, Cherry Tree, New Jersey (1995)
Barnesville Farms Inc., Marlboro, Maryland (1989 to 1995)
North Atlantic Spice Company, New York, New York (1985 to 1989)
Wayne Beverage, East Orange, New Jersey (1986 to 1987)
Triangle Foods, Murfreesboro, Arkansas (1985 to 1986)
Branch Foods, Gardenville, New Jersey (1984 to 1985)
Mitchell & Company, Memphis, Tennessee (1982 to 1984)
Triangle Foods, Gardenville, New Jersey (1979 to 1981)
Liberation Foods, Vineland, New Jersey (1977 to 1979)

NOTE: *From 1982 to 1984 employed directly by Mitchell & Company following their acquisition of Triangle Foods. Managed a large-scale production area with a staff of 80. Restructured portion control operation, implemented stringent production standards, and transitioned from $1.1 million loss to $1.5 million profit within first year.*

PROFESSIONAL TRAINING & DEVELOPMENT:

Graduate of more than 100+ hours of continuing professional education in:

- Production Management
- Personnel Management
- Training & Motivation
- Quality Management
- Resource Management
- Leadership Development
- Environmental Issues
- Logistics Management
- Team Building

Certification, Wastewater Pre-Treatment, State of Maryland, 1993

References Provided Upon Request

FRANK SANTIS

Home: (407) 555-1212   4256 S. Springfield Lane
Office: (407) 555-2121   Orlando, Florida 32000

SENIOR MARKETING / ADVERTISING EXECUTIVE

Expertise in Competitively Positioning Products & Services Globally

Dynamic management career leading start-up, turnaround, and high-growth organizations through explosive market growth and profitability. Combines extensive management experience in both marketing and advertising arenas. Consistently successful in conceptualizing, developing and orchestrating internal and external marketing initiatives to support top-producing national and international sales organizations. Core competencies include:

- Strategic Market Planning
- Competitive Product Positioning
- External Advertising Agency Management
- Organizational Leadership

- Revenue & Market Growth
- International Market Development
- New Product / Service Launch
- Market Identification / Penetration

PROFESSIONAL EXPERIENCE:

EXECUTEL CORPORATION, Orlando, Florida   1995-Present

(International company specializing in banking automation systems.)

Director of Marketing

Recruited as Senior Marketing Executive to spearhead start-up of internal marketing department and facilitate transition from external agencies for this $100 million privately held corporation. Challenged to redirect existing target market and lead major market penetration into world class organizations globally. Created new corporate vision and developed strategic and tactical business plans, marketing programs, and operating infrastructures to support new business development and rapid growth.

- Drove new market client base by 85% generating 60-70% of total revenues within two years.

FIRST TRUST BANK, Orlando, Florida   1990-1995

Assistant Vice President/Advertising Manager

Recruited to spearhead major change initiatives to resolve corporate image problems. Held full P&L responsibility for a $12 million advertising budget with accountability to 20 banks. Managed external advertising agency relationships, directed the creation, production and implementation of mass marketing advertising programs, and developed public relations strategies for new product launches.

- Restructured entire internal advertising department to facilitate improved quality and efficiency initiatives and cultivate effective working relationships with external agencies.
- Led negotiations with external advertising agencies in the reorganization and redeployment of talents to meet bank's quality and performance standards.

PROFESSIONAL EXPERIENCE (Continued):

TELECOM TELEPHONE, Altamonte Springs, Florida   1987-1990

Advertising Manager (1988-1990)

Community Relations Administrator (1987-1988)

Recruited to manage media and community relations programs throughout Northern and Central Florida regions and was promoted within one year to Advertising Manager. Held direct responsibility for a $6 million advertising budget, administration and implementation of advertising programs, external communications for new product introductions, and state-wide direct marketing initiatives.

- Built company awareness scores from 30-35% to 75-80% within 2 years.

MAIN STREET STATION, Orlando, Florida   1986-1987

Advertising/Public Relations Manager

Managed tactical advertising programs/campaigns for this privately owned entertainment attraction with responsibility for national and international public relations. Coordinated internal/external advertising programs.

- Launched the introduction of new collateral materials distributed internationally which significantly increased awareness, recognition and market share.

A. C. JACKSON INVESTMENT ADVISORS, INC., Orlando, Florida   1985-1986

Director of Communications

Directed the design, creation and production of PR and direct-response collateral materials and all marketing information for this multi-million dollar investment group.

EDUCATION:

Master of Arts – Communication – University of Central Florida, Orlando, Florida   1988

Bachelor of Arts – Communication – University of Central Florida, Orlando, Florida   1984
Summa Cum Laude

Associate of Arts – Journalism – Brevard Community College, Melbourne, Florida   1982

MEMBERSHIPS / ACTIVITIES:

Adjunct Professor, University of Central Florida (UCF) School of Communications
Chairman Marketing Committee/Board of Directors – UCF Alumni Association
President – Greater Orlando
Board Member – American Advertising Federation
Member – American Marketing Association

TARA BREEZE

2987 S. Atlantic Ave. Suite 806 • Daytona Beach Shores, FL 32118 • (904) 788-2003 • Fax: (904) 788-0408

MARKETING • ADVERTISING • SALES PROFESSIONAL

Visionary and creative professional with a proven track record of success from initial concept through project completion. High-energy, results-oriented leader recognized for unusual and fun-loving tactics and strategies. Combines passion for marketing with commitment to contributing to an organization's bottom line. Excellent negotiating, closing and communication skills among all types of people. Areas of expertise include:

- Strategic Market Planning
- Promotional Campaigns
- Direct Mail Campaigns
- Event Planning / Coordination

- Revenue & Market Growth
- New Product Launch
- Advertising Campaigns
- Media Buying / Selling

- Market Identification / Penetration
- Sponsorships
- Ad Layout / Design
- Research / Development

PROFESSIONAL EXPERIENCE

MAGIC MAGAZINE, Orlando, Florida   Present
Marketing Consultant
Managing market research and development of East Volusia County for *Magic Magazine*, the official magazine of the Orlando Magic Professional Basketball Team.

NORTH FLORIDA PUBLISHING COMPANY, INC., Gainesville, Florida   1997
Regional Sales Manager
Providing expertise in the development of new territories in the Central Florida region, for four state-wide publications, *Florida Living Magazine, Air Currents Magazine, Sports in Florida Magazine, Florida Naturalist Magazine.*

HALIFAX MAGAZINE & BEACH BRIEFS MAGAZINE, Daytona Beach, Florida   1997
Sales Director
Launched publication of a new monthly magazine, *Beach Briefs*, a sister publication of *Halifax Magazine* within a six-week deadline from concept through completion. Developed rate cards, marketing strategies and promotional materials. Designed layouts, sold advertising contracts and followed up on distribution.
- Secured $30,000 in advertising dollars for first issue of *Beach Briefs* and annual combined contracts totaling $118,094 within 4 months.

GREAT WESTERN DIRECTORIES, Santa Cruz, California   1995 to 1996
Advertising Consultant
Marketed yellow page advertising for the largest independent yellow pages directory in the nation with responsibility for Monterey, Santa Cruz, and Palo Alto phone books. Developed new accounts through cold calling and referrals. Consulted with prospective advertisers; developed strategic advertising concepts, designed ads and followed up with proofs, revisions and final approval. Recommended and maximized co-op advertising opportunities and programs.

THE COMPLETE PHONEBOOK, Daytona Beach, Florida   1991 to 1995
Advertising Consultant
Promoted yellow page advertising for an independent publisher of county-wide phone books with full responsibility for business development for two phone books covering Volusia and Flagler Counties (distribution of 265,000) and St. Johns County (distribution of 80,000). Evaluated and analyzed advertising program's effectiveness and recommended new and alternative strategies. Developed strategic marketing plans, designed ads and followed up with proofs, revisions and final approval.
- Ranked Top Sales Producer 1993 through 1995.
- Built annual revenues from zero to $.5 million through cold calling within five years.

TREASURE ISLAND INN, OCEANS ELEVEN RESORTS, INC., Daytona Beach, Florida   1989 to 1991

Business Development – Sales & Marketing

Launched new business development initiatives focused on conventions, banquets and meetings. Executed direct sales, telemarketing, and direct mail programs. Designed various collateral materials (brochures / flyers, print ads, direct mail pieces, yellow page, newspaper and trade magazine ads), and developed sales presentation tools. Facilitated event planning and coordination.

PREMIERE PUBLICATIONS, INC., Gainesville, Florida   1986 to 1988

Vice President – Shout! Magazine

Spearheaded market launch of a college-based magazine focused on student interests and activities. Established and managed all phases of initial publication from concept, layout and sales through printing and distribution including photography, interviewing and writing. Recruited and trained a staff for all operations.

- Expanded market to include the top 10 universities throughout the Southeast within 3 years.

CLUB LIDO BAR & GRILLE, Gainesville, Florida   1985 to 1986

Vice President – Publicity

Conceptualized, developed and implemented an 18-month multimedia advertising/promotional campaign for this restaurant/nightclub. Wrote and produced radio and print ads. Negotiated promotional events with large groups. Coordinated late-night entertainment program.

- Drove Wednesday night patronage from 4 to 150 people within first week, and up 450 patrons (maximum capacity, with lines waiting to enter) within one month. Created a renowned theme resulting in extensive media coverage and long-lasting notoriety.
- Increased average weekly attendance by 1,000 per week.

UNIVERSITY OF FLORIDA STUDENT GOVERNMENT PRODUCTIONS, Gainesville, Florida   1985 to 1986

Advertising Director

Promoted and booked indoor and outdoor concerts at the O'Dome Sports Arena for big name entertainment groups. Supervised a team of 8 responsible for all advertising campaigns.

EARLIER CAREER includes various positions in sales, marketing, promotionals, billboard advertising and event coordination for businesses, as well as photography / production assistant for a film company.

EDUCATION

UNIVERSITY OF FLORIDA, Gainesville, Florida
College of Journalism and Communications, Advertising Major / Art Minor, 1983-1986

RICHMOND COLLEGE, London, England, (University Of Florida), 1985

UNIVERSITY OF CINCINNATI, Cincinnati, Ohio, 1981-1982

AFFILIATIONS

DAYTONA BEACH ADVERTISING FEDERATION, 1989-Present
V.P. Programs, Board of Directors, Director of State Project, Addys Banquet Director, Committee Chairperson

---

AWARDS / HONORS

Silver Addy Award, Business Trade Publication Category – 1991
Addy Appreciation Award for Outstanding Personal Communication – 1991
Silver Addy Award, Direct Mail Category – 1990
First Place, Golden Flake Potato Chip Campaign – 1986

SAMANTHA WILLIAMS

5318 South King Street
Alexandria, Virginia 22203

Phone: (703) 485-5871
Email: swilliams@aol.com

CORPORATE MARKETING & BUSINESS DEVELOPMENT EXECUTIVE
Expertise in New Product Launch, Commercialization & Global Market Expansion

Successful management career spearheading marketing and business development programs throughout the U.S. and abroad. Delivered the strategies and tactical action plans that have generated significant revenue and profit improvements. Strong qualifications in industry deregulation and legal compliance.

- Strategic Market Planning
- Sales & Marketing Leadership
- Strategic Alliances & Partnerships
- New Market & Customer Development

- Competitive Analysis & Positioning
- Multimedia Campaign Design
- Recruitment & Training
- Multicultural Business Relations

PROFESSIONAL EXPERIENCE:

WILLIAMS MARKETING, Alexandria, Virginia   1995 to Present

Corporate Marketing Consultant

Founded an exclusive management consulting firm providing business, marketing, and sales solutions to technology-based growth businesses across a broad spectrum of industries. Advisor to senior management and operating executives to conceive, develop and launch global business development initiatives and long-term growth strategies in highly competitive markets.

- **Marketing to expand cross-border sales of leading technologies.** Designed marketing plan, capitalized on existing partnership with Canadian alliance and overcame international regulatory issues. Positioned U.S. telecommunications company as a leader in global business.
- **Marketing to gain competitive advantage in rapidly deregulating industry.** Restructured all sales, marketing and customer management communications to introduce new business development programs. Devised strategy to maintain existing accounts during transition from monopoly to competitive utility market.
- **Marketing emerging communications technology.** Analyzed sales channels, created distributor/dealer support tools and launched PCS products throughout 14 emerging countries for satellite communications company.
- **Marketing to increase customer awareness and change corporate identity.** Created team-based sales, marketing and customer service programs to meet the needs of a diverse customer base. Launched advertising and public relations campaigns to transform consumer perception of Mexican government-owned enterprise to private business operation.

MCI CORPORATION, Falls Church, Virginia   1988 to 1995

Promoted rapidly throughout seven-year career with this $6 billion global telecommunications organization. Advanced based on consistent success in capturing new business development opportunities, expanding distribution channels into alternative markets and positioning MCI as an industry leader in advanced voice and data communications technologies.

Group Manager - Business Services Group (1994 to 1995)

Senior Marketing Manager challenged to revitalize MCI's stagnant online and Internet services programs in response to emerging competition. Held full responsibility for analyzing the competitiveness of existing products, developing new technologies and redefining market niche. Restructured public relations strategy and created new sales collaterals, advertising and trade show materials to support market expansion. Directed a staff of marketing/product development professionals and managed annual advertising budget.

- Negotiated business partnerships with Lotus and Microsoft, and launched joint marketing and public relations campaigns to position MCI as a proactive multimedia technology provider.
- Revitalized existing customer relationships and enhanced sales promotions strategies to regain lost market share in this highly competitive market sector.
- Reorganized and streamlined order fulfillment and customer management systems to improve accuracy of data and operating efficiencies.

Program Manager - Business Services Group (1992 to 1994)

High-profile marketing position leading the aggressive expansion of MCI's Affinity Marketing Program throughout the association and commercial markets. Created sales and marketing strategies between MCI and leading businesses to drive market penetration with their members/employees. Developed customized marketing plans incorporating multiple sales channels (e.g., direct mail, telemarketing, field sales). Provided project support to teams responsible for mail-house, telemarketing, network, systems, billing and customer service.

- Built Affinity Marketing to $26 million in revenues within two years (200% annual increase).
- Awarded MCI's Business Services Group "Top Performer Award" in both 1992 and 1993 for outstanding performance in new business development and customer retention.
- Worked with several top advertising agencies to develop multimedia advertisements, trade show promotions and direct mail collaterals.

Sales Manager - Intermediaries Marketing Group (1990 to 1991)

Based on previous success in association sales, promoted to Sales Manager and challenged to create an in-house marketing and sales organization committed to expanding the association business segment through alternative distribution channel development.

- Closed 20 programs representing $8 million in new revenues (300% increase in sales).
- Designed and led on-site training in association networking, lead development and strategic selling for the entire field sales organization.

Major Account Representative - Business Services Group (1988 to 1990)

Sold/marketed a complete line of telecommunications services to commercial and association accounts throughout the Washington, DC metro region.

- Created an innovative sales strategy focusing on consultative selling and providing value-added services to maintain long-term client relationships. Increased association sales by 25%.
- Achieved 115% of revenue quota for two consecutive years. Ranked as a top revenue producer throughout the national sales organization.

EARLY CAREER EXPERIENCE   1985 to 1988

Fast-track promotion through a series of increasingly responsible sales and marketing management positions with start-up and emerging technology companies. Developed strategic business and marketing plans, established sales and marketing department infrastructure, and recruited/trained sales, marketing and technical support personnel.

- Achieved/surpassed all revenue, profit and account development goals for three years.
- Identified and structured strategic partnerships with Panasonic and Epson America.
- Launched a multimedia advertising campaign for a start-up PC repair organization which generated a significant increase in consumer awareness.

EDUCATION: **B.A., Business & Marketing**, The American University, Washington, D.C.

PROFESSIONAL AFFILIATIONS: American Marketing Association, 1994 to Present
American Society of Association Executives, 1990 to Present
Business Services Committee; Advisory Committee

JOHN S. DOE

3490 Montana Ridge Parkway, Blue Skies, Montana 99876
(987) 876-7473 • E-mail: johndoe@aol.com

PROFILE	

- **Over 20 years, senior-level Business Development, Sales / Marketing, and Public Relations experience.** Expert in building top-producing direct and distributor sales organizations for high-growth, startup, mature, and competitive business markets. **P&L responsibility: up to $600 million** generated from 250+ professional sales personnel. Open to an equity position for an emerging company. **Competencies:**

- domestic & international marketing	- startup organizations
- organizational development	- strategic & tactical planning
- new product development & pricing	- product packaging & product release
- marketshare & product positioning	- product management & life cycle
- market research & demography	- market segmentation
- customer focus groups	- consumerism & retail expansion
- marketing plan development	- cost / benefit analysis
- catalog & promotional material design	- marketing & advertising communications
- business alliance formation	- key account relationship management
- multichannel distribution	- process & productivity improvement
- vendor sourcing & negotiations	- contract development & negotiations
- multidimensional project management	- vertical integration
- human resource affairs	- unique ability to hire right persons
- training program design	- training program presentation

- **Entrepreneurial and forward-thinking.** Possess a sense of urgency as a change agent to identify new product and market opportunities for the profitable growth and diversification of the business unit.

- **Extensive creative project leadership background in trade shows, conventions and exhibitions** (from booth concept to day-of-event representation and orchestration).

- **Well-versed in Managed Care, Health Maintenance, Physician Provider (MCO, HMO, PPO) organizations, and integrated health networks protocols** (including DRG fixed reimbursement procedures).

PROFESSIONAL EXPERIENCE

1978 to Present

HORIZONS HEALTH ALLIANCE, INC., Blue Skies, Montana
Corporate Vice President Sales & Marketing (1987-present)
Regional Sales Manager: Northwestern United States (1978-1987)

- **Held full P&L responsibility for the strategic planning, development, direction, and leadership** of Horizon's global sales organization (with direct management of a 925-member national sales force). Served as liaison between sales force, manufacturing, management, and quality control.

- **Successfully grew fledgling company (which currently employs over 3500 people nationwide) from $3 million to over $850 million in less than 12 years.** Pioneered numerous strategic and tactical marketing campaigns including building a strong alliance with operating room nurses nationwide, and maximizing the internal competitiveness of each of Horizon's sales territories throughout the United States.

- **Conceived / delivered comprehensive sales training programs and provided executive leadership** to support corporate growth initiatives including management succession plans, leadership development, and continuous improvement programs.

- **Orchestrated key company marketing communication events** including trade show, conventions, annual meetings, and professional exhibitions. Interfaced with both internal departments (in a vertically-integrated environment), external agencies, graphic designers, writers, and printing resources.

- **Built startup, multidimensional Partner Alliance Division to a 75-member team which currently generates over $12 million annually.** Employed an inside sales force which realized a $6-$8 per sales call cost versus the industry average of $250 for use of an outside sales representative. **Competitively launched a retail distribution unit.**

PROFESSIONAL EXPERIENCE (continued)

1972 to 1978   MEDICO RESOURCES, INC., Forest Hills, Oregon
                      Director of Sales & Marketing: Startup Company

- **Matured start-up medical supplies organization to an $25 million enterprise** in five years (from $1 million) with a sales force of 87.
- **Productively transitioned company from a manufacturer's rep organization to one driven by a direct selling force.** Solidified company's competitive market position through employee relations development.
- **Honored with Medico's "Salesman of the Year Award"** for outstanding and innovative sales performance (of disposable surgical pack and gowns).
- **Ranked as nation's top producer for three consecutive years.** Increased sales by 150% within two years.

EDUCATION
- **Master of Business Administration**
  University of Montana, Blue Skies, Montana
- **Bachelor of Science - Marketing**
  University of Oregon, Mount Moriah, Oregon

PROFESSIONAL AFFILIATIONS

- Board Member: Healthcare Manufacturers & Marketing Council (HMMC)
- Exhibitors Advisory Board Member: Association of Operating Room Nurses
- Exhibitors Advisory Board Member: Emergency Nurses Association

Barbara O'Hara
789 Market Street
Appletown, NY 11111
(001) 987-5432

MARKETING/SERVICE PROFESSIONAL with several years of experience in diverse aspects of business, from college informational campaigns to marketing financial services. Trained in demographics, target marketing and research, with limited knowledge of graphic arts and design. Enthusiastic, self-directed, innovative individual with strong work ethic. Highly effective communication skills include demonstrated ability to satisfy client needs through troubleshooting, research and problem resolution. Functions successfully as liaison at all levels with staff, managers, and administration.

EDUCATION

Bachelor of Science: Business Administration (Minor: **Marketing**)   May 1992
St. Martha College, Teaville, NY
    Coursework included:

Marketing Management	Marketing Communications	Marketing Research
Graphic Arts/Designs	Marketing Policies and Problems	

PROFESSIONAL EXPERIENCE

FINANCE U.S.A., New York, NY   5/92 - Present
Senior Client Service Representative (1/94 - Present)
    First **Senior CSR** in a position created to utilize the skills of more experienced customer service personnel. Services major money management accounts, monitoring client checking accounts, VISA debit cards, investments, and money market accounts. Supervises service representatives; monitors and evaluates performance. Authorizes credit elevations and bank account adjustments. Conducts product research. Negotiates sales with brokers. Heavy client contact, servicing accounts and resolving customer problems.

Client Service Representative (5/92 - 1/94)
    Assisted clients and brokers with banking and money market accounts, assets and securities.

ST. MARTHA COLLEGE, Teaville, NY
Security Officer   1/90 - 5/92
Registrar's Office Assistant   1/90 - 9/91

ST. MARTHA INSTITUTE OF PUBLIC OPINION, Poughkeepsie, NY   9/88 - 5/90
Pollster
    Telephoned citizens nationally in random polls to collect public opinion information for political surveys.

RELATED ACTIVITIES

ST. MARTHA COLLEGE
Senior Project
    Market research covered demographics/target market identification, analysis and psychology of advertising.

Business Manager, *The Oval*   9/91 - 5/92
    Dealt directly with local businesses in all aspects of advertising, billings and collections. Recruited new ad accounts through referrals and cold calls; maintained regular customer accounts. Negotiated ad prices. Assisted in ad design.

Resident Student Council   9/89 - 5/90
    Organized numerous fund raising events, including t-shirt sales and dormitory Olympics. Created and conducted dorm surveys to determine student needs and desires.

St. Martha College Student Orientation Program   Summers, 1989 - 1991
    Conducted tours for prospective students, giving benefits presentations and answering questions concerning student life and college financing. Participated in playwriting and production of college life scenarios.

RALPH J. THOMPSON

985 South Park Lane
Kansas City, Missouri 67841
901-654-6541

EXECUTIVE SUMMARY

- ❖ Experience (12+ years) in new business development, marketing, and management achievements in the insurance industry, maximizing profit potential by increasing market penetration and member satisfaction rates
- ❖ Directing marketing efforts to promote visibility, negotiating lucrative contracts, and introducing new products
- ❖ Analyzing complex situations, designing practical solutions, and implementing cost-effective plans
- ❖ Developing personnel, motivating staff to exceed goal, and improving production and sales
- ❖ Revitalized stagnant or peaked-out related areas

EXPERIENCE AND ACCOMPLISHMENTS

HEALTHNET   1996 - Present
Kansas City, Missouri

SENIOR VICE PRESIDENT AND CHIEF MARKETING OFFICER
Direct the sales and marketing efforts and the development of sales account management teams for a provider owned managed care organization with 360,000 PPO members and 90,000 HMO members in Kansas and Missouri with 1998 projected revenue to be $220 million.
- ➢ Doubled HMO member to 93,000 from 47,000 in 15 months: 97%.
- ➢ Grew annual revenues run rate to $116 million from $28 million: 314%.
- ➢ Oversaw rollout of a new Medicare-RISK and Medicaid products; 18,000 total members.
- ➢ Introduced "open-access" HMO product.
- ➢ Spearheaded sale of many new large employers to include members of 2,000+: Sprint, TWA, Kansas City, Kansas School District, Shawnee County, Station Casino.

THE PRUDENTIAL INSURANCE COMPANY OF AMERICA   1985 - 1996
Denver, Colorado

MANAGING DIRECTOR OF COLORADO GROUP OFFICE
Manage the sales and service efforts of employee benefits to companies with 30+ employees in the Colorado, Wyoming and Montana territory.
- ➢ Increased Prucare HMO/Point-of-Service membership to 82,000 from 18,500 in 1990: annual average growth rate of 45%; plan grew to 3rd largest in the Denver area from 7th over four years.
- ➢ Improved annual new business revenues to $30.3 million in 1994 from $10.8 million in 1990: 328%. ???? 181%
- ➢ Enhanced total plan earnings to $10.8 million (1991-1994) from a 4-year loss of $600,000 (1987-1990): 8% return on premium.
- ➢ Expanded total employer groups serviced to 574 from 228 in 1990: 152%
- ➢ Increased average annual new cases to 111 (1991-1994) from 33 (1987-1990): 236%
- ➢ Reached highest member satisfaction rates of all Colorado's HMO's in 1993 and 1994: 93% each year. Benefit manager satisfaction rates rose to 93% in 1992 and 91% in 1993.
- ➢ Surpassed all company objectives every year.

EXPERIENCE AND ACCOMPLISHMENTS   (Continued)

> ➤ Originated several new large clients: State of Colorado, Colorado State University, Invesco Funds Group.
> ➤ Facilitated a full 3-year NCQA Accreditation for Prucare of Colorado, 1994.
> ➤ Spearheaded the development of a group practice delivery system: 5 exclusive health centers involving an initial $15 million in capital expenditures and $55 million over 5 years.
> ➤ Oversaw the conversion from a Denver area IPA network to a group model.

REGIONAL GROUP MANAGER   (1989-1990)
CHICAGO GROUP SALES OFFICE

> ➤ Managed 5 sales representatives whose combined production increased over 200%.
> ➤ Produced $24 million in new business revenues, leading the North Central region.
> ➤ Led all national group sales with 39 new large cases in 1989 and 27 in 1990, selling 6 cases with more than 1,000 employees.
> ➤ Established productive business relations with Towers Perrin, Wyatt & Company, Arthur Gallager and numerous other leading brokerage/consulting firms.

GROUP MANAGER (1988-1989)

> ➤ Managed 3 group sales representatives whose combined production increased 160%.
> ➤ Surpassed sales record for the most new large group cases sold in one year: 52 in 1988.

ASSOCIATE GROUP MANAGER   (1987-1988)

> ➤ Led North Central region with sales of 39 new large group cases in 1987.
> ➤ Produced $11 million in new business revenue in 1987.

GROUP REPRSENTATIVE   (1986-1987)

> ➤ Sold first group case 3 weeks after joining the office.
> ➤ Established sales standard with 15 large group case sales in first year in the field.

GROUP REPRESENTATIVE IN TRAINING   (1985-1986)

EDUCATION

Georgetown University   **Bachelor of Arts** - 1985
Washington, D.C.   Graduated Magna Cum Laude

Loyola Academy   **National Merit Scholar** - 1981
Wilmette, Illinois   Ranked 9th in a class of 441

Douglas M. Franz
3456 Cameron Road, Apt. 2
Athens, Ohio 45701
(614) 592-0000

" ... thank you for being so descriptive about the teams, courts and stadiums for the Athens games. I have been an Athens Bulldog fan since birth, but I have never been able to see the games with such clarity until you began broadcasting."

--Matthew J. Miller, legally blind since birth

RADIO EXPERIENCE

WATH-AM, Programming Department, Athens, Ohio   1996-present
Operations Manager/Program Director (12/96-present)
Morning Drive Air Talent (7/96-present)

WATH-AM/WXTQ-FM, Sports Department, Athens, Ohio   1994-present
Sports Director (7/96-present)
Morning/Afternoon Sportscaster (6/96-present)
Host/Director/Producer (7/96-present)
   • "970 Sportsfan" - hour-long call-in show
Play-by-Play Broadcaster (1994-present)
   • Athens High School Baseball, Basketball, Football, Soccer (1995-present)
   • Ohio University Baseball (1995)
   • Ohio University Women's Basketball (1994-1995)
Color Analyst (1994)
   • Athens High School Men's & Women's Athletics (1994)
Beat Reporter (1994-present)
   • Ohio Athletics

WATH-AM/WXTQ-FM, Sales Department, Athens, Ohio   1995
Account Executive
   • Established numerous new accounts and significantly increased sales

ACRN (All Campus Radio Network), Ohio University, Athens, Ohio   1991-1995
Sports Director (1993-1995)
Morning and Afternoon Sportscaster (1991-1995)
Beat Reporter (1991-1995)
   • Ohio Football, Basketball and Baseball
Host and Director (1991-1995)
   • "NFL First Look" – weekly football call-in show
   • "Infield Chatter" – weekly MLB call-in show
   • "In the NBA" – weekly pro basketball call-in show
   • "Collegiate Court Report" – weekly college basketball call-in show
   • "Best of the Bobcats" – weekly wrap-up show on Ohio Athletics

TELEVISION EXPERIENCE

AVW (Athens Video Works), Ohio University, Athens, Ohio
Host – Halftime report for Ohio University football and basketball

BELLBROOK HIGH SCHOOL, Bellbrook, Ohio
Host – "The Peer Connection" and "Spotlight on Eagle Athletics"

EDUCATION

OHIO UNIVERSITY, Athens, Ohio
Bachelor of Science in Telecommunications
Trained in Radio Broadcasting and Disc-Jockeying

ACTIVITIES

City League Sports – Soccer, Football, Basketball, Baseball, Broomball, Volleyball, Softball
D.A.R.E. Program Volunteer
Public Address Announcer for various fund-raisers and non-profit organizations

GREGORY A. JACOBS
97 Maple Street   Scarsdale, NY   10583
(914) 472-1998

OBJECTIVE

An entry level position in the Film Industry which will utilize exceptional detail orientation and benefit from my expertise in both post-production and editing of film and video.

PROFILE

☛ Possess hands-on experience working with a full range of professional camera and lighting equipment.
☛ Expertise in audio recording, audio post production, sound dubbing and sync-sound; knowledgeable in using ProTools for computerized digital recording.
☛ Proficient in using outboard equipment for sound enhancement.
☛ Experienced in equipment calibration and color adjustment.
☛ Proven ability to tell a story visually.
☛ Skilled in diverse transfer protocols including address track time code.
☛ Demonstrated proficiency in calibrating video color and sound.

EDUCATION

SCHOOL OF VISUAL ARTS, New York, NY
Bachelor of Fine Arts: *Film and Video*   May 1996
Acquired significant expertise in the following areas:
  ✧ Lighting techniques: control and angle
  ✧ Editing Systems: on-line and off-line; Steenbeck; Moviola
  ✧ Sound dubbing
  ✧ Video: camera & editing
  ✧ Video Post Production
  ✧ Character generators

SIGNIFICANT ACHIEVEMENTS

☛ Credited by Thesis Advisor with "*full understanding of how editing can save a scene and add meaning*." Recorded sound for 20 minute drama, under diverse and challenging locations. Edited film & sound and *placed appropriate sound effects*. *Repositioned dialog* into more appropriate locations. Transferred scene to interspersed flash-backs to *enhance over all flow and feel*.
☛ Wrote music and edited film & sound for 10 minute documentary. *Synched music* to dance sequence.
☛ Edited a "Gunsmoke" fight scene from provided footage,achieving desired level of drama/tension and climax. *Commended for fluency of action, pacing and timing*.

EMPLOYMENT
October 1993 - Present

CONSUMER VALUE STORES, Scarsdale, NY
Head Cashier
☛ Oversee floor management.
☛ Supervise cashiers.
☛ Count out drawers and facilitate bank deposits.

March 1990 -
October 1993

FOOD EMPORIUM, Eastchester, NY
Cashier

REFERENCES

Excellent references and a portfolio of accomplishments will be furnished upon request.

Alex Duart

P. O. Box 125 ❖ Prattville, Alabama 36000 ❖ ℘ [334] 555-5555

Value to Variety Press International: As a **writer and editor,** translate your vision into written words that are read, remembered and acted upon.

Capabilities you can use now:

❖ **Seasoned writer** who gets the best stories

❖ **Organized editor** who meets tight deadlines

❖ **"Turn around" specialist** with solid track record

Work history with selected examples of success:

Business owner, Champion Products, Montgomery, Alabama (92 – Present)

❖ Found and served specialty markets, met customer needs, developed promotion plans, and controlled costs.

Editorial Director, Norpress Publishers, Montgomery, Alabama (72 – 83, 90 – 93) *One of the first employees of this industry leader in natural resource magazines. Helped this aggressive company build a national circulation of 200,000.*

❖ Transformed unfocused collection of promotional literature into major resource book. Found and wrote the stories, did most of the editing. Handled promotion. *Results:* Sold nearly 30,000 copies of this $25 technical manual. **Won $50,000 advertising packages.**

❖ Helped build five magazines. Did it all, from hiring writers to setting details of layout. Spun off full-color, slick magazine from tabloid. *Results:* **Advertising up. Successfully converted free publication to paid publication.**

❖ Convinced nation's expert to let me do in-depth story on his one-of-a-kind system. *Results:* Although other competitors had tried and failed, I got *all* the information. Expert impressed. Our **25,000 audited readers very happy.**

Editorial Director, The Colophon Press, Atlanta Branch, San Francisco, California (83 – 90) *Key contributor to two magazines this 100-year old house publishes.*

❖ Major contributor and key researcher for flagship publications. *Results:* **Exceeded** corporate goals by **at least 15% every year for six years.**

❖ Developed and followed up on list of key decision makers in readers' markets. *Results:* **Always got the story. Manufacturers asked my opinion of their newest products.**

Computer literacy:

❖ Expert in Word for Windows 6.0c, WordPerfect 5.0, WordPerfect 6.1 for Windows
❖ Working knowledge of Excel, Lotus 1-2-3, Quicken, Peachtree Accounting, Windows

Skills that help build your productivity:

❖ Accomplished photographer comfortable with 35 mm and 2¼ x 2¼ formats
❖ Complete knowledge of paste-up procedures

Education:

❖ Attended Waller State University, Waller, Alabama: 30 semester hours in English

NATASHA ROSEN-LEVINSTEIN

1020 Artists Avenue, # 123, Harbor View, Georgia 87634
(555) 984-1234 • Email: levin4509@aol.com

VIDEO / AUDIO / PRINT PRODUCTION • CREATIVE PROJECTS • PROMOTIONS

PROFILE

- **Over five years project coordination experience in Creative Services and Communications. Current career interest in Video Production.** Talent for generating creative ideas, organizing, and bringing projects to fruition with very limited resources. **Willing to relocate.** Versed in:

  - corporate video production
  - pre & post production
  - story boarding
  - editing (inc. non-linear digital editing)
  - direction: special programs, news, others
  - camera operations / studio lighting
  - electronic graphic design
  - creative communications (print, broadcast)
  - promotional development
  - master of ceremony & on-air talent

  - instructional video production
  - production management
  - script writing
  - video editing
  - field shoots
  - audio switching
  - grip & gaffer work
  - equipment troubleshooting
  - PSAs, public relations
  - voice overs

- **Skilled professional writer.** Author and publisher of numerous articles for newspapers, trade publications, newsletters, literary journals, and ad copy for television and radio broadcasting.

EDUCATION

- **Bachelor of Science - Communications (Specialty: Broadcasting), 1992**
  Savannah University (SU), Newport, Georgia

ACHIEVEMENTS & HONORS

- "Outstanding Achievement in Video Production": SU College of Communications
- Licensed by the F.C.C. to operate a radio station (Level 1 broadcasting)
- Employed throughout college to fund expenses

SPECIAL COLLEGE PROJECTS

CORPORATE VIDEO
- Acquired hands-on knowledge of all aspects of video production for client project as freelance videographer.
- Assisted client in defining production goals and establishing parameters. Shot on-location footage, edited, produced, and mastered a broadcast quality video.
- Edited eight hours of footage into a series of informative tapes as well as into a single 45-minute overview program.

BROADCAST TELEVISION NEWS
- Invited by class professor to independently direct a weekly television newscast "Savannah View" for WSAV Channel 11. Wrote and edited scripts. Conceptualized, produced, and directed each show.
- Functioned as scriptwriter, talent coordinator, and set designer.
- Oversaw entire project: studio personnel activities, equipment, lighting, staging, sound work, props, scheduling.

BROADCAST MANAGEMENT
- Served on class project team for a collaborative venture between WSAV Channel 11 and Scripps-Howard to produce a regional cable network channel.
- Commissioned to design each phase of this project in the most cost-effective manner: staffing, studio location, funding, budget preparation, marketing, programming layout, etc.
- Produced a precise and informative presentation delivered to WSAV leadership and the entire class.
- Team received an "A" grade for outstanding effort.

SELECTED ACHIEVEMENTS

BERKINSHIRE MEDIA CENTER, Berkinshire, New Jersey (1992-present)
Publications Manager
On-Air Personality: WBKS NewsTalk Radio
Game Show Host / Producer: "LunchBox Hour"
Writer / Editor / Graphic Designer / Distribution Coordinator: CityLights Newspaper

WRITING & PRODUCTION LEADERSHIP

- Edited and produced several key publications as Publications Manager including: 16-page black/white newspaper "CityLights," a 64-page color "Community Planning Calendar", and two monthly newsletters for media conglomerate.
- Directed and coordinated the editing / rewrite, copy editing, design, composition, type specs, photo / illustration research and selection, proofing, and printing of "CityLights," a monthly feature-oriented newspaper.
- Approved mechanical preparation and cover design. Prepared camera-ready copy using Adobe Pagemaker.
- Established publications' style criteria; design and layout and designed style manual for reporters.
- Supervised and coordinated 20 project-related people (writers, printers, ad sales people, etc.).

CREATIVITY & PERFORMING SKILLS

- Served as on-air talent during all shifts of 24-hour programming.
- Produced commercials, promotional and public service announcements. Scripted promos and opens.

WNEW AM RADIO STATION, Savannah University Campus, Newport, Georgia
News Reporter / Anchor (1988-1992, during college)

COMPUTERS
- Platforms: IBM - Macintosh
- Operating Systems: Windows 95 - Windows - DOS - VAX
- Wordprocessing: MS Word - MS Works
- Task Management: MS Schedule - MS Money
- Languages: FORTRAN - BASIC
- Graphics & Desktop Publishing: Corel - Paintshop Pro - Adobe Pagemaker - Publisher - Power Point
- Other: Internet (Gopher, WWW, FTP, Telnet) - Navigator - Email - BBS - Newsgroups - D.A.D. (radio station software) - virus protection software - system back up protocols. Personally built a 486 multimedia computer system and peripherals from scratch. Proficient in purchase and installation of upgrades, memory, CD-ROM, Scanner, and Post-Script printer.

TECHNICAL EQUIPMENT
- Character generation: Chyron - Chyron IV with font compose and auto display
- Grassy Valley production switchers with effects memory
- Video tape editing (all)
- Audio mixing / soundtrack - 2, 4, 8 track, mono, stereo
- Digital: 8 track / DAT cassette
- Studio lighting, grip & gaff
- Teleprompting
- Video Toaster (video graphics and switching system)
- The Cube (non-linear editing system)

COMPOSURE UNDER PRESSURE • SENSE OF HUMOR • INDEPENDENT • RESOURCEFUL

LORRAINE A. LARSON

7890 Murray Lane · St. Louis, Missouri 63110
Office **(555) 333-8539** · Home **(555) 333-9027**

■ PROFILE SUMMARY

Conferences · Fund-raising · Trade Shows · Meeting Planning · Cultural Programs

Creative professional with expertise in all aspects of successful event/program planning, development and management. Excel in managing multiple projects concurrently with strong detail, problem solving and follow-through capabilities. Demonstrated ability to recruit, motivate and build cohesive teams that achieve results. Sourced vendors, negotiated contracts and managed budgets. Superb written communications, interpersonal and presentation skills.

■ SELECTED ACCOMPLISHMENTS

Special Events Management:

Planned and coordinated conferences, meetings and events for companies, professional associations, arts/cultural, and other organizations. Developed program content and administered budgets. Arranged all on-site logistics, including transportation, accommodations, meals, guest speakers and entertainers, and audiovisual support. Coordinated participation and represented companies at industry trade shows. Recognized for creating and planning some of the most successful events ever held state-wide.

- ♦ **Created cultural events for an arts organization that boosted membership enrollment.**
- ♦ **Organized 5 well-attended conferences for 2 national professional associations.**
- ♦ **Designed successful community educational campaigns promoting safety awareness.**

Fund-raising & Public Relations:

Created, planned and managed all aspects of several major fundraising campaigns resulting in a significant increase in contributions raised for each function over prior years. Recruited volunteers and developed corporate sponsorships. Generated extensive media coverage through effective promotional and public relations strategies. Created newsletters distributed to employees, customers and others.

- ♦ **Co-chaired capital fund campaign raising $3.5 million for new facility.**
- ♦ **Coordinated 3 auctions raising over $140,000 for an educational institution.**
- ♦ **Initiated successful publication generating $25,000 to finance community programs.**

Sales & Marketing:

Selected by management to spearhead opening of regional office, including all logistics, staff relocation and business development efforts. Designed and implemented creative sales and marketing strategies to capitalize on consumer trends and penetrate new market. Coordinated and conducted sales training.

- ♦ **Developed and managed 17 key accounts generating $10 million annually.**
- ♦ **Recognized for managing top revenue-generating program company-wide.**
- ♦ **Consistently exceeded sales forecast and led region to rank #1 out of 15 offices in profitability nationwide.**

LORRAINE A. LARSON

Office **(555) 333-8539** · Home **(555) 333-9027**

■ EVENTS MANAGEMENT EXPERIENCE

Special Events/Conference/Program Coordinator: 1983-Present

AREA ARTS COUNCIL · St. Louis, Missouri

UNITED COMMUNITY · St. Louis, Missouri

SAFETY COUNCIL · St. Louis, Missouri

BOTANICAL GARDENS · St. Louis, Missouri

NATIONAL ASSOCIATION OF INSURANCE WOMEN · St. Louis, Missouri

INSURANCE COUNCIL OF ST. LOUIS · St. Louis, Missouri

■ PROFESSIONAL EMPLOYMENT

MARCON FINANCIAL SERVICES COMPANY · St. Louis, Missouri   1988-Present
  Regional Manager
  Account Executive

SENTINEL BANK · St. Louis, Missouri   1985-1988
  Financial Underwriter

ROBERTS INSURANCE COMPANY · Springfield, Illinois   1980-1985
  Claims Analyst
  Senior Processor
  Health Claim Processor

■ EDUCATION

SPRINGFIELD COLLEGE · Springfield, Massachusetts
  B.A. in Business Administration · 1980

LEIGH WRIGHT
35 Royal Oak Court
Mystic, Connecticut 06355
Email: lnxl@msn.com

Home: 203-316-9114

Fax: 203-316-7126

SPECIAL EVENTS & ART SHOW MANAGEMENT

Seventeen-year career in the planning, promotion and management of special events for a nationally-recognized arts and crafts management company. Combines cross-functional expertise in Business Management, Event Management, Marketing, Promotions, Project Management and Finance. Excellent presentation, negotiation, organizational and administrative management skills.

PROFESSIONAL EXPERIENCE:

Board Director / Vice President / Treasurer / Show Director   1980 to Present
LEIGH WRIGHT ART SHOWS, INC., Mystic, Connecticut

Principal in one of the nation's leading commercial art show businesses, a venture that has grown from start-up to over $800,000 in annual gross revenues and dominated the Eastern Seaboard market for more than two decades. Recognized by Sunlight Artists as one of the "***best 100 traditional craft shows in the U.S.***" for five consecutive years (since annual awards inception). Dual responsibility as Business Manager and Show Director.

Marketing, Advertising & Promotions

- Lead the corporation's marketing, marketing communications, direct mail, advertising and promotional programs. Orchestrate projects from initial planning and concept through design, execution, production and media placement. Personally manage negotiations with broadcast and print media sales representatives, media buying agencies and graphic/design vendors. Negotiate rates and contracts with major media including *Boston Globe, Boston Herald, Hartford Courant, Sunlight Artists, The Craft Journal* and *The Craft Bulletin*. Instrumental in developing contacts resulting in local, regional and national feature articles and editorials.

Show & Special Event Management

- Direct the planning, marketing, scheduling, logistics, security and on-site management of up to 80 shows annually with total artist attendance surpassing 800. Events include arts & craft shows, antique & collectible shows and gun shows at more than 60 malls and exposition centers. Personally responsible for the largest annual event, a 350-exhibitor show in a 100,000 square foot exposition hall with more than 38,000 public attendees (Londonderry Faire in Massachusetts). Manage contract negotiations with mall management, negotiate group hotel reservations, and coordinate liaison affairs with local building departments, state tax departments, and regional law enforcement and fire departments. Manage site security, maintenance and janitorial contractors.

Financial Management

- Designed, implemented and currently manage all financial, accounting, budgeting, tax, payroll, income and expense reporting, cost analysis, contract negotiation and administrative functions. Delivered consistent operating cost reductions through strategic negotiations with vendors, insurance providers, material suppliers, graphic artists and print media to lower costs and improve net profitability.

Information Systems Technology

- Automated the entire corporation with the introduction of PC technology and several major upgrades. Currently operate under Windows 95 with Microsoft Office Suite. Designed and currently manage 13 databases with a total of 23,500+ contacts (artists and customers).

EDUCATION: **B.S., Criminal Justice**, Mount Holyoke College, 1979

James E. Stone

3515 Hartwood Lane
Melbourne, Florida 32934

(407) 752-0794

AIRPORT DIRECTOR

Profile

Well-qualified executive with twenty-one years experience managing multidisciplinary operations with increased responsibility directing extensive airport management, planning and design, organizational flight training and standardization.

Management

Actively directed the safe and efficient operation of one of the most active Army airfields in the world supporting over 1000 personnel and 130 assigned aircraft worth more than $1,000,000,000. Coordinated with various government officials and agencies on matters concerning future airfield design and development. Formulated local flight rules and airfield operating procedures for daily operations and all airfield emergencies including aircraft accidents and security violations. Directed studies and developed procedures on noise abatement resulting from complaints of excessive noise from low flying aircraft. Reviewed reports of expenditures for previous fiscal year, proposed improvements to facilities, and estimated operating costs in order to prepare budget estimates for the upcoming fiscal year. Managed the daily operation of the airfield in accordance with appropriate regulations and procedures.

Safety Management

Developed extensive safety and environmental programs that ensured airfield compliance with all applicable regulations. Received an overall exemplary rating on a recent Department of Defense Safety and Environmental inspection.

Project Management

Justified and developed long-range plans and airfield improvements, including the design of new runways, taxiways, an air traffic control tower and airfield operations facility, and two aircraft maintenance hangars valued at $15,000,000 each. Introduced several project changes which resulted in taxpayer savings of over $575,000.

Maintenance Management

Coordinated personnel involved with the repair and maintenance of airfield facilities and equipment to minimize equipment downtime. Established an extensive facilities preventive maintenance program which resulted in significantly lower maintenance repair costs.

Training Development

Formulated and managed an extensive flight training and air crew flight standardization program for an aviation organization with 325 flight crew members operating 126 aircraft. This program safely provided over 14,000 accident-free flying hours in 120 days during Operation Desert Shield and Desert Storm.

Personnel Management

Directly managed up to 41 personnel involved in air traffic control, airfield operations, fire department and airfield services. Developed job descriptions and personnel training programs which greatly improved airfield services and employee productivity.

James E. Stone

Employment	UNITED STATES ARMY	1975 to 1996

Commander (Airfield Director), Sabre Army Airfield (1992-1995)
Fort Campbell, Kentucky

	NATIONAL AIRLINES, Orlando, Florida	1973 to 1975

Flight Operations Agent

Education   **Bachelor of Science in Professional Aeronautics**
Embry-Riddle Aeronautical University – 1995

Airport Planning and Design
Embry-Riddle Aeronautical University – 1995

Operations and Safety Course
American Association of Airport Executives – 1994

United States Army Training:
Aviation Safety Course – 1992
Instrument Flight Examiner Course – 1987
Warrant Officer Advance Course – 1983
Instructor Pilot Course – 1982
Accident Prevention Course – 1979
Initial Flight Qualification Course – 1976

Certificates   Commercial Pilot-Instrument
Over 4,000 hours total flight time

Professional   Army Aviation Association of America
Associations   American Association of Airport Executives

Additional   Secret Clearance
Information   Willing to relocate

References   Available upon request

JOSEPH CZECH-KOW-SKI
21 Marjo Lane, Monterey, California 92056 ☎ (760) 555-1234

CAREER PROFILE

Confident, personable, and achievement-oriented sales and management professional offering personal skills honed by military service and refined by prior sales experience. Strong presentation skills are enhanced by substantial diverse experiences augmented by a graduate level education and specialized professional training. Computer literate in a wide variety of software applications including the ACT for Windows. Global perspective based upon extensive foreign travels and life abroad in 35 countries. Fluent in German, English, and conversational Hungarian. Qualifications and skills include superior interpersonal, motivational, and communications skills enhanced by an innate ability to transcend cultural and language differences.

EDUCATION AND PROFESSIONAL TRAINING

American University, San Bernardino, California
Master of Arts - Human Behavioral Science

Cleveland State University, Cleveland, Ohio
Bachelor of Arts - Major Emphasis: Economics and History

Uthkoss Technical Academy, Defochna, Germany
Vocational/Technical Schooling - Medical Equipment Manufacturing

PROFESSIONAL EXPERIENCE

Pfizer, Inc., New York, New York - 1994 to present

Healthcare Representative reporting to the District Manager, San Diego County, California. Scope of responsibility includes selling four classes of prescription medicine: antifungal, antihistamine, cardiovascular, and Aricept Alzheimer's medication. Primary focus was physicians, internists, and specialists located in hospitals, clinics, and private practices. Conducted sales presentations, coordinated lectures, and presented speaker programs.

- Transitioned into the private sector completing a 4-part training cycle within 1 year.
- Achieved 113% of market share for newly introduced Aricept Alzheimer's Medication.
- Nurtured and expanded client base by 20%+ within one year.

United States Marine Corps - 1974 to 1994

Lieutenant Colonel - Materials Management Officer whose professional responsibilities expanded to include areas of special projects analysis and planning, procurement activities, customer service support, supply and logistics administration, project and operations management, fiscal accountability, budget preparation and compliance, inventory control, and materiel, supplies, and equipment accountability in diverse classified assignments.

- Provided total logistical support to military organizations ranging in size from 600 to over 40,000 personnel. Assumed fiscal accountability of a $1+ billion account.
- Achieved a $110K savings by implementing a cost savings campaign on the annual budget.
- Attained 20% increase in equipment readiness; implemented sound and proven procedures.
- Awarded the prestigious Defense Meritorious Service Medal upon completion of Fellowship at the Pentagon, Department of Defense.

Wilson Readers Service, Indianapolis, Indiana - 1970 to 1974

Sales Representative reporting to the General Manager. Responsible for selling subscriptions for over 100 different magazines in a direct sales environment.

- Consistently achieved sales goals, earned high commissions, and received sales awards.
- Recognized as 1 of top 2 salespersons in the company within six months.

GEORGE BRIGGS
401 Jones Street • San Jose CA 95100
(408) 555-5555

OBJECTIVE: Position utilizing skills and experience gained as an Electronics Technician.

KEY QUALIFICATIONS:
- 5 years of hands-on experience and technical training as an Electronics Technician.
- Extensive background in troubleshooting, repair and maintenance of military low frequency test stations, camera systems and subassemblies.
- Proficient with electronic test equipment, including oscilloscopes, digital meters, counters, and circuit analyzers.
- Experience as a crew leader supervising other technicians; effective interpersonal skills.

TEST EQUIPMENT & PRODUCT KNOWLEDGE:
- BER Test Set, T-1, T-Berd 209A; BER Test Set, E-1, HP37742A
- Waveguide Fixed Attenuator, 65 dB
- Test Controller, 486 PC with VGA Monitor
- IDU'S with BNC (75 Ohm) line interface connections; IDU's with DB-25 line connections
- 4FSK & 2FSK IDU's ranging from 1X through 16X
- 13, 15, 18, 23, 26, 38 & 50 Ghz ODU's in 4FSK or 2FSK (E1 or T1); 4X2 or 16X2 data rates

PROFESSIONAL EXPERIENCE:

PTEK, San Jose, CA   Jan. 1997-Present
Millimeter wave radio systems for wireless telecommunications industry, consisting of outdoor unit (ODU), indoor unit (IDU), and single coaxial cable for the ODU-IDU interconnection.

SOAK TECHNICIAN/BURN-IN TECHNICIAN (cross-trained in Calibration)
- Perform required product quality verification tests for IDU/ODU system to ensure that performance specifications have been met in production.
- Identify faulty ODU/IDU through investigations and routing to ODU/IDU Test for back-up testing of unit to confirm bit error rate and hard failures or to Repair for appropriate rework.
- Earned promotion to swing shift Soak Technician Lead three months after joining company.

U.S. Navy   1993-Jan. 1997
AVIATION ELECTRONICS TECHNICIAN
- Supervised 2 technicians performing scheduled and unscheduled maintenance of test benches and avionics components.
- Tested components under simulated conditions to determine performance; isolated faults and repaired or replaced defective parts.
- Diagnosed, repaired and maintained aircraft camera, audio and video recorder systems.
- Performed necessary procedures for checkout, alignment, fault isolation, and disassembly of equipment utilizing functional, schematic and power distribution diagrams.
- Earned 2 awards for superior troubleshooting, repair and maintenance performance.

EDUCATION/TRAINING:
- Military electronics schools and technical training (52 weeks)
- General and technical education, University of California, Sacramento, CA (over 2 years)

CLEARANCE: Secret Clearance

SHELBY A. RICE
80 Boonsboro Avenue #418
Vienna, Virginia 22800
Residence (703) 615-6774   Business (202) 450-7611

PUBLIC RELATIONS STRATEGIST

Strategic Planning / Press Relations / Public Affairs / Multimedia Communications
Legislative & Regulatory Affairs / Industry Partnerships & Alliances

Dynamic career leading high-profile regional, national and international public relations program for JRI Communication, Inc., The United States Armed Forces, U.S. Press Federation, and other public and private organizations nationwide. Cross-functional expertise in strategic planning and competitive positioning with strong creative talent and campaign management skills.

PROFESSIONAL EXPERIENCE:

DYNAMIC STRATEGIES, INC.   1995 to Present
(Integrated media relations, corporate communications, public affairs & advertising group)

Press Officer

Key media contact, public affairs, image and policy strategist for one of DSI's most influential clients — JRI Communications, Inc., the parent company of South Communications Telephone and Pacific Communications. Define the strategies and create the programs to influence positive public support and industry relations. Plan and direct integrated press, communications and public affairs/public influence programs for the corporation and its operating companies. Coordinate efforts to ensure consistency of message and strategy implementation across business units to influence both state and federal legislation and regulations.

- Strengthened JRI's position as the company has successfully transitioned from a regulated utility to a leader in the competitive marketplace (100%+ revenue growth to $23.5 billion annually and 110,000+ employees). Won favorable support from major media, industry, public interest groups, and both state and federal legislatures.

- Member of team credited with influencing changes in state law in all five states in which JRI operates. Won support to transition from rate-of-return to price capital regulation, saving JRI hundreds of millions of dollars in annual operating costs.

- Built cooperative partnerships with other industry leaders (e.g., AT&T, MCI, U.S. West, Ameritech, Bell South, Bell Atlantic) to positively influence legislation, reduce regulatory control and improve corporate profitability.

- Defined/executed positive strategies to communicate messages across broad consumer, commercial, government, association, industry and private interest sectors. Authored media plans to favorably position the company as pro-competition.

- Catalyst for the development and launch of a new corporate image campaign, **"See You In The Marketplace!"**, a unique initiative leveraging competitive position.

PUBLIC RELATIONS CONSULTANT   1993 to 1995

Executive PR Consultant providing issues-driven public relations strategy, plans and programs.

- **Giles, Minton, Helvey & Myers, Inc**. — Developed and executed Congressional lobbying strategies for public and private sector transportation organizations.

- **The McAdams Group** — Wrote speeches and press releases, planned press conferences and managed media relations for this DC-based consulting group.

U.S. PRESS FEDERATION   1992 to 1993

Assistant Secretary for Public Affairs (1992 to 1993)
Deputy Assistant Secretary - Industry Affairs & Public Liaison (1992)

Joined USPF to lead the start-up of the new Office of Industry Legislature and Public Affairs, a public outreach initiative to improve USPF's relationships with industry and public interest groups. Promoted within four months to Assistant Secretary for Public Affairs and Chief Spokesperson. Directed media relations, public affairs activities, and both internal and external communications (e.g., speeches, press releases, briefing materials, publications, multimedia presentations). Managed a direct reporting staff of 30 and a total workforce of 120 in multiple locations. Administered a $3.5 million annual operating budget.

- Directed high-profile press relations campaigns addressing key issues before the organization (e.g., National Air's acquisition by London Airways, airport development and funding, inter-modal transportation initiatives, maritime union negotiations).

- At the request of the U.S. Armed Forces, directed public affairs and communications for the Commander's Task Force on Hurricane Hugo.

U.S. ARMED FORCES   1983 to 1992

Deputy Assistant to Commander/Director Office of Legal Affairs (1991 to 1992)
Special Assistant to the Commander & Deputy Publications Secretary (1989 to 1991)
Assistant to the Commander for Public Relations (1987 to 1989)
Special Assistant to the Foreign Affairs Secretary (1985 to 1987)
Director of Publications - Office of Commander Advance (1984 to 1985)
Staff Assistant to the Commander for Publications Advance (1983 to 1984)

Advanced through a series of increasingly responsible positions planning and directing press relations for two U.S. Commanders. Created communications strategies and programs to highlight Administration policy and initiatives. Briefed the Armed Forces Press Corps. Traveled worldwide.

Final promotion to Director of the Office of Legal Affairs, managing a 22-person White House Staff responsible for defense policy development strategy. Directed liaison affairs with Congress and prepared/reviewed statements and correspondence.

INTERNATIONAL WORLD SYMPOSIUM   Spring/Summer 1983

Special Assistant to the Deputy Director for Publications

Coordinated services provided to 3600 journalists from around the world. Assisted in liaison affairs with press officials and both domestic and foreign news organizations to manage coverage.

EDUCATION:

B.A., History, George Washington University, 1982
Daniel Smith Poole Award as Outstanding Student in Contemporary History

PUBLICATION:

Resurgence of 202, a 50-page pictorial narrative of the rebuilding of steam locomotive #202.

Kenda J. Kasin

975 Braddock Court, Apt. 2 • Athens, Ohio 45701 • (740) 593-0000

"highly creative when it comes to promotional ideas and planning ... creative, imaginative promotions mind ...
any organization with which you choose to affiliate will benefit from your wealth of ideas
and ability to express complex ideas in an understandable, imaginative manner ..."

--Kathy Smith, Director of Public Relations, Doctors Hospital
--Betty Brown, Director, Advertising & Media Relations, Roscoe Village

---

STRENGTHS

Public Relations · Marketing · Special Event Planning

Skilled public relations professional with 3+ years of successful experience and demonstrated enthusiasm, creativity and communication skills. Dedicated and dependable team player with strong work ethic.

EDUCATION & HONORS

OHIO UNIVERSITY, E.W. Scripps School of Journalism, Athens, Ohio – June 1995
Bachelor of Science in Journalism – Cum Laude · Major in Public Relations
Political Communication Undergraduate Certificate
   Dean's List · Dean's Scholarship · Golden Key National Honor Society

Computer Skills
Computer proficient with both IBM & Macintosh systems–Aldus Pagemaker ... Microsoft Word ...
QuarkXPress ... Photoshop ... WordPerfect ... Windows ... Excel

RELATED EXPERIENCE

Direct Marketing Coordinator – ABLE FINANCIAL SERVICING CORPORATION, Columbus, OH (1/96-present)
National billion-dollar financing company
- Head of Direct Department ranked in Top 5 out of over 50 offices nationwide in loan closings–directly involved with closing of over $10 million in loans
- Effectively market company to over 200 realtors and brokers throughout Ohio requiring knowledge of programs and excellent communication and interpersonal skills
- Provide superior service to clients while handling incoming inquiries, scheduling and providing information about programs and procedures

Marketing/Public Relations Intern – DOCTORS HOSPITAL, Athens, OH (9/95-12/95)
- Scope of position was focused on special event planning and promotion
- Played a key role in all phases of planning, preparation and execution of Golden Achievement Awards program
- Wrote over 15 news releases which appeared in various Columbus area newspapers
- Assisted with organizing Doctors Hospital Health Hotline with WOUB 10-TV
- Edited internal newsletter, brochures, news articles and press releases
- Developed strong working relationships with Athens-area media people

Public Relations Intern – ROSCOE VILLAGE, Chauncey, OH (11/94-1/95)
- Handled public relations activities for this historical village including writing news releases and designing ads for publication in local newspaper and educational magazine

Public Relations Intern/Special Events Coordinator – AMERICAN RED CROSS, Shade, Ohio (3/94-6/94)
- Performed a variety of public relations and special event planning functions while demonstrating an ability to work efficiently under deadlines
- Successfully planned and organized a major spring event within a strict budget–directed publicity, displays, presentations, catering and solicited local merchants for sponsorships; received front page recognition in local newspaper
- Wrote press releases, public service announcements and speech for presentation by director
- Assisted with recruitment of volunteers

Excellent References Provided Upon Request

WILSON P. WOODBRIDGE, APR

3934 Cecilia Lane
Los Angeles, California 90663
(210) 855-8749

PUBLIC RELATIONS & CORPORATE COMMUNICATIONS STRATEGIST
Extensive National & International Media Network

Dynamic senior management career as the Public Relations Executive & Corporate Spokesperson for organizations worldwide. Leads senior management through planning and situation analysis to decisive and immediate action. Combines cross-functional expertise in:

- Strategic Planning & Development
- Press Relations & Press Spokesperson
- Media Planning & Positioning
- Multimedia Advertising
- Regulatory & Government Affairs

- Issues Management
- Crisis Communications
- International Press Affairs
- Internal Communications
- Public Affairs & Presentations

PROFESSIONAL CREDENTIALS

Accredited Public Relations Professional (APR)
Guest Lecturer - University of California, University of Texas, University of Washington
Panel Member - Media Forum - Princeton University, Simon & Schuster Publishing

PROFESSIONAL EXPERIENCE

1995 to Present

Corporate Communications Director
THE SALVATION ARMY

Member of the Salvation Army's 20-person Senior Management Team and the most Senior Communications Executive for the organization's $1.2 billion housing and employment programs (largest operating group contributing over 80% of annual revenues). Challenged to improve the public's opinion and support to the organization. Lead a cross-functional communications, marketing, advertising, media and public relations team of up to 10. Manage a $2 million annual operating budget. Senior Public Relations Advisor to National Headquarters and CEOs at 38 locations nationwide. Senior Press, Corporate and Government Spokesperson.

- Built, staffed and currently direct the Division's first-ever communications department and won favorable press coverage (including front page news coverage) in major media publications nationwide.

- Dominated the competition with high-profile, action-driven campaigns.

- Developed and deployed preemptive strategic communications plan to eliminate hostile takeover attempts by competing organizations.

- Solidified and strengthened relations with the Congress and American public through positive press, government and public affairs initiatives nationwide.

- Created high-impact volunteer recruitment strategies and multimedia advertising campaigns in cooperation with internal advertising/marketing executives. Consistently improved public awareness and emergency response with a record number of first-time volunteers.

- Guided outside PR agency, human resources and legal counsel in communications strategies for high-profile labor relations and unionization issues.

- Championed development of the organization's first-ever Internet site to expand public outreach programs.

1992 to 1995   **Corporate Communications Director**
U.S. NAVY SUPPLY COMMAND

Planned and executed public relations, public affairs and corporate communications for a 75,000 person R&D and technology organization with operations in the U.S., Europe and Pacific Rim. Senior Advisor to top-level executives to favorably position media coverage of international trade and technology, crisis communications, environmental and hazardous materials issues.

- Personally orchestrated all national and international public relations and press affairs programs for U.S. Navy and Marine deployments in Haiti, Bosnia and other locations worldwide.

1992   **Senior Communications Associate**
WHITE HOUSE MEDIA RELATIONS

Directed senior communications staff managing public affairs and press relations with national and international media. Personally managed high-profile, sensitive and/or crisis issues. Corporate Media Spokesperson.

1990 to 1992   **Deputy Director - Public Affairs**
CENTER FOR WORLD RELATIONS

Directed a team of 20 professionals in the planning and execution of all public affairs programs throughout the European continent.

- Led efforts of 70 international public relations professionals during Rwanda Relief Operations. Won positive world media coverage of multinational humanitarian relief operations.

- Dispatched by DoD to Bosnia to establish an international media center.

- Primary press liaison and communications coordinator for the release of American hostages to US control.

SPECIAL PROJECT

VICE PRESIDENT - CONSUMER PUBLIC RELATIONS

First-ever U.S. Navy Officer to be selected for professional, year-long public relations assignment. Provided strategic planning, campaign development and public relations leadership in the consumer products, HBA products, banking and food/confectionery industries.

EDUCATION

Masters Degree in Public Administration, University of Georgia
Bachelors Degree in Liberal Arts, St. John's University

SHIRLEY J. JONES
12321 S. 19th Street
Wisconsin Rapids, Wisconsin 54494
(715) 325-5888

PROFESSIONAL PROFILE

Vendor Sourcing/Selection and Analysis   Internal Material Tracking Systems
Supplier Continuous Improvement Programs   Production Planning Systems
Materials Management   Inventory Planning and Control
New Product Development

EXPERIENCE

NATIONAL FOOD CORPORATION, Stevens Point, WI   July 1990-Present
Refrigerated Products Group

Purchasing Coordinator, March 1996-Present
Coordinate purchasing of all materials, ingredients, and supplies for a food processing facility. Work with the Material Control Manager on the establishment and certification of vendors. Prepare requisitions in conjunction with Corporate Purchasing Department for packaging materials and ingredients. Coordinate price changes and terms and conditions directly with vendors and supplier representatives. Manage the packaging orders and inventory of product being copacked and inform copackers of guidelines. Involved in the setting up of an EDI (Electronic Data Interchange) system with vendors. Member of TQM (Total Quality Management) Team, QIP (Quality Improvement Process) Team, Health Team, and the Company Picnic Committee.

<u>Accomplishments:</u>
- Reduced monthly inventory by $300,000 without any interruption to daily production of product.
- Achieved a 10% reduction in the 1996 budget for the packaging material account.
- Saved $5700 on one packaging material through blanket purchasing.
- Manage a continuous $1 million of packaging material inventory at all times.
- Secured a direct vendor manufacturing printer ribbons and labels, a savings of $18,000 annually.
- Obtained a national account vendor for rental items, a cost savings of $3,000.
- Used inventory control forecasting to minimize the absolute write offs during 1996 by $100,000.

<u>Special Projects:</u>
• Researched, coordinated, and implemented a capital improvement project involving the installation of an inkjet system on each line for inline barcode printing onto plain fiber boxes.
• Coordinate yearly holiday program that enables customers to purchase products in a plastic container or crock. Used new fiber design creating a cost savings on materials and shipping in 1996.
• Key player involved with launching a new product. Involved in creating the packaging material for the new product consisting of fiber, outerwrap, and innerwrap. Purchased materials for start-up and full scale operation.
• Coordinate purchasing for yearly summer promotion involving inpacking of coupons, offers, and prizes.

Purchasing Assistant, September 1994-March 1996
Reviewed inventory levels of routine stock items and initiated purchase orders. Worked with MRO Supervisor in maintaining and ordering MRO supplies. Maintained vendor relationships to ensure best pricing, appropriate quantities, and delivery terms to meet production scheduling requirements.

Checked purchase requisitions and applied payment and freight terms. Processed purchase orders and maintained purchase order files.

Purchasing Clerk, March 1993-September 1994
Maintained computerized stock and packaging inventories. Reconciled invoices, placed approved purchase orders with vendors, maintained purchasing files, inventories, and sample packaging files. Entered vendors into new computer system including shipment and payment terms. Assisted shipping department in implementing new computer system including training two hourly assistant supervisors.

Lab Clerk, July 1990-March 1993
Sampled, examined, and prepared up to 50 sample orders per week for shipment. Maintained written reports on all products produced in the plant. Worked with Quality Control on product evaluation and hold determinations. Set up weekly comparison test for customer service with National Kitchens.

EDUCATION

Small Private College, Port Edwards, WI
Associates Degree - Communication Graphics, 1989

The Essentials of Credibility, Composure, and Confidence, 1996
How to Be a Better Buyer, 1994,
Take-Charge Purchasing Assistant, 1994

PROFESSIONAL ACTIVITIES

Financial Women International - Member
Big Brothers/Big Sisters of Portage County

References Available Upon Request

John H. Smithers
16 Terryville Avenue
Bristol, CT 06010
(860) 583-7500

TOP-PRODUCING RETAIL BUYER/SALES MANAGEMENT PROFESSIONAL with:

- Nearly ten years of experience in the strategic planning, implementation and management of sales and merchandising programs in a high-profile, high-growth retail operation.
- Proven ability to capitalize upon merchandise trends and achieve market dominance.
- Success in increasing profitability through astute market projections, attention to customer needs and ability to capitalize on market niches.
- Demonstrated leadership skill in the training, development and motivation of sales staffs.

PROFESSIONAL EXPERIENCE

MAJOR RETAIL COMPANY, Dallas, TX   9/86 - Present
Fast-track promotions through a series of increasingly responsible positions.

Senior Merchandise Manager/Buyer (8/92 - Present)
MEN'S DEPARTMENT: Bristol, CT
Manages entire operation of $6.5M retail department. Buyer for complete line of men's wear including accessories, sportswear, tailored clothing and athletic apparel. Oversees item development, merchandise mix and floor layout; interfaces with outside sales representatives. Key areas of responsibility include budget, inventory control, personnel recruitment, training/development, with a staff of 15-40 employees. Coordinates extensive retail computer MIS operation.
- Hand-picked by District Manager to participate on 3-member Men's Buying Committee, providing complete merchandising recommendations for 22 retail stores in the Northeast.
- Increased departmental revenues by $1M through astute buying, capitalizing on market trends and designing highly effective merchandising strategies.
- Increased sales of college merchandise by 300% in past twelve months by recognizing and acting on sports trends.
- Consistently ranked in top 4 performers district-wide.

Senior Merchandise Manager/Buyer (2/89 - 8/92)
CHILDREN'S DEPARTMENT: New York, NY
Promoted to senior merchandising position after only six months.
- Increased revenues by 80% in three years, successfully developing departmental sales upward from $2.5M to $4.5M.
- Instrumental in departmental remodeling, creating merchandising strategies and interacting with contractors. Subsequently assisted with new store opening in Salem, NH.

Merchandise Manager/Buyer (8/88 - 2/89)
SOFT HOME and CHILDREN'S DEPARTMENTS: Hartford, CT
- Coordinated departmental buying, strategic planning, merchandising and staffing for new store opening.

Merchandise Manager/Buyer (9/86 - 8/88)
WOMEN'S LINGERIE, SLEEPWEAR and CHILDREN'S DEPARTMENTS: Hartford, CT

EDUCATION/CONTINUING EDUCATION

MAJOR RETAIL COMPANY   1986 - Present
Company-sponsored workshops: Workforce Diversity, Senior Merchandising, Merchandise Manager

UNIVERSITY OF CONNECTICUT, SCHOOL OF MANAGEMENT, Storrs, CT   1986
B.A. Business Management
Dean's List all semesters; GPA: 3.5

JARED W. THORNTON, CPM

3499 Garden Grove
Manassas, Virginia 22330

Home (703) 288-8779
Office (202) 409-6226

SENIOR PURCHASING DIRECTOR
MRO & Capital Equipment Purchasing / Materials Management / Inventory Planning & Control
Multi-Site Warehousing / Regional & National Distribution / Barter & Trade Operations

Delivered over $100 million in total cost savings throughout career through expertise in planning, staffing, budgeting and directing large-scale domestic and offshore purchasing operations. Spearheaded development of regional and national purchasing programs, fixed price contracts, and vendor sourcing plans to expand supplier base and reduce acquisition costs. Keen negotiation and vendor/subcontractor management skills.

PROFESSIONAL EXPERIENCE:

FABRICATIONS INTERNATIONAL, Washington, D.C.   1990 to Present
($120 million consumer products manufacturer)

Director of Purchasing

Promoted from Purchasing Manager to Director with full responsibility for the planning, staffing, budgeting and operations of a diversified purchasing and inventory management function (e.g., stainless steel, aluminum, parts, packaging, MRO, POP). Managed a large off-shore purchasing and vendor management program. Directed a staff of six purchasing agents, buyers and support personnel. Negotiated $55+ million in annual purchasing contracts.

- Introduced MRP technology (BCPS system) to the corporation to upgrade the quality, control and availability of parts, equipment and support services. Resulted in a 14% reduction in annual inventory volume/costs.

- Structured and negotiated multi-year, fixed price contacts for major raw material expenditures, resale goods and components. Resulted in an 18% reduction ($1.7 million) in annual purchasing costs.

- Spearheaded the transfer of parts manufacturing from U.S. to offshore facilities, significantly enhanced design performance, and saved 12% in annual purchasing and subcontractor costs.

- Directed a $10 million addition to physical plant. Brought project in on time and within budget despite problems with contractor performance and materials availability.

UNIVERSAL APPAREL CORPORATION, Philadelphia, Pennsylvania   1987 to 1990
($18 million, privately-held custom uniform & career apparel manufacturer)

Director of Operations & Sales

Recruited to this family-owned business to introduce sound operation, purchasing and general management strategies as part of the management team's commitment to accelerated growth. Challenged to introduce the systems, processes and operations to support expansion and improve financial performance. Demonstrated success within a fast-paced, entrepreneurial and customer-driven organization.

Held full planning, budgeting and operating management responsibility for purchasing, inventory control, warehousing, subcontract production, scheduling, customer service, mail order processing and fulfillment, shipping and receiving, and divisional sales.

- Negotiated over $10 million annually in subcontractor manufacturing agreements and an additional $3 million in general purchasing contracts.

- Launched an aggressive expansion of computer technology to automate general business, customer service, purchasing, inventory and distribution management functions.

NATIONAL RENT A CAR, INC., New York, New York   1980 to 1987
($2 billion automotive rental & fleet management company)

Director of Purchasing & Distribution

Directed the purchase of over $250 million in parts, components, equipment and support services utilizing a centralized national contracts system. Supported three major corporate facilities and three major operating divisions generating $2+ billion in annual sales revenues. Concurrently, directed all purchasing, vendor relations and subcontractor negotiations for the purchase of direct mail, promotional, printing and fulfillment programs.

- Delivered a 3% annual reduction in purchasing costs ($6-$7 million) through the introduction of the corporation's first regional and national purchasing contracts with complete internal purchasing audit function. Negotiated firm fixed price contracts to control accelerating costs and expanded vendor sourcing worldwide.

- Assumed additional responsibility for the planning, staffing, budgeting and management of telecommunications, support services, invoice audit and travel departments.

NORTHSTAR SYSTEM, INC.   1973 to 1980

Director - Field Purchasing & Administrative Services (1974 to 1980)
Northstar Truck Rental, Inc., Alexandria, Virginia *($3 billion corporation)*

Led the start-up of a complete purchasing function as Northstar transitioned from third party to in-house materials management. Recruited/trained 12 buyers and support personnel responsible for the cost-effective acquisition of parts, replacement equipment, tires, shop equipment, chemicals and fuel storage/dispensing equipment.

Assumed concurrent responsibility for management of the Administrative Services function (e.g., accounting, graphic arts, records management, word processing, micro-graphics, mail & supply space planning, facilities management, inventory control). Directed Services team of 25-30.

- Structured, negotiated and executed $150 million annually in national and regional purchasing contracts. Supported company growth from $900 million to $3+ billion in revenues.

Director of Purchasing (1973 to 1974)
Supplies, Inc., Alexandria, Virginia

Joined newly-created subsidiary established to provide a national buying source for the entire Northstar system. Directed $25+ million in annual purchasing volume and operated four distribution centers nationwide supplying over 600 locations. NOTE: Company was liquidated in 1974 and all purchasing functions were transitioned in-house to Northstar System.

Previous Professional Experience:

Purchasing Manager, Norfolk & Southern Railroad, Inc., Richmond, Virginia
Purchasing Agent to Superintendent, Swisher Company, St. Alamos, Texas

EDUCATION:

VIRGINIA POLYTECHNIC INSTITUTE – B.S., Chemical Engineering
HARVARD UNIVERSITY – NAPM Executive Purchasing Program
AMERICAN INTERNATIONAL COLLEGE – MBA Program
REGISTERED PROFESSIONAL ENGINEER – Virginia & Texas
CERTIFIED PURCHASING MANAGER (CPM)

PAUL K. RATHER
432 First Street, Monroe, MI 48162
(313) 555-5432

Quality Assurance Management

- A 20-year record of accomplishment in Quality Management, with emphasis in the automotive industry. Solid background in new program management and new vehicle launches. Experience includes both original equipment manufacturers and suppliers.
- Developed quality systems at plant locations that achieved the GM Targets for Excellence, Ford Q1, Chrysler QE award, and Isuzu Motors quality award.
- Trained as ISO-9000 Lead Auditor/Assessor.
- Strong TQM background with hands-on experience developing and implementing total quality management system.
- Experience in supplier development, systems auditing, procedures writing, strategic planning, and budget development.
- Training and hands-on experience in statistical process control, quality operating systems, Just-in-Time, problem solving, and continuous improvement programs.

1996-1997

QST STEEL COIL PROCESSING, Trenton, Michigan

Quality Systems Manager (5/96-2/97)
- Managed quality system and customer concerns for major auto industry supplier. Tracked cost of quality by analyzing data on cost of repairs and replacements.
- Trained and supervised quality supervisors and a technical service representative.
- Finalized existing Quality System and Quality Procedures to meet ISO-9002 requirements.
- Achieved ISO-9002 certification assessment November, 1996.
- Developed a document traveler procedure which controlled distribution, revision levels, and sign-off of all quality procedures and work instructions.
- Implemented a Non-Conforming Status Log which documented and tracked rejects and provided full directions on repair, rework, and cost of quality activities.

1993-1996

KENTON AUTOMOTIVE PRODUCTS COMPANY, Nashville, Tennessee

Manufacturing Assembly Manager (Promotion) (2/96-5/96)
- Managed five welded assembly lines producing front engine cradles, rear trailing axles, frame side rails, and lower suspension arms.
- Managed five line supervisors, weld technicians, and line technicians.

Quality Assurance Manager (11/93-1/96)
- Instituted plant-wide QS-9000 Quality Improvement Program after a major downsizing. Reengineered Quality Department into customer-specific areas of responsibility, which resulted in a significant improvement in customer communication.
- Improved quality and productivity by revamping existing quality programs: Introduced front-line responsibility for quality – manufacturing workers became on-site inspectors; Quality Department performed less line inspection and more data analysis and auditing.
- Cross-trained quality staff in advance quality planning activities, and in proactive participation in launching new programs.
- Managed staff of 18, including Quality Specialists, SQA Engineers, and Line Auditors.

1991-1993 | **AUTOMOTIVE PANELS, INC.,** Toledo, Ohio

Quality Assurance Manager (10/91-9/93)
- Developed a continuous Quality Improvement Program, introducing systems and procedures directed by GM's Targets for Excellence and Ford Motor Company's Q1.
- Revised existing quality program to meet automotive/truck quality requirements.
- Wrote manuals for corporate quality systems and vendor requirements. Modified existing systems to meet and comply with the ISO-9002 standard.

1988-1991 | **STEEL INTERNATIONAL,** Toronto, Canada (U.S. Stamping Supplier)

Quality Systems Manager (2/90-10/91)
- Transferred from group level to division level to revitalize, develop, and implement quality systems to meet pending Japanese truck manufacturer quality requirements.
- Developed Statistical Process Control, Employee Involvement Teams, and Just-in-Time manufacturing techniques which surpassed customer requirements and led to supplier quality award within one year of implementation.

Group Quality Systems Manager (9/88-2/90)
- Developed and implemented continuous Quality Improvement Programs at a group level and interfaced with five divisions in refining existing programs.
- Lived and worked in Japan during 1989 as Quality Team Facilitator for a joint venture between Magna International and Isuzu Motors.

1980-1988 | **HARLEY-DAVIDSON MOTOR COMPANY,** Milwaukee, Wisconsin

Corporate Quality Assurance Engineer (12/82-8/88)
- Implemented a statistical quality summary for all vehicles on roll test.
- Increased vehicle quality through assembly line responsibility system.
- Originated dealer questionnaire resulting in significant product improvement.
- Quality Programs Manager for new vehicle programs.
- Prior positions at Harley-Davidson (1980-1982): Liaison Engineer, National Field Service Representative.

EDUCATION & TRAINING | **TRAINING:**

ISO/QS-9000 Lead Auditor Assessor Training; The Rational Approach to Problem-Solving (TOPS), Coaching and Teambuilding Skills for Managers and Supervisors, Reliability Engineering, Quality Functional Deployment, Fundamentals of Management for Quality Control Supervisors, Advanced Statistical Process Control, Cost of Quality, Measurement Systems Evaluation.

MILWAUKEE TECHNICAL COLLEGE, Milwaukee, Wisconsin
Associate in Science & Technology - Metallurgy

Member, American Society for Quality Control

Q.A. NGINEER

Home: 650/123-4567
Work: 650/595-2514

1601 El Camino Real, #301
Belmont, CA 94002

PROFILE   **Senior Software Quality** professional with substantial expertise in systematically decreasing the development cycle time and improving the quality of software.

QUALIFICATIONS SUMMARY

Highly motivated quality professional with experience in designing, implementing and managing software quality systems. Utilize strong theoretical and practical aspects of quality with a solid software development background. Special expertise includes:

- Quality team development
- Software process development, documentation, and analysis
- Software quality, effectiveness, and schedule metric use and analysis
- ISO 9000 and Malcolm Baldrige National Award auditing and preparation

PROFESSIONAL EXPERIENCE

Database Software Incorporated, Small Town, CA   1992 - Present
Senior Software Quality Engineer, Software Metrics Lead

- Managed team of three to four engineers in establishing, providing, training, and the analysis of software metrics.
- Partnered with Development, Testing Engineers, Porting, Program Management, Technical Support and Project Management to monitor and project defect capture and leakage rates.
- Assisted development and test teams in the application of testing metrics such as code complexity and code coverage.
- Provided overall high level trend analysis for executive level management.
- Applied root cause analysis techniques to assist several organizations in process improvement.
- Lead trainer, defect tracking database system. Developed and delivered hands-on training for entering, querying, and updating the status of software defects.

XYZ, Computer Systems Division, Small Town, CA   1990 - 1992
Senior Systems Quality Assurance Engineer

- Coordinated 10 cross-functional teams in preparation for XYZ's Quality Systems Review (QSR), ISO 9000 Certification, and then reached consensus on the development process requirements.
- Designed and developed an on-line documentation system, accessible to all employees, that was compliant to ISO 9000 Quality Manual Standards.
- Assisted development teams in designing and collecting software metrics in order to measure the effectiveness of their processes.
- Co-prepared the Computer Systems Division's portion of the Malcolm Baldrige Award applications.
- Verified compliance to release specifications on all products prior to first customer shipment.

Ultrasonic Company, Silicon Valley, CA   1989 - 1990
    Software Quality Assurance Engineer

Major Corporation, Silicon Valley, CA   1988 - 1989
    Senior Requirements and Software Test Analyst

Major Aerospace, Silicon Valley, CA   1987 - 1988
    Senior Software Engineer

ABC Government Systems, Silicon Valley, CA   1985 - 1987
    Member, Technical Staff II - Software Development

ABC Aerospace Center, Silicon Valley, CA   1980 - 1985
    Software Engineer II - Real Time Satellite System Programming

TECHNICAL EXPERTISE

Languages:	C, SQL, HTML, Fortran, Pascal, Assembly, COBOL, Ada, Informix NewEra
Operating Systems:	UNIX, Windows, DOS, Apple, VMS
Applications:	Excel, Wingz, Quattro Pro, FrameMaker, MS Word, WordPerfect, QA Partner, MS Project, MacProject

EDUCATION

B.A. Applied Mathematics, San Francisco State University; 1980

Candidate, Masters of Business Administration - Computer Information Systems Option, California State University, Hayward

Continuing Education:
- Process Mapping and Analysis • Design/Code Reviews • Code/Document Inspections
- Human Factors and Team Dynamics for Quality Management • Strategic Planning
- Understanding Six Sigma • Successful Negotiations • Management Techniques
- Methods of Applied Quality Management (I & II) • Project Management
- Assessor Training for Motorola's Software Quality System Review

CERTIFICATIONS AND AWARDS

• ASQC, Certified Quality Manager • ASQC, Certified Quality Engineer
• ASQC Certified Quality Auditor • Database Outstanding Contributor Award, 1995
• Certificate (*with Distinction*) in Continuous Improvement for Total Quality, UC Berkeley Ext.

PROFESSIONAL ASSOCIATIONS AND AFFILIATIONS

American Society for Quality Control (ASQC)
Association for Computing Machines
Member, Small Town Elementary School District Board, elected to second 4-year term

PRESENTATION OF QUALIFICATIONS

BRUCE G. HARTWELL

- **MARKETING SERVICES**
- **REAL ESTATE DEVELOPMENT**
- **CONSTRUCTION MANAGEMENT**

Post Office Box 6789
Anywhere, AZ 12345
Phone: 555.555.5555
E-mail: bruce@land.com

BRUCE G. HARTWELL

PROFILE

Accomplished Marketing Executive with *Fortune 500* senior management expertise, as well as entrepreneurial marketing skills and development of competitive business strategies. Goal oriented and results-driven with ability to utilize cutting edge technologies in generating new markets. Strong decision maker with proactive management style.

QUALIFICATIONS

- Million Dollar Circle member of the National Association of Home Builders.

- Adept negotiator and closer, excel in business development, new market penetration, equipped to compete in a fast-paced, aggressive sales environment.

- Interfaced with state and local government officials on an advisory level concerning land use policy and planning, business retention and economic development, resulting in over 25,000 new jobs.

- Excellent management and leadership skills resulting in top team performance.

- Published author on land use, environmental, economic development, and homebuilding issues.

- Persuasive and articulate communicator, functions effectively as a part of a decision making team.

- Proficient at launching new ventures with responsibility for conceptual development, marketing campaigns, distribution strategies including www exposure.

SELECTED PROJECTS

❑ *Pine Valley Ranch*   Resort, AZ
Exclusive gated community of 57 homesites in a national pine forest setting

❑ *Ocean View Estates*   Major City, CA
256 beach side, ocean view single family homes in prestige coastal area

❑ *Mili Makani*   Kauai, HI
A development including 63 plantation-style homes in prime beachfront golf resort community overlooking Hanalei Bay

❑ *Butte Park*   Butte, OR
Lead builder-developer in Butte's first master-planned residential community

❑ *Lake Butte View Estates*   Butte, OR
163 view, lake and waterfront homes and home sites

❑ *Lincoln Creekside Estates*   Big City, OR
Suburban community of 73 custom homes on wooded, creek side junior acreage parcels

LICENSES

CONSULTANT - Real Estate, Land Acquisition, Development Impact   California, Arizona
REAL ESTATE BROKER   Oregon, California, Arizona
GENERAL CONTRACTOR   Oregon, Hawaii, California, Arizona

BRUCE G. HARTWELL

PROFESSIONAL EXPERIENCE

A-P DEVELOPMENT GROUP   1994 to present   Resort, AZ
PRINCIPAL/OWNER
Provide business development, public relations and consulting services to clients engaged in land acquisition, real estate development and homebuilding.

C-P DEVELOPMENT GROUP   1981 to 1993   Major City, CA
PRESIDENT
Developed and built custom high-end single family residences, provided marketing and consulting services to builders and other firms engaged in real estate development.

K-P DEVELOPMENT GROUP   1987 to 1992   Kauai, HI
PRINCIPAL
Completed a 63-home residential development in the resort community of Princeville. Also served as local government liaison for the developer, Linezek, Ltd. (Australia), and its offshore financial partners.

RIVERVIEW HOMES   1971 to 1981   Big City, OR
PRINCIPAL
Involved in real estate, land development and other business activities including the development and marketing of learning programs and automated electronic controls. Built over eleven hundred homes in the Portland and Seattle markets.

SCM CORPORATION   1961 to 1971   New York, New York
VICE PRESIDENT - MARKETING
Senior management with a stellar track record . . . responsible for profitable product line marketing through 550 sales offices, dealers and distributor outlets.

EDUCATION/PROFESSIONAL DEVELOPMENT

CONTINUING EDUCATION   1970 to present   Oregon, California, Hawaii, Arizona
Courses: Construction, Real Estate, Land Use Development (2,100 hours)

UNIVERSITY OF OREGON   1960   Eugene, OR
BACHELOR OF ARTS DEGREE Major: Marketing, Finance

CREDENTIALS

SAN DIEGO COUNTY BAR ASSOCIATION   San Diego, CA
Expert Witness - Real estate contract and construction defect litigation

SAN DIEGO ECONOMIC DEVELOPMENT CORPORATION   San Diego, CA
Governmental and public affairs liaison

STATE OF OREGON   Salem, OR
Economic development and business retention advisory team

PROFESSIONAL ASSOCIATIONS

National Association of Home Builders
National Association of Realtors
U.S. Chamber of Commerce

Artie Fufkin

11 Polymer Drive • Chicago, Illinois 60601 • (555) 221-5995

Real Estate...Construction Management...Company and Franchise Development

Site Layout / Site Design and Selection / Lease Negotiation / Permitting / Zoning / General Contracting / Bidding / Negotiations / Contractor Relations / Executive Leadership

Vice President of Development for California Pizza Kitchen, a major PepsiCo-owned chain with retail outlets in 19 states. Promoted to higher levels of responsibility over the last 10 years, gaining expertise in all phases of construction, franchise development, and management of real estate for renovation and business expansion in national and international markets. Key management skills include:

Purchasing	Logistics/Strategic Planning	Vendor Relations
Team Building	Customer Service	Sales/Promotions
Training/Development	Cost/Risk Analysis	Budgeting
Market Research	Brand Expansion	Project Planning

A process-oriented leader whose ability to consistently streamline operations has resulted in significant cost savings, increased productivity and business capacity, and million-dollar gains in profitability.

PROFESSIONAL EXPERIENCE

PEPSICO INC., 1985-Present

California Pizza Kitchen (CPK), Los Angeles, California, 1996-Present

VICE PRESIDENT OF DEVELOPMENT SERVICES: Oversee the national development strategy for this casual dining restaurant with annual revenues of $180 million. Supervise facilities department that provides service to 77 stores with a $3.5 million repair/maintenance budget and a $4 million capital improvement budget.

Scope of accomplishments:

- Reduced service costs in facilities department from 3.7% of sales to 3.2% in six months, working toward a goal of 2.5%.
- Established the company's first real estate penetration strategy. Currently analyzing demographics in key markets and their respective trade areas to facilitate the future growth of franchises and company stores. Manage staffing, site selection, quality control, site development, and franchisee relations.
- Created and implemented a national construction program using a proven project management approach. Developed a tracking system and convinced the company to leverage the purchasing power of PepsiCo Food Services as an added cost control measure. Sought national contractors that resulted in an immediate annual cost savings of $150,000.
- Launched an effective franchise development strategy to increase and control the growth of new businesses with uniform high-quality standards. Provided comprehensive training from real estate development to initial store opening.
- In conjunction with the CFO, helped lay the groundwork to establish an international presence for CPK in the Pacific Rim.
- Currently involved in the effort to modernize the store's image and expand into new business segments. Designed and implemented a new channel for brand expansion (ASAP) to compete in the express dining market.
- Disposed of excess properties that yielded a net gain of $1.2 million.

PROFESSIONAL EXPERIENCE (cont.)
PEPSICO INC., 1985-Present

PepsiCo Food Services (PFS), Irvine, California, 1994-1996
DIRECTOR OF EQUIPMENT MARKETING AND SUPPORT, NORTH AMERICA: Directed activities for 40 sales, expediter, and project management professionals supporting $120 million procurement and supply business for Taco Bell, Hot n Now, Chevys, and CPK.
- Aligned strategic direction of PFS with that of Taco Bell, KFC, and Pizza Hut. Consolidated non-sales activities from four venues to one, achieving a $3-5 million cost savings through the elimination of redundant functions and satellite offices.
- Implemented multi-functional teams to improve the efficiency of service delivery. Created new delivery strategies and project management positions into the service cycle. Reduced backorders from an average of 10% to less than 2%.
- Positioned sales and marketing teams to focus on franchise development. Instilled project management techniques, expanded licensing capabilities, and implemented extensive skills training.
- Established new business and distribution channels to elevate the company to a full-service organization, resulting in additional revenue of $6 million for PepsiCo and non-PepsiCo concepts.

Taco Bell Corp., Marlton, New Jersey, 1985-1994
DIRECTOR OF DEVELOPMENT SERVICES, NORTHEAST AND CANADA: Supervised 14 construction engineers in the development of a $150 million dollar real estate portfolio. Served as national liaison for equipment procurement and delivery issues. Recruited to reengineer internal delivery processes as well as strategically plan and execute the construction of new restaurants. In 1985, only 9-12 new stores were being built per year in this region and 85-100 stores nationally.
- Increased staff 150% and developed the first national training program for construction managers. Program consisted of multi-level training in development processes, field investigation, and team problem solving, resulting in a more skilled talent base and a newly created pipeline of experienced workers for future projects.
- Spearheaded the rebuilding of a Taco Bell store destroyed during the Los Angeles riots. Store was fully-operational in 48 hours, generating $5-7 million of free advertising and marketing spin.
- Streamlined the entire development process to facilitate unprecedented regional and national growth. By 1994, 125 free-standing Taco Bell stores and an additional 100 Express units had been opened in the same regional geography. Nationally the company approached the capacity to build 800-1000 stores annually, representing an increase of 700-900% with lower costs and higher quality standards.

Previous positions held at Taco Bell Corp. include: **SENIOR MANAGER OF CONSTRUCTION; MANAGER OF FRANCHISE DEVELOPMENT; CONSTRUCTION MANAGER**

ADDITIONAL EXPERIENCE, 1980-1985

Partner and Vice President of Construction for two New Jersey-based entrepreneurial ventures. Directed all phases of multi-story, mid-rise residential building as well as commercial/light industrial projects including fast food restaurants, warehouse facilities, and strip shopping centers.

EDUCATION

Bachelor of Arts Degree in Metropolitan Studies & Architecture
Ramapo College of New Jersey, Mahwah, New Jersey

References Available Upon Request

CHRIS L. HAMILTON

Growth-Oriented... Profit Building... Business Development

118 KENDALL WAY ■ LAKELAND, FLORIDA 33810 ■ (941) 555-1212

COMMERCIAL REAL ESTATE DEVELOPMENT

Commercial Development / Sales / Leasing / Property Management / Construction Supervision
Site Selection / Financing / Due Diligence / Strategic Expansion / Financial Analysis
Staff Development and Training / Contract Negotiation / Acquisitions

Diversified commercial real estate developer with over 14 years' experience in all phases of property development, management, financing, leasing, and construction. Managed over $60 million in projects and over 1 million square feet of retail and office properties. Successfully placed a number of local, regional, and national tenants while meeting both landlord and tenant objectives. Strong work ethic; unmatched drive and ambition.

CAREER HIGHLIGHTS

➤ Increased occupancy from 20% to 85% within one year of taking over management responsibility for Lakeland Towne Center in Lakeland, Florida. Utilized creative marketing techniques to successfully secure over 25 new national and regional tenants. Renegotiated anchor tenant's lease from month-to-month to A 20-year term lease. Created consumer excitement and interest, filled a void in the community, and increased the bottom line to yield a positive net operating income. Sold the Center at a 150% profit.

➤ Served as manager and marketing consultant to high-profile organizations: First Winter Haven Savings, Mulberry Loan & Trust, Citibank, Rhiannon Financial, Inc., Garden Terrace Savings Bank, and Lakeland Trust Corporation.

➤ Took over the operations of The Land Group (a real estate and investments firm) to position the company for sale. As part of the company's manufacturing entity, conducted site analysis, negotiation, and placement of water vending machines at over 160 convenience stores.

AREAS OF EXPERTISE

Property Development
- Locate, acquire, and develop real estate; perform site selection based on assessment of demographics, traffic count, property values, zoning, population growth, existing occupancy/tenant mix. Prepare financial analyses and market feasibility studies.
- Negotiate lease/purchase contracts; secure interim and permanent financing.
- Work with representatives of local government, other businesses, community and public interest groups, and public utilities to eliminate obstacles to the development of the land and to gain support for the planned project.

Property Management/Construction Supervision
- Negotiate lease/rental agreements; oversee building management/maintenance, capital improvements, marketing, leasing, tenant relations/retention, financial reporting, budgeting, and collections.
- Secure financing for new development projects; work with architectural firms to draw up plans.
- Solicit and assess bids from construction companies and subcontractors; meet with county officials to secure permits and establish construction schedule.
- Inspect projects during and after construction to ensure building code standards are met; provide progress reports to owners.
- Set up temporary rental facilities; work with advertisers in the print, radio, and television media to coordinate marketing campaigns and promotions.

EXPERIENCE SUMMARY

Executive Vice President	**The Land Group,** Lakeland and Winter Haven, Florida	**1993-Present**
President	**Hometown Realty,** Raleigh, North Carolina	**1989-1993**
Real Estate Consultant	**Northern Virginia Savings,** Winchester, Virginia	**1987-1989**
Real Estate Consultant	**Chris L. Hamilton,** Richmond, Virginia	**1987**
President/Owner	**Chris L. Hamilton & Associates,** Richmond, Virginia	**1983-1987**
General Partner	**Greater Virginia Development Co.,** Richmond, Virginia	**1980-1983**
President	**C.L.H. Investment Group,** Richmond, Virginia	**1979-1980**
Project Superintendent	**Andrew Properties,** Martinsburg, Virginia	**1978-1979**

EDUCATION/TRAINING

Florida Insurance License
Florida School of Insurance, Tampa, Florida

**Completed courses required to test for the
Florida Real Estate Broker License**
Bob Hogue School of Real Estate, St. Petersburg, Florida

Salesman License
North Carolina School of Real Estate, Raleigh, North Carolina

Construction Technology
North Carolina State University, Raleigh, North Carolina

PROFESSIONAL AFFILIATIONS

American Management Association ■ International Council of Shopping Centers
Florida Association of Life Underwriters ■ Tampa Association of Life Underwriters

REFERENCES

"Without reservation, I can highly recommend Chris Hamilton..."
Jonathan George, Senior Vice President and Trust Officer
Raleigh Federal Savings & Loan, Raleigh, North Carolina

"[Chris'] most outstanding characteristics, however, are his willingness to work and his tenacity to see his goals accomplished."
Herbert E. Tannenbaum, Former Mayor
City of Raleigh, North Carolina

"...honest, hard worker, and candid in his business dealings."
Kyle Aaron, Executive Vice President
First Raleigh Federal, Raleigh, North Carolina

Project Portfolio Available Upon Request

Robert S. Mitchell, Jr.

3456 Richview Road
Lexington, Kentucky 41000
(606) 555-5555

PROFILE

Over 20 years of successful experience in all phases of construction in progressively responsible positions. Strong background in supervision and management of large construction projects. Possess knowledge of building practices and codes. Seeking a management position in the construction industry which will utilize this background and experience.

SUMMARY OF QUALIFICATIONS

Construction Manager
◆ Supervised and coordinated all phases of construction of housing in $70,000-$140,000 range
◆ Contracted and supervised up to 30 subcontractors
◆ Estimated and purchased materials
◆ Conducted site evaluations; reviewed and revised plans
◆ Maintained construction supervision of up to 6 sites simultaneously

Construction Supervisor
◆ Supervised both company employees and subcontractors during construction of custom homes ($280,000 to $3,000,000) and production homes ($110,000-$225,000)—maintained construction supervision of up to 16 sites simultaneously
◆ Interacted directly with clients regarding design, construction and decorating requirements
◆ Serviced 16-50 homes

Lead Carpenter
◆ Supervised a crew of 5-8 employees
◆ Gained hands-on experience in all phases of construction from start to completion—framing, remodeling, concrete, drywall, interior and exterior trim, siding, roofing, block laying

Heavy Equipment Operator
◆ Experienced in operation of 953 Loader, D-3 & D-4 Dozer, Dump Truck—possess current C.D.L.

EMPLOYMENT HISTORY

KAUFMAN, INC., Edgeville, Kentucky	1992-present
PHILLIPS DEVELOPMENT, Edgeville, Kentucky	1989-1991
DON RHODES BUILDER, Fort Mitchell, Kentucky	1987-1989
COLLIN CONSTRUCTION, Dallas, Texas	1984-85; 1986-87
SELF-EMPLOYED, Grayson, Kentucky	1976-1984

References Available Upon Request

BRIAN J. EDMONDS, Ph.D.

325 Haines Road
Bedford Hills, NY 10507
(914) 242-1998

OBJECTIVE

A challenging **Laboratory Research/Research Management** position with a high-growth pharmaceutical or biotechnology company committed to pioneering research and product development.

SUMMARY OF QUALIFICATIONS

⊹ *Well-qualified and technically-proficient Research Scientist* with more than eight years laboratory experience and strong academic qualifications.

⊹ *Diverse experience* working from *whole animal* to *molecular modeling*; bring a broad perspective to all research and development projects.

⊹ *Organized*, take-charge professional with *exceptional follow-through* abilities and *detail-orientation*; able to plan and oversee projects from concept to successful conclusion.

⊹ *Analytical problem solver*; proven expertise in assembling and organizing data.

⊹ Demonstrated ability to efficiently prioritize a broad range of responsibilities in order to achieve maximum level of operating effectiveness.

⊹ Expertise in lab and field research, data collection/analysis and project management.

⊹ Substantial experience in sophisticated research techniques and technologies.

⊹ Strong planning, organizational and communications skills.

⊹ Extensive experience working with cross-functional scientific and research teams.

⊹ **Clinical Laboratory Skills**

Ecology	Molecular Biology	Physiology
Cellular Biology	Bio-Chemistry	

⊹ **Computer Technology**

⊹ **Skills and Techniques**

 ✓ All forms of protein purification and biophysical characterization including FPLC, HPLC, gel electrophoresis, antibody production, and western blot.

 ✓ All types of molecular genetic manipulation including cloning, neuronal and somatic cellculturing and transfection, library construction and screening, transgenics.

 ✓ Confocal imunofluorescence and video microscopy; electron microscopy

 ✓ Ligand binding assays and enzyme kinetic analysis using fluorescence spectroscopy

AREAS OF EFFECTIVENESS

Direct /Restructure Research Plans - teach new, more productive techniques.

Identify and Target Alternate Avenues of Pursuit - assess and evaluate previous progress.

Organizational Effectiveness - funnel resources into more productive direction; proven ability to sort out the wheat from the chaff in a number of scientific disciplines.

EDUCATION

INTERNATIONAL SCHOOL OF NEUROSCIENCE, Padua, Italy
Coursework: *Developmental Neurobiology*   1990

STATE UNIVERSITY OF NEW YORK, Buffalo, NY
Ph.D. : *Physiology*   1988

UNIVERSITY OF ROCHESTER, EASTMAN SCHOOL OF MUSIC, Rochester, NY
Master of Arts: *Music*

BOWLING GREEN STATE UNIVERSITY, Bowling Green, OH
Coursework towards M. Mus   1980

HOBART and **WILLIAM SMITH COLLEGES**
Bachelor of Arts   1980
          Major: Biology
          Minor: Music

**COMPETITIVE
AWARDS
AND HONORS**

⟐ **National Research Service Award** (1991 - 1994)
⟐ **Howard Hughes Medical Institute Associate** (1988 - 1991)
⟐ **Fidia Research Foundation Fellow** (1990)
⟐ **Interdisciplinary Graduate Group in Neuroscience Fellow** (1986 - 1987)
⟐ **Delta Chi Educational Foundation Scholar** (1976 - 1980)

**PROFESSIONAL
EXPERIENCE**
1991 - Present

ALBERT EINSTEIN COLLEGE OF MEDICINE, Bronx, NY
Senior National Research Service Fellow/Project Leader

⟐ **Achievements:** A characterization of the regulation by the cytoskelaton of G protein-mediated gene expression, protein synthesis, and metastic breast cancer.
⟐ *Manage the training and research focus* of postdoctoral fellows, graduate students and technicians.
⟐ *Resurrected a floundering project* and designed a new research plan to maximize efficiency resulting in the identification of several new initiatives requiring the assimilation of new technologies for protein purification, characterization and enzyme kinetic analysis.
⟐ *Established and manage collaborations* with outside investigators in enzymology, protein structure/function, cancer biology, and molecular genetics.
⟐ *Achieved substantial recognition* by the National Institute for Health and the U.S. Army, *receiving awards* totaling *$1 million* over five years.

1988 - 1991	**UNIVERSITY OF TEXAS SOUTHWESTERN MEDICAL CENTER** **HOWARD HUGHES MEDICAL INSTITUTE** , Dallas, TX

Research Fellow
- ✤ *Credited with identification of genomic regions* undergoing active transcription during development of the mouse nervous system.
- ✤ *Recipient of nationally competitive awards* from HHMI and NIH-NINDS to develop two independent projects using biochemical and molecular genetic techniques to identify genes and proteins important for the growth of the mammalian nervous system.
- ✤ *Identified important genes, that would escape detection* by traditional strategies utilizing a bacterial transgene whose expression is dependent upon mouse regulatory sequences adjacent to the locus of transgene insertion.
    - ✤ Out of 13 established mouse lines, two displayed transgene expression in discrete areas of the nervous system during neuritogenesis: the afferent auditory pathway and pyramidal cortical neurons.
    - ✤ The *cloned mouse regulatory elements* can now be ***used for gene targeting*** to specific mammalian neuronal subpopulations *in vivo*.

1982 - 1988	**STATE UNIVERSITY OF NEW YORK: DIVISION OF NEUROBIOLOGY,** Buffalo, NY

Graduate Research Assistant: Department of Physiology
- ✤ *Successfully characterized a novel form of neuronal intracellular motility*.
- ✤ *Investigated relationship* between the organization of the cytoskeleton and certain motile phenomena by employing goldfish retinal ganglion cell axons.
    - ✤ *Determined* that *movements of large varicosites*, containing membranes and cytoskelatal elements, are linked in a "piggyback" manner to movements of smaller organelles and are *powered by at least two different molecular "motors".* This work was prescient of an exploding field: discoveries of the neuronal molecular motors *kinesin* and *cytoplasmic dynein*.
    - ✤ *Successfully showed* that *transmembrane signals* generated by a small subset of membrane receptors *alter the organization* of the actin cytoskeleton and *interfere with organelle motility*.
    - ✤ *Results suggest* that *metabolite supply*, within neurons, *can be modified by extracellular factors*.

PROFESSIONAL **AFFILIATIONS**	American Society for Cell Biology American Society for Neuroscience American Association for the Advancement of Science New York Academy of Sciences
REFERENCES	*Excellent References and detailed Curriculum Vita Will Be Furnished Upon Request*

DARRIN M. PEPIN, Ph.D.

1990 34th Street
Hartford, Connecticut 06430

Phone/Fax: 505-662-5651
Email: darinpin@comnet.att.net

SENIOR SCIENCE, TECHNOLOGY & RESEARCH DIRECTOR
U.S. & International Research & Technology Development Projects, Laboratories & Organizations

Twenty-year leadership and management career leading the development of high-quality, state-of-the-art research, systems, technologies and applications to meet emerging market demand worldwide. A catalyst for change, technological innovation, global teaming and product/technology delivery in energy, manufacturing, materials, environmental and defense applications. Strong leadership performance across diverse functional organizations in the corporate, university and government sectors. Featured in "American Men & Women in Science."

MANAGEMENT & LEADERSHIP EXPERTISE

Dynamic track record of performance in energizing multidisciplinary technology and scientific R&D teams through defined vision and decisive management of new discoveries, systems integration and large-scale development projects. Delivered measurable gains in the productivity, efficiency, quality and results of research programs, projects and tasks by building cooperative, value-driven relationships with diverse business partners and funding organizations. Successful in balancing technology with human resources and corporate culture. Innovative marketer able to identify and capture emerging opportunities within technology sectors. Participative management style. Risk-taker and technology champion.

- Organization & Lab Design/Development
- Team Leadership & Technical HR Development
- Public/Private Partnerships & Alliances
- New Product & Technology Commercialization
- Resource & Technology Acquisition

- Multi-Million Dollar Project Management
- Proposal Development & Price Negotiations
- Project Planning, Scheduling & Management
- Inter-Organizational Liaison Affairs
- Public Speaking, Meetings & Presentations

TECHNICAL EXPERTISE

Creative and innovative Scientist, Technologist and Engineer with cross-functional experience in the conceptualization, research, development, discovery, testing, evaluation, management and commercialization of advanced programs. Powerful creative analysis and technical troubleshooting skills. Expertise in technology transfer across industries and technical disciplines. Credited with continuing individual and team contribution to the development of more than 150 new discoveries, prototypes, technologies, systems and applications to support product development in:

- Ultrasonics & Acoustics Engineering
- Electrical & Dielectric Engineering
- Specialty Ceramic & Alloy Development
- Cryogenic & High-Temperature Applications
- Semiconductor Technology & Manufacturing
- Passive & Smart Sensor Engineering
- Defense & Space Applications

- Nuclear Engineering & Radiation Effects
- Reliability & Quality Management
- Mechanical & Chemical Engineering
- Energy & Environmental Engineering
- Employee Health & Safety (EH&S)
- Nondestructive Testing & Evaluation (NDT&E)
- Microwave Technology

PROFESSIONAL EXPERIENCE:

Staff Member / Physicist   1996 to Present
Devening Technical Services, Inc. - HNL Operations, Hartford, Connecticut

Created new environmental remediation technology with potential global impact for accelerating eradication of hazardous organics from soil. Developed pioneering instrumentation, testing and measurement methods to move project forward. Catalyst for successful team effort followed by Motorola/Hartford National Laboratory (HNL) partnership. Prepared annual report documenting project success. Reinstatable DOE "Q" Clearance.

Technical Staff Member - Project Leader / Principal Investigator / Task Leader 1984 to 1995
Hartford National Laboratory, Hartford, Connecticut

Revitalized technology and scientific R&D projects, infused new direction and new vision, and focused teams on growth, technology and commercialization in materials and device development. Led vigorous program management and technology development efforts. Oversight responsibility for project teams of up to 24 across broad engineering disciplines and organizations worldwide, with concurrent responsibility for enhancing the professional development of 20 technical professionals. Led or contributed to 15 projects.

- Authored/co-authored 24 proposals and co-generated $3.5 million in funding from public and private sectors.
- Staffed and directed pioneering research, engineering and testing programs across broad technical disciplines in cooperation with national and international project teams. Invented four new materials testing technologies and authored/co-authored 40+ technical papers and reports.
- Led design, development, start-up and management of new electrical testing and lab facility, acquired all technology and instrumentation, recruited staff, and led sophisticated R&D programs and experimentation.

Chief Physicist / Senior Scientist 1981 to 1984
STB-Hoelter Industries, Inc., Burlington, Vermont

Provided scientific direction and leadership for a 4-year, 10-person, international R&D project funded by the Electric Cooperative Facilities (ECF) to enhance energy transmission capabilities. Matrix management for 18.

- Championed a series of internal process, productivity, quality and efficiency improvement initiatives through redesign of laboratory, office, research and information resources/facilities.
- Wrote 450-page report integrating and synthesizing data from 100 projects and presented findings on technology/process development, applications and commercialization.

Project Scientist / Researcher 1977 to 1981
Livingston Research Laboratory - The Massachusetts State University, State College, Massachusetts

Recruited to establish and direct the University's first nondestructive testing laboratory. Built from concept into a fully-funded, fully-operational, fully-staffed, advanced research and development facility.

- Secured or co-generated over $500,000 in funding for multi-year projects to develop new testing technologies.
- Invented and prototyped new ultrasonic hardware, developed product applications and awarded U.S. patent.

Health Research Physicist 1975 to 1977
Food & Drug Research Center, Baltimore, Maryland

Participated in original research on core issues impacting public health and the regulatory oversight of the health care and dental care industries. Provided strong scientific leadership and technological innovation.

Early Career: Several years of scientific and engineering research, development, testing and evaluation.

EDUCATION:

FORDHAM UNIVERSITY
Ph.D., Physics (GPA 4.0), 1974 ... M.S., Physics (GPA 4.0), 1969 ... B.S., Physics, 1964

Graduate, 200 + contact hours of continuing Management, Technology & Leadership Training.

PROFESSIONAL PROFILE (*full information including publication lists provided upon request*):

Patents	Co-Author of 3 U.S. technology patents.
Publications	Author/Presenter of more than 90 oral & written publications.
Affiliations	Member of numerous scientific and engineering professional associations.

MICHAEL L. BOWDEN

6908 Brookhollow
New Haven, Texas 72220

(333) 555-6688 (Residence)
(333) 522-5533 (Business)

AREAS OF EXPERTISE

♦ Rapid Bioassessment (RBA) ♦ Nonpoint Source Pollution (NPS) ♦ Project Management
♦ Public Speaking / Presentations ♦ Classroom / Hands-On Training
♦ Budget Management ♦ Environmental Quality Control

HIGHLIGHTS OF QUALIFICATIONS

♦ **Highly qualified Aquatic Biologist / Biology Educator**; M.S. degree in **Biology** and six years of experience in **biological research** and **classroom training**. Excellent **presentation/speaking** abilities.

♦ Thoroughly cognizant of TNRCC and EPA regulations related to water quality; **OSHA Advanced Hazardous Materials Emergency Response** and **OSHA HAZWOPPER certifications**.

♦ Proficiency in use of Spectrophotometer 70, Gas Chromatography Spectrophotometer, Atomic Absorption, Ultraviolet-Visible, Infrared, nutrient chemistry analyses, slide preparation/keys to identify zooplankton, fish, and benthic macroinvertebrate organisms.

♦ Knowledgeable of statistical programs (SAS, SPSS); IBM/MAC (WordPerfect, Quattro Pro, Harvard Graphics, MS-Works, Word, Excel, Greatworks, Aldus PageMaker, Delta Graphics), Internet.

♦ Exceptional **communication** and **interpersonal** skills; easily establish positive rapport with people of diversified socioeconomic backgrounds, cultures, and personalities. Conversational Spanish.

EDUCATION / PROFESSIONAL DEVELOPMENT / CERTIFICATIONS

STEPHEN F. AUSTIN STATE UNIVERSITY – Nacogdoches, Texas
Master of Science Degree With Thesis (1993)
Major: **Biology**; Minor: **Applied Statistics**; Overall GPA: 4.0

Bachelor of Science Degree (1990)
Major: **Biology**; Minor: **Chemistry**

EPA Rapid Bioassessment Training

Valuing Diversity in the Workplace – TNRCC

OSHA Advanced Hazardous Materials Emergency Response Course (24 Hours) – **Certification**

OSHA HAZWOPPER Training (40 Hours) – **Certification**

RESEARCH PROJECTS / PRESENTATIONS

Annual Report–Baseline Monitoring Results for the Lake Simpson Reservoir Project (1995)
(Compilation report for highly technical scientific project)
Presented to EPA Regional, TNRCC (Statewide), and USDA (Statewide) Conferences (1995-96)

Annual Report–Review of Data for Lake Simpson Reservoir Project (1994)

Thesis: The Effects of Dairy Farm Effluents on the Benthic Macroinvertebrate Communities of Two Streams in Harris County, Texas (1993); **Presented at Texas Academy of Science** (1992)

A Complete Analysis of the Productivity of Lake Simpson Reservoir, Texas (1991)

Stability of Sodium Ferrate in an Aqueous Solution (1990) – **Research/Presentation**

PROFESSIONAL EXPERIENCE

TEXAS NATURAL RESOURCE CONSERVATION COMMISSION (TNRCC)　　　　Austin, Texas
Project Manager / Environmental Quality Specialist IV　　　　August 1994 – Present

- Monitor streams in the Lake Simpson Reservoir watershed to determine impacts of nonpoint source pollution on water quality. Responsible for security of $50,000 automated sampling equipment in the field.
- Determine sampling locations; establish trusting relationship with landowners to obtain permission to gain access to and set up equipment on private property (reduces occurrence of vandalism).
- Collect data using routine water and sediment samples, EPA Rapid Bioassessment Protocols, and ISCO automated stormwater sampler. Analyze data; prepare highly technical reports required by EPA.
- Responsible for quarterly reports and budgetary issues. Project expenditures. Write specifications and submit bids for purchasing equipment. Manage $30,000 annual budget; coordinate budget overruns.
- Work closely with state and federal agencies regarding reservoir; present project information at various professional and non-professional meetings/workshops. Made presentations at three conferences in 1996.
- Serve as **Volunteer Spill Response team member** (one of 4 out of 50 in office); work with local authorities in coordination and remediation of hazardous materials.
- **Instrumental in design of sampling program** and **QA Project Plan revisions. Authored two annual reports.**
- **Designed/constructed stands for equipment**; enhanced protection of equipment.
- **Successfully negotiated/established 20 monitoring locations on private property.**

TEXAS INSTITUTE FOR APPLIED ENVIRONMENTAL RESEARCH (TIAER)　　　　Waco, Texas
Research Biologist　　　　December 1993 – August 1994

- Opened branch office in Harris County; set up/equipped office.
- **Created/implemented Stream Monitoring Program** using chemical, macroinvertebrate, and stormwater samples for nonpoint source pollution study in Lake Simpson Reservoir watershed.
- **Instrumental in development of sampling protocols** using EPA protocols.

STEPHEN F. AUSTIN STATE UNIVERSITY　　　　Nacogdoches, Texas
Graduate Teaching Intern　　　　August 1992 – May 1993

- Established course outline/presentation. Lectured, tested, and graded 500 students in Concepts of Biology, Introductory Zoology, and General Ecology courses on full-time basis.
- Supervised four teaching assistants.

SUPERIOR INTERNATIONAL CORPORATION　　　　Lufkin, Texas
Environmental Summer Intern　　　　May 1992 – August 1992

- Performed stack gas sampling using modified VOST method; sampling of effluent, sludges, and fish tissue for dioxin and AOX analysis; stormwater sampling required by EPA; analysis of microbes in MLSS.
- Reviewed/**revised analytical laboratory methodology.**
- **Participated in classification of Paper Mill Creek** for TWC.

STEPHEN F. AUSTIN STATE UNIVERSITY　　　　Nacogdoches, Texas
Teaching Assistant　　　　August 1990 – May 1992

- Introduced material and supervised students in Biology, Botany, Ecology, Limnology, and Chemistry Lab.

PROFESSIONAL AFFILIATIONS

Member, TEXAS ACADEMY OF SCIENCE
Member, CADDO LAKE INSTITUTE (ISIS Foundation sponsored by Don Henley)
Member, SIGMA Xi – Scientific Research Honorary Society

JOAN MCCALL, CNA

(333) 222-1111
555 North Spencer Street • Liberty, Iowa 55555

SUMMARY

Skilled direct patient care provider seeking to transition biology degree and knowledge of laboratory research methods to a **Research** or **Laboratory Assistant** position.

Additional skills, personal attributes and accomplishments include:

√ Proven sense of responsibility and self-reliance—financed 50% of college education through employment and scholarships.

√ Solid communication abilities—competent in asking appropriate questions to effectively and completely carry out instructions from RNs, administrators, clients, and other patient care providers ... skilled in medical charting ... comfortable introducing self to new clients.

√ Flexible, adaptable and dependable—willing to work odd or consecutive shifts; frequently called to work within 2 hours' notice.

√ Willing to display leadership qualities—seriously focused on working as part of a scientific research team.

EDUCATION

THE UNIVERSITY OF IOWA, Iowa City, Iowa
BA—Biology, May 1997

Lectures: **Electron Microscopy Techniques ... Confocal Light Microscope**

Project: *Confirmation of a Novel Prognostic Marker in Breast Cancer*
√ Confirmed cell culture results involving live tissue using immuno-fluorescence, immunohistochemistry, and cryosectioning.
√ Received an A on project and placed first in presentation out of approximately 30 students, the majority of which were post-grads.

Relevant Coursework:
√ Biochemistry ... Cell Biology ... Developmental Biology
√ Fundamental Genetics ... Statistics ... Medical Terminology

HEALTHCARE EXPERIENCE

ALL STAFF, INC., Creston, Iowa
Certified Nursing Assistant June 1997 to Present
• Temporary CNA assignments include residential long-term care facilities throughout Eastern Iowa.

HOMER MEMORIAL HOME, Liberty, Iowa
Certified Nursing Assistant December 1996 to Present
• Invoke high-level skills in teamwork, communication and organization.

VISITING NURSE ASSOCIATION, Iowa City, Iowa
Certified Nursing Assistant May to August 1996
• Functioned as the primary care giver for an individual in end-stage AIDS.

UNIVERSITY OF IOWA HOSPITALS & CLINICS, Iowa City, Iowa
Certified Nursing Assistant August 1994 to May 1996
• Gained experience in the cardiothoracic and post-anesthesia care units.

NURSE'S HOUSE CALL, Coralville, Iowa
Certified Nursing Assistant August 1993 to July 1994
• Promoted independence to clients in their homes.

SKILLED IN WORD ... POWERPOINT ... LASER SHARPE ... E-MAIL USE

BARBARA MORGANSTERN
1543 West Chester Pike
Paoli, Pennsylvania, 01908
(610) 387-7698

SCIENTIST / RESEARCHER / EDUCATOR

- Statistical Theory & Analysis
- Information Technology
- Quality & Efficiency

- Data Collection, Analysis & Reporting
- Project Planning & Administration
- Curriculum Design & Development

Combines analytical and research expertise with strong public speaking, presentation, writing, communications and interpersonal relations skills. Direct, decisive and action-oriented. Recognized for innovation and superior performance in program development and implementation. Lived and worked in Italy, Saudi Arabia and Japan. Traveled worldwide.

CORE COMPETENCIES:

Statistical Analysis & Methodology

- Currently completing undergraduate studies in Statistics. Key courses include Statistical Methods, Probability, Statistical Computing, Statistical Design and Analysis of Experiments, Regression Analysis, Sample Survey Methods and Mathematical Statistics.

- Extensive working knowledge of design and analysis methods for Single Factor, Factorial, Randomized Block, Nested, and Latin Square Designs including Fixed, Random and Mixed Models.

- Hands-on use of Bivariate and Multiple Regression Analysis with Graphics, One and Two-Way Analysis of Variance, and Trend Analysis in addition to Bonferroni, Scheffe, Tukey, Tukey-Kramer, Dunnett, Bonferroni-Welch and Protected LSD simultaneous test procedures for contrasts and comparisons.

- Well-qualified in the application of Simple Random, Stratified Random, Post Stratification, Systematic and Cluster Sample Survey Designs and Simple, Ratio, Regression and Difference Estimation procedures.

Information Technology

- Extensive use of Minitab and SAS® data programming including the creation of data sets and data manipulation, statistical analysis of data, and the reporting of data set information and analysis in graphs, tables and written reports. Familiar with Macro coding and SQL.

- Strong hands-on experience with VAX mainframe systems. PC literate with IBM and Apple software applications including word and data processing, graphics and spreadsheets.

Medical Background

- Fourteen-year career in Medical Technology. Strong working knowledge and fundamental education in hematology, biochemistry, serology, histology, urinalysis, bacteriology and blood banking.

- Certified Medical Technologist by the Registry of Medical Technologists of the American Society of Clinical Pathologists.

Academic Training

- Selected from a competitive group of candidates for a series of training programs to change the focus of Mathematics and incorporate National Council of Teachers of Mathematics (NCTM) curriculum and evaluation standards. Implemented leading edge information technology into the classroom to lead education into the 21st century.

- Mathematics, Science and General Teaching certifications in secondary and elementary education. Continuing education in cooperative learning, special education, the Study of Teaching and new technologies for the classroom.

- Took advantage of unique field experiences to enrich and broaden scientific expertise. Completed an environmental study of Kenya, an ecological study of terrestrial and marine environments in Puerto Rico and a geological study of National Parks of the Southwestern United States.

Special Projects

- Member of faculty steering committee at Okinawa American High School to review and compile a series of reports for evaluation by the North Central Accreditation team for institutional certification.

- Appointed Building Based Facilitator of Department of Defense Dependent Schools (DoDDS) Pacific Region program for the Study of Teaching. Maintained regular study groups, coordinated peer observations and led faculty presentations to foster experimentation and collegiality throughout the school.

- Participated in the School Improvement Program (SIP), a cross-functional team of educators and administrators with the goal of designing and implementing programs to improve the quality of educational curricula, enhance parent and community relations, and increase student participation both inside and outside the classroom.

- Championed the introduction of a course to teach students technical research and presentation techniques. Developed and taught this two-semester course to guide students through development of a proper scientific experiment including collection, analysis and interpretation of data, technical writing, and written and oral presentation of the results. Assumed additional responsibility for mentoring individual students entering in the Pacific Region Science Symposium.

PROFESSIONAL EXPERIENCE:

DEPARTMENT OF DEFENSE OFFICE OF DEPENDENTS EDUCATION   1982 to 1996

Secondary Education Teacher - Math & Science (1987 to 1995)
Okinawa American High School, Okinawa, Japan

Member of an eight-person Science department. Taught Life, Earth and Physical Science to middle school and high school students. Introduced hands-on activities into classroom to provide a unique learning experience and adapted textbook materials to meet the needs of special students. Incorporated computer technology into the curriculum.

Subsequently transferred to the Mathematics Department with full responsibility for teaching 7th grade Math, General Math, Algebra and Geometry. Introduced computer-based applications (e.g., spreadsheets, graphs, data analysis) to enhance the educational program.

Secondary Education Teacher - Science (1984 to 1987)
Substitute Teacher (1982 to 1983)
Dhahran American High School, Dhahran, Saudi Arabia

Designed, developed and instructed courses in Life Science, Physical Science and Biology to students in grades 7 - 12 at this 650-student school for military dependents. Acted as Advisor to the National Honor Society and Sophomore Class.

AMERICAN SCHOOL OF NAPLES, Naples, Italy   1980 to 1982

Substitute Science Teacher for this private American school.

REGIONAL MEDICAL LABORATORIES, King of Prussia, Pennsylvania   1971 to 1980

Laboratory Supervisor / Medical Technologist

Led team of 15 medical technologists and managed the daily operations of a full-service medical testing and laboratory facility for this 150-bed hospital. Scope of responsibility was diverse and included scheduling, inventory management, procurement, quality control, preventative maintenance, employee safety, training and laboratory compliance with OSHA standards.

EARLY CAREER EXPERIENCE (1966 to 1971) as a **Medical Technologist** with Chester County Hospital and Community Hospital in West Chester, Pennsylvania. Participated in special project to design and test new procedures for triglycerides, barbiturates and fluorometric chemistry.

EDUCATION & CERTIFICATIONS:

Candidate for B.S in Statistics, April 1997
WEST CHESTER UNIVERSITY, West Chester, Pennsylvania

B.A., Biology, 1965
COLLEGE OF ST. CATHERINE, St. Paul, Minnesota

Continuing Certificate in Education, 1989
STATE OF PENNSYLVANIA DEPARTMENT OF EDUCATION

General Elementary K-6 Endorsement to Michigan Teaching Certificate, 1987
WEST CHESTER UNIVERSITY, West Chester, Pennsylvania
(All Subjects)

Provisional Certificate in Secondary Education, 1984
WEST CHESTER UNIVERSITY, West Chester, Pennsylvania
(Major in Biology, Minor in Chemistry)

National Certificate in Medical Technology, 1966
REGISTRY OF MEDICAL TECHNOLOGISTS OF THE AMERICAN SOCIETY OF CLINICAL PATHOLOGISTS

Certificate in Medical Technology, 1965
CHESTER COUNTY HOSPITAL SCHOOL OF MEDICAL TECHNOLOGY

SAMUEL L. NEUMANN

1800 Bayfront Avenue North
St. Petersburg, Florida 33700
(813) 896-2211

SALES MANAGEMENT / RETAIL OPERATIONS

Business Development ◆ Marketing ◆ Merchandising ◆ Strategic Planning ◆ Financial Management
Technical/Production Operations ◆ Motivational Training ◆ Personnel Management

---

CAREER PROFILE

Top-Producing, District Sales Manager with dynamic career reflecting progressive advancement, superior accomplishments, and talent for maintaining profitable operations of multiple retail store locations. Goal-oriented, proactive *Sales Leader*, successful in capitalizing on emerging growth opportunities, implementing consumer-oriented sales/marketing initiatives, and upholding fiscal efficiency. Self-directed, entrepreneurial minded individual exhibiting high-level business ethics and performance standards. Excellent facilitator, provide results-driven attitude focused on attention to bottomline and generating personnel productivity. Keen organizational, analytical, problem-solving and decision-making ability. Articulate communicator with effective interpersonal and presentation skills. Computer literacy includes MacIntosh, Windows-based programs: Quicken, Word Perfect, Word, Claris Works.

EXPERIENCE SUMMARY

Sales Management

- **Led effective market penetration** of one-hour photo finish retail chain in the State of Florida; oversaw development/management of up to 29 retail locations. Presently accountable for generating $5MM+ annually in gross volume sales.

- **Produced high-level sales increases** concurrently with maintaining labor costs below district target and overall company average within multi-state territory consisting of Connecticut, New York, Pennsylvania and New Jersey.

- **Demonstrated strengths in business management**, customer-focused service, executing strategic action plans, delineating well-defined sales goals/incentive programs, and tracking industry trends.

- **Established customer relations program** in Florida District instituting standards for consistency in service, customer follow-up, and resolving complaints.

- **Expertise in P&L analysis,** budgeting, implementing cost controls, calculating weekly/area sales, evaluating sales performance, formulating sales projections and long-range planning.

- **Key role in marketing**, merchandising, advertising, and planning national/seasonal promotions or special events at the local level; able to effectively assess needs and recommend/deploy applicable action plans.

- **Positioned Florida District as a** *"Top-Producing Territory"* via employing motivational sales training for hourly/management staff, cultivating top-notch sales teams, and building employee relations. Currently oversee 17 managers/trainers and 70 hourly employees.

Retail Operations

- **Directed and implemented innovative procedures** for retail operations of all one-hour photo locations within territory that optimized production/efficiency levels and increased sales volume.

- **High-level technical knowledge** along with hands-on management and production experience in professional photography led to serving as advisor for production design, installation, construction, and opening new store locations in the central and east coast regions of the U.S.

- **Well-honed skills in purchasing and inventory control,** quality assurance, equipment/property maintenance, and maintaining smooth flow of operations; *set all-time production record and exceeded performance expectations*.

- **Conversant with the legal aspects of human resources**; well-versed in presiding over policy enforcement, hiring/termination/ training procedures for management and hourly staff, performance evaluations, salary decisions, and review/approval of raises.

SELECTED ACHIEVEMENTS

Tenure with XYZ/AAA Photo is comprised of numerous accomplishments recognizing my outstanding performance as a District Manager. Selected from a group of 60 professionals as the recipient of the Company's most prestigious award on two separate occasions.

- **1996** - Pinnacle Award for top performance, dedication, sales performance and best overall increase in net operating contribution.
- **1996** - Largest Film Sales Dollar Average Increase Award
- **1996, 1990, 1987** - Top Award - Customer Add-on Sales
- **1996** - Largest Percentage Increase in Gross Profit
- **1996** - Second Place Award for Enlargement Sales Average Increase
- **1995, 1996** - Increased district film sales by 50%+
- **1992, 1990, 1987** - Top Territory Award for Enlargement Sales Average Increase
- **1990** - Top Award for Consistent Excellent Performance in Customer Service, Sales, Gross Profit, Net Contribution
- **1988** - Second Place Territory Award - Highest Percentage of Gross Profit Increase
- *"District of the Month Award"* 19 times, represents increased sales averages over last year, effective cost controls and gross profit contributions in stores currently managed.

EMPLOYMENT HISTORY

Exceptional track record of consistently surpassing corporate objectives resulted in successive promotions and assuming highly demanding, pivotal roles of diverse responsibilities augmented by mergers and acquisitions and the restructuring of managerial and operational parameters.

AAA PHOTO, INC. - St. Louis, MO *(Joint venture between National Film and XYZ Photo)*   **7/84 - Present**
District Manager - State of Florida - Headquartered in Tampa, FL (1986 - Present)

East Coast District Manager (XYZ Photo Finish) - Headquartered in Philadelphia, PA (1984 - 1986)

PHOTOMART, INC. - Tampa, FL *(Acquired by XYZ in 1984)*   **12/82 -7/84**
Group Area Manager/Technical Advisor/Operations

ONE-HOUR PHOTO - Kansas City, MO *(Merged with Photomart , Inc.)*   **1/82 - 12/82**
Technical Advisor/Store Manager

MOBLEY PHOTO COMPANY - Kansas City, MO   **1/81 - 1/82**
Production Supervisor

SLN PHOTOGRAPHY - Kansas City, MO   **1/78 - 10/81**
Owner/Manager-Professional Studio

EDUCATION

Central Missouri State University, Major: Criminology
(Two years of undergraduate study via scholarship endowment)

PROFESSIONAL TRAINING

Dale Carnegie, Management Training Course. . .Stephen Covey Leadership Seminar. . .Kodak Process Management Seminar. . .Employee Selection and Recruiting. . .30-second Retail Selling. . .Manager Training / Training the Trainer. . .Human Resources, Legal Aspects of Employee Relations. . .Understanding Profit & Loss Budget Analysis

MILITARY

U.S. Navy / Honorable Discharge
Rank at Discharge: E-5

James Mueller

Bleibtreustr 80
10590 Berlin, Germany
Tel. 0114-930-555-2222
Fax 0114-930-555-8888

US contact information
5840 Roselawn Way
Cincinnati, Ohio 45202
Tel. (513) 555-0550 • (513) 555-0440

Profile

Fashion retailing professional with a solid background in all aspects of merchandise selection and retail management.

- Proven ability to apply **exceptional fashion knowledge** and unerring taste to upgrade store's fashion image and increase sales.
- Thoroughly familiar with **major fashion designers** through buying activities that include travel to major fashion events in the US and Europe.
- Effective manager with demonstrated ability to **improve sales and operations** to achieve higher profitability.
- **Outstanding sales skills** and the ability to train and supervise sales staff to increased performance.

Professional Experience

Manager/Buyer • FRANZ HOLZ, Berlin, Germany • 1992-Present

Management

- Total store management responsibility and accountability including profit and loss, financial record keeping, staffing, scheduling, and management reporting.
- Presided over increased sales from 1.7 million marks to 3 million marks in 4 years primarily due to upgrading the quality and stylishness of the merchandise mix and promoting through imaginative window and in-store displays.
- Manage a 10 million marks annual buying budget for 5 stores.
- Supervise and train 5-person sales staff, instilling a customer service focus and ensuring thorough knowledge of merchandise.

Fashion Direction

- Design original fashions and contribute to the selection process for merchandise carried under the private-label "Franz Holz Collection."
- Creative window and display designer skilled at promoting new and avant garde fashions in all store areas.
- Earned reputation as one of the best fashion stores in Berlin through aggressive promotion of high-quality and cutting-edge fashions.
- Select and buy store merchandise for 5-store chain. Conduct regular buying trips to Paris, New York and Milan, buying from such designers as Kiton, Brioni, Giorgio Armani, Versace, Calvin Klein, Gucci, Prada, Donna Karan, and Christian Dior.

Sales/Customer Service Representative • DELTA AIRLINES, Cincinnati, Ohio • 1989-1992

Sales Representative • DUKE'S CLOTHING STORE, Cincinnati, Ohio • 1984-1989

Additional Information

- Born 7/20/65 in Casablanca, Morocco.
- American citizen.
- Two years full-time business studies, University of Cincinnati.
- Fluent in English, German, French; some Spanish.
- Computer-proficient in business applications including word processing.

BRENDA MONDE

1647 Richmond Terrace
Great Neck, New York 11345
(718) 222-1211

RETAIL SALES & MANAGEMENT PROFESSIONAL

Self-motivated retail manager and sales associate with a solid track record of spearheading company growth and increasing profits. Able to envision goals and implement procedures to achieve them. Expertise in:

- ◆ Customer Service
- ◆ Sales
- ◆ Merchandising
- ◆ Bookkeeping
- ◆ Marketing
- ◆ Advertising

Effectively use motivational techniques to train employees to excel. Enthusiastic salesperson with a talent for generating new and repeat business. Experience devising security measures that reduce shoplifting and improve store safety. Knowledge of MS Word, WordPerfect, Excel, Lotus 1-2-3, and Quicken.

EXPERIENCE

Manager, 1996 to present　　　　　**Rite Value Home Centers,** New York, NY
Manage Building Materials Department. Train and supervise 5 employees and coordinate scheduling.

- Implemented security procedures that decreased theft by 75%.
- Initiated employee retraining plan that elevated the level of customer service.
- Increased monthly sales by $17,000 after 2 months of employment.

Department Manager, 1994 to 1996　　　**Sampson's Home Store,** Brooklyn, NY
Managed Floor and Wall Department and supervised 8 employees.

- Revamped operating procedures which boosted monthly rug sales by $37,000.
- Selected from among 30 managers to receive company merit award.
- Frequently received letters of commendation from satisfied customers.

Sales Associate, 1993 to 1994　　　　**Carpet Emporium,** Flushing, NY
Learned the rug and carpet business, including history, symbolism, and models.

- Recommended redisplay of merchandise which stimulated sales.
- Sold previously stagnant line of rugs worth $60,000 within 3 weeks.
- Provided excellent customer service to all customers.

Assistant Manager, 1991 to 1993　　　**Ace Video Company,** Boston, MA
Oversaw store operations and supervised 20 employees.

- Implemented systems that helped increase sales from $2.5 to $3.3 million.
- Enhanced corporate image by involving the company in charitable giving.
- Assisted with new store openings and assumed Manager role in his absence.

EDUCATION

Bachelor of Arts in Psychology, 1991　　**Russell Sage College,** Troy, NY
- Minor in Business Administration

"Ms. Monde's leadership has been central to the department's growth...her knowledgeable assistance sets us apart from the competition and keeps the customers returning to our stores..." — Jonathan Q. Childs, Chairman of the Board, Rite Value Home Centers

MARILYN WONDER

2 Green Meadow Drive • Snellville, Georgia 30278 • (404) 979-7777

PROFILE

A seasoned professional with experience in selling and merchandising a wide variety of gift items and home furnishings. Ability to scout new lines, identify, and anticipate industry fashion and trends. Execute multiple responsibilities simultaneously, set priorities, and act decisively.

- Comprehensive knowledge of, and participation in, major gift trade shows in Atlanta, Dallas, Chicago, New York, and San Francisco; toured Europe to identify buying trends and marketable imports.

- Capable of growing customer base through implementation of high customer service standards, educating consumers, training sales staff, and ensuring consistent quality of product.

EXPERIENCE

1984 to Present

ARRAY OF WONDER, Norcross (Atlanta Market Area), Georgia
Owner/Manager
- Selected wide variety of merchandise for unique gift and decorative accessories boutique; designed both store layout and visual merchandising displays, creating vignettes specific to merchandise.
- Facilitated major change of product mix and focus three times — from American Country, to Victorian, to Country French.
- Conceived and developed quarterly newsletter to effect customer awareness of new products and promotions.
- Organize basketweaving classes that run concurrently for various skill levels; coordinate teachers, schedules, and inventory.
- Supervise staff of three.

In conjunction with
1988 to Present

SUPERIOR MARKETING, INC., Atlanta, Georgia
Administrative Director and Consultant
- Conceptualized and developed plan to establish sales and marketing rep base for ten manufacturing companies of gift items and decorative accessories.
- Assessed growth and potential market; steered business from total field rep orientation to establishment of showroom concept in Atlanta Gift Mart.
- Act as liaison between showroom customers and manufacturers, and between outside sales reps and showroom staff, to minimize and resolve problems.
- Train sales force and telemarketing staff on proper presentation of products and appropriate sales techniques.

ASSOCIATIONS

Who's Who in Georgia, 1994
Norcross Business Association, Member
Gwinnett Basketweavers Guild, Founding Member
North Carolina Basketweavers Association, Member

REFERENCES AND PRIOR EXPERIENCE AVAILABLE UPON REQUEST

667 Colonial Circle
Briarwood, Massachusetts 01956
(508) 807-3456

Summary of Qualifications

A senior marketing and merchandising professional with an eye towards bottom line profit requirements. Domestic and international experience in the following areas:

- Product Development
- Project Management
- Brand Management

- Corporate Buying Programs
- Point of Purchase Advertising
- Newspaper Advertising

- Direct Mail Advertising
- Supervision and Training
- Vendor Negotiations/Presentations

Professional Experience

Macys, Boston, MA   1995-Present

Divisional Merchandise Manager (Housewares, Candy Division)

- Responsible for all financial aspects of the Division including sales, gross margin, stock levels, and mark up. Annual volume $35.0 million.

- Supervise a staff of 11 employees including 4 buyers.

- Oversee all direct mail and newspaper advertising.

Achievements:

- Increased Housewares sales 19% in Fall 1995 to $18.2 million. Ranked No. 2 within Mays Company.

- Increased gross margin .5% in Fall 1995 to 33.9%. Ranked No. 1 within Macys Department Stores.

Mikassa, USA, Flemington, NJ   1993-1995

Director of Marketing

- Responsible for the following areas: sales, gross margin, product development, point of sale materials, collateral, and production on the international level.

- Work closely with corporate headquarters in Japan to develop a world-wide marketing concept.

- Supervise marketing personnel. Interface with graphics staff and advertising agencies.

Achievements:

- Instrumental in obtaining an 11% sales increase within one year. Increased gross margin by 3% in 1994.

- Chosen as part of the team responsible for the current redevelopment and repositioning of the Mikassa Brand.

- Developed and implemented a three-year business plan to increase Mikassa from 19 to 27 patterns and increase cost shipments from $20.7 million to $27.2 million.

J.C. Penney Company, New York, NY   **1987-1993**

   Divisional Merchandise Manager (Housewares Division)   1991-1993

- Oversaw sales and gross margin for the entire Housewares Division for all J.C. Penney department stores.

- Supervised all Housewares Market Representatives.

Achievements:

- Created seasonal merchandising programs. Handled negotiations with senior management of major houseware companies including Krups, Braun, Libbey, and Pfaltzgraff.

- Directed product development in both the European and Asian markets.

- Traveled extensively to perform hands-on supervision of Market Representatives.

- Led division to a gross margin improvement of 1.5% in 1992 (over 1991) with sales of $225 million, exceeding target sales projections by 6%.

- Developed excellent communication skills (both up-line and down-line) particularly with regard to intense, frequent teleconferencing activities.

   Market Representative (China/Crystal)   1988-1991

- Managed and developed the China and Crystal departments for the May Company resulting in an outstanding employment rating and a promotion to Division Merchandise Manager.

- Developed and marketed "Giftable" concept within the Crystal Department that helped achieved double digit increases two years in a row.

   Market Representative (Gift/Tabletop Housewares and Stationery)   1987-1988

Caldor, Inc., Newark, NJ   **1981-1987**

   Group Manager   1985-1987
   Assistant Buyer   1983-1985
   Department Manager   1981-1983

Lord & Taylor, New York, NY   **1980-1981**

   Assistant Buyer (Handbags, Small Leather Goods)

Education

Salve Regina University, Newport, RI
Bachelor of Science in Business Management
Minor Concentration in Public Speaking, 1982

Captain, Men's Varsity Basketball Team
Co-Captain Men's Varsity Soccer Team

SALLY ANNETTE SEVENSON

2457 US Hwy 48 South ❖ Mesa, MN 65345 ❖ (819) 898-1045

OBJECTIVE:

HOME FASHIONS BUYER

PERSONAL PROFILE:

19 years of experience in the retail industry with an emphasis on buying . . . Strongly self-motivated, enthusiastic and committed to professional excellence . . . Inspires, motivates and supports others to work at their highest level of productivity. . . Able to pull together and manage all aspects of complex projects and assignments . . . Readily project a professional, fashionable image . . . Exceptional communication and interpersonal skills with the ability to relate warmly with people, generating trust and rapport . . . Equally effective working in self-managed projects and as a member of a team . . . Sharp and creative in problem solving and needs assessment . . . Strong skills in organization and time management priorities . . . Able to handle a multitude of details at once, meeting deadlines under pressure . . . Possess a working knowledge of computer software to include Windows 3.1, Lotus and AmiPro.

PROFESSIONAL EXPERIENCE:

MARTINDALE DEPARTMENT STORES, INC.

Group Cosmetic Buyer - Treatment/Fragrance, Mesa, MN   1990 - Present
Purchase for and manage multi-million budget throughout 40 stores throughout Minnesota, Wisconsin and North Dakota.

❖ Supervise all aspects of retailing, from product purchasing through merchandising, to floor presentation.

❖ Formulate and administer departmental objectives, as well as promotional strategies, effectively increasing sales volume.

❖ Make personal visits to each store on a monthly rotation basis for the purpose of:
   — meeting with management and sales associates to address concerns, as well as new concepts and ideas that will meet the needs of store clientele;
   — assisting in creating tasteful merchandise designs and displays;
   — reviewing stock books to ensure accurate maintenance and inventory.

❖ Work directly with vendors in planning and implementing special events.

❖ Maintain open communication with each store on a daily basis, assisting sales associates in matters that may arise in meeting the needs of clientele, troubleshooting problems and creating effective resolutions thereto.

❖ Monitor progress of all sales and focus on improving areas of weakness.

❖ Attend semi-annual cosmetic market in New York selecting treatments and fragrances within the lastest fashion trends and demand of clientele.

❖ Select promotional products and assist in designing appealing ads that generate sales.

❖ Responsible for seven account coordinators who are shared by Martindale and vendors.

❖ Resolve merchandise marking and receiving problems utilizing daily action list from computer system.

Divisional Manager of Home Fashions, Mesa Regional Mall, Mesa, MN   1975 - 1992
Prepared merchandising plans to include sales, inventories and open to buy for entire home fashions department in a mall environment.

❖ Successfully built a cooperative work team consisting of 17 full- and part-time employees and promoted a productive work environment by:
  — scheduling hours and delegating jobs in accordance with employees' skills and abilities;
  — welcoming constructive input on departmental matters;
  — assisting in the hiring phases of all employees within department;
  — conducting fair assessments and evaluations based on overall performance.

❖ Attended home fashions markets in New York, Atlanta, Chicago and Charlotte, implementing knowledge of georgraphic location and demand in selecting merchandise.

❖ Worked directly with clientele in meeting their needs and resolving problems.

EDUCATION:

NEW YORK SCHOOL OF HOME FASHION AND DECOR, New York, NY; 1975
Certificate in Home Fashion and Decor

MESA COMMUNITY COLLEGE, Mesa, MN; 1973
A.A.S. Degree in Business Administration

Excellent References Available Upon Request

ANN SELLER
319.441.3200

666 North Devil's Glen
Iowa City, Iowa 52255

e-mail:
ASELLER@online.net

SALES PROFILE

Assertive, customer-driven professional experienced in **face-to-face selling** and **sales team leadership** in a retail setting. Confident communicator offering high-caliber presentation, negotiation and closing skills. Able to draw upon excellent decision-making skills, the ability to perform under deadline pressures and well-developed listening skills.

EDUCATION

Bachelor of Arts—Communication Studies • August 1997
THE UNIVERSITY OF IOWA, Iowa City, Iowa

- Media Studies course track; GPA: 3.14
- Production emphasis
  - √ Developed production video currently used as part of standard undergraduate communications curriculum.
- French minor
  - √ Selected to participate in a unique educational immersion program … completed final semester at Sofogest Pitiot, Lyon, France as 1 of 40 participants chosen from a state-wide applicant pool.

RETAIL SALES MANAGEMENT EXPERIENCE

BEST ELECTRONICS COMPANY • 1991 to Present
Initially hired in **Customer Service** (Milan, Illinois store); secured transfer to Iowa City, Iowa store and gained specialist experience in entertainment software and audio / visual product lines; worked full-time while attending college. Selected to open new stores in key Georgia and Florida markets and gained comprehensive experience as **Media Trainer** and **Sales Team Leader**. Subsequently **appointed to Management School** and accepted **Merchandising Manager** position in Atlanta, Georgia upon completion. Accepted lower position after 15 months to return to Iowa City location and complete college degree.

Audio Senior Specialist • Iowa City, Iowa (September 1997 to Present)
- Returned from Europe after 2 1/2 months of study and was quickly **promoted to Senior status to turnaround lagging department sales.**

Merchandise Specialist • Iowa City, Iowa (September 1996 to May 1997)
- Coordinated with marketing and advertising departments the strategic placement of products within customer sight lines (e.g., mass displays, register lanes, endcaps, sidecaps, planograms).
- Ensured proper pricing, ordered adequate product, and developed weekly print advertisements.

Video Senior Specialist • Iowa City, Iowa (August 1995 to September 1996)
- Managed entire employment cycle of 10 department employees while meeting all department sales quotas set by store management.
- **Assumed Temporary Assistant Manager status to assist with 4-month 1995 Christmas season rush.**

continued …

RETAIL SALES MANAGEMENT EXPERIENCE, *cont.*

BEST ELECTRONICS COMPANY • **1991 to Present**

Merchandise Manager • Atlanta, Georgia (April to August 1995)
- Accepted this Sales Team Leader management position in Atlanta market and held full responsibility for overall supervision of 150 employees as well as sales coaching, competitor analysis, customer relations, profitability analysis, and employee recruiting and retention.
- **Created and implemented a warranty sales drive which included competitive spiffs and prize giveaways to motivate sales staff.**

Management In Training • Atlanta, Georgia (February to April 1995)
- Chosen from a field of 30 applicants as 1 of 7 participants from same district to be sent to management school. This 8-week course involved 27 students of which only 3 were women.

Entertainment Software Supervisor • Savannah, Georgia (May 1994 to February 1995)
- Hired and trained 20 employees; managed labor, scheduling, merchandising, vendor relations, drop shipments, inventory control and ensured consistent delivery of quality customer service.
- **Realigned inventory and product stocking system to ensure rapid and cost efficient product placement.**

Audio Product Specialist • Milan, Illinois (February to May 1994)
- Took semester off from college to work full-time in hometown store and save money for college expenses.
- **Within 3 months was asked to open store in Savannah, Georgia.**

Video Product Specialist • Iowa City, Iowa (May 1993 to February 1994)
- Acquired product knowledge and further developed sales skills.
- **Chosen as Video Trainer for new hires in 5 Georgia stores**. Training curriculum for 100 employees included product knowledge, selling techniques, company history, etc.

Entertainment Software Specialist • Iowa City, Iowa (September 1992 to May 1993)
- Gained merchandising, stocking and sales experience.

Customer Service • Milan, Illinois (July 1991 to September 1992)
- Developed excellent customer service skills in a variety of customer interaction settings: staffing cash register, receiving product returns, preparing finance applications and resolving customer concerns.

A / V PRODUCTION EXPERIENCE

UNIVERSITY OF IOWA MEDIA DEPT. • **1995 to 1997**

As **Director / Producer**, gained diverse practical experience in managing extensive scope of responsibility involved with heading numerous TV, radio, video and screenplay projects.

COMPUTER SKILLS

Proficient in MS Word 7.0 / Excel / Publisher ... Windows 95 ... Novell Perfect Office
Netscape Navigator ... Internet and e-mail use

HERBERT R. MAGRATH

13 Hillcrest Court
Troy, Illinois 62294
(618) 555-4295

- Top-notch sales producer with 13 years of proven success in commissioned sales, including automotive and industrial advertising markets.

- Possess dynamic people skills and a solid reputation for maintaining above-average profit contributions with uncompromising regard for customer retention and first-class service quality.

- Additional background in retail sales management, with strong track record of individual and multi-unit performance, handling all operations including finance, public relations, and human resources.

RECENT PERFORMANCE

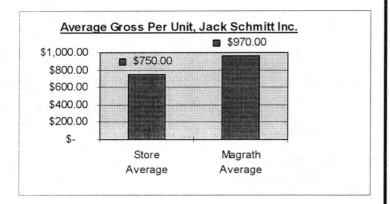

"My customers know that I will take care of them. Making a sale is one thing...gaining their trust and keeping them satisfied is what makes me successful."

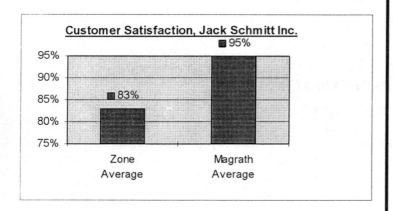

SALES EXPERIENCE

JACK SCHMITT INC., 1991-1996
- Ranked #3 in highest gross per unit.
- Consistently rated 95% in customer satisfaction, exceeding company average by more than 10%.

MEYER ON MAIN, 1990-1991
- Ranked #1 in Pontiac sales.
- Ranked #6 out of 155 salespeople in five states.
- Maintained 96% customer satisfaction rate.

THOMAS REGISTER INC., 1989-1990
(sold advertisements for an industrial buying guide)
- Increased territory 20% over previous year.
- Achieved a 95% renewal rate.

M & M MARKETING, 1983-1989
(The Waterbed Store: Sales Associate; promoted to Assistant Manager and Sales Manager with concurrent responsibility for financing, floor sales, ordering, purchasing, scheduling, merchandising, and customer service.)
- Consistently ranked in top 3 in sales and the #1 selling manager.
- Trained three of the top five sales producers.
- Managed the #1 producing store for two years with revenues of $1 million.
- Supervised operations of as many as three stores during company restructuring.
- Featured in and wrote copy for T.V. advertisements.

EDUCATION

Management/Marketing Coursework, Southern Illinois University at Edwardsville
Numerous continuing education seminars from top sales professionals

References Available Upon Request

Robert Dane

132 New Road ■ Newton, New Jersey 07860
(973) 555-5555

Value Offered

■ Establish positive relationships and effective sales strategies to cultivate emerging markets, while expanding existing markets.

■ Possess uncompromising consideration for customer retention and premier service.

■ Recognized for ability to diffuse and reverse potentially volatile situations utilizing strong negotiating and conflict resolution skills.

■ Effectively motivate staff to drive sustained revenue and earnings growth.

Dynamic, team-building management professional with proven expertise in market identification and penetration; key account management; human resource development; customer relationship management; budget administration; waste stream assessment and profiling; compliance control. Excellent qualifications in team leadership.

Recent Sales Performance

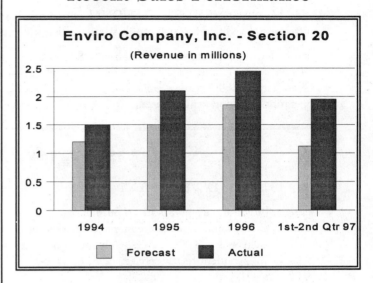

Challenged to revitalize stagnant sales territory to accelerate revenue growth and improve market position.
■ Delivered 25% revenue growth in first 6 months.
■ Grew Merck account from $76,000 to 1.2 million in 3 years.
■ *Sales Quality Club*, 1996. Ranked #2 in New York branch in overall revenue for 1997 YTD.

Previous Sales/Management Experience

WASTE MANAGEMENT CONSULTANTS, Seaside, NJ (1990-1994)
Coordinator, Transportation and Disposal
■ Excellent project management qualifications including hands-on field service supervision.
■ Extensive regulatory knowledge and federal/state agency interface.
■ Streamlined transportation function, achieving 25% cost reduction in the first 8 months.

GORDON HUMUS COMPANY, Southtown, NJ (1989-1990)
Field Operation Manager for 15-person field crew operating heavy machinery to harvest peat humus. Developed effective production strategies and manpower cross-functional training methods resulting in 20% increase in productivity. Conducted monthly performance reviews and compensation evaluations.

DANE'S GARDEN CENTER, Southtown, NJ (1977-1989)
Entrepreneur. Established successful garden center/nursery niche market utilizing innovative organic growing techniques.

Education

Bachelor of Arts, Biological Sciences, Cook College - Rutgers University, New Brunswick, NJ (1975)

OWEN W. MICHELSON

234 East Wellington Avenue ~ Bentville, OR 94545 ~ (345) 234-2345

SALES / MANAGEMENT PROFESSIONAL with more than 14 years' experience building and directing customer-driven organizations. Qualified for high-profile positions that will benefit from:

♦ **Sales talent** to cultivate strategic relationships, expand customer base, and maximize account sales.
♦ **Business savvy** to anticipate contingencies, control expenses, stretch operating dollars, and maximize profitability.
♦ **Change agent** skills to analyze global organizational needs, influence change among tenured employees, and retool operations/support staff to excel in competitive environments.

REPRESENTATIVE ACCOMPLISHMENTS

SALES / BUSINESS DEVELOPMENT

Challenge: Build sales in service-driven business catering to corporate clientele.
Action: Created and implemented targeted marketing, advertising, and promotional strategies.
Result: Delivered $78,000 increase in higher-profit segment of operation. Achieved 91% rating (above average) from Independent review service.

Challenge: Recruited to turnaround operation with stagnant sales and declining patronage.
Action: Brought business-driven initiatives to non-profit setting for operation typically viewed as a "loss leader."
Result: Increased sales by 46% and 24% in major revenue categories; total increase represented $320,000 in added operating revenue.

MANAGEMENT / OPERATIONS / BUSINESS ADMINISTRATION

Challenge: Maintain uninterrupted member services during 10-month, $6.5 million construction project.
Action: Set-up temporary business office, maintained access to key materials, designed alternate operating procedures.
Result: Accommodated all events without inconvenience, including premiere sporting competition attended by 2,000.

Challenge: Inherited operation performing below par for service and quality.
Action: Recruited new talent, retrained service staff, designed new quality/cost controls.
Result: Lowered operating costs, increased facility usage by an overall 34%, and earned favorable scores on recent member survey.

PROFESSIONAL HISTORY

♦ **MANAGER** ~ Not-For-Profit Member Organization, Bentville, Oregon   8/93-Present
Recruited as Chief Operations Officer for 750-member private club. Accountable for budget preparation ($2.5M), financial controls, policy development, daily operations, member relations, and Board reporting. Direct a staff of 50-60 in performing a full range of administrative, food and beverage, aquatics, building and grounds maintenance functions.

♦ **ASSISTANT MANAGER** ~ Premiere Properties, Portland, Oregon   1989-1993
Management accountability extended to operations, purchasing, and business office functions. Supervised staff of 20-30.

♦ **ASSOCIATE MANAGER** ~ Retail Ventures Limited, Seattle, Washington   1983-1988
Managed profit performance through cost controls, staff development, and service enhancements. Directed staff of 35-40.

EDUCATION

University of Washington, Pullman ~ Coursework emphasis in Business, Accounting, Economics

---

SCOTT P. HAMILTON

2934 Oak Tree Drive • Roanoke, VA 23552 • (804) 265-8748

CAREER PROFILE:

Top-Performing **Sales, Marketing & Customer Service Professional** with 10+ years experience across broad industries, markets and accounts. Expert qualifications in identifying and capturing market opportunities to accelerate expansion, increase revenues and improve profit contributions. Equally strong experience in planning, operations management, finance, logistics, inventory management and quality control. PC proficient.

CORE COMPETENCIES:

New Business Development & Customer Relations
- Managed the entire sales cycle from lead generation and client assessment through proposal preparation and presentation to contract negotiations, project scheduling, product/service delivery and follow-up.
- Doubled account base, expanded representation in new markets and introduced product offerings to meet diverse client needs. Delivered a $600,000 increase in sales over two years.

Contract Negotiations
- Consistently met or exceeded all sales and performance objectives. Captured 275 new accounts within two years in fast-paced, highly-competitive environments.
- Direct liaison between client and financing companies to evaluate potential financing options. Provided client recommendations to maximize discounts and reduce interest on purchases.

Account Management & Retention
- Pioneered innovative account management program integrating pre-call planning, objective setting and relationship management strategies.
- Recognized for commitment to quality service and client satisfaction through creative problem-solving and customer-driven sales initiatives.

Marketing & Merchandising
- Launched a comprehensive direct mail and promotions campaign that captured a 20% increase in prospective clients and significantly enhanced market awareness.
- Evaluated product inventory levels and developed merchandising strategies for product placement and advertising. Managed large vendor relationships.

Operations Management
- Designed a series of reports (e.g., lead/sales tracking, financial analysis, inventory management) to provide management team with critical performance criteria.
- Directed personnel scheduling, payroll, logistics and distribution functions for a large retail chain.

Training & Team Leadership
- Designed and instructed a series of sales, customer service and product training programs for more than 20 new hires.

PROFESSIONAL EXPERIENCE:

Sales Manager	Gorman Construction	1995 to Present
Inventory Control Manager	Harris Teeter Supermarkets	1990 to 1995
Customer Service Supervisor	Grand Piano & Furniture	1988 to 1989
Sales Representative	Shelor Automotive Company	1984 to 1988

EDUCATION:

Currently enrolled in a BA Marketing Degree Program through Virginia Polytechnic University.

Completed numerous continuing professional education programs throughout career. Courses included Strategic Selling, Key Client Management, Negotiations and Advanced PC Technology.

JAMES WESTBROOK

3075 West Street
Salem, Massachusetts 02065
(555) 222-5785

CAREER FOCUS: Sales / Marketing / Account Relations

STRENGTHS and SKILLS:

- Highly creative, self-motivated professional with sales, marketing and customer relations experience.
- Ability to conceptualize and generate new ideas, analyze problems and develop effective solutions.
- A dependable team player who relates well and works cooperatively with diverse personalities.
- Fast learner with demonstrated initiative and dedication to the achievement of organizational goals.
- Focus on providing exceptional service resulting in customer satisfaction and repeat business.
- Computer capabilities include Windows 95, Microsoft Office Suite, Publisher, and Lotus 1-2-3.

EDUCATION:

B.S. in Marketing • ROGER WILLIAMS COLLEGE • Bristol, Rhode Island • 1996
Courses included:
**Marketing Principles ... Marketing Research ... Consumer Behavior
Advertising Principles ... Advertising Campaigns ... Sales Management**

ACCOMPLISHMENTS:

*Sales &
Promotions*
- Consistently achieved high sales volume for a sporting equipment retail business.
- Recognized by management for sales performance, surpassing productivity levels of full-time associates store-wide.
- Promoted and sold products at Fenway Park for the Red Sox, earning more than $5000 in commissions and tips to contribute to college expenses.

*Marketing
& Research*
- Organized and launched successful direct mail marketing campaign for new product.
- Created an advertising campaign for Levi jeans from concept development through copywriting for a college advertising project.
- Earned top grade for designing comprehensive business, marketing and sales plan as well as management structure for a college marketing project.
- Researched and compiled target database of 100 clients representing diverse industries.

*Customer
Relations
& Service*
- Addressed customer inquiries, serving as an informational resource and referring calls to appropriate staff for technical support.
- Commended by management and customers for ability to build trust and confidence, resulting in repeat business and increased sales.

EXPERIENCE:

Carpenter's Assistant • NBP, INC., Weymouth, Massachusetts • 1996-Present
Sales Associate • NATIONAL SHOES, Kingston, Massachusetts • 1995-1996
Marketing Intern • COMPUTER SOLUTIONS, Boston, Massachusetts • 1994
Sales Associate • BROWN & STEVENS, INC., Boston, MA • 1991-1994

PATRICIA M. LUTHER
2110 Whirlpool Lane
Austin, Texas 78700
(512) 888-7777

CAREER TARGET: PHARMACEUTICAL SALES

AREAS OF EXPERTISE

- Key Account Acquisition / Retention
- Sales / Marketing / Account Management
- Negotiating / Influential Selling
- Presentation / Communications

- Public Relations / Customer Service
- Strategic Planning / Development
- Critical Problem Resolution
- Scheduling / Time Management

- **Highly self-motivated, dynamic Sales Professional** with demonstrated **Sales / Account Management** expertise and the **confidence** and **perseverance** to succeed/exceed in all endeavors.

- **Impact Award Winner. Top 10 Achiever.** Consistently exceed sales dollar/volume quotas.

- Exceptional **presentation**, **negotiation**, **communication**, and **interpersonal** skills; quickly develop positive rapport with healthcare/business professionals; comfortable in healthcare environment.

- Outstanding **organization**, **time management**, and **problem-solving** abilities; strategically manage time and expediently resolve problems for optimal productivity, improvement, and profitability.

- Computer literate: WordPerfect, Lotus 1-2-3, CAD, Graphics.

- **Goal-** and **success-driven. Focused. Tenacious. Team-spirited. Profit-oriented.**

EDUCATION / PROFESSIONAL DEVELOPMENT

UNIVERSITY OF TEXAS AT AUSTIN – Austin, Texas
Bachelor of Applied Arts and Sciences Degree (1994)
Major: **Technology**; Minor: **Business Management**
GPA: 4.0/Major; 3.85/Cumulative

Map for Action (Sales / Account Management Training Program)
Power Sales Negotiating Training Program (Intense 5-day Program)

PROFESSIONAL SALES EXPERIENCE

SOUTHERN FREIGHT COMPANY
Sales Account Manager

Austin, Texas
1996 – Present

- Recruited to manage all marketing/sales efforts in Austin area; report to Regional Sales Director.
- Efficiently manage 200 face-to-face accounts; call on manufacturing firms to promote motor freight services and solicit new accounts; perform monetary analysis of companies; prepare proposals; negotiate contracts/pricing.
- Extensively interface with customers and team members (drivers and operational personnel) to ensure superior customer service; quickly resolve problems/conflicts. **Maintain impressive customer satisfaction record.**
- Make presentations at Mini Customer Conferences, business meetings; host golf tournaments/dinners for clients.
- **Selected by Regional Sales Director** (one of two chosen out of 20) to participate in Power Sales Negotiating Training Program (specialty program for potential top-level sales management professionals).
- **Impact Award Winner** six times within one year for highest Sales Performance (out of 20 sales reps).
- Member of **Gold Rush Program**; **exceeded quota every month**.

AMERICAN TRANSFER   Austin, Texas
Account Representative   1994 – 1996

- Called on businesses in Austin and surrounding area to market motor freight services for family-owned agency representing 23 companies. Established/maintained congenial, profitable business relationships with clients.
- Planned, organized, and hosted business luncheons, dinners, golf outings for clients/prospective clients; **increased levels of commitment to American was attained through superior customer service**.
- **Accelerated client base by 98% during first year.**
- **Increased intrastate outbound shipments from 12% to 58%.**

ROSE COSMETICS   Austin, Texas
Sales Associate   1988 – 1989

- Held part-time position as sales associate for major cosmetic company while pursuing degree.
- Greeted/consulted with clients; performed makeovers. **Influential in generating increase in sales volume**.
- Assisted counter manager with day-to-day store operations; generated monthly sales reports.
- Planned, coordinated monthly sales promotions and events.
- Organized and managed client records.

INTERNSHIP

APPLE COMPUTER COMPANY   Houston, Texas
Events Coordinator – Marketing and Sales Division   1990 – 1992

- Selected as sole candidate (out of 600 applicants) for prestigious internship (determination based upon scholastic ability, aptitude, communication skills, and personality).
- Trained, directed, and supervised support staff of five engaged in planning and coordinating seminars for up to 500 professionals. Coordinated up to 20 seminars simultaneously.
- Interacted with Apple sales force to determine seminar topics; coordinated dates; selected business partners.
- Compiled lists of possible attendees, using SIC codes and Apple mainframe computer.
- Designed/created invitations; compiled and orchestrated mailouts for up to 500 professionals.
- Recipient of **award for design/creation of computer training system/manual**; received **award for significantly increasing revenue and productivity**.

MONEY MAGAZINE   Austin, Texas
Advertising Sales Intern   1989 – 1990

- Accompanied/observed sales representatives during sales calls. Assisted with various tasks in office.

♦ ♦ Professional References Furnished On Request ♦ ♦

ELAINE M. HARRIS
400 Shelton Way
Dallas, Texas 75200
(214) 555-9999

PROFESSIONAL OBJECTIVE: HEART SALES REPRESENTATIVE

HIGHLIGHTS OF QUALIFICATIONS

- **Dynamic, enthusiastic Sales Professional** with comprehensive experience and expertise in areas of: **Customer Service ❤ Product Knowledge ❤ Industry Trends ❤ Influential Selling ❤ Presentations**.

- Avid advocate for and in-depth knowledge of **Heart products**! Professional development: "Heart on the Road" seminar.

- **Intuitive. Persuasive. Creative.** Know what customers want to buy; **strong negotiating / closing ability**.

- Outstanding **leadership, organizational, time management**, and **problem-solving** abilities. Effective **motivator**.

- Exceptional **public relations, communication**, and **interpersonal** abilities; outgoing personality with positive, "can-do" attitude. Persistence in achieving goals and professional success.

PROFESSIONAL EXPERIENCE

MERLE NORMAN COSMETICS
Manager / Buyer / Heart Consultant
Dallas, Texas
1992 – Present

- Manage operations and promote Merle Norman cosmetics, Heart accessories, and various clothing lines.
- Train, direct, and motivate three sales associates.
- **Increased Heart sales by 147% during first year**, and **consistently achieved increases each year** due to **personal enthusiasm and outstanding conception of Heart products**.
- Attend market 3-4 times annually; purchase marketable, trendy merchandise.
- Efficiently manage $350,000 inventory.

CHARLES PETERSON'S FINE JEWELRY
Sales Associate / Buyer
Dallas, Texas
1990 – 1992

- Provided prompt, courteous service to customers; sold fine jewelry and gifts.
- Attended market several times a year; purchased jewelry and gifts. Maintained $475,000 inventory.

METRO PACKAGE STORE
Manager
Dallas, Texas
1982 – 1993

- Managed successful product distribution business with annual sales of approximately $325,000.
- Responsible for personnel recruitment, training, supervision; purchasing; advertising; receiving/stocking; and financial aspects of business.
- Negotiated competitive pricing with vendors. Managed $125,000 inventory.

❤ ❤ **References Furnished On Request** ❤ ❤

Sales Representative

PROFILE

Highly successful Manufacturer Representative for wide variety of animal/poultry feeds and supplements around New England. Outstanding customer relations skills strong ability to persuasively relate new concepts and ideas. Successful and proven ability to "cold call close" sales. Expertise in the following:

Quality Control	*Batch Mixing*	*Inventory Control*
Nutritional Consulting	*Purchasing*	*Order Tracking*
New Product Introductions	*Telemarketing*	*Commodity Sales*

HIGHLIGHTS OF QUALIFICATIONS

- Over 12 years experience in the sales and marketing field.
- Proven record in effectively handling difficult situations, negotiating, developing and implementing solutions.
- Thorough knowledge of the animal and poultry feeds.
- Responsible for hiring/firing and training staff.
- Personally sold to and serviced regional accounts.
- Highly adaptable to rapidly changing requirements and situations
- Provided continual follow-up to potential customers in order to ensure future sales.
- Basic computer skills in Lotus 123.

RELATED WORK HISTORY

Feed Sales and Service Representative, K&L Feeds, Franklin, CT 1993-1997
➤ Expert Nutritional Consultant. Duties included direct personal relations with animal and poultry farms around New England, scoring livestock conditions, sampling forages, reading sample results and balancing ration for maximum production. Recommended management practices and telemarketing for commodity sales.

Sales for Animal and Poultry Feeds, Beacon Feeds, Cauga, NY   1983-1988
➤ Duties included nutritional services, scoring, sampling and management of feed formulas and in and out of house customer service.

Office Manager, Agway Inc., Franklin, CT 1971-1983
➤ Duties included sampling of product for quality control, inventory control and ordered, order tracking, processing invoices, operating truck scales and batch mixer, operated pellet mill, dispatching and managing liquid feed division at the Franklin mill. Coordinated vitamin and mineral supplement ordering. Liaison between sales staff and purchasing department.

ADAM R. WILLIAMS

3368 Shannon Way
Plain City, Ohio 43064

Phone: (614) 555-0105
Voice Mail: (800) 555-3123 x 2347

PROFILE

Dynamic sales and management career marketing products and technologies within high-growth, emerging, mature and competitive business markets. Expert in building top-producing sales organizations. Outstanding presentation, negotiation and closing skills. Demonstrated achievements in:

- Key Account Relationship Management
- Strategic Sales/Market Planning
- Goal Attainment/Revenue Growth

- Sales Coaching/Motivational Training
- New Account Prospecting
- Sales Recruitment

*Achieved strong and sustainable revenue improvement
during first eight months with Digital Inc.*

PROFESSIONAL EXPERIENCE

DIGITAL INC., Dublin, Ohio   **1/95 to Present**
Manufacturing "giant" of computer and office equipment with annual revenues in excess of $3.2 billion.

Branch Manager
Senior sales management executive with full P&L responsibility for the strategic planning, development and leadership of Digital's Copier Division in the Dublin, Cincinnati and Indiana territories.

- Manage 21 total staff consisting of 2 sales managers, 4 office managers and 15 sales reps.
- Transitioned division from $35,000 average monthly revenue to over $100,000; highest month being $137,000. Accomplished growth with only 2 veteran sales people and 13 rookies.
- Recruited, hired and trained 11 new reps bringing total sales force to 15.

XEROX INC.   **9/82 to 3/84 and 8/85 to 12/94**
Marketer of office products such as copiers, fax machines, typewriters, time clocks, digital products, color copiers with annual sales of over $19 million.

Met or exceeded 100% of quota during entire history with Xerox.

District Manager, Elk Grove Village, Illinois (10/89-12/94)

- Spearheaded ground floor opening of 2 new branch operations. Ranked #1 and #3 in percent of quota.
- Led fastest growing branch in company's history, experiencing revenue growth of $190,000 (1990) to over $914,000 (1994) and ranking of #3 (out of 11) in highest sales volume.
- Achieved "President's Club" status 3 out of 5 years winning several trips for highest sales.

Major Account Representative, Cicero, Illinois (4/88-10/89)

- Marketed office equipment to Fortune 500 companies, national accounts, government offices, banks, educational facilities and medical communities.
- Established largest account in company's history by selling 125 copiers to Landview Hospital. Another significant sale was 60 fax machines to Johnathan National Life.

Copier Sales Representative, Schaumburg, Illinois (8/85-4/88)

- Achieved #1 sales rep status 1986-1988
- Won Xerox's national demo contest "Runner-Up" award (4,200 participants).
- Won Xerox's national "Pursuit of Excellence" award 8 times.

Typewriter Sales Representative, Schaumburg, Illinois (9/82-3/84)

- Developed new territory to $350,000 in annual sales.

PROFESSIONAL EXPERIENCE (continued)

STATEWIDE FINANCIAL SERVICES, Carbondale, Illinois 3/84 to 8/85
Financial services of investments, annuities, variable life insurance products, mutual funds, stocks, bonds, life, health, property and casualty insurance. Billion dollar company.

Agent
- Marketed and sold financial products to consumers.
- Completed Securities License Series 6 (Life, Health, Property & Casualty).

TRAINING SEMINARS

- Applied Concepts, Sales Management Leadership Program (MVP)
- NOMDA, How to Hire and Train, Major Account Penetration (MVP)
- Xerox, Selling Skills (MVP)
- Xerox, Selling in Vertical Markets

ACTIVITIES

- Vice President, P.T.A. Board, Highland Park Elementary School
- Coach, Youth Soccer
- Enjoy baseball, golf and skiing

CONNOR JAMESON

118 West Parker Place
La Jolla, California 92037
(888) 555-1212

DISTRICT / REGIONAL SALES MANAGEMENT

**Sales Support / Allocations / Advertising / Marketing and Promotions / Negotiation / Communication
Customer Satisfaction Practices / Profit and Loss Forecasting / Organization / Market Surveys
Strategic Planning / Staff Training and Development / Conflict Resolution**

EXPERIENCE

BAYSIDE CHEVROLET — La Jolla, California   **1994-Present**
General Sales Manager/New Vehicle Sales Manager/Customer Relations and F&I Manager

Ignite declining business operations and avoid loss of franchise. Increase sales efficiency, sales volume, inventory earning rate, and market lease penetration while maintaining bottom-line profitability.

Conducted a thorough analysis of operation, prepared a cost vs. return prospectus, and implemented significant changes in planning, forecasting, and expenditure control. Developed new marketing strategies which included a complete redirection of all advertising approaches (newspaper, radio, television, direct mail) and promotional campaigns. Completely revamped the earning rate of inventory. Evaluated existing market lease penetration, implemented a thorough training program to educate sales staff regarding every aspect of leasing vs. buying, which enabled staff to more confidently present leasing as an option to prospective customers.

Results
- Tripled the sales efficiency rating from 1995 to 1997 and increased sales volume four times that of 1995.
- Increased new car sales volume by 184% while maintaining gross margin 120% of industry average.
- Improved the company's inventory position. Reduced 60-day supply in 1995 to 16-day supply in 1997.
- Significantly increased market lease penetration and achieved higher customer retention. Sustained integrity of the leasing program, resulting in no lease disclosure actions filed against the dealership.

Develop a non-confrontational selling policy. Establish a competitive sales force focused on customer service and retention, sales volume, and product knowledge. Reduce employee turnover.

Completely revamped sales philosophies and strategies. Developed a comprehensive compensation plan. Worked with an outside consultant to create an extensive training program geared specifically to sales philosophies and commitment to customer service. Recruited and hired the initial sales force, oversaw introductory training, and led all aspects of continuing training. Established sales recognition and incentive programs.

Results
- Built an effective sales team with focus on improved sales as well as customer service and retention. Created a positive work environment through employee empowerment. Enabled employees to focus on their jobs, which created a harmonious atmosphere for customers.

Enhance the Customer Satisfaction Index (CSI) rating.

Evaluated and hired a prospecting company to manage long-term customer mailing campaign. Worked with the company to develop a series of letters targeted at past, present, and prospective customers. Assisted the owner in establishing a policy adjustment/goodwill account to ensure every measure was taken to exceed customer expectations and guarantee satisfaction.

Results
- Doubled the survey responses in all CSI categories (encompassing sales satisfaction, customer referrals, service and follow-up performance, and delivery of quality), placing the dealership above the benchmark in all measurable categories.
- Refined customer base, allowing future marketing plans to be targeted toward the most active customers.
- Developed a delivery process which prepped customers for post-sales activity, including overview of the automobile's owner's manual and features, an introduction to the parts/service department, and a review of the financing agreements.

CONNOR JAMESON

EXPERIENCE

BAYSIDE CHEVROLET — La Jolla, California *(continued)*   1994-Present

Restructure the F&I department, establish sales philosophy and process, and increase F&I market penetration. Protect dealer against potential misrepresentation and financial loss. Educate consumers regarding the value of post-sales products.

Led in-depth F&I training seminars; directed staff in the promotion of after-sales contracts (extended warranties, credit/life insurance, prepaid maintenance agreements, and guaranteed accident protection).

Results   • Significantly enhanced the F&I profit center and increased penetration by 417%. Currently lead the district in after-sales product penetration.

LAGUNA COMMUNICATIONS, INC. — Laguna Hills, California   1993-1994
Account Executive
• Marketed cellular service to corporate prospects; serviced a client base of over 360 and closed an average 30% of all prospects. Effectively managed accounts receivable while consistently meeting corporate objectives.
• Achieved 110% of projected monthly sales goals during entire tenure with the company.
• Nominated for the "Service Excellence" award; selected as a mentor to assist in the development of new associates.

LAGUNA GENERAL CONSULTING, INC. — Laguna Beach, California   1988-1993
Operations Manager
• Directed an average of 7 to 10 custom residential construction projects annually, with each project ranging from $180,000 to $500,000 in cost.
• Evaluated and administered all sublet contracts, ensuring quality control under stringent time and budget constraints, monitoring labor cost and proper use of company resources.
• Managed all post-sales customer service and warranty programs.
• Implemented marketing strategies including project portfolio, company image, and field advertisement.

EDUCATION

BACHELOR OF SCIENCE - FINANCE   1991
University of California • Long Beach, California

DIPLOMA - GRADUATED WITH HIGH HONORS   1987
Long Beach High School • Long Beach, California

PROFESSIONAL TRAINING

Pacific Chevrolet Sales Management College
Pacific Area Finance and Insurance Training
Chevrolet Sales Qualified
California Service Management Excellence
  Completed Marketing and Advanced Financial Analysis of the four colleges offered.

MICHAEL S. GRAHAM

2001 Parkland Street
Baltimore, Maryland 20832

Home (301) 223-6655   Mobile (301) 221-7689   Office (410) 998-3549

SENIOR EXECUTIVE PROFILE

General Manager / Strategic Business Unit Executive / National Sales & Marketing Leader
Start-Up, High-Growth & National Organizations

Dynamic leadership career building top-performing business organizations. Strong general management, P&L, multi-site operating, technology, information systems and human resources qualifications. One of Trent's most prestigious sales and marketing track records. Innovative in conceptualization and tactical execution of successful business development campaigns, product/technology launches and customer management programs. Extensive leadership training and mentoring.

PROFESSIONAL EXPERIENCE

TRENT CORPORATION - Maryland, Virginia & Washington, D.C. - 1977 to Present

High-profile general management and sales/marketing management career distinguished by rapid advancement through a series of increasingly responsible positions in several start-up and early stage business ventures with this Fortune 1000 company. Provided with the unique entrepreneurial opportunity to build and lead new business units with the financial, marketing and organizational support for a large, global corporation. Recipient of numerous corporate honors and awards including:

- **TCS President's Award**, 1994 and 1995 (*One of only five Trent management executives worldwide.*)
- **President's Club Award**, 1977-97 (*Only Division executive to win 20 consecutive Club Awards.*)
- **#1 General Manager in the U.S.**, 1994 (*Ranked in Top 5 in 1995 and 1996.*)
- **#1 District Manager in the U.S.**, 1991, 1992 and 1993
- **#1 District Manager for Customer Satisfaction**, 1989-92

General Manager - TCS Maryland Operation (1994 to Present)

Senior Management Executive with full responsibility for the strategic planning, development, operations, sales, marketing, customer service, human resources, administration, technology and P&L performance of Trent's newest business unit - a comprehensive strategic outsourcing and document management organization. Challenged to transition new business concept into a viable, credible and profitable business servicing major accounts throughout Baltimore and the State of Maryland. Created infrastructure, launched an aggressive recruitment campaign, devised innovative sales and business development initiatives, and rapidly positioned Trent as the area's leading provider of strategic outsourcing operations.

Currently lead a 6-person senior management team, a staff of 150 and strategic outsourced operations at 70 client sites. Establish P&L objectives for each individual client operation to increase accountability and profitability of site management teams.

- Built new venture from concept to the #1 business unit in the U.S. within first year (growth, revenue, profitability, client and employee satisfaction). Delivered unprecedented results:

  -- 300% revenue growth and 400% profit growth in 1994.
  -- 153% revenue growth and 225% profit growth in 1995.
  -- 160% revenue growth and 254% profit growth in 1996.
  -- 170% revenue growth and 185% profit growth projected in 1997.

- Captured key accounts including USF&G, Blue Cross Blue Shield of Maryland, Alexander & Alexander, Maryland National Bank, Black & Decker and numerous other major corporations. Personally negotiated and developed strategic client relationships.

317

National Manager of Systems - Federal Government Operation (1992 to 1994)
District Manager of Systems - Federal Government Operation (1989 to 1992)

Nationwide responsibility for the strategic planning, vision, operating leadership and P&L performance of Trent's new Document Systems, Printing Systems and Business Operations Division for the Integrated Systems Operation. Created an entirely new business unit, consolidated disparate functions under a common organization, launched several high-profile product introductions, and transitioned Trent from a marketer of stand-alone systems technology into a totally integrated systems solution provider. Achieved phenomenal success.

- Built new venture to #1 in the U.S. for three consecutive years with growth from start-up to $75 million in profitable annual sales revenues.
- Honored as #1 in the U.S. for customer satisfaction results in 1989 through 1992.

Manager, Federal Systems Technical Support - Federal Government Operation (1988 to 1989)

Planned, budgeted and directed the deployment of technical resources to service more than 100 federal government accounts throughout the U.S. Devised innovative plans and processes to expedite systems installation, enhancement and support to meet Trent objectives and client technology performance goals.

National Sales Operations Manager - Federal Government Operation (1988)

Trained, developed and led a 10-person national account sales, technical and support team targeting federal government accounts nationwide. Provided the strategic and tactical leadership critical to competitive wins, successful technology installations, and long-term, profitable client retention.

- Honored as the Top Federal National Accounts Manager in the U.S. in 1988.

District Sales Manager - Commercial (1985 to 1987)
Region High Volume Sales Operations Manager - Commercial (1984 to 1985)
Major Account Sales Manager - Commercial (1982 to 1984)
High Volume Marketing Executive - Commercial (1980 to 1982)
Sales Representative - Commercial (1977 to 1980)

Fast-track promotion through a series of increasingly responsible field sales, major account and sales management positions marketing Trent products and office systems throughout the DC/Maryland/Northern Virginia market. Consistently delivered revenue and profit results significantly over plan. Honored with numerous corporate awards including:

- #1 District Sales Manager in the U.S., 1987. #1 District Sales Region in 1986.

EDUCATION

BS - Marketing & Management, University of Maryland, 1977

Graduate of more than 500 hours of continuing professional education:

- Trent Advanced Management School
- Managing People & Processes
- Leading Cross-Functionality
- Quality Improvement Process

- Leading the Enterprise
- Systems & Docutech Training
- The Leadership - Baltimore
- Problem Solving Process

PERSONAL PROFILE

Active Leader and Board Member with civic and charitable organizations including Maryland Boy Scouts, Fire/Police Coalition, Association of Charities and Greater Baltimore Chamber of Commerce.

ROBERT A. ALLEN

115 North Union Boulevard • Colorado Springs, Colorado 80909 • **(719) 632-9050**

CAREER PROFILE

- Top-performing senior executive with unique tactical planning skills
- Proven record of leading organizations through growth and expansion periods
- Competent strategic planner with a record of maximizing employee productivity
- Able to deliver significant revenue and profit gains within competitive markets
- History of igniting stagnant and declining operations into profitability
- Experienced in working within the constraints of limited resources to effect change

FORMAL EDUCATION

Master of Business Administration, Growth Management, Boston University
(Graduated in top 10% of Class with a 4.0 GPA)

Bachelor of Arts, Business Administration, Boston University
(Graduated, cum laude and a member of Sigma Phi Honor Society)

RELEVANT PROFESSIONAL EXPERIENCE

President   1970 - Present
American Uniform Service, Colorado Springs, Colorado
(A $72 million retailer and wholesaler of law enforcement uniforms. Second largest dealer in the United States.)

- Manage all daily operations with full P&L responsibility
- Direct forecasting-administration of a $4.5 million annual operating budget
- Responsible for long-range strategic planning and product development
- Accountable for monitoring and controlling sales and marketing functions
- Oversee imports and all international operations
- Spokesperson for the company both nationally and internationally

◆ **Special Achievements:**

  ◆ Developed catalog sales program with $2.3 million in annual sales
  ◆ Reduced inventory by over 60%
  ◆ Increased product turnover by 800%
  ◆ Expanded profit margins from 31% to 46%
  ◆ Increased sales by over 84% from $11.0 million to $72.0 million
  ◆ Grew company from virtual obscurity to 2nd largest of its type
  ◆ Control materials and labor costs to obtain 12% annual net return

REFERENCES AND FURTHER DATA UPON REQUEST

**Uniquely
Qualified
for . . .**

- **CEO**
- **General Manager**
- **Regional Manager**

or other leadership
positions with an
organization that
needs to ignite
stagnant or declining
operations.

PROFESSIONAL
TRAINING

Dale Carnegie Sales Training

Karrass Negotiation Seminar

Computer Applications for
Inventory Intensive Companies

AFFILIATIONS

Toastmasters International

UNIQUE SKILLS

Fluent French and German

(Ideal for International
business negotiations)

NICHOLAS CHANDLER

118 Cordova Way, Austin, Texas 74960
Phone: (888) 555-1212 ■ Fax: (888) 732-0005
E-Mail: NChandler@aol.com

EXECUTIVE PROFILE

CORPORATE PLANNING / RETAIL OPERATIONS / P&L FORECASTING / HR MANAGEMENT
QUALITY CONTROL / EXPENDITURE ANALYSIS AND MANAGEMENT / MARKET DEVELOPMENT

➤ Vision-driven leadership; team-oriented management style focused on employee motivation and morale.
➤ Strategic and financial planning expertise under stringent budgetary controls; emphasis on maximizing personnel and financial resources while focusing on bottom-line profitability.
➤ Strong analytical decision-making skills; effective problem identification, analysis, and resolution.
➤ Ability to effectively manage all aspects of cash flow, sales growth, and costs for operations, consumables, maintenance, and labor; consistently achieved highest margin of controllable profit over long-term period.
➤ Instrumental in reviving business and expanding operations into previously undeveloped territories.
➤ Extensive knowledge of computer hardware/software, including Internet and Web-based applications as well as Web site design.

EXPERIENCE

PRESIDENT / CHIEF EXECUTIVE OFFICER
1986-PRESENT
BIG BLUE MUFFINS *dba* MAMA CORBIN'S BAKED GOODS, Austin, Texas
Central Texas franchise operation for one of the nation's leading baked goods retailers.

Direct all aspects of the daily operations of the franchise, including site prospecting/selection, lease review and negotiation, planning, construction, staffing, cost control, quality control, sales, marketing, merchandising, P&L, balance sheets, in-house accounting, and outsourced legal activities. Develop innovative sales/marketing strategies, product promotions, cross-promotions, and corporate sponsorship agreements designed to increase revenue and enhance company image. Assemble a loyal, results-oriented management team and improve long-term employee retention through top-down motivation, incentive, and satisfaction programs.

CAREER HIGHLIGHTS:

- Joined the one-year-old company as the Executive Vice President and Chief Operating Officer. Promoted to President and CEO in March 1995.
- Ignited stagnant business operations by defining long-term company goals and utilizing employee motivation to attain those goals.
- Expanded operations from 2 to 10 store locations in just 5 years; took the company from a loss in its first year to a profit each subsequent year.
- Developed and wrote the company's computer-based cost control program.
- Wrote the company's employee handbook, safety manual, and all control related system material.
- Increased company sales 226% over the first 10 years by developing a sales analysis system designed to examine in greater focus consumer purchasing trends, enabling locations to center on products that were "hot" at any given time (similar to a "just-in-time" inventory).
- Developed a detailed employee and location review process which focused on increasing sales and customer satisfaction. Later implemented a company-wide feedback system targeting the same areas.
- Reduced payroll by 8% in the first year by developing and implementing an ongoing efficiency training program which incorporated the use of efficiency guidelines for all job descriptions.
- Reduced product cost by 5% in first year as COO by evaluating existing supply expenditures and implementing a cost control system.
- Sustained operating/payroll costs among lowest in industry while maintaining high customer service level.
- Developed original programs to enhance loss control and inventory control functions.
- Completely computerized the company's home office by analyzing existing processes and anticipating future growth needs.

EXPERIENCE
(continued)

CENTRAL REGIONAL MANAGER   **1979-1986**
MAMA CORBIN'S BAKED GOODS, Austin, Texas
Recruited as Store Manager for the company's 7th location (now has over 380)... promoted to Austin District Manager after 2½ years... promoted to Central District Manager/Director of Training after 4 years.

Directed company-owned and franchise store operations encompassing 50 to 70 locations in a 9-state region. Assisted in the development and implementation of company policies and procedures; maintained quality control measures and profit/sales revenue objectives. Recruited, hired, trained, and evaluated management personnel; motivated employees through effective and open communication. Prepared and analyzed P&L statements; ensured that all stores performed effectively, efficiently, and profitably.

CAREER HIGHLIGHTS:

- Coordinated 50 new store openings, including site planning, staffing, and development and implementation of marketing and promotional campaigns.
- Facilitated the monumental task of converting over 50 stores to a new product. Retrained over 500 store managers and staff in the handling and production of the new product.
- Served as business advisor to corporate management and franchise owners.

NEIL D. RHODES
56 Kenny Avenue
Redondo Beach, California 92126
Email: Nrhos@msn.com

Phone: (714) 331-8975   Fax: (714) 331-8976

SENIOR EXECUTIVE PROFILE
President / Chief Executive Officer / Chief Operating & Financial Officer
Early Stage, High-Growth & Turnaround Organizations

Cross-functional, cross-industry leadership success in General Management and Financial Management. Keen ability to conceive strategy, execute business plans and deliver profitable financial results in competitive markets nationwide. Dynamic leadership, mentoring, negotiations and investor relations performance. Successful in developing systems and processes to improve productivity, quality and efficiency. MBA Degree.

PROFESSIONAL EXPERIENCE:

PRESIDENT & CHIEF OPERATING OFFICER   1986 to 1997
CASUAL SHOPPE STORES, INC., Los Angeles, California

<u>Scope of Responsibility</u>: *$347 Million, 577-Store Retail Chain, 22 States Nationwide (Publicly-Held)*

Promoted from Executive Vice President to President & COO within first six months of hire with full strategic planning, operating, marketing, technology, human resources, distribution and P&L responsibility. Leveraged market and product opportunities to lead the organization through a period of accelerated growth and nationwide expansion.

Organizational Leadership & Financial Achievements

- Built Casual Shoppe from 220 stores, 1600 employees and sales of $110 million to **577 stores, 5000 employees and annual sales of $347 million**. Positioned Casual Shoppe as a dominant player in markets nationwide.
- Created the corporation's Investor Relations function, expanded market coverage and led road show presentations in the U.S. and London.
- **Delivered up to 15% annual pre-tax profit** in one of the most competitive industries in the U.S.
- Integrated and automated administrative and support functions for a **20% ($5 million) cost reduction**.
- **Negotiated over $40 million** in corporate credit facilities at favorable rates and fees.

Operating, Technology & Marketing Achievements

- Implemented state-of-the-art information systems to automate core business, financial control and reporting, merchandising, store operations, real estate and administrative functions. Upgraded technologies to meet growth demands.
- **Increased private label product mix from 5% to 20%**, improving customer perceived merchandise value and supported long-term revenue and profit gains.
- Leveraged inventory investment by expanding distribution center capacity, increasing throughput 50% and **improving overall productivity 30%**.
- Established human resource function to enhance recruitment and training competencies, enrich employee benefit and compensation programs, and strengthen employee retention while reducing annual costs.
- Launched a high-profile, multimedia marketing campaign and captured preeminent market positioning in the greater Los Angeles and Orange County region. **Operated one of the most successful and most profitable retail chains in the area.**

SENIOR EXECUTIVE VICE PRESIDENT - OPERATIONS & FINANCE 1983 to 1986
HALGREN STORES CORPORATION, New York, New York

Scope of Responsibility: *$700 Million, 800-Store Chain, 49 States & 10,000 Employees (Privately-Held)*

Member of 3-person Senior Executive Team and Chief Operating Officer directing finance, systems, distribution, human resources, construction and store operations nationwide. **Joint P&L** responsibility.

- Spearheaded an aggressive operations, revenue and profit improvement program to strengthen competitive market lead and deliver world class operating, financial management and merchandising systems.
- **Delivered pre-tax profit margins of 15%**, reduced store labor costs 12% and significantly enhanced quality of customer service. Revitalized store renovation program and reduced costs 24%.
- Innovated first computerized point-of-sale system, revolutionizing the company's product sales and financial systems.

VICE PRESIDENT - FINANCE & SOURCING 1982 to 1983
ASHWORTH, LTD. , New York, New York

Scope of Responsibility: *Corporate Finance, Systems & Global Product Sourcing (Publicly-Held)*

- Turned around loss at domestic manufacturing facility to **20% ROI within six months**.
- Acquired Hong Kong agent to reduce product costs, improve apparel quality and expedite U.S. delivery.

PRESIDENT & CHIEF EXECUTIVE OFFICER 1979 to 1981
EXECUTIVE VICE PRESIDENT - OPERATIONS 1975 to 1979
LAWSON'S SPORTING GOODS, Trenton, New Jersey

Scope of Responsibility: *$230 Million, 92-Store Retail Chain, 13 States Nationwide (Publicly-Held)*

- Led the organization during rapid expansion, including five acquisitions and an aggressive internal growth program. **Increased revenues 130% over six years**.
- Initiated private label program and successfully launched new marketing campaign to expand penetration.

Several years' previous **financial management** experience with two other W.R. Grace divisions.

MANAGEMENT SKILLS PROFILE:

- Strategic Planning & Development
- Acquisitions & Strategic Alliances
- Financial Planning, Control & Analysis
- Multi-Site Operations Management
- Information Systems & Telecommunications

- Manufacturing & Retail Operations
- New Business & Venture Development
- Marketing & Sales Leadership
- Training & Leadership Development
- Multi-Channel Global Distribution

EDUCATION & CERTIFICATION:

MBA - Finance - New York University
BBA - Accounting, City University of New York
Certified Public Accountant - New York & New Jersey

QUENTIN GONZALEZ

1355 East 188th Street
New York, NY 10037
(212) 555-8795 ☎ (212) 555-7891 [FAX]

HIGH-IMPACT ENTERTAINMENT INDUSTRY EXECUTIVE
Music • Television • Advertising
Lifestyle/Image Development • Management • Marketing • Team Building • Start-ups

Multi-dimensional management and marketing professional with a comprehensive understanding of the culture, operations and practices of the marketplace. A strong, resourceful leader and decision maker with a record of new product success and established product enhancement. Accomplished negotiator, expert at networking key decision-makers at the highest levels. Financial, strategic analysis/planning and problem-solving acumen combine to assess, establish and master new and existing markets.

PROFESSIONAL HISTORY

A.H.O.R.A. (A Host Of Raza Artists) Recordings, New York, NY   1995 - Present
Independent, fully-funded start-up record company, marketing bilingual artists to the pop audience.

Executive Vice President/General Manager
Report to President. Manage day-to-day operations of fully-funded, independent start-up record label distributed through Pentagram Group Distribution. Supervise staff of 20 professionals in Marketing, Promotion, Sales, Publicity Finance, Legal and Business Affairs, A&R, Creative Services, Production and Administration. Direct liaison with *Pentagram Holdings Inc.* senior management to maximize potential of joint venture. Hired all staff, including CFO. Negotiated artist contracts and approved all marketing strategies and budgets. Ran weekly meetings with distribution company to ensure priorities and release dates.

- Designed the strategy and led the label to viability in 18 months; exposed young, bilingual talent to the mainstream and established strong market niche in radio, retail and the media.

- Led development of initial five year business plan in concert with president and Goldman Sachs investors; determined templates for artist and producer agreements; developed company benefits package and employee manual.

AVANTI RECORDS GROUP, New York, NY   1989 - 1994
East coast record label with $175MM in annual sales, 120 employees, and an artist roster of 88.

Senior Vice President of Marketing
Reported to Chief Executive Officer. Supervised marketing of recording artists. Managed a staff of 22 in the development and implementation of all strategic planning and marketing. Accountable for budgets in excess of $28MM.

- Spearheaded the creation and implementation of innovative television advertising campaigns for major roster artists.

- Created and supervised the artist development and marketing of major pop artists to multi-platinum sales.

RCA VICTOR RECORDS, New York, NY   1986 - 1989
East coast label that developed new artists and marketed the renowned *Village Gate* jazz label. Annual sales of $75MM and 36 employees.

Vice President of Marketing

Headed Marketing Department in newly established division. Hired a staff of six to support the marketing of 54 artists. Conducted weekly Marketing and Planning meetings. Created and delivered monthly sales presentations to distribution company's branch network. Conceived and presented large scale audio/visual presentations to the industry.

- Led and directed hands-on marketing and artist development of Enrico Caruso, Rudy Vallee, Little Richard, Dale Evans, Sons of the Pioneers and Mick Jagger to superstar sales levels.

- Conceived and implemented retail marketing promotions and unique cross merchandising programs that accessed and accrued sales beyond the standard distribution channels.

CHROME PONY RECORDS, New York, NY   1983 - 1986
One of the most celebrated "boutique" labels in the music industry.

National Director of Marketing

Managed all marketing. Determined strategy, control, and implementation of marketing plans; accountable for multimillion dollar budgets. Worked closely with Branch Distribution executives to distribute releases through SONY Records. Established and managed freelance creative staff in the design of all merchandising materials, advertising, and album packaging.

- Supervised marketing during transition from independent to major (***CBS***) distribution to realize biggest yearly sales ever of over $90MM in 1985.

- Created and directed marketing campaigns for Mariah Carey, Billy Joel, and Linda Ronstadt that achieved multi-million unit sales levels.

EMI RECORDS, New York, NY   1981 - 1983
Major international record label, with over $250MM annual sales, a subsidiary of *EKG Entertainment*.

Product Manager

Developed and implemented marketing strategies for roster of 15 new artists; determined budget, sales plans, and advertising campaigns for each release. Researched and recommended video producers and directors. Subsequently assigned to stars Donna Summer and Aretha Franklin. Developed marketing plans for multi-platinum debut album.

JACK SPRAT TELEVISION PRODUCTIONS, Burbank, CA   1977 - 1982

Associate Producer

Programmed music and booked talent for a one-hour weekly series.

Concurrently, **Associate Producer** for several specials:
- New Years' Rockin' With the Stars (NBC)
- American Music Awards (ABC), Academy of Country Music Awards (NBC)

EDUCATION

B.A., Marketing, New York University, Stern School of Business   1977

DEBRA SHADE, C.P.A.

(904) 738-2146 • 660 Forest Lane • DeLand, Florida 32724

SENIOR OPERATING, MANAGEMENT & FINANCE EXECUTIVE
Startup, Turnaround, High-Growth Organizations

MBA, BSBA and demonstrated record in the successful development, leadership and improvement of:

- Behavior Health Care Organizations
- Pharmaceutical Organizations
- Clinical Laboratories
- Foundations
- Primary Care & Physicians Offices
- Capital Financing thru Bond Issues

- Standard & Poor Financial Ratings
- Profit & Not-For-Profit Organizations
- Entitlement Programs
- Partial Hospitalization Programs
- Environmental Services
- Insurance / Billing Programs

Financial Management

- Held full accountability for overall financial management of multi million dollar companies reporting directly to President/CEO.
- Constructed industrial revenue bonds and health facility revenue bonds of $13 million.
- Established an Annual Gift Giving Campaign for a not-for-profit organization.
- Managed and oversaw all audits and accounting records for 2 HUD operations.
- Created, formulated and implemented a Foundation for a not-for-profit organization.
- Structured, negotiated and managed complex financing, investment, lending and contractual agreements.
- Restructured financial structures for a Standard & Poor rating.

General Management

- Created and developed organizational models and lead matrix management systems transcending all core business, operating, financial, and human resource functions.
- Coordinated and directed all construction, capital improvements and renovation initiatives for 4 buildings from concept through Certificate of Occupancy (5,000-75,000 sq. ft.).
- Conducted MIS feasibility studies, prepared RFPs, managed installation of IBM 23/IBM36/Risk 6000 systems, LAN/WANs, and coordinated all conversions while maintaining data integrity.
- Developed and established models and infrastructures for the launch of 3 pharmacies and 2 laboratories.
- Structured, instituted, and monitored Medicare/Medicaid Entitlement Programs.

Operations Management

- Oversaw all cross functional operations for wellness, dietary, safety and security programs, housekeeping operations, facility maintenance, and business office operations.
- Structured and instituted transportation systems for large multi-site health care facilities.
- Managed a staff of 17 department managers and 150 staff members.
- Established a Resource & Development Committee to create a separate foundation titled "Because I Care".

Human Resources

- Setup corporate-wide incentive compensation programs to improve employee morale and productivity.
- Coordinated paperwork and applications for immigration to hire aliens.
- Recruited, selected and appointed Board Members for not-for-profit organizations.

Regulatory / Credentialing

- Positioned start-up and existing facilities for JCAHO compliance.
- Established and conducted Physician Credentialing programs for managed care contractors.
- Oversaw Department of Children & Family Services' contracts and administrator monitorings.

Industry-Wide Leadership

- Serve as Chair and member of numerous state-wide committees formed to improve outcome measures, performance issues, contracting, and select MIS endorsements.
- Conduct numerous state-wide workshops on all phases of health care facility management.

PROFESSIONAL EXPERIENCE:

CONSULTANT
Consulting For Financial Solutions, Inc., DeLand, Florida   1995 to Present
    Manatee Glens, Bradenton, Florida
    Mental Health Care Inc., Tampa, Florida
    ACT Corporation, Daytona Beach, Florida

SENIOR VICE PRESIDENT / CFO
Lakeside Alternatives, Inc., Orlando, Florida   1990 to 1997

CHIEF FINANCIAL OFFICER
Act Corporation, Daytona Beach, Florida   1986 to 1990

TREASURER / CONTROLLER
Modernage Kitchens, Inc., Holly Hill, Florida   1981-1986

EDUCATION / PROFESSIONAL DEVELOPMENT:

MBA – ROLLINS COLLEGE – 1997

BSBA – UNIVERSITY OF CENTRAL FLORIDA – 1977

Hundreds of courses primarily in Health Care including Managed Care and Medicaid Managed Care

PROFESSIONAL ASSOCIATIONS:

National Society of Fund Raising Executives
American Institute of Certified Public Accountants
Florida Institute of Certified Public Accountants
Florida Council for Community Mental Health

CIVIC AFFILIATIONS:

Mental Health Association, Orange County Member
Center for Visually Impaired, Past Treasurer and Board Member
Daytona Beach Community College, Adjunct Instructor

SAMUEL MAYES

777 Circle Drive
Savannah, Georgia 30000

(222) 222-2222 home
(222) 222-1111 office
mayes@aol.com E-mail

EXECUTIVE MANAGEMENT
CFO / Controller / Strategic Planning
Certified Public Accountant

PROFILE

Dynamic management career in growth, start-up, turnaround, or crisis environments. Significant background in problem identification, problem solving, and strategy development. Proven and verifiable success in arbitrating conflict, negotiating attainable goals, and implementing informative programs. Entrepreneurial, energetic, and committed.

- Unify diverse groups to achieve corporate goals; outstanding interpersonal, communication, motivational, and organizational skills.

- Analyze organization's philosophy, how it relates to management techniques, and the historical impact it has rendered through observation of attitudes and ethics of management and staff. Devise recommendations and procedures to reposition company and correct functional as well as operational disorders (MBO).

- Combine strategic planning and business development expertise with strong technical qualifications to establish financial operations responsive to long-range corporate objectives for growth and profitability.

- Direct and manage investments for venture capitalists. Interpret vision and examine operational elements to evaluate enterprise's potential for success.

- Maintain interests and knowledge in a wide realm of business applications including retail, wholesale, software, distribution, manufacturing, consulting, and management.

EXPERIENCE

MAYES & ASSOCIATES, Savannah, Georgia   1985 to Present
President
- Perform functions of CFO, Controller, Tax Advisor, and Administrator for clients.
- Evaluate and structure mechanism for turnarounds, start-ups, bankruptcy, mergers, and acquisitions; compile business plans and business valuations; prepare industrial authority loan packages and prospectus.
- Create more efficient information systems, identify strengths, and determine strategic plan for cost effective operations in the *medical, healthcare, distribution, computer software, manufacturing, retail and wholesale industries.*

SAMUEL MAYES

EXPERIENCE *(Continued)*

MAYES & ASSOCIATES *(Continued)*

<u>Accomplishments</u>
- Envisioned and developed customized management consulting services; marketed services via writing newspaper columns, public speaking, radio, and TV appearances.
- Redirected and instituted strategic plans to bring irrigation equipment manufacturing company out of Chapter 11 Bankruptcy within 3 years.
- Activated totally integrated manufacturing software package with forecasting capacity and real time information ability (TQM); reorganization attracted high-level investors for this state-of-the-art railcar repair and manufacturing facility.
- Instituted activity based cost analysis of wholesale and retail parts distribution company resulting in realignment of all pricing policies and procedures to regain market share and return to profitable operations; grew from $10M to $20M in sales in 6 years.

ALL AMERICAN DESIGN, Atlanta, Georgia   1984 to 1985
   Controller
- Reengineered software development company; established chart of authority, opened cross-departmental communications, and implemented zero-based budgeting to improve profits.

THE PEPSI-COLA COMPANY, Dallas, Texas   1977 to 1984
   Assistant Controller, The Wine Spectrum
   Senior Internal Auditor, Soft Drink Company

PROFESSIONAL AFFILIATIONS

American Institute of Certified Public Accountants
Georgia Society of Certified Public Accountants
Institute of Management Accountants, *Past President*
Who's Who in Executives and Professionals

EDUCATION

NORTH CAROLINA STATE UNIVERSITY, Raleigh, North Carolina
   Bachelor of Science, Business Administration

FREDERICK MANSFIELD

3256 West Mountain View
Denver, Colorado 50333

Phone   (303) 744-9829
Fax   (303) 744-4450

SENIOR EXECUTIVE PROFILE
President / Chief Operating Officer / General Manager
Start-Up & Emerging Growth Ventures / Operating Turnarounds / High-Growth Corporations
MBA Degree

- Strategic Planning & Direction
- Capital Investment & Financing
- Road Show & Investor Presentations
- Mergers, Acquisitions & Alliances

- Sales & Marketing Leadership
- Key Account Relationship Management
- Multi-Site Operations & Distribution
- Information Systems & Technology

PROFESSIONAL EXPERIENCE:

BLUE CHIP COMPANY, Denver, Colorado   1995 to Present

President / Chief Operating Officer / Minority Owner
Recruited by Board Chairman to lead 1995 merger with Specialty Foods Company. Challenged to integrate two diverse corporate cultures into a consolidated organization, spearhead expansion, develop new opportunities and lead the organization through accelerated growth. Full strategic, marketing, operating and P&L responsibility.

- Created new $70 million corporation with 250 employees. Expanded distribution throughout Ohio, New York, Pennsylvania and West Virginia and delivered a 9% increase in total revenue.
- Presented major retail customers with new and innovative marketing concepts including "Store-Within-The-Store." Led to specialty food sections in 50 stores region-wide.
- Developed strategic direction and operating plans to deliver 67% growth over next five years.
- Won Board approval and led implementation of a $400,000 capital investment in information technology. Resulted in a $120,000 reduction in purchasing costs, $150,000 savings in distribution costs and 9% gain in productivity. Launched EDI initiative with key customers.

NOTE: *Board Member & Minority Owner of Blue Chip Company since 1993. Selected for operating management position by Chairman following merger.*

VIE DA LIVRE, INC. (dba Pizza Experience), Chicago, Illinois   1992 to 1995

President / General Manager / Owner
Launched an entrepreneurial venture with business partner. Identified niche market opportunity, negotiated financing, acquired franchise and established full service operations. Spearheaded high-profile advertising/promotions, negotiated leasing agreements and contracts, and created innovative employee recruitment and retention programs. Supervised up to 100 employees.

- Built new venture from start-up to $7 million in annual sales and 8 operating locations.
- Achieved and maintained unit sales twice the industry average based on consistently superior product quality and customer service.

NOTE: *Resigned full-time operating management position to accept opportunity with Blue Chip Company. Continue as Majority Owner & Board Director.*

NORTHERN OHIO BOTTLING COMPANY, Toledo, Ohio   1986 to 1992

Vice President / General Manager - PepsiCo (1990 to 1992)
President / General Manager - Private Investor Group (1986 to 1990)
Senior Operating Executive with full P&L for the strategic planning, marketing, customer service, human resources, operations and finance of this $241 million division. Responsible for 12 distribution centers, 2 production facilities, 700 associates and annual case sales of 26.2 million.

- Increased sales by 80% over six years. Recognized as the only major bottler in the region to achieve market share growth and positive share swings against all major competition.
- Improved cash operating profit by an average of 21% annually and 300% over six years.
- Trained, developed and led a team of top-producing sales and management professionals.

NOTE: *Led transition following 1990 acquisition by PepsiCo. Retained full operating, marketing and P&L responsibility under new ownership.*

MID-SOUTH BEVERAGE COMPANY, Dallas, Texas   1985

Vice President Marketing & Sales
Recruited by President of regional Coca-Cola bottler to revitalize and expand sales, marketing and promotional campaigns. Reversed stagnant sales performance, restored credibility with key accounts and generated strong profit performance.

- Delivered 15% revenue growth in one year to achieve $300 million in annual revenues.

NATIONAL BOTTLING COMPANY OF ST. LOUIS, St. Louis, Missouri   1983 to 1985

Vice President Marketing & Sales
Led successful turnaround and market expansion for this $85 million bottler. Orchestrated new product launches, revitalized sales and marketing teams, and streamlined internal reporting and administrative processes.

- Returned company to profitability following five years of consecutive losses. Increased sales 32% and gained equal market share with major competitor.

BALL CORPORATION, San Ramon, California   1978 to 1983

Vice President & General Manager - West Coast Operations
Established market research and consulting firm providing advertising and promotional services to consumer packaged goods companies. Established West Coast operation, recruited/trained staff, and launched an aggressive marketing and business development initiative.

- Captured a 600% increase in sales revenues over five years.

SCHWEPPES BOTTLERS, Carmel, Indiana   1977 to 1978

Vice President Marketing & Sales

- Increased regional sales volume by 30% and developed 2 key middle managers into key account positions, further accelerating revenue performance across all key accounts.

COCA-COLA ENTERPRISES   1972 to 1977

Region Manager, Chicago, Illinois (1975 to 1977)
District Manager, Minneapolis/St. Paul, Minnesota (1974 to 1975)
District Manager, McLean, Virginia (1973 to 1974)
Assistant Marketing Manager, Purchase, New York (1972 to 1973)

KRAFT FOODS INTERNATIONAL - DAIRY DIVISION   1968 to 1972

Assistant Southern Region Manager, White Plains, New York (1972)
Account Manager, Los Angeles, California (1971)
Sales Supervisor, Los Angeles, California (1970 to 1971)
Sales Representative, San Francisco, California (1968 to 1970)

EDUCATION: **SANTA CLARA UNIVERSITY**, Santa Clara, California
              MBA (Marketing & Management), 1968
              BA (History), 1965

DAVID WATSON
250 Christmas Court • Los Gatos, CA 95000
(408) 555-0000

OBJECTIVE: Position as a Golf Course Superintendent.

QUALIFICATIONS:
- Over 20 years of relevant experience, including four years as golf course superintendent and two years as assistant superintendent.
- Knowledgeable in all facets of turfgrass maintenance: grow-in to full-scale operations.
- Proven management/leadership, organizational, and project completion skills.
- Effective financial planning skills; ability to prepare and maintain budgets.
- Experience in handling purchasing, including negotiating price and delivery with vendors.
- Ability to identify and resolve problems; follow up as needed to ensure completion.
- High level of self-motivation and ability to motivate others to achieve goals.

PROFESSIONAL EXPERIENCE:

First Tee Golf Center, San Jose, CA   1994-Present
SUPERINTENDENT
Directed initial development and currently manage all aspects of 26-acre golf center operation and golf club maintenance.
- Assumed responsibility for completion of grow-in process after contractor left project unfinished and improperly done; tasks included replanting extensive areas of greens/tees and finalizing entire irrigation system.
- Maintain 3.5 acres of driving range grass tees in first-class condition, topseeding one acre per month on an ongoing rotational basis.
- Develop and implement plans that enable the center to remain open without interruption.
- Conduct center activities in accordance with strict budgetary requirements, making best possible use of available resources.

Lost Horizon Golf Course, Los Altos, CA   1992-1994
SUPERINTENDENT
Managed 9-hole golf course and club house maintenance.
- Constructed two lakes and raised greens quality to level not attained in 25 years, using personal technique which involved verticutting, regular fertilization, and light top-dressing monthly.
- Installed 550-foot well and connected it to existing irrigation system.
- Relocated twenty 25-foot palm trees to new site using only in-house labor to control costs.

Reef Islands Hotel Properties   1982-1992
Largo Marina Resort/Royal Cruise Hotels, Reef Islands Harbor, CA
DIRECTOR OF MAINTENANCE & GROUNDS SERVICES
Directed maintenance of 14-acre grounds and administration/supervision of 3 kitchens, 2 restaurants and 275 guest rooms at full-service, four-star resort hotel. Supervised 14 employees.
- Re-landscaped several areas around hotel, including re-design of large patio.
- Directed $420,000 restaurant/bar renovation and supervised major renovation of hotel facilities while supporting ongoing operations.

Prior Experience:

Jefferson Golf and Country Club, Jefferson, IL (2 years)
ASSISTANT SUPERINTENDENT
Assisted golf course superintendent in administration/coordination of 235-acre championship course, driving range, swimming pools, tennis courts, and club house.
- Supervised crew of eight employees; established and maintained regular program for all pesticide spraying.
- Acted as mechanic, maintaining essential equipment in satisfactory condition.

Hedges Nursery, Capitola, CA (8 years)
LANDSCAPER, CONSTRUCTION, SALES

EDUCATION:
- Turf Management Short Course, Cal Poly, San Luis Obispo, CA
- Hotel Management Short Course, Cornell University, New York
- Physical Education/Horticulture, Cabrillo College
- AA Hotel & Restaurant Management, Lakeland Community College

CERTIFICATIONS:
- Qualified Applicator, certified by California Department of Pesticide Regulation
- California Certified Nurseryman

PROFESSIONAL AWARDS & AFFILIATIONS:
- "Coral Reef Beautiful" Award, 1987 & 1988
- Golf Course Superintendents Association of America
- Golf Course Superintendents Association of Northern California
- United States Golf Association
- Northern California Golf Association
- Association of Facilities and Plant Operating Engineers
- Professional Grounds Maintenance Society of America
- California Association of Nurserymen

COMMUNITY INVOLVEMENT:
- Served on Cabrillo College Horticultural Curriculum Advisory Board.
- Delivered presentations to local garden clubs.

Stephen Marney

3 Higgins Street
Belleville, Illinois 62220
(618) 555-4242

Golf Course Superintendent
Public, Private, and Championship Courses

*Renovation • Construction • Maintenance
Start-Up Course Management
Environmental/Wildlife Preservation*

Key Projects

CHAMPIONS TRAIL, Fairview Heights, Illinois   1996-Present

Superintendent: Manage construction and grow-in of this Bob and Ky Goalby design featuring zoysia fairways, bluegrass rough, and Caddo/Crenshaw greens. This 27-hole facility opened on schedule to the public in September 1997.

THE MISSOURI BLUFFS GOLF CLUB, St. Charles, Missouri   1995-1996

Superintendent: Completed the grow-in of this Tom Fazio design featuring zoysia fairways and tees, bluegrass/fescue roughs, and Crenshaw greens. Course was cleared from 300 acres of mature timber resting atop a 120-foot bluff overlooking the Missouri River. Course required extensive environmental and wildlife management. Ranked the #1 public facility in Missouri and third Best New Public Course by Golf Digest in Dec. 1995. Host of the Gateway Nike Tour event.

EASTERN HILLS COUNTRY CLUB, Dallas, Texas   1993-1995

Superintendent: Brought in as part of a new management team to rebuild all areas of this 40-year-old, 18-hole private golf club. Directed the reconstruction of tees, greens, bunkers, and irrigation system. Initiated a long-range plan and rebuilt the maintenance facility. This property is on the largest lake in the metroplex with an extensive fish and game population and is considered an environmentally-sensitive area that requires great care regarding chemical usage and run-off.

BENT TREE COUNTRY CLUB, Dallas, Texas   1992-1993

Assistant Superintendent: Managed all aspects of daily operations for one of the metroplex's premier golf clubs, including scheduling, inventory, crews, mechanics and tournament set-up. Annual budget: $987,000. Home of the Reunion Classic Senior PGA event (1985-1988) and the LPGA Mary Kay Classic (1981-1984).

Key Projects (cont.)

FOUR SEASONS RESORT & CLUB, Irving, Texas   1991-1992

Assistant Superintendent: One day a week, managed 36 holes; five days a week, managed 18 holes and 25 people. Responsible for chemical programs, budgeting, monthly Greens Committee presentations to Mr. Byron Nelson, and all scheduling of duties. Annual budget: $1 million. Home of the PGA's GTE/Byron Nelson Classic.

Involved with major drainage projects, greens renovation and expansion, tree program, and grow-in responsibilities of a D.A. Weibring re-design of hole #15. *This was the first Caddo/Crenshaw green played in the country.*

Maintained Tif 419 fairways and roughs, penncross bentgrass greens, and rye overseed in winter for the spring tournament. Built a research green for Dr. Engelke of Texas A&M with six varieties of bentgrass.

COUNTRY CLUB OF MISSOURI, Columbia, Missouri   1990-1991

Second Assistant: Completed major bunker renovation projects. Annual budget: $275,000 (+capital). Grounds consisted of zoysia japonica fairways, fescue rough, and penncross bentgrass greens. Home of the Shelter Insurance Open mini-tour event.

TWIN OAKS COUNTRY CLUB, Springfield, Missouri   1988

Grounds Staff *(during college)*

Education

UNIVERSITY OF MISSOURI - COLUMBIA
B.S. in Horticulture (Turf Grass Emphasis), December, 1990

DRURY COLLEGE, Springfield, Missouri
B.A. in Biology/Chemistry, May, 1989

Honors/Activities: Golf Course Superintendents Association of America, Class B Member; Jacobsen Turf Internship, 1990 (one of 30 students selected nationwide); 4-year scholarship letterman, All-District Honors, Drury College Golf Team; Founder & President, Drury College Environmental Club; 4-year Co-Captain, Drury College Soccer Team; Soccer Coach, YMCA

Coursework: Plant Biology, Plant Physiology, Field Zoology, Biochemistry, Woody Ornamentals, Plant Propagation, Plant Environments, Soils, Turf, Garden Flowers, Agriculture, Advanced Plant Pathology & Entomology, Advanced Genetics, Microbiology

References, Testimonials, and Portfolio Available Upon Request

RACHEL B. SALIZAR

457 Tee-Off Drive
Milton Square, Missouri 65321
(647) 548-3117

PLAYER PROFILE

Golf professional with a successful tournament track record, managing pro shop, providing golf instruction, coordinating tournaments, and directing golf course operations with a strong knowledge of business aspects.

- ❖ Golf Instruction: Instructing (12 years) individuals, groups, clinics, juniors and playing lessons; experience with all skill levels (beginners to tour players); knowledge of state-of-the-art video equipment.
- ❖ Tournament Administration: Coordinating tournaments; organizing corporate and small business tournaments; facilitating league play; supervising men's club activities and tournaments
- ❖ Pro Shop Management: Supervise personnel; price and promote sales; represent equipment and services; merchandising and inventory control; club fitting, repair, regrip, and reshaft
- ❖ Golf Course Operations: Directing golf club activities; maintaining course, club building, and equipment

Certification/Professional Designation
PGA of America Class A-8
Scoring Average 72.54

PLAYER EXPERIENCE

SOUTHVIEW GOLF COURSE   April 1993 - Present
Belton, Missouri

ASSISTANT GOLF PROFESSIONAL
Manage pro shop, coordinating tournament and junior golf programs, and overseeing snack bar operations of an 18-hole privately owned public facility with 40,000+ rounds per year, open 364 days a year. Supervise a staff of 18 and monitor a $500,000 operating budget.
- ➢ Schedule an annual average of 103 golf lessons, 28 series lessons, 9 playing lessons, and 5 clinics/29 juniors.
- ➢ Coordinate 59 corporate and small business tournaments annually and 11 weekly league plays consisting of 25/60 players each.

PIPER DRIVING RANGE   March 1992 - April 1993
Lee's Summit, Missouri

HEAD TEACHING PROFESSIONAL
Directed all teaching programs, planning and conducting individual and group lessons/clinics.
- ➢ Within 7 months, instructed 125 lessons, 37 series, and 15 playing lessons.

PLAYER EXPERIENCE   (Continued)

BOB STONE DRIVING RANGE   January 1990 - March 1992
Independence, Missouri

ASSISTANT TEACHING PROFESSIONAL

Coordinated all junior golf programs.
➤ Assisted in the design, promotion and start-up of the facility.
➤ Averaged annually 140 lessons, 46 series, 22 playing lessons, and 3 junior clinics for high schools with 35/40 students.

CRACKERNECK GOLF COURSE   January 1980 - January 1990
Independence, Missouri

ASSISTANT GOLF PROFESSIONAL

Managed golf shop operations of a privately owned public golf facility to include a golf cart fleet (65) and staff of 15.
➤ Increased play 200% by improving operations and developing techniques to eliminate slow play.
➤ Opened and managed the first pro shop at Crackerneck Golf Course.

CONTINUED PROFESSIONAL DEVELOPMENT

PGA of America
■ Business School I (GPTP Level I)   November 1995
■ Business School II (GPTP Level II)   March 1996

OTHER SIGNIFICANT ENDEAVORS

PGA Midwest Section: Tournament Committee   1996-1997

Tournaments:	Midwest Section, PGA Assistant's Championship	1997
	River Oaks Golf Course, Grandview, MO (Course Record 61)	1995
	Carthage Invitational - 1st Place (69)	1995
	Chapel Woods Golf Course, Lee's Summit, MO (Course Record 64)	1991
	Pro-Pro - 1st Place (62)	1990
	Crackerneck Golf Course, Independence, MO (Course Record 61)	1990
	Midwest Tournament of Champions - 1st Place (70)	1989
Qualified:	Western Regional PGA Club Professional Championship	1997

DARREN M. MILLER

3928 Greensview Drive • Athens, Ohio 45701 • (614) 589-0000

"Darren is excellent at creating innovative lessons to provide cooperative learning opportunities for his students to think, explore, develop and share their own understandings ... he would make an excellent addition to any school staff."

– Susan Duncan, Supervisor
The Ohio State University, College of Education

PROFILE

Dedicated, resourceful teacher skilled in building rapport and respect with students. Possess a unique ability to establish a creative and stimulating classroom environment. Seeking a Social Studies teaching position with an interest in coaching high school debate.

EDUCATION & HONORS

THE OHIO STATE UNIVERSITY, Columbus, Ohio
Bachelor of Science in Education • Major in Social Studies Education

Major GPA: 3.36/4.0 • Dean's List • 1994 Barton Scholar • Golden Key National Honor Society

Certification: History, Economics, Political Science (9-12) • Comprehensive (7-8)

FIELD EXPERIENCE

Student Teacher – JEFFERSON HEIGHTS HIGH SCHOOL, Jefferson Heights, Ohio   Winter/Spring 1994
 • Taught US Government for general and college-prep students building a strong rapport and respect.
 • Developed and implemented creative lesson plans to foster interaction and participation by all students.

Freshman Early Experience Program – REDHALL HIGH SCHOOL, Redhall, Ohio   Spring 1991
 • Observed psychology and sociology classes and led class discussions.

PROFESSIONAL EXPERIENCE

Substitute Teacher – OREGON CITY SCHOOLS, Oregon, Ohio   1994-present
 • Effectively develop and implement lesson plans on short-term notice
 • Maintain a positive learning environment for students
 • Team-teach and fulfill day-to-day duties of regular teachers

Assistant Speech and Debate Coach – MIDDLEVILLE HIGH SCHOOL, Middleville, Ohio   1996-1997
Speech and Debate Advisor – MASON HIGH SCHOOL, Mason, Ohio   1994-1995
 • Supervised all functions of speech and debate teams from budgeting team funds to coaching practices
 • Coached practices for students of varied skills levels
 • Developed tournament schedule, coordinated transportation and chaperoned students on overnight tournaments
 • Directed and participated in various research projects
 • Completed team and school administrative tasks
 • Served as Assistant Speech & Debate Advisor 1995-96 school year for Middleville High School

ACTIVITIES & AFFILIATIONS

National Council for the Social Studies
National Debate Coaches Association
Ohio Council for the Social Studies
Volunteer Assistant Debate Advisor – Middleville High School, Middleville, Ohio, 1995-96

LORRAINE HAYSON

5432 Lake View Drive
Vickson, WA 98754
Home: 213-211-2111
Work: 213-213-2321

PROFESSION

Experienced Elementary Educator -- Career highlights include:

- Strengths in literacy development and early language acquisition for 2nd-language learners.
- Excellent record with multi-cultural, special needs, and at-risk students.
- Award-winning classroom management skills.
- Three years' experience as Mentor Teacher.

EDUCATION, CREDENTIAL

Master of Arts Degree in Education: Reading & Language Arts -- Redlands College
Bachelor of Arts Degree -- Wellington College
Undergraduate Credential Program -- University of Washington, Seattle
Multiple Subject Teaching Credential

PROFESSIONAL EXPERIENCE

VICKSON SCHOOL DISTRICT, Vickson, Washington   1983-Present

Fourteen years' teaching experience at Cleveland Elementary in assignments ranging from grades 1-5, including six years in Grade 2 and four years in Grade 5. Multi-ethnic population includes Hispanic, Asian, African-American, Pacific Rim, and East Indian, with a high percentage of Limited-English-Proficient (LEP) students.

- **Teaching Style:** Create an engaging learning environment featuring literature-based units with integrated curriculum, hands-on interactive lessons, multi-media technology, and use of portfolios to document students' growth. Structure whole group, small group, and individual instruction to accommodate different academic levels and learning styles. Encourage parent involvement through regular communications, biannual parent-teacher conferences, and classroom volunteerism.

- **Language Arts, Science, Math:** Facilitate emerging literacy through thematic units, SDAIE, Natural Approach, Language Experience Approach, Total Physical Response, Sheltered English, whole language, phonics-based reading instruction, and writing workshops. Wrote and received grant to establish classroom library for literacy. Employ AIMS activities to develop students' critical thinking skills. Emphasize real life applications in lesson planning.

- **Special Needs, At-Risk Students:** Experienced success with at-risk and learning disabled students (aggressive behavior, hyperactivity, dyslexia, dysphasia). Apply cooperative learning, cross-age tutoring, and peer tutoring to increase learning, self-esteem, and cross-cultural understanding. Advocate for RSP children, accessing resources which enabled them to improve test scores and graduate from RSP program.

- **Community Partnerships:** Partnered with community and business resources-- linked students with Boys and Girls Clubs, obtained volunteers for reading support, referred needy families to community agencies, worked with law enforcement and parents to form a much-needed traffic squad, secured representatives from business, government, and the medical community as guest speakers.

LANGUAGE

Speak conversational Spanish . . . international orientation ... extensive and frequent travel (Europe, Asia, Africa, South America, Canada) ... broad life experiences.

One hundred years from now it will not matter what my bank account was, the sort of house I lived in, or the kind of car I drove, but the world may be different because I was important in the life of a child.

--Anonymous

JERRY WILLS, MBA, Ph.D. • 115 North Union Boulevard • Colorado Springs, CO 80909
• Office - (719) 632-9050 • E-Mail: Jwills@MSN.com • WWW.jwills.com

FORMAL EDUCATION

Ph.D., Business Ethics - 1997
American University

MBA, Finance - 1981
Commencement Speaker
LaJolla University, LaJolla, California

Graduate Degree
Graduate School of Savings and Loan
Indiana University - 1979

Accredited in Accounting & Taxation
Accreditation Council for Accountancy &
Taxation, Inc.

Graduate, The Mediation Process - 1997

[A Training program in the theory and practice
of conflict management, utilizing Theocentric
values designed to measurably aid the system
of justice and the prospects of peace between
and among people in their daily lives.]

Lifetime Teaching Credential
State of California
Real Estate Finance and
Ethics in Real Estate Sales

Adjunct Faculty Member
Pikes Peak Community College
Blair College - City College
Mesa College - Southwestern College

AFFILIATIONS & MEMBERSHIPS

Member of the Board of Directors
Rotary Club of Colorado Springs

Chairman, Membership Development
Rotary Club of Colorado Springs

Member, Credentials, Ethics and Convention
Planning Committees
Rotary Club of Colorado Springs

PROFESSIONAL PROFILE

- Unique qualifications for Adjunct Faculty in Accounting, Bookkeeping and Ethics
- An accomplished public speaker and professional motivator
- Certified as a Teacher of Accounting, Bookkeeping and Business Ethics
- Extensive experience in writing, revising and consulting on tax issues
- Long-term consulting experience in Home-based Business Operations

RELEVANT PROFESSIONAL EXPERIENCE

Owner - Operator   *2/83- Present*

Home-Based Business Consultants, Colorado Springs, Colorado
- Prepare monthly write-up and business plans for small to large firms
- **Special Achievements:**
  - **Author of numerous professional articles on business plans**
  - **Co-author,** *"Code of Business Ethics for Small Businesses"*
  - **Featured public speaker in college classrooms**
  - **Quoted on a regular basis in** *The Wall Street Journal*

Adjunct Faculty   *5/62- Present*

Various Colleges in the Pikes Peak Region
- Instruct Finance, Accounting, and Computer Operations to college students
- **Special Achievements:**
  - **Adjunct Faculty Member of the Year - 1996**
  - **Twice honored as "Most Inspirational Teacher"**

President and Chief Executive Officer   *3/82- 3/85*

Fidelity Federal Savings and Loan Association, Galesburg, Illinois
- Directed all operations for this 25 office and $850,000,000 financial institution
- **Special Achievements:**
  - **One of the top 10 most profitable institutions in the United States**

President and Chief Executive Officer   *3/80-2/82*

Equality Savings and Loan Association, San Diego, California
- Directed all operation of this 2 office and $50,000,000 financial institution
- **Special Achievements:**
  - **Responsible for all start-up operations**
  - **Successfully sold this institution with a 300% return to investors**
  - **Twice served a Chair of the Secondary Market Committee**

Vice President and Manager, Major Lending   *3/75-3/80*

Old Dominion Federal Savings and Loan Association, San Diego, California
- Directed all Major Lending operation for this $1 billion dollar financial institution
- **Special Achievements:**
  - **Honor graduate, Graduate School of Savings & Loan**
  - **Successfully lead this organization to profitable status**

VOLUNTEER EXPERIENCE

- Past Vice-President, Rotary Club of Colorado Springs, Colorado
- Member, Membership, Credentials, Ethics and Convention Planning Committees
- Loaned Executive, United Way of Colorado Springs
- Soccer Coach, Pikes Peak Recreation District

REFERENCES AND FURTHER DATA ON REQUEST

JENNIFER L. PRINCESS

111 Skyland Drive
Snellville, Georgia 30278
(770) 999-0101

*"Jenny's empathy and ability to work with students certainly made her an effective tutor.
If there is such a person as a "natural born teacher," then Jenny is certainly one."****
Assistant Professor of Mathematics

Objective

To create an energized Mathematics learning environment which focuses on individual understanding and expression and results in improved performance and knowledge.

Education

GEORGIA STATE UNIVERSITY, Atlanta, Georgia
Bachelor of Science, 1994 GPA: 3.8
Major: Mathematics Minor: Education

Activities and Honors
Outstanding Student Award for Drama, **Four Year Scholarship**
Dean's List
Eta Sigma Alpha Honor Society
Archonties Society for Outstanding Performance
Tutor / Math Help Session Leader***
Secretary of SPAGE and Peer Counselor

Related Experience

NEW HIGH SCHOOL, Decatur, Georgia   Fall 1994
Student Teacher for Fundamentals of Algebra and Applied Math
- Knowledgeable of newly required Algebra curriculum, related teaching materials, and objectives.
- Actively instructed and independently designed lesson plans; assumed full charge of classes.
- Set standards of conduct and accomplished goals through one-on-one consultations and open communication with students; built positive class rapport.
- Participated in inservice days and open house; conducted parent meetings.
Volunteer Activities
- Pre-school planning and classroom set-up.
- Tutored students before and after school hours to assure their full understanding of mathematical principles.
- Attended all departmental meetings and Mathematics Conference at Rock Eagle to expand effective teaching techniques.
- SWAT (to create student awareness of tragedies resulting from drug abuse).

General Experience

TARGET, Snellville, Georgia   1988 to Present
Supervisor, 1994 to Present
Supervise Service Desk, Cashiers, and Garden Center as needed.
Cashier, 1988 to 1994 (Part-time and Seasonally)

SHEILA MORRIS
88 Diamond Avenue
Cortlandt Manor, NY   10566
(914) 739-1998

OBJECTIVE

A position as an Elementary School Teacher which will allow me to utilize creative, multi-channel strategies in meeting the educational and social needs of students with differing styles of learning.

PROFILE

- *Enthusiastic educator* with proven four year track-record fostering academic learning and enhancing student creativity.
- Possess strong people orientation; sensitive to students' specialized and changing needs.
- Demonstrated expertise in taking academic subject matter and "*making it come alive*" for the student through well-planned projects; fostering development of creative and critical thinking skills.
- *Versatile*; diversified experience with school populations from pre-school through grade twelve, in both regular and special education settings.
- Possess significant experience in *coordinating multiple activities*.
- Demonstrated ability to *consistently individualize instruction*, based on students' interests and needs, at the most appropriate level.
- Proven ability to develop effective working relationships with fellow staff and parents, alike. Maintain strong communication channel with parents. Foster strong inter-teacher cooperation and exchange of ideas.

CERTIFICATIONS

Elementary Education K - 6: New York State (Permanent)
Special Education K - 12: New York State (Permanent)

MAJOR ACCOMPLISHMENTS

- *Developed strategy* of using "rap song" to teach rounding-off of numbers to low math group.   Strategy worked so well that these same students taught the rap to their peers in other classes which greatly *enhanced their* own *self esteem*.
- *Utilized* dinosaur *research project, incorporating* a *diversity of skills*: i.e. main idea in development of research reports, vocabulary, etc., to *motivate lower ability readers*. Project completion increased student self-confidence and gained their trust.
- *Utililze Differentiation* of *learning* to *maximize student performance* at own level. During class-wide reading unit on "Mystery", *encouraged students* to *write their own mystery stories, sharing* with fellow students.
- Utilized video equipment to "*capture*" *culminating class-presentations* based on Native American research unit. *Video taped presentations* to be *shared with parents*.

EXPERIENCE
1994 - Present

GEORGE WASHINGTON ELEMENTARY SCHOOL, Lake Mohegan, NY
Teacher of Fourth Grade <u>regular education</u>
- Transitioned into regular education from special education, a change of tenure area. *Selected out of a field of 800 candidates*.
- Team teach with remedial reading and remedial math teacher.
- Provide significant input, as *Fourth Grade Teacher-Leader*, into district's Committee on *Setting 4th Grade Benchmarks* for State Curriculum.
- Implemented Multi-Sensory Reading program, a holistic approach which also involves writing and spelling and *hits upon each student's strength*. Program provides reinforcement via all learning modalities and ensures retention, in that *students take the concepts with them*.
- Provided significant input into developing school's first science fair.   Encouraged own student participation which helped them develop presentation skills through cooperative learning.

1993 - 1994	**GEORGE WASHINGTON ELEMENTARY SCHOOL,** Lake Mohegan, NY **Teacher of Fourth Grade Special Education**
1992 - 1993	**GEORGE WASHINGTON ELEMENTARY SCHOOL,** Lake Mohegan, NY **Teacher of Sixth Grade Special Education**
1978 - 1994	**LAKELAND SCHOOL DISTRICT** and **PRIVATE PRACTICE** **TUTOR** • Provided individualized instruction, elementary through 12th grade levels, to home bound regular and special needs students. • Provided instruction to students requiring additional, out-of-classroom reinforcement.
1976 - 1977	**PUTNAM/NORTHERN WESTCHESTER BOCES,** Yorktown Hgts, NY **Resource Room Teacher: Grades K - 6**
1975 - 1976	**LAKELAND SCHOOL DISTRICT,** Lake Mohegan,NY **Teacher Aide: Special Education**

EDUCATION

COLLEGE OF NEW ROCHELLE, New Rochelle, NY
Master of Science: Special Education 1992

WHEELOCK COLLEGE, Boston, MA
Bachelor of Science: Elementary Education 1975
Double Minor: Psychology/Theatre Arts

CONTINUING EDUCATION

Recent Courses plus ten in-service credits
Classroom Management   Multi-Sensory Writing
Math Manipulatives   Literature through Media
Multi-Sensory Reading   Dimensions of Learning
Science is Elementary - Janet VanCleve

REFERENCES   Available upon request.

COMMITTED TO THE CARE AND EDUCATION OF YOUNG CHILDREN

ELIZABETH MELCHER
18 Bayshore Drive
Hometown, Arizona 86301
520.555.5555

PROFILE

Enthusiastic, degreed professional with experience in primary educational field, creating and implementing lesson programs. Committed to professional ethics, standards of practice and the care and education of young children.

SUMMARY OF QUALIFICATIONS

- Exhibits creativity in preparing and implementing lesson plans and teaching tools.
- Utilizes solid organizational, work and time management skills.
- Proficient at producing quality, accurate and timely work.
- Performs effectively both as an autonomous, self-motivated individual and as an active, contributing team member.
- Demonstrates decision making skills with problem-solving abilities.
- Positive coaching and motivational proficiencies.
- Strong interpersonal relations, effective oral and written communication skills with colleagues, principal, parents and individuals on all levels.
- Displays enthusiasm and willingness to develop continually evolving skills to maximum efficiency.
- Noted for resourcefulness with ability to handle diverse situations and perform well under stressful situations.

Computer Skills: Knowledgeable in Mac, DOS, Word Processing and Internet search procedures.

ACHIEVEMENTS

CERTIFICATE

- Developmentally Appropriate Music Experiences for Young Children

Originated and developed CHILDREN'S ACTIVITY GROUP CENTER

- Provided children from the age of 4 to 12 with educational activities.
- Designed and implemented programs for crafts and science experiments
- Planned and directed field trips encompassing *"How The World Works"* venues.

EMPLOYEE OF THE MONTH AWARD, *CONDE NASTE RESORT*

EDUCATION

MAJOR UNIVERSITY   Hometown, Arizona
   BACHELOR OF SCIENCE DEGREE - 1996
      Major: Elementary Education

MINOR COMMUNITY COLLEGE   Hometown, Arizona
      Courses: Mathematics for Elementary School, Spanish, Music, Computers, English

UNIVERSITY OF OTHER TOWN   Other Town, Arizona
      Major: Elementary Education; *Minor*: History

SMALL TOWN MEADOWS COMMUNITY COLLEGE   Small Town, Arizona
   ASSOCIATE OF ARTS DEGREE
      Major: Early Childhood Development, Education

CERTIFICATIONS

ARIZONA DEPARTMENT OF EDUCATION, 1997

   Elementary K through 8
      Endorsement: Early Childhood

TEACHING EXPERIENCE

LITTLE TOWN SCHOOL DISTRICT, 1996   Little Town, Arizona
STUDENT TEACHER, KINDERGARTEN

- Prepared materials in accordance with lesson plans, and often improvised creatively when no lesson plans were available.
- Led storytelling sessions. Followed up with thoughtful questions to make sure children understood concepts correctly.
- Monitored children in playground activities.
- Designed space and set up class room according to reading, art, and music areas
- Kept records of grades and attendance.
- Interacted with community resource and child support personnel.
- Adept at working with special needs children; behavioral problems, ADD needs.

ANOTHER STATE COUNCIL OF GOVERNMENTS, 1992 to 1993   Anywhere, U.S.A.
TEACHER

- Assisted in all preschool classes from three years through five years old.
- Planned arts & crafts projects to complement weekly educational theme.
- Developed, designed and implemented indoor and outdoor children's activities and teaching lessons.
- Supervised children in playground activities
- Interact with parents delivering and picking up children. Communicated special requests and information to staff.
- Performed home visits.
- Extensive knowledge of community resources, support systems and social services.

COUNTY SCHOOL DISTRICT, 1986 to 1990   Anywhere, U.S.A.
TEACHER AIDE - *ADD and Behavioral problemed children*

- Performed evaluations and assessments for referral and mainstreaming.
- Designed and implemented programs to involve children in creative expressions of art and music.
- Maintained a structured, monitored environment.

ADDITIONAL EXPERIENCE
CONDE NASTE RESORT, 1994 to present   Other Town, Arizona
RESTAURANT SUPPORT SERVICES

- Performs all aspects of retail restaurant operations including public contact, effective communication, order processing, food service, inventory control, and maintaining proper health and cleanliness standards.

Business, management and supervisory experience.
Spanish language competency.

PROFESSIONAL AFFILIATIONS

Big Brother - Big Sister   Member
National Teachers Association   Member

CONTINUING EDUCATION AND PERSONAL DEVELOPMENT

SEMINARS, WORKSHOPS AND SPECIAL TRAINING

1997	**G.E.M.S. Society - Math and Science Workshop** *BIG TOWN UNIVERSITY* ▸ Using Math and Science to solve "real world" problems ▸ Environmental Issues and Our Children
Fall, 1996	**Teaching the Solar System to Children** *SMALL TOWN COMMUNITY COLLEGE* ▸ A method course constructing Saturn w/rings and 17 moons
August, 1995	**Project Wild - Creating environmental activities** ▸ People, Culture and Wildlife ▸ Responsible Human Actions
August, 1995	**North Central AZ Mathematics & Science Consortium** ▸ Problem Solving in Math and Science
March, 1995	**More Creative Art Activities With Books** ▸ Making and Wearing Masks in a Musical Skit ▸ Making Collages, Creating a Play
February, 1993	**Early Childhood Education Conference** ▸ Early Learning Difficulties ▸ Assessment in Early Childhood Education ▸ Creative Thinking for Early Learners **Teaching Music in the Pre-Kindergarten Set** ▸ Administering Music Programs ▸ Developing Age Appropriate Materials ▸ Understanding Young Children's Music Behaviors
May, 1993	**Early Childhood Music (In-service presentation)** ▸ Using Creative Arts to Make People Feel Good About Themselves
February, 1993	**Child Fine - Arts for Children With Special Needs** ▸ The Power of Music ▸ Music Therapy Techniques ▸ Creative Dance and Movement
August, 1992	**Accepting Individual Differences and Change** ▸ Insights into Listening and Communication ▸ Developing Appropriate Activities For Special Needs Children ▸ Family Changes in Changing Times
April, 1989	**Linguistic Bias** ▸ Language Reflecting Culture Values ▸ Gender Bias Relating to Interaction With Children ▸ Traditional and Historical Usage of Language

Chapter 8

12 Unique Resumes

EVE TEIGER
14 Sunnybrook Farm Way
New Paltz, NY 12569
(914) 555-0936

AWARD-WINNING AGRICULTURAL OPERATIONS & MARKETING EXECUTIVE
Chemicals • Fertilizer • Plant Disorders & Diagnostics • Treatment Solutions
Market-driven • Sales/Territory Management • Industry Consultant

Senior agricultural chemicals sales and marketing professional and horticultural diagnostician. Superior technical knowledge and strengths in plant sciences result in sales and product management strategies that build customer confidence, loyalty and the bottom line. Extensive experience with ornamental plant care, fruit, vegetable and diverse crop farmers. Owned and managed successful business; forged familiarity and working relationships with industry leaders. Strong closer with excellent interpersonal and communications skills. Builder of motivated, productive teams.

PROFESSIONAL HISTORY

ET CONSULTING, Highland, NY   1997 - Present
Consultants to crop growers, ornamental care professionals on Integrated Pest Management (IPM) and fertility programs, including crop scouting, soil testing and computerized treatment recommendations.

Representative Projects:

- **Serenity Gates**, Valhalla, NY: Prestigious cemetery had serious turf maintenance problems. Assessed needs, devised a soil testing program, accounted for all variables (sun/shade/traffic patterns), and current maintenance budget and program. Created and implemented a long-term improvement program, within budget. Growth and resiliency improved visibly since implementation, with higher success rate for newly-seeded areas.

- **Canterbury Farms**, Winston, NY: A diversified bedding plant, fruit and vegetable growing operation selling primarily at New York City green markets. Engaged to assist with crop growth management. Tested soils, recommended crop by crop fertility and pest control strategies. Increased productivity and profitability. Improved marketable corn yield 25%; cut input costs by 3%.

EARTHFARMS GROWERS, INC., Rhinebeck, NY   1996
A $300MM, 500 employee agricultural chemical distributor/manufacturer, purchaser of **Glendale Agservice, Inc.**

Field Sales Representative/Sub-Location Manager
Sold *Glendale Agservice* to *Earthfarms* and assisted management takeover. Diagnosed crop disorders and planned corrective/curative products for proper treatments, using IPM. Marketed crop protectants, fertilizers, and seeds to retail dealers, crop producers, and ornamental plant care professionals. Devised strategic plan to develop long term business relationships. Planned and spoke at company-sponsored sales meetings.

- Converted former *Glendale* accounts and transitioned customer base smoothly to new company and systems; strengthened retail dealer relations and increased one account by $200,000+ in one year through added sales, product performance and technical support.

- Created PC-published "Crop Growing Tip Sheets" customized for major client company's individual vegetable crop needs; booked $15,000 in new sales in one day's travel with client sales representative.

GLENDALE AGSERVICE, INC., Winston, NY   1991 - 1995
A $1MM crop-protectant, fertilizer and seed supply company to crop producers, retail dealers and ornamental plant care professionals.

Founder/President

Diagnosed, detailed corrective steps for proper resolution and control of crop disorders. Managed, coordinated and performed sales forecasts for territory. Oversaw inventory, coordinated ordering and accounting. Created strategic business alliances with other suppliers. Devised and implemented marketing/advertising programs. Computerized management, customer newsletters and sales presentations.

- Grew start-up company with no initial capitalization to $1MM+ sales revenue in under four years.

- Created a strategic alliance with fertilizer manufacturing giant to use their specialized blending equipment and delivery network in exchange for marketing, billing and technical assistance.

- Spearheaded application of research on apple tree pest control in partnership with major university research project and apple growers; generated data and adaptations that gave new solution a competitive sales advantage over older, less successful applications.

AGWAY, INC., Syracuse, NY   1986 - 1991
$2 billion cooperative and manufacturer/distributor of agchemicals, seeds and fertilizer.

Horticultural Sales Specialist

Sold crop protectants, nutrients, & seeds to fruit, vegetable and sod producers through diagnosis of crop care problems and consultation with farm manager to select proper crop care program. Organized and scheduled productivity within assigned territory. Recommended generative soil testing and fertility outcomes.

- Rebuilt sales territory and doubled sales volume to $400,000 in first year; built territory to over $1MM within five years.

EDUCATION

B.S., Horticulture, University of California, Davis, Davis, CA   1986

AFFILIATIONS/HONORS

NYS Ag-Business Association Representative to the NYS Dept. of Environmental Conservation's Pesticide Task Force

Co-Chaired Production Committee of the Columbia County Vegetable Growers' Association Improvement Initiative

Served on Board of Directors of the Sullivan County Farm Bureau

Featured speaker at two Agway internal sales meetings

Winner of joint Agway/Rahway Laboratories sales contest

Served on joint Exxon/Agway computer programming project

Delta Tau Alpha National Agricultural Honor Society

Melanie W. Jones

123 Main Street
Anytown, Ohio 45454
(513) 555-5555

Airline Crisis Management Specialist / Consultant

FOCUS   Communication and assistance to families of accident victims.

STRENGTHS

◆ **Ability to take control** and make sound decisions in crisis situations.

◆ **Interpretation of disaster-management plans** and rapid revision in response to the unique circumstances of each incident.

◆ **Extensive airline experience** that contributes to a sound decision-making process and helps to balance the needs of the families with the best interests of the airline.

◆ **Organizational and management skills:** the ability to oversee multiple activities and focus on hundreds of small but essential details.

◆ **Communication skills:** empathy and concern to grieving families; sensitivity to cultural and religious beliefs; training and communication to crisis management team members.

◆ **Leadership:** guiding, motivating and supporting inexperienced disaster team members; directing overall program operations to assure timely, responsible, and professional crisis management.

Crisis Management Experience

Jan. 1997   National Airways Flight 3272 — Buffalo, New York

Due to previous experience with Circle Air incidents, my assistance was requested for several weeks following the National Airways flight 3272 tragedy. Primary role was to guide an inexperienced team of relative-assistance representatives. Interpreted the company's disaster-management plan; contributed to overall direction and decision-making; provided on-site guidance to as many as 35 reps.

Sept. 1994   Circle Air Flight 427 — Provo, Utah
July 1994   Circle Air Flight 1016 — Portland, Oregon

Helped to establish direction in the Relative Assistance Center by providing daily communication from corporate management to relative-assistance representatives during search and recovery of accident victims. Maintained focus on delivering correct information in as timely a fashion as possible.

Guided reps in providing support and assistance to the accident victims' families. Assistance was tailored to the individual needs of each family and included air and ground transportation, emotional and religious support, memorial or funeral arrangements, short-term monetary aid, and accident recovery information. Approached these communications with empathy, sensitivity and professional insight.

Transitioned from on-site locations to Consumer Affairs. Worked directly with families of the deceased.

◆ Flight 1016/Portland — assigned to a family that lost 5 members in the crash.

◆ Flight 427/Provo — supported the families of 4 separate victims, maintaining daily contact for an extended period of time due to the lengthy recovery period from this incident.

Airline Experience

1987-Present   CIRCLE AIR

Reservation Sales Agent (1996-Present)

Sales Support (1995-1996)
Provided assistance and support to the upper-tier accounts within Circle Air's sales department. Dealt with problems requiring immediate resolution at various locations within the company's route structure.

Team Leader, Priority Gold Department (1994-95)
Directed 25-35 agents servicing the company's most valued clientele. Provided technical assistance; trained agents in motivational selling techniques; held final authority for resolving customer complaints.

Team Leader, Convention Sales (1992-1994)

Reservations Service Desk Agent (1987-1992)

1973-1987   VALLEY AIRLINES

Assist Desk (1985-1987)

Reservationist (1973-1985)

Technical Expertise

Word processing — TTY — Frequent Traveler database

JASON W. ALEXANDER

1928 Oak Knoll Lane
Knoxville, Tennessee 54061

Home: (423) 720-3657
Fax: (423) 720-8994
Office: (423) 890-8415

SENIOR ENERGY INDUSTRY EXECUTIVE

Uniquely qualified business development and management executive with exemplary start-up and new business achievements. Able to perceive and capitalize on market opportunities to launch successful new ventures. Highly focused, accomplished creator and manager of profitable non-regulated business units. Expert at project/program design, implementation and delivery. An adept and aggressive problem-solver with strong operating and leadership skills. Energy marketing and sales expertise includes:

- Team Building & Leadership
- Relationship Marketing
- Organizational Development

- Strategic Market Positioning
- Customer & Partner Development
- Wholesale/Retail/Sales Management

Guest Speaker at Industry Conferences & Symposia Nationwide:

- American Public Gas Association
- National Association of Gas Consumers
- Fort Smith Association of Petroleum Landmen

- American Gas Association
- Gas Daily Conference
- Panhandle National Gas Association

PROFESSIONAL EXPERIENCE:

UNITED ENERGY INC., Knoxville, Tennessee   1994 to 1997
($2 billion diversified energy company with 12 domestic & international distribution operations)

Vice President of Business Development - Total Energy Venture

Member of 6-person Senior Executive Team recruited to plan and orchestrate the start-up of the first retail energy brand in America. Challenged to build new venture and position Total Energy as a dominant market leader. Expanded and managed the non-regulated activities of business units worldwide and launched successful new initiative with market potential of $300 billion.

- Led the utility founding partner team that defined the business opportunity, objective, positioning, differentiation, strategy and critical success factors. Developed the national commodity energy delivery platform for Total Energy brand for the retail marketplace and created commodity energy products.

- Negotiated 10-year contract for construction of an intrastate pipeline, generating $6 million in revenue.

- Grew annual profits by $700,000. Developed municipal market penetration plan for commodity energy. Championed United Energy's non-regulated sales force to secure contracts with 18 municipalities.

- Transitioned a proposed divestiture from $1.5 million loss to 20% pre-tax ROI by negotiating a non-regulated natural gas storage partnership which significantly lowered corporate risk.

- Led task force that identified opportunities to leverage resources across United Energy's wholesale and retail business units, reducing managed costs by more than 50%.

- Prepared a structured response to curtailment, authored the policy and directed follow-up for successful execution.

353

NATURAL GAS, INC., Anchorage, Alaska   1993 to 1994
(Integrated natural gas gathering, processing & marketing company with 10,000+ miles of interstate pipelines)

General Manager - Market Development

Recruited to plan and direct an aggressive expansion of marketing and business development efforts throughout unregulated markets in the Northwestern and Southwestern U.S. Created innovative, market-driven development programs to facilitate improved customer/partnership relations.

- Doubled prior years' net margins to over $12 million in first year.

- Negotiated, structured and closed 20-year contract for new cogeneration load.

NEW ENERGY COMPANY, Seattle, Washington   1988 to 1993

Vice President - Business & Market Development

Spearheaded 500% growth for this natural gas marketing company.

- Drove municipal marketing effort to supply 70+ municipalities and generating $2 million in annual revenue.

- Closed over $3 million annually in new business revenues through well-targeted market expansion initiatives.

- Initiated market support and enabled $45+ million in long term project financing for construction of natural gas pipeline (subsequently sold for $25 million profit in 1995).

- Led development of purchasing consortium for colleges and hospitals. Built new venture to $500,000 in gas sales margins.

BLACK GOLD PETROLEUM, Dallas, Texas   1987 to 1988

Vice President Marketing for high-growth unregulated energy company.

CRUDEX CORPORATION, Dallas, Texas   1986 to 1987

Vice President Marketing for entrepreneurial start-up venture in the unregulated energy industry.

LONGWELL OIL COMPANY, Dallas, Texas   1981 to 1986

Manager - Oil & Gas Sales / Investor Relations

BEDFORD COUNTY SCHOOLS, Bedford, Virginia   1971 to 1981

Senior High School Principal / Teacher

EDUCATION:

VIRGINIA POLYTECHNIC UNIVERSITY, Blacksburg, Virginia

M.S., Administration, 1976
B.S., History/Geology, 1970

ROBERT MICHAELSON

22 Marsh Landing
New Haven, CT 06221

Home   (203) 325-3214
Office   (203) 596-3322

CAREER PROFILE:

SENIOR FACILITIES REPRESENTATIVE with over 15 years professional experience. Expert in the feasibility analysis, design, specification, construction and management of multi-million dollar land, property and facility development projects. Qualifications include:

- Property/Business Transactions
- Site Assessment/Acquisition
- Due Diligence Assessment
- Facilities Leasing/Build-Out
- Industrial Engineering
- Contract/Investment Negotiations

- Project Scheduling/Budgeting/Controls
- Asset/Portfolio Management
- Government/Regulatory Affairs
- Environmental Impact Assessment
- Capital Improvement Projects
- Mixed-Use Property Portfolio Management

PROFESSIONAL EXPERIENCE:

INTERNATIONAL MARINE, Hartfod, Connecticut   1985 to Present

PROGRAM MANAGER - NEW FACILITIES CONSTRUCTION (1987 to Present)

Multi-faceted assignment directing nationwide facilities construction, renovation and lease build-out program. Direct projects from planning and feasibility analysis through design, specification, engineering, internal funding, external regulatory approval, budgeting, scheduling, construction, completion and delivery. Source and select subcontractors for architectural design, engineering and field construction.

Administer an average of $35 million in annual capital improvement and new construction projects, and an additional $5 million in tenant build-out and renovations. Establish strategic plans and objectives for facilities management, research market and economic trends to determine the continued use and/or disposition of specific properties, and coordinate all related MIS functions. Negotiate leases, lease buy-outs and the disposition of excess property/space.

Accepted additional responsibility in February 1994 for the management of all Hartford office facilities (total of 650,000 sq.ft.). Operate within a matrix team environment coordinating personnel from in-house legal, purchasing, contracts, engineering, estimating and operations on a per-project basis.

Project Highlights & Achievements:

- Planned, directed and completed (on-time and within budget) five major construction projects including a technology center, office expansion, blast and paint facility, lead bonder's facility and radiological control training facility. Total footage exceeded 200,000 sq.ft. Project values exceeded $28 million.

- Controlled a portfolio of 35 office facilities with a total of more than 1.5 million sq.ft. of leased office space. Launched a massive consolidation program to integrate common facilities and saved more than $5.6 million in annual lease costs. Subsequently downsized facilities to 11 sites nationwide.

- Directed engineering and construction of a $2.5 million fiber optic network integrated into the Hartford facility, and a series of leading edge telecommunications and data network projects for off-site facilities.

- Orchestrated relocation of Corporate Office and Corporate Flight Operations from St. Louis, Missouri to Falls Church, Virginia ($4 million project).

- Consulted with Smith Barney to develop divestiture strategy for 98-acre heavy industrial facility. Projections indicate a $12 million cash payment for sale of obsolete facility.

- Coordinated marketing efforts to divest two major properties, one manufacturing site and one undeveloped site. Estimated value of $8 million cash.

INTERNATIONAL MARINE *(Continued)*:

- Identified new business opportunity for the first defense conversion contract. Negotiated with Harris Construction to build digester and storage tanks for a large sewage treatment facility in Norfolk, Virginia. Generated over $21 million in new sales.

- Wrote and prepared Hartford Motor Inn business plan and performed total project management for the construction of a berthing facility for Naval pre-commissioning crews (valued at $6.1 million).

- Established an extensive network of contacts and built cooperative working relationships with local, state and federal government agencies, chambers of commerce, state economic development agencies, environmental protection and remediation agencies, and other organizations involved in site regulation, use and approval.

- Spoke before government, professional and civic organizations.

SENIOR ADMINISTRATOR - OPERATIONS & MODULAR CONSTRUCTION (1985 to 1987)

Managed a team of 125 engineering, testing, operations and support personnel in the construction of specific components for nuclear submarines. Managed project scheduling, budgeting, work sequence planning, materials, installation planning, and all specialty trades. Administered annual construction budget of approximately $50 million.

- Introduced quality circles and JIT manufacturing concepts which significantly enhanced learning curve, speed, accuracy and performance in the construction cycle.

AMERICAN REFINING COMPANY (Marine Engineering Department), Houston, Texas   1978 to 1985

CHIEF ENGINEER

Progressed through the ranks from Second Engineer to First Engineer to Chief Engineer licensed by the U.S. Coast Guard. Commissioned as Engineering Officer aboard tanker vessels travelling worldwide providing technical and operational direction for the construction, maintenance and retrofit of tankers, steam propulsion plants, cargo handling equipment and related components. Trained and directed operational teams of project designers, engineers and managers. Worked with Houston office, American Bureau of Shipping, U.S. Coast Guard and shipboard officers as required to transport company products.

INTERNATIONAL MARINE (Boat Division), Groton, Connecticut   1974 to 1978

NUCLEAR PROJECT ENGINEER

Designed sophisticated radioactive effluent and resin discharge collection systems and facilities. Wrote procedural documentation to meet regulatory restriction requirements, coordinated design/engineering teams, monitored project performance, and coordinated field engineering modifications. Appointed to Joint Work Group to advance procedures review to decrease radiation exposure to shipyard personnel.

EDUCATION & LICENSES:

MBA / Marketing, University of New Haven, 1992
BS / Marine Engineering, Maine Maritime Academy, 1970
Chief Engineer (Unlimited H.P.), United States Coast Guard, 1983
National Board Commission (Boilers & Unfired Pressure Vessels), 1974

PROFESSIONAL AFFILIATIONS:

- Member, Rotary International
- Member, Society of Naval Architects and Marine Engineers
- President, Connecticut Chapter, Maine Maritime Academy Alumni
- Member, Board of Directors, Maine Maritime Academy Alumni

GEORGE STEPHENSON

P.O. Box 6388
Washington, DC 20221
Home (202) 483-5548
Office (202) 382-2320 / (202) 382-5418

PROFESSIONAL PROFILE:

Over 15 years experience in Security and Intelligence Operations worldwide. Combines strong planning, analysis, organizational and communications skills with excellent qualifications in the development of security operations. Skilled personnel manager and budget administrator. Expertise includes:

- Scientific & Technical Intelligence
- Tactical Assessment/Planning
- Document Security/Control
- Security Training & Team Leadership

- Operations & Personnel Security
- Counter-Terrorism
- Counter-Espionage
- Reporting/Analysis/Communications

Excellent knowledge of the Freedom of Information Act and security policies of U.S. and foreign governments. Familiar with general security practices followed by major industries and corporations nationwide. Held highest level U.S. Government security clearance and positions of trust. PC proficient.

PROFESSIONAL EXPERIENCE:

Intelligence & Security Officer, U.S. Intelligence Office | 1981 to Present
Logistics Officer, U.S. Intelligence Office | 1977 to 1981

Fast-track promotion throughout career. Advanced through a series of increasingly responsible security and intelligence positions with organizations operating worldwide. Won numerous honors and commendations for capabilities in threat analysis, intelligence collection/analysis, security operations planning and personnel training. Career highlights include:

Security Operations Planning & Management

- Authored several major documents impacting security and intelligence operations worldwide. Provided the strategy, organizational structure and processes for security operations development, management and expansion in response to changing demands of worldwide operations.

- Hosted two intelligence planning committees of multi-disciplinary intelligence and operating management personnel challenged to enhance security and operations planning worldwide.

- Provided high-level security and intelligence support to technologically advanced systems and engineering projects.

357

Intelligence Collection & Analysis

- Directed large-scale intelligence research, collection, analysis and dissemination operations to provide top management with critical information regarding potential threats, breeches to security and technical intelligence.

- Initiated processes to overcome shortcomings in intelligence collection and analysis vital for the success of major projects.

- Authored reports, led executive-level presentations and coordinated information flow between various public and private organizations.

Personnel Training, Supervision & Development

- Designed and led training programs in security and intelligence for operative personnel, management and executives worldwide. Created customized presentations to meet specific operating requirements of each organization.

- Trained, scheduled, supervised and evaluated work performance of up to 85 personnel.

Budgeting & Financial Management

- Participated in the long-term administration of a $7 million annual budget. Provided timely and accurate input to high-level reports and discussions addressing operations planning and budget requirements.

Achievements & Project Highlights:

- Developed processes to maintain control of more than 70,000 sensitive security documents.

- Managed systems development and implementation project to computerize a large technical scientific library and integrate advanced optical data technology for long-term document retention.

- Built cooperative working relationships with government agencies worldwide to facilitate the timely exchange of information critical to intelligence and security operations.

- Extensive technical knowledge of chemical, biological and radiological security threats, electronic surveillance technology, electronic counter-measures and munitions technologies.

EDUCATION:

Pursuing Certificate of Specialization in Hospitality Management
The American Hotel & Motel Association Educational Institute

Bachelor of General Studies, Kent State University, 1976

Completed 350+ hours of continuing professional training in Security and Intelligence. Programs included scientific and technical intelligence collection/analysis, leadership and supervisory skills, and tactical assessment.

GREGORY A. STEVENSON

8754 Riverview Court
Kansas City, MO 64312
(610) 647-6412

PROFESSIONAL PROFILE

Extensive law enforcement background (25+ years); 10 years as a commander (5 years being at an executive level), with expertise in leadership, administration, human resource development, strategic planning, systems development, emergency management, and management reporting

♦ Leadership Skills: Preparing and developing programs of action to accomplish objectives; demonstrating a positive attitude, strong work ethic, loyalty, and dedication; considering the impact of decisions on the department, its members and community; obtaining cooperation; utilizing logic and sound judgment in decision-making; diplomatic, setting an example of integrity

♦ Administrative Skills: Ensuring accountability of subordinates related to conduct and productivity; quick to recognize problems and execute solutions; systematically securing relevant information and identifying key issues; paying attention to detail; structuring tasks, plans and objectives to establish priorities and set goals

♦ Human Resource Skills: Interacting effectively with individuals at all levels; fostering a spirit of cooperation and respect; leading by example; making recommendations based on research and familiarity with various elements; soliciting ideas/opinions of others and utilizing input on key issues; encouraging training

♦ Communication Skills: Expressing ideas (written and orally) in an articulate, clear, concise and effective manner; addressing large groups; persuasive

PROFESSIONAL EXPERIENCE

KANSAS CITY, MISSOURI POLICE DEPARTMENT   December 1970 to Present
Kansas City, Missouri

MAJOR - COMMANDER, NORTH PATROL DIVISION (April 1996 - Present)
Direct the largest geographic precinct in the city (162 square miles), providing day-to-day police services to 94,000 residents to include a community policing program.
- Formulated plan to address the inordinate man-hours on responses to alarm calls.

MAJOR - COMMANDER, SPECIAL OPERATIONS DIVISION (March 1993 - April 1996)
Direct activities of the division (175+ personnel and a $8.1M budget) comprised of three units (Traffic, Tactical Operations (SWAT), and Helicopter) to include all aspects of traffic and security for special community events, visiting dignitaries, civil disorders and disasters.
- Increased level of responsiveness, reducing traffic fatalities by 36% and traffic accidents by 9% in 1994.
- Reduced overtime cost by $200,000 through close monitoring of overtime expenditures and utilization of flexed schedules when appropriate.
- Negotiated the training of 4 helicopter pilots, resulting in significant savings ($7,600 vs. $100,000).
- Initiated request to Missouri Division of Highway Safety, resulting in reinstatement of full funding ($88,177 vs. $50,000) of Multi-offender Grant. Letter of Commendation from Chief of Police.
- Revised and implemented an advanced and comprehensive Critical Incident Management Plan which included the Field Force concept and the Critical Incident Committee, receiving a "Special Unit Citation".
- Developed a comprehensive staffing configuration, combining the Traffic and Tactical Operations Divisions, resulting in expanded and more uniformed coverage, reducing division personnel by 20% while maintaining previous levels of support.
- Developed and implemented the Gun Suppression Program (community policing initiative) resulting in a reduction of homicides by 62.5% in target areas and an overall 24% reduction in homicide citywide compared to a national reduction of 12%.
- Formulated guidelines to maximize staffing levels while providing a fair and equitable leave policy.

PROFESSIONAL EXPERIENCE (Continued)

- Established a Division Training Committee to identify training issues and to provide on-going training to include "Monthly Training Topics".
- Coordinated presidential visits (4) with recognition from the Secret Service for receiving outstanding cooperation, along with other letters of appreciation.

MAJOR - COMMANDER, EAST PATROL DIVISION (August 1992 - March 1993)
Direct activities of the division (150+ personnel) in response to law enforcement needs covering approximately 35 square miles with 87,000 residents, addressing specific neighborhood issues.
- Developed and implemented a project to address crime problems/patterns associated with prostitution, resulting in reduction of activities as outlined in Letter of Appreciation from The Ministerial Alliance of Kansas City.
- Researched actual personnel vs. authorized personnel, establishing staffing guidelines to ensure optimal response to calls-for-service.
- Designed plan to address growing problem of gangs and related community crime issues, resulting in Letter of Commendation from the Chief of Police.

MAJOR - EXECUTIVE OFFICER, PATROL BUREAU (December 1990 - August 1992)
Provided administrative support relevant to operations and procedures of a 750-member uniformed personnel to include human resources, training requirements and evaluations. Participated in the preparation of documentation for disciplinary matters, expenditures, staff responsibilities. Served as Acting Bureau Commander when required.
- Chaired, Probationary Officer Review Panel.
- Chaired, Firearms Review Committee.
- Chaired, Awards Committee
- Revised Field Training Officer Program.
- Addressed slow response time of city tow trucks, identifying problem and implemented solution with the Communications Unit Commander.
- Assisted in the implementation of McGruff Safe House Project in the Kansas City, Missouri School District by obtaining assistance of the Records Unit Commander.
- Developed and presented a training module at Pre-Sergeant's School titled "Supervisors' Responsibilities to the Public, Departments and Subordinates".
- Attended Executive Committee and presented Board Report in Bureau Commander's absence.

CAPTAIN - COMMANDER, PLANNING AND RESEARCH (July 1990 - December 1990)
CAPTAIN - COMMANDER, CRIMINAL ENFORCEMENT UNIT (April 1989 - July 1990)
CAPTAIN - COMMANDER, COMMUNICATIONS UNIT (May 1987 - April 1989)
CAPTAIN - EXECUTIVE OFFICER, TRAFFIC DIVISION (June 1986 - May 1987)
CAPTAIN - WATCH COMMANDER, CENTRAL PATROL DIVISION (July 1985 - June 1986)
- Established Back-up Communications Center, procuring an automatic call distributor.
- Led investigation resulting in the arrest/prosecution of the largest drug operation in Kansas City history.
- Received "Special Unit Citation" for transferring communication functions to alternate site during headquarters fire.
- Received "Special Unit Citation" for participation in dismantling ongoing criminal enterprises, particularly in the illegal drug trade.
- Chaired task force to evaluate communications unit procedures regarding vehicle pursuits.
- Academic Selection Board Member.

SERGEANT - PUBLIC AFFAIRS (March 1984 - July 1985)
SERGEANT - COMMUNITY ASSISTANCE UNIT (February 1983 - March 1984)
SERGEANT - PATROL (January 1982 - February 1983)
POLICE OFFICER (December 1970 - January 1982)

EDUCATION

Federal Bureau of Investigation National Academy
Quanitco, Virginia

December 1990
Certificate of Completion

Webster University
Kansas City, Missouri

Master of Arts - July 1987
Management

University of Missouri
Kansas City, Missouri

Bachelor of Science - May 1978
Major: Administration of Justice

Other Training

Dealing with the Media — November 1995
Integrated Emergency Management Cause — September 1995
Law Enforcement Traffic Safety Advisory Council — August 1994
Sexual Harassment — January 1994
Area Command Field Force Training — January 1994
C.A.R.E. Team Training — May 1993
Law Enforcement Incident Command System — June 1992
Team Task Leadership Training — April 1991
Labor Management Leadership — March 1991
Secret Service Dignitary Protection — January 1990

MILITARY BACKGROUND

United States Coast Guard Reserve — 1978-1980
United States Marine Corps Reserve — 1967-1973

MEMBERSHIPS

Federal Bureau of Investigations National Academy Associates
Kansas City Police Credit Union, 1983-Present
    Chair - Board of Directors (1994), Vice Chair - Board of Directors (1995)

DEPARTMENT RELATED COMMUNITY SERVICE

Special Olympics Broadway Bridge Run (Coordinator)
Missouri Police Chief's Law Enforcement Run for Special Olympics (Committee member)
Care Team (Career Crisis Support Group)
United Way Campaign (Co-Chaired)

SALLY BUTLER

114 Sky Road • Anytown, California 91040 | 818 555-1387

Creative **Music Librarian** with 18 years experience and a background in **Post Production**. Combination of expertise in research, staffing, and project coordination. Talented negotiator and team leader with substantial contributions in innovative problem solving, decision making, and crisis management. Natural communicator with strong motivational skills and the ability to produce and succeed. Consistently effective in streamlining and upgrading operations, and improving productivity. Personable and enthusiastic with a sense of humor.

SUMMARY OF QUALIFICATIONS

Management

Act as liaison between composers, music copyists, editors, and post production.
Deal effectively with difficult people; qualified for client/staff interaction at all levels.
Handle budgets of $20,000+ (time allocation, musicians and copyists costs).
Created a standardized music sheet for use by composers and music editors; production manual was implemented company-wide.
Issue directives to editorial people.
Can organize and focus the efforts of others; train operations-level staff.

Research

Thorough understanding of
- composers' needs both technically and artistically
- source music, public domain, and music clearance.
Very resourceful at finding data and developing primary and secondary sources.

Administration

Assist producer in choice of composer and music.
Coordinate schedules, meetings, and licensing agreements.
Exceptional organizational skills; capable of prioritizing and managing a heavy work flow without direct supervision.
Accustomed to handling diverse responsibilities resourcefully.
Execute multiple jobs simultaneously.

Computer Skills

IBM: Microsoft Word, Excel, Access, Calendar Plus, FileMaker Pro.
Macintosh: FileMaker Pro, Claris Works, MacWrite Pro.

PROFESSIONAL EXPERIENCE

MUSIC COORDINATOR / POST PRODUCTION   1995 - Present
MTM/INTERNATIONAL FAMILY ENTERTAINMENT

Supervise replacement or deletion of all music cues throughout the entire MTM/Family Channel Library. Analyze revision of music and, when appropriate, recommend either no replacement or sound creativity. Gather proper master elements for work (NTSC, PALS, syndication). Analyze cue sheets, implement new cue sheet standard, and update inventories with new revised music masters.

Assist Vice President of Post Production in daily operations. Oversee development and preparation of telecine dailies and distribute tapes accordingly. Coordinate ADR sessions, insert stages, and second unit photography as needed. Improved company inventory tracking system for all film, video, and audio elements.

MUSIC LIBRARIAN / MUSIC PREPARATION 1979 - 1991
MOVING PICTURES MUSIC LIBRARY

Catalogued **all** of Columbia's music for motion pictures and television produced since 1928. Created card file to cross reference by composer and movie title. Organized and handled all music preparation for motion pictures, mini-series, movies of the week, and episodic television. Arranged for music to be picked up from composer and delivered to copyist. Prepare music for recording date; list all music and timings on breakdown sheets. Double check all instruments. Created books (music folders) for recording sessions, ensured all music was at recording date and picked up afterwards.

MUSIC LIBRARIAN 1979 - Present
INDEPENDENT PROJECTS (Concurrently)

Beverly Hills POP — Music Librarian (1990)
Spelling and Spelling/Goldberg (1979-1985)

MUSICAL SKILLS
Piano and clarinet

PROFESSIONAL AFFILIATIONS
Member, Musician Union Local 47

EDUCATION
San Joaquin Delta College, Stockton, California
Private studies in music

DANIEL J. ROGERS
185 Summer Drive
Miami, Florida 99887
(680) 442-0098

TRANSPORTATION INDUSTRY EXECUTIVE
Start-Up, Turnaround & High-Growth Operations Nationwide

Senior Operating & Management Executive with 15+ years of senior-level experience building and directing profitable, large-scale, multi-site, multi-modal transportation operations. Recognized for expertise in creative solutions and action to meet complex operating challenges and competitive demands. Strong analytical, negotiations, strategic planning and change management performance. Excellent performance in new business development, mergers, acquisitions, joint ventures and other corporate initiatives. Harvard Masters Degree.

PROFESSIONAL EXPERIENCE:

HARTMAN SHIPPING COMPANY, Miami, Florida   1981 to Present

Distinguished 16-year management career with this 110-year-old shipping agency and stevedoring operation. Promoted through increasingly responsible operating and general management positions to **Senior Vice President (#2 in the company)**. Delivered strong and sustainable profit improvement through leadership of strategic turnaround, revitalization and business development initiatives.

Senior Vice President (1995 to Present)

Member of 4-person Board of Directors operating this 400-employee, 26-office shipping agency and stevedoring company. Hold full P&L responsibility for West Gulf Operations (previous position) in addition to national corporate functions (e.g., business development, customer service, cost reduction and avoidance, information technology, mergers, acquisitions, strategic alliances, joint ventures). Focusing on rebuilding the corporation and negotiating unique partnerships in response to dramatic industry changes.

- Created national sales program and recruited national account team which won major corporate clients nationwide (e.g., Dow Chemical, DuPont, Exxon, Goodyear). Captured a 16% volume increase for one major shipping line through targeted account development.

- Championed acquisition and implementation of $3 million investment in emerging information systems to revolutionize operations, centralize bookings and customer service, and enhance the entire planning, operating and financial functions of the corporation. Projecting 5-year project payback.

- Architected a unique plan to integrate, streamline and consolidate both agency and stevedoring operations. To date, delivered $2.5+ million in annual savings in recurring expenses (e.g., purchasing, travel, facilities leasing, staffing). Transitioned from office to home-based, implemented 800 number and significantly enhanced customer service delivery.

Member of the **Board of Directors of Hartman Shipping Company** and several affiliates including:

- **Allen Transport** (1995 to Present). **Co-Founder & Managing Director** with full P&L responsibility for agency services joint venture between Hartman and Allen Agency. Merged each company's operations and transitioned from $400,000 operating loss to $400,000 profit in first year.

- **Oceana Services** (1995 to Present). Alternate Board **Director** of holding company with seven operating stevedoring and terminal subsidiaries.

- **King Oceanic Agencies** (1994 to Present). **Co-Founder & Managing Director** with full P&L responsibility for multi-agency joint venture for crew, marine products and spare parts distribution.

- **Maritime Shipping, Inc.** (1991 to Present). **President & Board Director** for NVOCC.

- **T.C. Cranes, Inc.** (1990 to 1996). **Board Director** providing general management and operating leadership to crane and forklift rental partnership.

HARTMAN SHIPPING COMPANY (*Continued*):

Vice President - West Gulf (1990 to 1995)

Promoted to lead an aggressive turnaround and revitalization of the largest agency and stevedoring operation in the company. Challenged to reverse previous losses by upgrading operations, personnel, new business development initiatives, and overall efficiency, productivity and quality of the business unit. Scope of responsibility was diverse and included 13 profit centers (e.g., agency, stevedoring, container terminals, freight handling, chassis leasing, container repairs), 135 employees (including ILA union personnel), a direct management team of 15 and complete P&L responsibility.

- Achieved/surpassed all turnaround objectives.

- Captured a 42% reduction in overall operating costs within first 12 months, transitioning from $1 million loss to $600,000 profit.

Vice President - State of Florida (1985 to 1990)
Local Manager - Miami, Florida (1981 to 1985)

Recruited to Hartman to manage their Port Everglades facility, including all operations, accounting, sales, traffic, documentation, new business development, cost control and revenue enhancement programs. Promoted to Vice President for the entire State of Florida (four offices and 65 employees). Challenged to revitalize and streamline operations, enhance staff performance, and restore profitability. Full P&L.

- Delivered annual revenue growth of 20% despite increasing market competition.

- Restored key account relationship and increased carrier volume by 500%.

WESTIN LINE AGENCY, Miami, Florida   1978 to 1980

Port Manager (1979 to 1980)

Planned and directed the start-up of a new port facility with complete rail, trucking, marine and CFS operations. Created the infrastructure and operating systems to support growth from start-up to $24 million in first year revenues (2000 containers per month).

Operations Manager (1978 to 1979)

Full operating management responsibility for all port operations including vessel loading, equipment control, maintenance and repair, scheduling and expense management. Supervised staff of seven.

NEVILLE LINES, Miami, Florida   1977 to 1978

Manager - Marine Operations

Managed vessel operations (breakbulk, bulk, semi-container, tanker) in Miami. Supervised cargo loading/discharging, stevedoring and stowage layout. Prepared production rates, cost control analyses, budgets and long-term projections.

EDUCATION: **Masters Degree - Yale University** - 1976
Concentration in Program Planning & Management

Bachelor of Arts Degree - Trinity College - 1975
Concentration in Comparative Politics & Economic Development

AFFILIATIONS: Board of Directors, United Marine Association
Board of Directors, Greater Miami Bureau

MILITARY: U.S. Army - Marine Transportation - Honorable Discharge - 1967 to 1970

Jeri Goodhands

123 Oak Avenue   San Mateo, CA 94444   415/123-4567

Objective   Massage Therapist for a Chiropractic Office

Strengths

- Effective Communicator
- Planning
- Manager
- Customer Service
- Coordinator
- Sales
- Trainer
- Negotiator
- Supervisor

Training

National Wholistic Institute

▸ Over 400 hours of formal training in the following forms of bodywork:
- Swedish • Shiatsu • Sports Massage • Deep Tissue • Foot Reflexology
- Hydrotherapy • Active and Passive Stretches • Trigger Point Work
- Cross Fiber & Longitudinal Release •

▸ Completed western internship and externship; currently serving eastern externship at San Mateo County AIDS program; will begin eastern internship in August.

Professional Experience

Customer Service
- Significantly improved customer satisfaction on a continuous basis.
- Assist customers with phone and walk-in orders, provided quotes, pulled orders for shipment.
- Successfully resolved shipment, return and warranty problems.
- Revised customer service and training procedures.
- Selected and trained customer service staff.

Sales Representative
- Successfully sold cutlery products, increased amount sold and customer satisfaction.
- Demonstrated products and provided training.
- Distributed sales leads; supervised five sales employees.

Secretarial • Receptionist • Bookkeeping
- Handled large volume of calls and successfully distributed messages.
- General office responsibility.
- Updated and maintained accounting records.
- Journalized and posted transactions; performed trial balance.

Employment History

11/90 - 10/95	Senior Customer Service Rep.	Happy Corporation, Foster City
08/88 - 11/90	Coordinator	All-State Corporation, San Mateo
02/87 - 09/88	Sales Representative	Rector Marketing Corporation, San Jose
03/86 - 02/87	Receptionist/Cashier	Chrysler Ford, Redwood City
06/85 - 03/86	Customer Service/Accts Rec.	A&B, Tool & Die, San Juan

Professional Organization

Member, American Massage Therapy Association

DREW KANNY OVERLAND
SSN: 555-55-5555

2121 High Mountain Loop
Somewhere, Arizona 82222

Ph: 555.555.5555
e-mail: drewkan@aol.com

OBJECTIVE   Career pilot

CERTIFICATES AND RATINGS

Airline Transport Pilot:	Airplane Multiengine Land
Commercial Privileges:	Airplane Single Engine Land
Flight Engineer Written Exam:	Completed 9/97, score of 98%
Ground Instructor:	Advanced, Instrument
FAA First Class Medical Certificate:	Issued with no waivers

FLIGHT TIMES   TOTAL 3,629

Pilot-in-Command	1,677	Turboprop	1,651	Actual Instruments	126
Instructor	1,374	FW Multiengine	1,916	Night	279
Second-in-Command	1,770	FW Single Engine	1,713	Cross Country	2,360
Student	268	Hood Simulated Instruments	77	Simulator	130

WORK EXPERIENCE

02/96 - Current	West Airlines 11 Flight Path Big Town, AZ 82222	**FIRST OFFICER:** BE-1900D. Part 121 scheduled passenger transport operations in the Southwest as West Airlines feeder.
08/95 to 02/96	Flight Safety 25 Approach Blvd. City Airport City, FL 33333	**FLIGHT INSTRUCTOR:** Taught primary, advanced, instrument, and multiengine under Part 141; provided private and commercial instruction.
12/94 to 04/95	Mountain Air 58 Mountain Drive College Town, WA 91111	**FIRST OFFICER:** Piper Chiefton. Part 135 scheduled passenger transport operations between College Town and Business Town.

(Mountain Air no longer in business)

09/91 to 04/95	Town Community College 66 Community Way College Town, WA 91111	**FLIGHT INSTRUCTOR:** Taught private, commercial, instrument, and private pilot ground school to CFI and CFII students under Part 141.

ACHIEVEMENT: Developed and implemented curriculum for private pilot ground school.

09/88 to 09/91	United Parcel Service 66 Community Way College Town, WA 91111	Preloader: Load and unload delivery trucks.

FORMAL EDUCATION: BACHELOR OF SCIENCE DEGREE

08/93 to 01/94	Big Town College College Town, WA 91111	Managerial Leadership major

ASSOCIATE OF ARTS AND APPLIED SCIENCE DEGREE

09/86 to 06/91	Town Community College College Town, WA 91111	Flight Technology major
08/87 to 09/88	University of Big Town College Town, WA 91111	General Studies

PROFESSIONAL TRAINING

6/12/95 to 6/19/95	West Airlines Big Town, AZ	Airline Transport Pilot Training

AVAILABILITY   Immediate

DAVID L. INMAN

265 Belvedere Avenue
Lakeland, Ontario
Canada K5P 3L2

Phone: (613) 525-4439
Mobile: (613) 525-4776
Email: InmanD@atgn.lakeland.net

GLOBAL SECURITY MANAGEMENT PROFESSIONAL
Personnel / Property / Technology / Facilities

Over 15 years experience in the strategic planning, development and tactical leadership of comprehensive security operations worldwide. Combines strong training, resource management, budgeting and technology skills with excellent performance in international liaison affairs, international negotiations, investigations and data analysis. PC proficient. Dual British & Canadian citizenship. EEC Eligible. Security Clearance.

PROFESSIONAL EXPERIENCE:

NATIONAL SERVICES & AFFILIATED AGENCIES   1989 to Present

Chief Security Officer - Bangkok, Thailand (1996 to Present)
Senior Field Security & Logistics Officer - Kigali, Rwanda (1994 to 1996)
Field Security & Logistics Officer - Phnom Penh, Cambodia (1993 to 1994)
Field Security & Logistics Officer - Kabul, Afghanistan (1989 to 1993)

High-profile security management position supporting operations, programs, projects, personnel, facilities, properties, technologies and other assets of National Services in regions worldwide. Scope of responsibility is significant and includes long-range planning, security operations, security systems, personnel identification systems, NS headquarters reporting, personnel training and development, VIP protection, advance security, international liaison affairs, budgeting and a comprehensive crisis management program.

- Current supervisory responsibility for a team of 48 NS, General Services and contract security professionals responsible for the safety and protection of 2900 NS personnel within 12 NS agencies and a 99,000 square meter NS complex.
- Manage security liaison affairs with NS agencies, diplomatic missions, intelligence organizations and local government agencies. Coordinate special security arrangements for NS meetings and visits of high-ranking dignitaries and delegates for both national and cross-border missions.
- Author annual security plans and crisis/emergency response plans. Lead security briefings for new staff. Travel throughout Asia to conduct security assessments and participate in NS official missions.
- Manage a sophisticated NS communications network, including technology acquisition, integration, systems operation and cooperative efforts with local telecommunications companies and government agencies.

Special Projects & Achievements:

- Achieved 100% success in providing 24-hour surveillance for the U.S. Diplomatic Community.
- Developed the first-ever NS security plan for Cambodia (new station). Designed organizational infrastructure, created security information database prototype incident reporting and tracking system, and recruited/trained security force and support personnel.
- Orchestrated immediate personnel evacuations and relocations in response to volatile local country political and terrorist activity.
- Conducted discrete criminal investigations allegedly involving NS personnel and/or their dependents. Investigated major counterfeit currency operation, several homicides and large theft case following personnel evacuation from Afghanistan.

UNITED STATES EMBASSY, Kabul, Afghanistan   1988 to 1989

Security & Logistics Officer / Operations Manager
Recruited and trained 800-person U.S. Embassy security force for diplomatic installations throughout the country.   Designed and delivered training programs on physical security, asset protection, personnel/VIP protection, crisis response and international liaison affairs.   Controlled expense budgets, administrative and security reporting functions.   Managed cooperative investigations with local law enforcement agencies.

LARGE CANADIAN POLICE FORCE, Lakeland, Ontario   1979 to 1988

Constable
Promoted through a series of increasingly responsible patrol, investigation and management positions during 10-year career to final position as Constable leading a 10-person joint forces team.   Directed the "largest and most indepth undercover narcotics operation in the Force's history."

Seconded to Ontario Police College (1984 to 1986) as an **Instructor of Provincial Studies, Self-Defense and Arrest & Search Techniques**.   Taught police recruits from forces throughout Canada and from various provincial ministries.   Co-wrote training manuals, participated in developing training videos, and authored journal articles.

EDUCATION:

Currently Pursuing MA in International Relations, Knightsbridge University, London
BA in Social Sciences, Law & Sociology, Queen's University, Lakeland, Canada, 1978
General Police Studies, Canadian Police College, 1988
Advanced Police Studies Certification, Ontario Police College / University of Western Ontario, 1986
General Police Studies Certification, Ontario Police College / University of Western Ontario, 1984
Teaching Certification in Methods of Instructional Techniques, Ontario Police College, 1983
Diploma - Probationary Constable, Ontario Police College, 1981

Additional training in the U.K., Canada, Europe, Australia, Japan and the U.S. including:

National Services Field Security Officer Training, Turin, Italy, 1994 & New York City, 1992
Technical Surveillance Training, London, England, 1988
Study Tour of Northern Ireland & Scotland, Ulster Constabulary & Scottish Police, 1988
Attorney General's Conference on Terrorism, FBI Academy, Quantico, Virginia, 1986
FBI Training Academy, Quantico, Virginia, 1984
Canadian Ministry of Environmental Certification, 1976

PERSONAL PROFILE:

Publications	*National Services Field Security Handbook, National Services, 1993*
	Armed & Unarmed Defense Tactics Manual, Griffin House Publishers, Toronto, 1985/1986
	A Woman's First Defense Manual, Griffin House Publishers, Toronto, 1985/1986
	Ontario Police College Self-Defense Training Manual, Ontario Police Department, 1985
Affiliations	International Police Assn ... Justice System Training Assn ... Assn of Law Enforcement Instructors
	Canadian Director, International Non-Lethal Weapons Assn
Licenses	Certified NAUI Scuba Diver ... Black Belt- 2nd Degree Judo ... Commercial Pilot's License
Competitions	Silver Medalist in Judo, Law Enforcement Olympics, Australia
	Manager / Team Member, Canadian National Judo Team

ROGER M. SMITH

987 South Manitoba Lane, Big Vista, North Dakota 78964
(555) 123-4567 • Email: planbtr@usit.net

PROFILE	• **Career interest in Urban Planning.** Strong academic background combined with diverse experience. **Strength in creative problem solving,** blending idealism with political reality, and devising new methods to improve procedural and system efficiency. **Big-picture oriented.** Willing to relocate. Core competencies:

- zoning administration
- site plan review & approval
- subdivision regulation
- waste water distribution
- design ordinance administration
- economic development
- historic preservation
- environmental impact & planning
- policy analysis
- training presentations

- community development
- stormwater drainage
- surface hydrology
- parking lot design
- environmental impact
- public relations
- urban redevelopment
- administrative management
- leadership & motivation
- media spokesperson

- **Proven communications ability that is straightforward, honest, articulate, yet tactful and diplomatic.** Sincere sensitivity to unique needs and aspirations of all segments of a community. Active listening and consultation skills with talent for respecting and responding to divergent opinions and interests. **Highly organized.**

EDUCATION

- **Master of Science - Urban Planning,** 1996
  University of North Dakota • GPA 3.7/4.0
- **Master of Arts - Anthropology (Major: Archaeology),** 1992
  University of North Dakota • GPA 4.0/4.0
- **Bachelor of Arts - Archaeology,** 1989
  Indian State University • GPA 3.8/4.0
- **Officer Candidate School: United States Army,** 1983
  - Commandant's List (top 10%)

SELECTED ACHIEVEMENTS

WAUTENEKA DEVELOPMENT AUTHORITY (WDA), Wauteneka, North Dakota
Urban Planner (1995-present)

- **Reviewed development proposals** for adherence to county zoning and other ordinances and aesthetically-based design guidelines.
- **Researched rezoning requests** in the development area to ensure conformance with published long range plans and community needs.
- **Employed skills in persuasive communications and negotiations** with property developers, architects, and citizens in administering design guidelines.
- **Facilitated public involvement in planning decisions** by communicating merits of project(s) which in turn, promoted community good will and continued support.
- **Successfully gained support from influential community leaders** relating to the impact of WDA's agenda on their property values and quality of life.
- **Independently orchestrated a highly productive meeting** which formed alliances between the WDA, property owners, and businesses.

KENETAQUA TRIBAL ARCHAEOLOGY PROJECT, Mineotalla, South Dakota
Director of Field Operations / Private Consultant (1994-1995)

- **Oversaw historic archaeological project** for joint venture between Big Rock Community College and Kenetaqua Tribal Foundation. **Recruited and technically trained work crew of 135 volunteers** consisting of local community college students, elementary school children, and others to survey, test, and excavate site.
- **Developed all project policy and operational procedures.** Directed site mapping, photography, and field documentation activities. Effectively led well-received project to completion **on time and under budget with all volunteer staff.**
- **Coordinated a significant public education program** for the local historical society and area elementary schools.

SELECTED ACHIEVEMENTS (continued)

BIG ROCK COMMUNITY COLLEGE, Mineotalla, South Dakota
Adjunct Professor (1994-1995, concurrent)

- **Led classes of 30 students in basics of field archaeology and excavation technique** for intensive field school in New Vista, South Dakota. Lectured in classroom and field setting on the prehistory of the Midwest.
- **Taught two courses per semester at Big Rock County Community Colleges** (Chief Eagle C.C. and Mineotalla College) in Anthropology and Archaeology. Designed curricula which ensured credit transferability to South Dakota State University.

UNIVERSITY OF NORTH DAKOTA (UND), Narrow Ridge, North Dakota
Lab Director: UND Archaeology Field School (1992)
Crew Chief: UND Archaeology Field School (1990-1992)
Graduate Teaching Assistant (1990-1992)

- **Directed field laboratory** for 1992 field season. Returned from field with all artifacts through primary processing.
- As Crew Chief, for the Narrow Ridge Prehistory Project, **instructed and supervised work crews** at Wolf's Peak State Park in excavation techniques, mapping, recording, and the preservation of archaeological materials and sites.
- **Performed public relations / awareness activities**: site tours and educational classes.

MILITARY ACCOMPLISHMENTS DEMONSTRATING ADMINISTRATIVE MANAGEMENT SKILLS

UNITED STATES ARMY, Honorably Discharged
Executive Officer (Army Reserves)
Article 32(b) Investigating Officer
Platoon Leader

- **Trained company of drill sergeants in classroom and field settings** in all aspects of professional bearing, leadership acumen, and administrative protocol.
- **Educated 950 West Point cadets** on Army vehicular driving and maintenance in the field and achieved a 100% "pass" and 100% incident-free record.
- **Served as a one-person Grand Jury** for a jurisdiction of over 20,000 soldiers and families on Administrative Law violations to determine eligibility for general court martial and military dismissal.
- **Presided over 87 hearings yearly.** Orchestrated pre-trial investigations including witness interrogations, acquired sworn testimony, and authored over 100 technically-complex investigative reports.

COMPUTERS

- MICROSOFT: Windows 97 - Office Suite - Word - Excel
- NOVELL OFFICE: WordPerfect - Quattro Pro
- INTERNET APPLICATIONS: E-mail - FTP - Web applications - browsers - HTML
- OTHER: LAN - GIS familiarity

COMMUNITY

- **Initiated a community garden project** in South Mineotalla which involved site planning, recruiting and motivating volunteer staff, orchestrating public relations activities, and coordinating materials acquisition.
- **Coordinated Archaeology Days, a collaborative public education project** for three Big Rock County cities.
- **Invited as guest speaker for numerous community groups** on topics relating to Midwestern Archaeology.

Chapter 9

Get Started!

This chapter includes several resume development forms to assist you in writing your resume. Take the time to complete each form and be as detailed in your responses as possible. Then use these sheets as the baseline data for developing your resume, cover letters and other job search communications.

---

*The time you devote to completing this information is
directly correlated to the final quality,
caliber and impact of your resume.*

PROFESSIONAL SKILLS SHEET

Use This Professional Skills Sheet to highlight your professional skills, competencies and knowledge. Then integrate this information into the Summary and Job Description sections of your resume, as they may be appropriate to your current search objective(s).

PERSONAL ATTRIBUTES

(Circle all that apply.)

Adaptable	Determined	Persistent
Aggressive	Driven	Persuasive
Assertive	Dynamic	Pioneering
Competent	Efficient	Polished
Competitive	Energetic	Positive
Conceptual	Enterprising	Practical
Confident	Enthusiastic	Productive
Conscientious	Independent	Progressive
Creative	Innovative	Resourceful
Decisive	Intelligent	Sophisticated
Dedicated	Motivated	Strategic
Dependable	Opportunistic	Successful

OTHERS CHARACTERIZE ME AS:

_____

_____

_____

_____

TECHNICAL / COMPUTER SKILLS:

(Fill in the blanks with a complete listing of all of your computer skills.)

Hardware: _____

Software: _____

Networks: _____

Languages: _____

INDUSTRY EXPERIENCE:

(Fill in the blanks with a comprehensive listing
of all of your industry experience.)

_____

_____

_____

_____

PROFESSIONAL SKILLS:

(Fill in the blanks with a detailed listing of your specific professional skills. For example, if you are a CFO, your skills will include finance, accounting, treasury and tax. For a sales executive, your skills include negotiations, presentation, account management and new product introduction. Be comprehensive. Many of these skills are the KeyWords that you will use in your resume.)

_____   _____

_____   _____

_____   _____

_____   _____

_____   _____

_____   _____

_____   _____

_____   _____

_____   _____

_____   _____

_____   _____

EMPLOYMENT HISTORY SHEET

Use the following Employment History Sheets as the starting point for writing your job descriptions. Fill out a sheet for each position you have held throughout your entire career. Be sure to be comprehensive and detail everything that you can think of about each position. Then use these sheets to evaluate and prioritize the information, using what is most notable to create your job descriptions.

The first sheet is completed to give you a precise example of how best to use these preparation tools.

Company Name: The XYZ Manufacturing Company

City & State: Omaha, Nebraska

Job Title: Vice President of Operations

Dates: February 1996 to Present

Co. Description: Single site manufacturer of industrial heating & ventilation equipment with $125 million in revenue, 400 employees and nationwide sales/distribution.

Challenge: Although profitable for 14 years, since 1994 the company had lost over $10 million annually, shareholder confidence was low, customer quality and satisfaction ratings were poor, and creditors were threatening potential action. Company required strong and immediate turnaround to survive.

Responsibilities: Full P&L responsibility for ALL operations – production planning and scheduling, manufacturing, assembly, warehousing, distribution, transportation, purchasing, inventory, quality, personnel (union and non-union), union negotiations, budgeting, capital improvements, industrial engineering, facilities management, energy & building systems, safety, risk management, new product engineering, R&D,

administration, manufacturing automation, information systems and telecommunications.

- $25 million annual operating budget.
- $15 million annual capital budget.
- 6-person direct management team.
- $500 million in capital assets.
- 1 manufacturing plant, 2 assembly facilities & 1 warehouse

Achievements:
- Led successful turnaround and returned to profitability.

- Decreased manufacturing costs $5 million annually.

- Decreased inventory holding costs $1 million annually.

- Improved productivity 35% and efficiency 22%.

- Increased customer satisfaction to a consistent 98%.

- Reduced turnover 12% and Workers' Compensation costs 28%.

- Implemented MRP, JIT and Kanban techniques.

- Automated key areas of production and optimized yields.

EMPLOYMENT HISTORY SHEET

Company Name: _____

City & State: _____

Job Title: _____

Dates: _____

Co. Description: _____

_____

_____

Challenge: _____

_____

_____

Responsibilities: _____

_____

_____

_____

_____

Achievements: _____

_____

_____

_____

_____

EMPLOYMENT HISTORY SHEET

Company Name: _____

City & State: _____

Job Title: _____

Dates: _____

Co. Description: _____

_____

_____

Challenge: _____

_____

_____

Responsibilities: _____

_____

_____

_____

_____

_____

Achievements: _____

_____

_____

_____

_____

_____

EMPLOYMENT HISTORY SHEET

Company Name: _____

City & State: _____

Job Title: _____

Dates: _____

Co. Description: _____

_____

_____

Challenge: _____

_____

_____

Responsibilities: _____

_____

_____

_____

_____

_____

Achievements: _____

_____

_____

_____

_____

_____

EMPLOYMENT HISTORY SHEET

Company Name: _____

City & State: _____

Job Title: _____

Dates: _____

Co. Description: _____

_____

_____

_____

Challenge: _____

_____

_____

Responsibilities: _____

_____

_____

_____

_____

Achievements: _____

_____

_____

_____

_____

_____

EMPLOYMENT HISTORY SHEET

Company Name: _____

City & State: _____

Job Title: _____

Dates: _____

Co. Description: _____

_____

_____

Challenge: _____

_____

_____

Responsibilities: _____

_____

_____

_____

_____

Achievements: _____

_____

_____

_____

_____

_____

INFORMATIONAL WORKSHEET

Complete all of the information below that is pertinent to you. Then prioritize the information that supports your current career objective(s) and integrate, as appropriate, into your resume. Remember, this information can be included in separate sections, consolidated into one section and/or integrated with other information already presented on your resume.

Consulting Projects: _____

_____

_____

Certifications: _____

_____

_____

Licenses: _____

_____

_____

Foreign Languages: _____

_____

_____

Professional Affiliations: _____

_____

_____

Civic Affiliations: _____

_____

_____

Academic Honors: _____

_____

_____

Professional Awards: _____

_____

_____

Publications: _____

_____

_____

Presentations: _____

_____

_____

Patents: _____

_____

_____

Military Service: _____

_____

_____

International Travel: _____

_____

_____

Additional Information: _____

_____

_____

RESUME & JOB SEARCH RESOURCES

THE ADVANTAGE INC.

Executive Resume & Career Management Center

The Advantage, Inc., one of the nation's foremost resume and job search centers, was founded by Wendy S. Enelow in August 1986. The firm specializes in resume development, job search and career coaching for professional, management, senior management and executive job search candidates. To date, The Advantage has worked with more than 5000 professionals worldwide to plan and manage their successful job search campaigns!

Professional writers and coaches work one-on-one with you to explore your professional goals, develop career strategies, create winning resumes and implement action plans that competitively position you to:

> **Win in Today's Competitive Job Search Market!**

Executive Resume Development   **Targeted Direct Mail Campaigns**
Cover Letter Writing Services   **Internet Online Services**
Executive Career Planning & Coaching   **Interview Counseling**
Executive Job Lead Publications   **KeyWord Presentations**

Consultations with Wendy Enelow are by scheduled appointment. If you are interested in executive resume, career coaching or job search management services, fax the form below with your resume to (804) 384-4700 or phone (804) 384-4600.

- -

❑   **YES!**   Please contact me regarding your services and pricing.

My resume is attached.

NAME: _____

ADDRESS: _____

PHONE: _____

FAX: _____   *Is this a private fax?*   **YES**   **NO**

CAREER RESOURCES

C ontact Impact Publications to receive a free annotated listing of career resources or visit their World Wide Web (Internet) site for a complete listing of career resources:

http://www.impactpublications.com

The following career resources are available directly from Impact Publications. Complete this form or list the titles, include postage (see formula at the end), enclose payment, and send your order to:

IMPACT PUBLICATIONS
9104-N Manassas Drive
Manassas Park, VA 20111-5211
Tel. 1-800-361-1055 (orders)
Tel. 703/361-7300 or Fax 703/335-9486
E-mail: *impactp@impactpublications.com*

Orders from individuals must be prepaid by check, moneyorder, Visa, MasterCard, or American Express. We accept telephone, fax, and e-mail orders.

Qty.	TITLES	Price	TOTAL
Author's Resume and Cover Letter Books and Audio			
___	100 Winning Resumes For $100,000+ Jobs	$24.95	_____
___	201 Winning Cover Letters For $100,000+ Jobs	$24.95	_____
___	1500+ KeyWords For $100,000+ Jobs	$14.95	_____
___	Resume Explosion (audio)	$29.95	_____
___	Resume Winners From the Pros	$17.95	_____

Resume Books

___ 100 Winning Resumes For $100,000+ Jobs	$24.95	_____
___ 101 Best Resumes	$10.95	_____
___ 101 Great Resumes	$9.99	_____
___ 101 Resumes For Sure-Hire Results	$10.95	_____
___ 175 High-Impact Resumes	$10.95	_____
___ 1500+ KeyWords For $100,000+ Jobs	$14.95	_____
___ Adams Resume Almanac	$10.95	_____
___ America's Top Resumes For America's Top Jobs	$19.95	_____
___ Arco's Electronic Resumes That Get Jobs	$12.95	_____
___ Asher's Bible of Executive Resumes	$29.95	_____
___ Best Resumes For $75,000+ Executive Jobs	$14.95	_____
___ Blue Collar and Beyond	$8.95	_____
___ Building a Great Resume	$15.00	_____
___ Complete Idiot's Guide to Crafting the Perfect Resume	$16.95	_____
___ Designing the Perfect Resume	$12.95	_____
___ Dynamite Resumes	$14.95	_____
___ Electronic Resumes: Putting Your Resume On-Line	$19.95	_____
___ Electronic Resumes For the New Job Market	$11.95	_____
___ Encyclopedia of Job-Winning Resumes	$16.95	_____
___ Gallery of Best Resumes	$16.95	_____
___ Gallery of Best Resumes For Two-Year Degree Graduates	$14.95	_____
___ Heart and Soul Resumes	$14.95	_____
___ High Impact Resumes and Letters	$19.95	_____
___ How to Prepare Your Curriculum Vitae	$14.95	_____
___ Internet Resumes	$14.95	_____
___ Just Resumes	$11.95	_____
___ NBEW's Resumes	$11.95	_____
___ New Perfect Resume	$10.95	_____
___ Portfolio Power	$14.95	_____
___ Power Resumes	$12.95	_____
___ Quick Resume and Cover Letter Book	$12.95	_____
___ Real-Life Resumes That Work!	$12.95	_____
___ Resume Catalog	$15.95	_____
___ Resume Pro	$24.95	_____
___ Resume Shortcuts	$14.95	_____
___ Resume Solution	$12.95	_____
___ Resume Winners From the Pros	$17.95	_____
___ Resume Writing Made Easy	$10.95	_____
___ Resumes & Job Search Letters For Transitioning Military Personnel	$17.95	_____
___ Resumes For Advertising Careers	$9.95	_____
___ Resumes For Architecture and Related Careers	$9.95	_____
___ Resumes For Banking and Financial Careers	$9.95	_____
___ Resumes For Business Management Careers	$9.95	_____

___ Resumes For Communications Careers	$9.95	_____
___ Resumes For Dummies	$12.99	_____
___ Resumes For Education Careers	$9.95	_____
___ Resumes For Engineering Careers	$9.95	_____
___ Resumes For Environmental Careers	$9.95	_____
___ Resumes For Ex-Military Personnel	$9.95	_____
___ Resumes For 50+ Job Hunters	$9.95	_____
___ Resumes For the Healthcare Professional	$12.95	_____
___ Resumes For High Tech Careers	$9.95	_____
___ Resumes For Midcareer Job Changers	$9.95	_____
___ Resumes For the Over 50 Job Hunter	$14.95	_____
___ Resumes For People Who Hate to Write Resumes	$12.95	_____
___ Resumes For Re-Entry: A Woman's Handbook	$10.95	_____
___ Resumes For Sales and Marketing Careers	$9.95	_____
___ Resumes For Scientific and Technical Careers	$9.95	_____
___ Resumes in Cyberspace	$14.95	_____
___ Resumes That Knock 'Em Dead	$10.95	_____
___ Resumes, Resumes, Resumes	$9.99	_____
___ Sure-Hire Resumes	$14.95	_____

Resume Books With Computer Disk

___ Adams Resume Almanac With Disk	$19.95	_____
___ New 90-Minute Resume	$15.95	_____
___ Ready-to-Go Resumes	$16.95	_____

Resume CD-ROMs

___ Adams JobBank Fast Resume Suite	$49.95	_____
___ ResumeMaker	$49.95	_____
___ Win-Way Resume 4.0	$69.95	_____

Resume Software (specify disk size and system)

___ Perfect Resume Kit (Individual Version)	$49.95	_____
___ Perfect Resume Kit (Counselor Version)	$259.95	_____
___ Perfect Resume Kit (Lab Pack Version)	$639.95	_____
___ Perfect Resume Kit (Network Version)	$999.95	_____

Cover Letters

___ 175 High-Impact Cover Letters	$10.95	_____
___ 200 Letters For Job Hunters	$19.95	_____
___ 201 Dynamite Job Search Letters	$19.95	_____
___ 201 Killer Cover Letters	$16.95	_____
___ 201 Winning Cover Letters For $100,000+ Jobs	$24.95	_____
___ Adams Cover Letter Almanac and Disk	$19.95	_____
___ Complete Idiot's Guide to the Perfect Cover Letter	$14.95	_____

___	Cover Letters For Dummies	$12.99 ___
___	Cover Letters That Don't Forget	$8.95 ___
___	Cover Letters That Knock 'Em Dead	$10.95 ___
___	Cover Letters, Cover Letters, Cover Letters	$9.95 ___
___	Dynamite Cover Letters	$14.95 ___
___	NBEW's Cover Letters	$11.95 ___
___	Perfect Cover Letter	$10.95 ___
___	Sure-Hire Cover Letters	$10.95 ___

Interviews, Networking, and Salary Negotiations

___	101 Dynamite Answers to Interview Questions	$12.95 ___
___	101 Dynamite Questions to Ask At Your Job Interview	$14.95 ___
___	101 Dynamite Ways to Ace Your Job Interview	$13.95 ___
___	201 Answers to the Toughest Job Interview Questions	$10.95 ___
___	Adams Job Interview Almanacs	$10.95 ___
___	Ask the Headhunter	$14.95 ___
___	Dynamite Networking For Dynamite Jobs	$15.95 ___
___	Dynamite Salary Negotiation	$15.95 ___
___	Dynamite Tele-Search	$12.95 ___
___	Great Connections	$19.95 ___
___	How to Work a Room	$9.95 ___
___	Interview For Success	$15.95 ___
___	Interview Kit	$10.95 ___
___	Interview Power	$12.95 ___
___	Job Interviews For Dummies	$12.99 ___
___	NBEW's Interviewing	$11.95 ___
___	Networking For Everyone	$16.95 ___
___	People Power	$14.95 ___
___	Power Networking	$14.95 ___
___	Power Schmoozing	$12.95 ___
___	Quick Interview and Salary Negotiation Book	$12.95 ___
___	The Secrets of Savvy Networking	$11.99 ___
___	What Do I Say Next?	$20.00 ___

Skills, Testing, Self-Assessment, Empowerment

___	7 Habits of Highly Effective People	$14.00 ___
___	Career Satisfaction and Success	$9.95 ___
___	Chicken Soup For the Soul	$12.95 ___
___	Common Sense For Uncommon Times	$14.95 ___
___	Discover the Best Jobs For You	$15.95 ___
___	Do What You Are	$16.95 ___
___	Do What You Love, the Money Will Follow	$10.95 ___
___	Get a Job You Love!	$19.95 ___
___	Gifts Differing	$14.95 ___

___	Heart at Work	$14.95 ___
___	Love Your Work and Success Will Follow	$12.95 ___
___	P.I.E. Method For Career Success	$14.95 ___
___	Real People, Real Jobs	$15.95 ___
___	A Second Helping of Chicken Soup For the Soul	$12.95 ___
___	Starting Out, Starting Over	$14.95 ___
___	Stop Postponing the Rest of Your Life	$9.95 ___
___	A Third Helping of Chicken Soup For the Soul	$12.95 ___

Dress, Appearing, Image

___	110 Mistakes Working Women Make and How to Avoid Them: Dressing Smart in the 90's	$9.95 ___
___	John Molloy's New Dress For Success (men)	$12.99 ___
___	The New Women's Dress For Success	$12.99 ___
___	Red Socks Don't Work! (men)	$14.95 ___
___	The Winning Image	$17.95 ___

Job Search Strategies and Tactics

___	101 Great Answers to the Toughest Job Search Problems	$11.99 ___
___	110 Biggest Mistakes Job Hunters Make	$19.95 ___
___	303 Off the Wall Ways to Get a Job	$12.99 ___
___	Change Your Job, Change Your Life	$17.95 ___
___	Complete Job Finder's Guide to the 90s	$13.95 ___
___	Five Secrets to Finding a Job	$12.95 ___
___	How to Get Interviews From Classified Job Ads	$14.95 ___
___	Job Hunter's Catalog	$10.95 ___
___	Job Hunting For Dummies	$16.99 ___
___	Job Hunting For the Utterly Confused	$14.95 ___
___	Job Hunting May Easy	$12.95 ___
___	Job Vault	$20.00 ___
___	Joyce Lain Kennedy's Career Book	$29.95 ___
___	Knock 'Em Dead	$12.95 ___
___	Me, Myself, and I, Inc	$17.95 ___
___	New Rites of Passage At $100,000+	$29.95 ___
___	The Pathfinder	$14.00 ___
___	Professional's Job Finder	$18.95 ___
___	Strategic Job Jumping	$13.00 ___
___	SuccesssAbilities	$14.95 ___
___	Very Quick Job Search	$14.95 ___
___	Welcome to the Real World	$13.00 ___
___	What Color Is Your Parachute?	$16.95 ___

Electronic Job Search and the Internet

___	Adams Electronic Job Search Almanac 1998	$9.95 ___

__ CareerXroads: 1998 Directory to the 500 Best Sites on WWW	$22.95	_____
__ Employer's Guide to Recruiting on the Internet	$24.95	_____
__ Finding a Job on the Internet	$16.95	_____
__ Getting on the Information Superhighway	$11.95	_____
__ Guide to Internet Job Searching	$14.95	_____
__ How to Get Your Dream Job Using the Web	$29.99	_____
__ Internet Resumes	$14.95	_____
__ Point and Click Jobfinder	$14.95	_____
__ Resumes in Cyberspace	$14.95	_____
__ The Three R's of E-Mail	$12.95	_____
__ Using the Internet & the World Wide Web in Your Job Search	$16.95	_____
__ Using WordPerfect in Your Job Search	$19.95	_____

Best Jobs and Employers For the 90s

__ 100 Best Careers For the 21st Century	$15.95	_____
__ American Almanac of Jobs and Salaries	$17.00	_____
__ Best Jobs For the 21st Century	$19.95	_____
__ Hidden Job Market 1998	$18.95	_____
__ Hoover's 500 (annual)	$29.95	_____
__ Hoover's Top 2,500 Employers	$22.95	_____
__ Jobs 1998	$16.00	_____

Key Directories

__ American Salaries and Wages Survey	$110.00	_____
__ The Big Book of Minority Opportunities	$39.95	_____
__ Business Phone Book USA	$155.00	_____
__ Careers Encyclopedia	$39.95	_____
__ Complete Guide For Occupational Exploration	$39.95	_____
__ Dictionary of Occupational Titles	$39.95	_____
__ Directory of Executive Recruiters (annual)	$44.95	_____
__ Directory of Outplacement Firms	$89.95	_____
__ Encyclopedia of Careers and Vocational Guidance	$149.95	_____
__ Enhanced Guide For Occupational Exploration	$34.95	_____
__ Free and Inexpensive Career Materials	$19.95	_____
__ Internships (annual)	$24.95	_____
__ JobBank Guide to Computer and High-Tech Companies	$16.95	_____
__ JobBank Guide to Health Care Companies	$16.95	_____
__ Job Bank Guide to Employment Services (annual)	$200.00	_____
__ Job Hunter's Sourcebook	$69.95	_____
__ Moving and Relocation Directory	$179.95	_____
__ National Job Bank (annual)	$320.00	_____
__ National Trade and Professional Associations	$129.95	_____
__ Minority Organizations	$49.95	_____

__	Occupational Outlook Handbook	$21.95 ____
__	O*NET Dictionary of Occupational Titles	$49.95 ____
__	Personnel Executives Contactbook	$149.00 ____
__	Places Rated Almanac	$21.95 ____
__	Professional Careers Sourcebook	$99.95 ____

International, Overseas, and Travel Jobs

__	Careers in International Affairs	$17.95 ____
__	Complete Guide to International Jobs & Careers	$13.95 ____
__	International Jobs Directory	$19.95 ____
__	Jobs For People Who Love Travel	$15.95 ____
__	Jobs in Paradise	$14.95 ____
__	Jobs in Russia and the Newly Independent States	$15.95 ____
__	Jobs Worldwide	$17.95 ____
__	Teaching English Abroad	$15.95 ____

Public-Oriented Careers

__	Complete Guide to Public Employment	$19.95 ____
__	Directory of Federal Jobs and Employers	$21.95 ____
__	Federal Applications That Get Results	$23.95 ____
__	Federal Jobs in Law Enforcement	$14.95 ____
__	Find a Federal Job Fast!	$15.95 ____
__	Government Job Finder	$16.95 ____
__	Jobs and Careers With Nonprofit Organizations	$15.95 ____
__	Jobs For Lawyers	$14.95 ____
__	Non-Profit's Job Finder	$16.95 ____

Videos

__	7 Day Professinal Update	$99.00 ____
__	Attitude!	$149.00 ____
__	Career Evaluation	$69.00 ____
__	Career Exploration	$99.00 ____
__	Careers Without College	$79.95 ____
__	Chicken Soup For the Soul Video Series	$59.95 ____
__	Common Mistakes People Make in Interviews	$79.95 ____
__	Dialing For Jobs	$139.00 ____
__	Dynamite Interview Questions and Techniques	$149.95 ____
__	Effective Resumes	$79.95 ____
__	Exceptional Interviewing Tips	$79.00 ____
__	Extraordinary Answers to Common Interview Questions	$79.95 ____
__	First Impressions	$99.00 ____
__	How to Present a Professional Image (2 videos)	$149.95 ____
__	Information Superhighway Video Series	$149.95 ____
__	Job Search—Interviewing Success	$195.00 ____

___	Looking Sharp Video Series	$249.00	_____
___	The Miracle Resume	$99.00	_____
___	Networking on the World Wide Web and Beyond	$79.00	_____
___	Networking Your Way to Success	$89.95	_____
___	Resume Zone	$129.00	_____
___	Super Self-Esteem	$149.00	_____
___	Ten Commandments of Resumes	$79.95	_____
___	Ten Ways to Get a Great Job	$79.95	_____
___	Very Quick Job Search	$129.00	_____
___	The Video Resume Writer	$102.95	_____
___	Why Should I Hire You?	$129.00	_____
___	You're Hired!	$129.00	_____

Military

___	From Air Force Blue to Corporate Gray	$17.95	_____
___	From Army Green to Corporate Gray	$17.95	_____
___	From Navy Blue to Corporate Gray	$17.95	_____
___	Jobs and the Military Spouse	$14.95	_____
___	Resumes & Job Search Letters For Transitioning Military Personnel	$17.95	_____

CD-ROMs

___	Ace the Interview	$99.00	_____
___	Adams JobBank Fast Resume	$49.95	_____
___	America's Top Jobs	$295.00	_____
___	Encyclopedia of Associations	$595.00	_____
___	Encyclopedia of Careers and Vocational Guidance	$199.95	_____
___	Interview Skills For the Future CD-ROM	$199.00	_____
___	Job Browser *Pro*	$295.00	_____
___	Ultimate Job Source	$199.95	_____

SUBTOTAL   _____

Virginia residents add 4½% sales tax   _____

POSTAGE/HANDLING ($5.00 for first
title and 8% of SUBTOTAL over $30.00) $5.00

8% of SUBTOTAL over $30.00 ----------------------   _____

TOTAL ENCLOSED -------------------------   _____

SHIP TO:

NAME _____

ADDRESS _____

_____

_____

❏ I enclose check/moneyorder for $ _____ made payable to IMPACT PUBLICATIONS.

❏ Please charge $ _____ to my credit card:

❏ Visa ❏ MasterCard ❏ American Express ❏ Discover

Card # _____

Expiration date: _____/_____

Signature _____

We accept official purchase orders from libraries, educational institutions, and government offices. Please attach copy with official signature(s).

The On-Line Superstore & Warehouse

Hundreds of Terrific Career Resources Conveniently Available On the World Wide Web 24-Hours a Day, 365 Days a Year!

Ever wanted to know what are the newest and best books, directories, newsletters, wall charts, training programs, videos, CD-ROMs, computer software, and kits available to help you land a job, negotiate a higher salary, or start your own business? What about finding a job in Asia or relocating to San Francisco? Are you curious about how to find a job 24-hours a day by using the Internet or what to do after you leave the military? Trying to keep up-to-date on the latest career resources but not able to find the latest catalogs, brochures, or newsletters on today's "best of the best" resources?

Welcome to the first virtual career resource center/bookstore on the Internet. Now you're only a "click" away with Impact Publication's electronic solution to the resource challenge. Impact Publications, one of the nation's leading publishers and distributors of career resources, has launched its comprehensive "Career Superstore and Warehouse" on the Internet. The bookstore is jam-packed with the latest resources focusing on several key career areas:

- Alternative jobs and careers
- Self-assessment
- Career planning and job search
- Employers
- Relocation and cities
- Resumes
- Cover letters
- Dress, image, and etiquette
- Education
- Telephone
- Military
- Salaries
- Interviewing
- Nonprofits
- Empowerment
- Self-esteem
- Goal setting
- Executive recruiters
- Entrepreneurship
- Government
- Networking
- Electronic job search
- International jobs
- Travel
- Law
- Training and presentations
- Minorities
- Physically challenged

"This is more than just a bookstore offering lots of product," say Drs. Ron and Caryl Krannich, two of the nation's leading career experts and authors and developers of this on-line bookstore. *"We're an important resource center for libraries, corporations, government, educators, trainers, and career counselors who are constantly defining and redefining this dynamic field. Of the thousands of career resources we review each year, we only select the 'best of the best.'"*

Visit this rich site and you'll quickly discover just about everything you ever wanted to know about finding jobs, changing careers, and starting your own business—including many useful resources that are difficult to find in local bookstores and libraries. The site also includes what's new and hot, tips for success, monthly specials, and a "Military Career Transition Center." Impact's Web address is:

http://www.impactpublications.com